NATIONALISM IN EASTERN EUROPE

Nationalism in Eastern Europe

Causes and Consequences of the National Revivals and Conflicts in Late-Twentieth-Century Eastern Europe

Søren Rinder Bollerup
Head of Section
Danish Ministry of Foreign Affairs

and

Christian Dons Christensen
Head of Section
Danish Ministry of Foreign Affairs

First published in Great Britain 1997 by
MACMILLAN PRESS LTD
Houndmills, Basingstoke, Hampshire RG21 6XS and London
Companies and representatives throughout the world

A catalogue record for this book is available from the British Library.

ISBN 0–333–69941–6

First published in the United States of America 1997 by
ST. MARTIN'S PRESS, INC.,
Scholarly and Reference Division,
175 Fifth Avenue, New York, N.Y. 10010

ISBN 0–312–17332–6

Library of Congress Cataloging-in-Publication Data
Bollerup, Søren Rinder, 1968–
Nationalism in Eastern Europe : causes and consequences of the national revivals and conflicts in late 20th-century Eastern Europe / Søren Rinder Bollerup and Christian Dons Christensen.
p. cm.
Includes bibliographical references and index.
ISBN 0–312–17332–6 (cloth)
1. Europe, Eastern—Politics and government—1989–. 2. Europe, Eastern—Autonomy and independence movements. 3. Nationalism–
–Europe, Eastern. 4. Europe, Eastern—Ethnic relations.
I. Dons Christensen, Christian, 1969– II. Title.
DJK51.B65 1997
320.54'0947—dc21 96–37767
CIP

This book is printed on paper suitable for recycling and made from fully managed and sustained forest sources.

10 9 8 7 6 5 4 3 2 1
06 05 04 03 02 01 00 99 98 97

Printed and bound in Great Britain by
Antony Rowe Ltd, Chippenham, Wiltshire

Contents

List of Figures

List of Abbreviations

ASSR	Autonomous Soviet Socialist Republic (*Avtonomnaya Sovetskaya Sotsialisticheskaya Respublika*)
CDC	Croatian Democratic Community (*Hrvatska Demokratska Zajednica – HDZ*)
CDF	Croatian Defence Forces (*Hrvatske Odbrane Snage – HOS*)
CDP	Civic Democratic Party (*Občanská Demokratická Strana – ODS*) (Czech)
CF	Civic Forum (*Občanské Fórum – OF*) (Czech)
CIS	Commonwealth of Independent States (*Sodruzhestvo Nezavisimykh Gosudarstv – SNG*)
CLC	Croatian League of Communists (*Savez Komunista Hrvatske – SKH*)
CM	Cooperation Movement (*Arkalyk*) (Gagauz)
CMEA	Council for Mutual Economic Assistance
CPC	Communist Party of Czechoslovakia (*Komunistická Strana Československa – KSČ*)
CPE	Communist Party of Estonia (*Komunisticheskaya Partiya Estonii – KPE*)
CPHR	Croatian Party of Historical Rights (*Hrvatska Stranka Prava – HSP*)
CPM	Communist Party of Moldavia (*Komunisticheskaya Partiya Moldavii – KPM*)
CPSU	Communist Party of the Soviet Union (*Komunisticheskaya Partiya Sovetskogo Soyuza – KPSS*)
DM	Democratic Movement in Support of Perestroyka (Moldovan)
GP	Gagauz People (*Gagauz Khalky – GKh*)
KGB	*Komitet Gosudarstvennoy Bezopasnosti* (The Committee for State Security)
MDS	Movement for a Democratic Slovakia (*Hnutie za Demokratické Slovensko – HDS*)
OSCE	Organization of Security and Cooperation in Europe (until 1994 named the Conference on Security and Cooperation in Europe – CSCE)
PAV	Public Against Violence (*Verejnost Proti Násiliu – VPN*) (Slovakian)

PFE	Popular Front of Estonia (*Eesti Rahvarinne*)
PFM	Popular Front of Moldova (*Frontul Popular din Moldova*)
RSFSR	Russian Soviet Federated Socialist Republic (*Rossiyskaya Sovetskaya Federativnaya Sotsialisticheskaya Respublika*)
RSK	Republic of Serbian Krajina (*Republika Srpske Krajine*)
SARK	Serbian Autonomous Region Krajina (*Srpska Autonomna Oblast – SAO Krajina*)
SDP	Serbian Democratic Party (*Srpska Demokratska Stranka – SDS*)
SLC	Serbian League of Communists (*Savez Komunista Srbije – SKS*)
SNP	Slovakian National Party (*Slovenská Národná Strana – SNS*)
SSR	Soviet Socialist Republic (*Sovetskaya Sotsialisticheskaya Respublika*)
UCWC	United Council of Work Collectives (*Ob'edinneny Sovet Trudovykh Kollektivov – OSTK*) (Russian)
UNPROFOR	United Nations Protection Force (in the former Yugoslavia)
USSR	Union of Soviet Socialist Republics (*Soyuz Sovetskikh Sotsialisticheskikh Respublik – SSSR*)
UWC	Union of Work Collectives (*Soyuz Trudovykh Kollektivov – STK*) (Russian)
YLC	Yugoslavian League of Communists (*Savez Komunista Jugoslavije – SKJ*)
YPA	Yugoslavian People's Army (*Jugoslovenska Narodna Armija – JNA*)

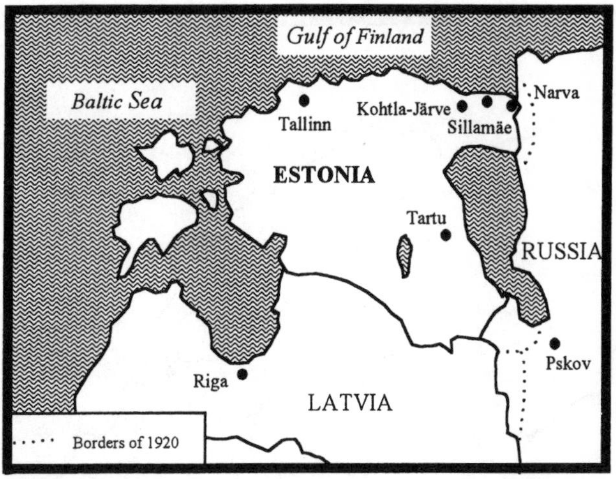

Map 1 Estonia

Map 2 Moldova

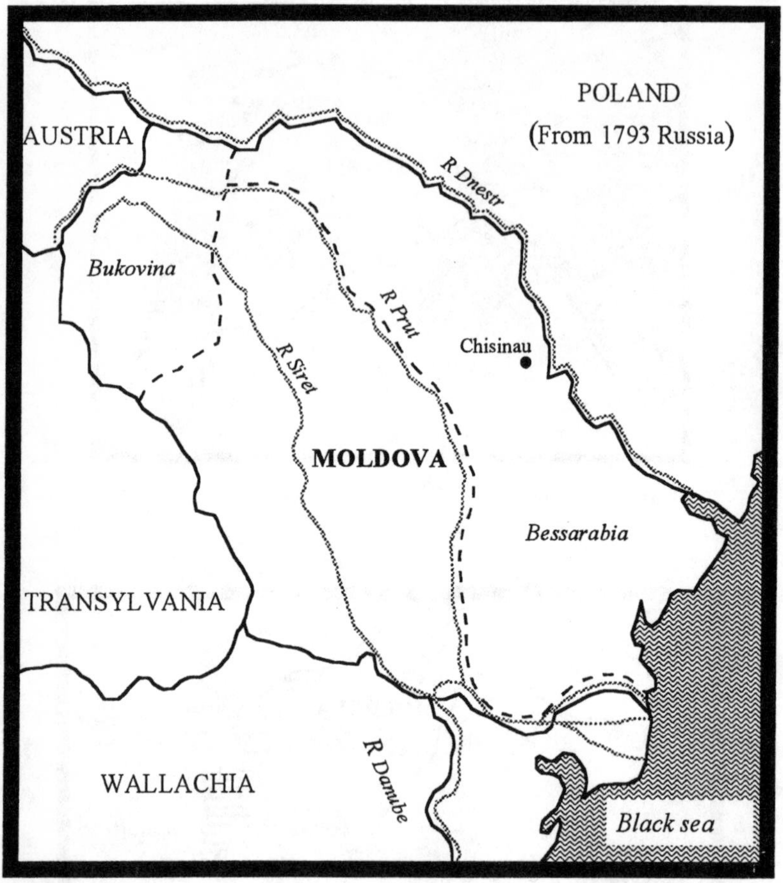

Map 3 Principality of Moldova, End of 18th and Beginning of 19th Centuries

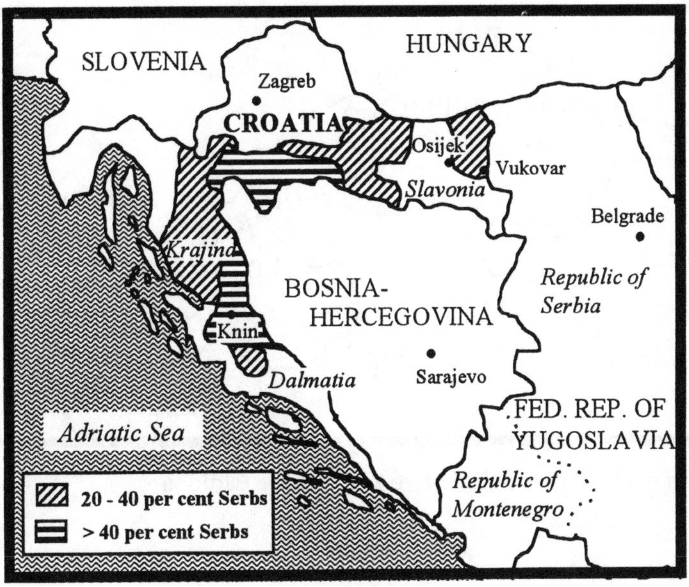

Map 4 Croatia, with Present Borders and Serb Inhabited Areas by 1989

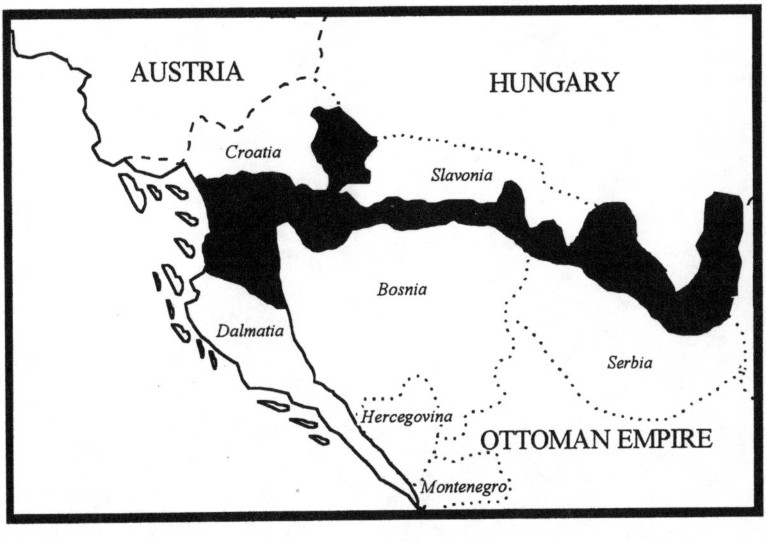

Map 5 The Austrian Military Frontier (*Vojna Krajina*)

Map 6 Czechoslavakia, before and after the Partition

1 Introduction

1 OUTLINE OF THE ANALYSIS

The wave of national revivals that spread quickly across Eastern Europe and the former USSR was one of the most notable consequences of the collapse of the communist regimes. And, like numerous other national revivals in the history of the modern world, the resulting upheavals have been profound and sometimes disastrous. These two facts, the prevalence and the fatality of nationalism, have served as an appetizer in the writings of most analysts who have set out to explain the origins of nationalism in general and the causes of the recent national revivals in particular. However, while they all arrive at an explanation of nationalism and its prevalence, they almost always stop short of fulfilling the second promise, namely to explain *why* nationalism sometimes has these disastrous consequences – that is, why only some instances of national upheavals lead to violent conflict while others do not.

This comparative analysis of the nationalism in Estonia, Moldova, Croatia, and the former Czechoslovakia is an effort to fulfil both promises. We do this by answering the following two questions:

1. *Why did the **national revivals** of the late 1980s and early 1990s occur among Estonians and Russians in Estonia, Moldovans, Gagauz and Slavs in Moldova, Croats and Serbs in Croatia, and Czechs and Slovaks in Czechoslovakia?*
2. *Why were the consequences of the **national conflicts** in the four countries so different: violent conflict between Croats and Serbs in Croatia and between Moldovans and Slavs in Moldova, and non-violent conflict between Moldovans and Gagauz in Moldova, between Estonians and Russians in Estonia, and between Czechs and Slovaks in Czechoslovakia?*

On the basis of theoretical discussions and empirical investigations of the above-mentioned cases, we seek to generate explanations of national revivals and national conflict intensity that are generalizable at least to other cases in the East European setting.

In order to explain national revivals fully, we suggest that the two main groups of macrosociological explanations, primordial and instrumental, should be combined, and that this is consistent with social identity theory as the microsociological theoretical foundation of the explanation. More precisely, we think that primordial and instrumental explanations should be regarded not as mutually exclusive categories, but as complementary variables.

Furthermore, understood in this way, the primordial and instrumental explanations provide a fruitful framework for an explanation of the different consequences of the national conflicts. On the basis of this framework, our theory is that the potential for intense (and, ultimately, violent) conflict is highest when two nation-groups perceive that they have strong and conflicting primordial and instrumental interests.

2 METHODS

2.1 Definitions

By setting out to analyze the causes and consequences of nationalism we enter a minefield of 'essentially contested concepts'. Therefore, in order to escape terminological confusion, it is necessary to define some of the central terms. For some terms, their relevance is obvious already as a consequence of the formulation of our two questions; for others, the relevance will become clear as our argument proceeds.

By a **national revival** we mean the resurgence of nationalism in an ethnic group that has already experienced a wave of nationalism at least once before. By this analytical definition of national revivals we hope to avoid any *a priori* suggestions of an age-old national identity being awakened from its hibernation. **Nationalism** for its part can be defined as 'an ideological movement for attaining and maintaining autonomy, unity and identity on behalf of a population deemed by some of its members to constitute an actual or potential "nation"' (Smith, 1991: 73). Like Pandora's box, this definition reveals yet another concept, namely a nation. This term, however, has been employed in very different ways. In the theoretical literature (as in the quotation from Smith), it most often connotes 'a group of people who feel themselves to be a community bound together by ties of history, culture, and common ancestry' (Kellas, 1991: 2). However, in common language, the term 'nation' is often used in several other ways – most often as synonymous with the term 'state'. To avoid any misunderstanding, we shall specify the meanings of a 'nation' by introducing some closely interrelated concepts. First of all, we preserve **nation** with no suffix for the few instances when we refer to the *idea* which is the core of the ideology of nationalism, namely the idea of national autonomy, unity, and identity. Secondly, we follow Nielsson (1985: 28) and employ **nation-group** to emphasize Kellas's sense of a group that perceives itself to be a community bound together by ties of history, culture, and common ancestry. The common use of 'nation' as a state populated by one nation-group is, finally, captured by the term **nation-state**. However, due to our focus on national revivals and conflicts *within* the borders of specific republics or states, we need to distinguish further between those of a certain national group who live within the borders of the state and those who live outside. We do this pragmatically by using 'nation-group' about our primary object of inquiry – national groups within the territory of a state (such as the Serbs in Croatia) – and by introducing a **mother-nation** to denote *all* members of a national group regardless of their residence (such as all Serbs). Finally, we let the **nationality** of an individual denote the mother-nation rather than the nation-state to which he or she belongs.

The concept of **conflict** is at least as contested as the concepts pertaining to national revivals. The main distinction is between those who advocate a broad definition of conflict, including both latent and manifest conflict, and those who advocate a narrow definition encompassing only manifest conflict. We do not wish to dwell upon the numerous possible definitions of conflict available in the sociological conflict literature (for a thorough discussion see Fink, 1968: 431ff). Our definition is taken from Pruitt and Rubin who define conflict simply as 'perceived divergence of interest' (1986: 4). A **national conflict**, then, involves conflict between two or more nation-groups. When we examine the intensity of a national conflict, we refer to the groups relevant to a specific national conflict as **opposing nation-groups**. Finally, a means in a national conflict is **policies of nationalism** which we define as 'actions taken by a state-bearing nation-group that influence the status of other nation-groups living within the territory of the state'.

2.2 The Comparative Method

We believe that a comparative approach is essential if we are to infer generalizable conclusions from an analysis of the causes and consequences of nationalism in late-20th-century Eastern Europe. The alternatives are the experimental and the statistical methods or an in-depth examination of one specific case (Lijphart, 1971: 683). With nation-groups as our object of inquiry, the experimental method is obviously both impracticable and unethical.

Instead, the optimal solution might be the statistical method. However, as our primary interest is the macrosociological relationships between variables in total systems, we shall in many respects regard nation-groups as units of these systems. This approach lowers the number of available cases to a level where only the crudest cross-tabulations are merited. Yet, in some instances, it is possible to regard nationality simply as an additional variable in line with other individual attributes instead of treating each nation-group as a case by itself. In these instances, the statistical method is clearly preferable as the large number of nation-group members obviously makes control for several key variables possible. However, in the effort to conduct statistical analyses in the East European context, we would encounter extensive problems with respect to the available data. In the period of communist rule in Eastern Europe, only very few surveys were conducted. And those that were made public are at best questionable with respect to reliability and validity since research of this kind was under strict control and often employed to serve the interests of the regimes. Only shortly before and especially after the fall of the communist regimes, at a time when most national revivals had already begun, did some independent Western and newly established domestic survey agencies begin to conduct opinion polls. However, even these surveys rarely posed the analytical questions that we would have preferred, and the statistical evidence was even more rarely comparable across nation-groups.

Given these limitations, the choice is between individual case studies or a comparative analysis. As the former approach gives us only isolated knowledge about the functioning of nationalism and as we search for generalizable explanations, we are left with a comparative analysis as the single feasible choice. The problems of a low number of cases can then be reduced by choosing cases in a limited historical period and within a well-defined geographical area so that many variables can be held constant.

Having said this, however, we should be careful to emphasize that our conclusions are restricted to the late-20th-century East European socio-political setting, and that our cases include only a minor part of the large number of potential and actual national revivals and conflicts in this setting.

2.3 Choice of Cases

The area from which we have selected our cases of national revivals and national conflicts is Eastern Europe. Our definition of Eastern Europe is geographical rather than political. This implies that Eastern Europe not only includes all the former socialist satellite states but also the western part of the former USSR, the so-called Soviet West (the Baltic republics, Belarus, Moldova, Ukraine, and Russia west of the Ural mountains).

As for the choice of national revivals, we have divided Eastern Europe into three regions in order to take advantage of the differences that existed within the area. In each area, then, we have chosen both national revivals among titular nation-groups and the concomitant revivals among minority nation-groups living in the territory claimed by the titular nation-groups. Firstly, with regard to the republics of the Soviet West, we have chosen the revivals among the Estonians and the Moldovans to represent the revivals of the titular nation-groups. The national revivals among minority nation-groups are represented by the Russians in Estonia and the Slavs and the Gagauz in Moldova. Secondly, with regard to the East European satellite states of the USSR, we have chosen the revivals in Czechoslovakia[1] among the Czech majority and the Slovakian minority. Finally, with regard to the Titoist break-away Yugoslavia, we have chosen the revivals among the Croatian majority and the Serbian minority in Croatia.

As for national conflicts, our choice of cases follows from the pairing of the above-mentioned nation-groups. In our choice of these nation-groups, we have, of course, also paid attention to the importance of assuring sufficient variance in the dependent variable of national conflicts. Thus, we have selected conflicts which differed with regard to the extent to which violence was employed by the opposing nation-groups. At one end of the violent–non-violent continuum of national conflicts, the Croatian–Serbian and the Moldovan–Slavic conflicts represent the category of conflicts which resulted in large-scale warfare and deadlocked situations (in this category only the conflicts in Bosnia-Hercegovina are omitted). At the other end of the continuum, the Estonian–Russian, the Moldovan–Gagauz, and the Czech–Slovakian conflicts represent the category of conflicts which did not escalate into the use of violence. While the last of these three conflicts resulted in a negotiated partition of Czechoslovakia into two independent states, the first two resulted in a (so far) peaceful *modus vivendi* between the opposing nation-groups.

3 STRUCTURE OF THE ANALYSIS

This book consists of two main parts. Part One deals with national revivals, and Part Two deals with national conflicts. Both parts are structured in the same way. Thus, each part is introduced by a *theoretical* analysis of national revivals and conflicts in general. This is followed by an *exploratory* analysis of the social context of the national revivals and conflicts in late-20th-century Eastern Europe. Then we provide an *explanatory* analysis of each case of national revival and conflict. And finally, we draw conclusions about the national revivals and conflicts in Eastern Europe on the basis of a *comparative* analysis of theories, hypotheses, and empirical evidence.

The first two chapters in each part are theoretical: one discussing microsociological theories about national revivals and conflicts – that is, theories originating mainly from the individual and group level of analysis – and one discussing macrosociological theories of national revivals and conflicts – that is, theories originating mainly from the group and intergroup level of analysis. The main emphasis is laid on testing the hypotheses deduced from the macrosociological theories, as the empirical evidence needed for testing the microsociological theories in an East European context is fragmentary and in some cases totally absent.

The microsociological theories, however, are not at all inconsequential. Apart from providing the theoretical foundation necessary for turning societal correlations into real explanations, they provide some important points about the interplay between the societal level and the individuals which do not follow from the macrosociological theories alone. The interplay between the societal level and the individual is the subject of the third chapter in each part (Chapters 4 and 12). These chapters provide an exploratory analysis of the social context of Eastern Europe as seen from the individuals' perspectives, and for this purpose we use some of the microsociological theories and concepts presented in the microsociological theoretical chapters.

The analysis of the social context is then followed by an explanatory analysis of the nine national revivals and five national conflicts under examination. For practical reasons, this analysis is divided into four chapters in each part: one for each country. In these chapters, we test the hypotheses deduced from the macrosociological theories.

Finally, each part is concluded by a comparative analysis. On the basis of a comparison of the explanatory power of the different theories, these chapters proceed with a discussion of some theoretical implications of the results. At the end of the concluding chapters, we present our view of the causes of national revivals and national conflict intensity in two integrative theoretical models.

This general structure results in the following concrete plan of the book. In Part One, we deal with the first of our main questions. This implies an analysis of different kinds of explanation of the rise of nationalism. Chapter 2 on the proclivity for nationalism discusses whether the joining of human beings in nation-groups or national movements – or at least their tendency to be ethnocentric – is the result of a predisposition or a rational choice. Chapter 3 on the causes of national revivals then turns to the formulation of hypotheses about the causes of national revivals testable in the East European societies. In Chapter 4, we use microsociological theories to explore the social context of the late-20th-century national revivals. More specifically, we examine whether any general social conditions in the modern world in general and in Eastern Europe in particular were conducive to the promotion of nation-groups as opposed to individual action or promotion of alternative groups. In Chapters 5 to 8, the macrosociological hypotheses are tested systematically on the national revivals in Estonia, Moldova, Croatia, and Czechoslovakia. Finally, in Chapter 9, the results are used for comparisons and conclusions.

In Part Two, we turn to our second question about the consequences of nationalism. This implies a search for some kind of generalizable reason why national conflicts develop in a particular way. Chapter 10 provides the microsociological foundation for this search by a discussion of some psychological and group processes involved in the escalation of group conflicts and an examination of important actors of escalation involved in national conflicts. Chapter 11 develops different hypotheses about the causes of the varying intensity of national conflicts. Paralleling Part One, the next chapter explores the social context of the national conflicts by examining how important actors of escalation influenced and characterized the general East European political climate in the late 1980s and early 1990s. Then, in Chapters 13 to 16, the deduced macrosociological hypotheses are tested for each of the selected national conflicts. Chapter 17 concludes Part Two with a theoretical discussion and an integrative theoretical model of national conflict intensity on the basis of a comparison of the results from the empirical chapters. Finally, in Chapter 18 which concludes the whole book, we sum up and discuss the results of our analyses.

Part One: The Causes of National Revivals

2 The Proclivity for Nationalism

1 INTRODUCTION

That the ideology of nationalism is ubiquitous in the present world is obvious. But how can the ideology of nationalism come to command the loyalty of such large numbers of individuals? What induces the individual member of a nation-group to participate in or sympathize with a national movement? In this chapter, we examine two basically different types of answers to this question. One group of theories sees nationalism as resulting from, or at least building on, some kind of human predisposition, whereas the other group of theories sees nationalism as the result of a rational choice. Both groups are microsociological theories – that is, they take as their point of departure primarily the individual and group level of analysis.

Now, only a few of the theories see a direct causal link between the predisposition or the rational choice of the individual and the national movements on the societal level. Therefore, we begin by introducing the concept of ethnocentrism which plays the role of an intervening variable in the relation between the individual person and the national movement. The ethnocentrism of the individual and of groups of individuals is only a precondition for nationalism. In our view, the reasons why some national movements flourish while others do not should be found at the societal level of analysis using macrosociological theories. This level of analysis is discussed theoretically in Chapter 3.

The study of the motivations, behaviour, and attitudes of human beings in and towards groups has resulted in an overwhelming amount of literature and theories primarily in the domain of psychology and social psychology. The limits of this book, however, permit us to present only a few of the most well-known theories of ethnocentrism. The theories that presuppose some kind of human predisposition for ethnocentrism comprise one sociobiological theory and two psychodynamic theories, whereas rational choice theories are treated under a single heading. Finally, we argue that social identity theory includes a predispositional element while at the same time allowing for contingent factors such as conscious decisions, historical developments, and social structure.

2 ETHNOCENTRISM

2.1 The Concept of Ethnocentrism

The concept of ethnocentrism was introduced by Sumner:

> Ethnocentrism is the technical name for this view of things in which one's own group is the center of everything, and all others are scaled and rated with reference to it.... Each group nourishes its own pride and vanity, boasts itself superior, exalts its own divinities, and looks with contempt on outsiders. Each group thinks its own folkways the only right ones, and if it observes that other groups have other folkways, these excite its scorn.... Ethnocentrism leads a people to exaggerate and intensify everything in their own folkways which is peculiar and which differentiates them from others. (1959 [1906]: 13)

This quotation, however, does not exhaust Sumner's understanding of ethnocentrism. In fact, as LeVine and Campbell note, Sumner's concept of ethnocentrism is actually a syndrome of attributes of social life, and they list 23 such attributes as an initial overview (1972: 12). Furthermore, Sumner postulates several causal relationships between these attributes. To avoid the discussions of all the causally and functionally related elements of Sumner's concept of ethnocentrism (e.g. LeVine & Campbell, 1972; Brewer, 1979), we have chosen the shorter and more descriptive definition provided by Adorno, Frenkel-Brunswik, Levinson and Sanford in their famous study of the authoritarian personality:

> Ethnocentrism is based on a pervasive and rigid ingroup–outgroup distinction; it involves stereotyped negative imagery and hostile attitudes regarding outgroups, stereotyped positive imagery and submissive attitudes regarding ingroups, and a hierarchical, authoritarian view of group interaction in which ingroups are rightly dominant, outgroups subordinate. (1950: 150)

Thus, ethnocentrism as an ideal type involves strong group stereotypes (which we shall examine more closely in Chapter 10), attitudes of ingroup loyalty and outgroup hostility, and a moral preference for ingroup dominance. But it should be noted that it is possible to imagine weaker instances of ethnocentrism involving, for example, group stereotypes, ingroup favouritism and outgroup derogation, and a moral resistance to outgroup dominance; or involving only some of these elements. Thus, in our view, ethnocentrism must be regarded as a variable.

2.2 The Scope of Ethnocentrism

Reflecting the scientific predilection of his day for universal statements, Sumner generalized that all groups display the syndrome of ethnocentrism (LeVine & Campbell, 1972: 8). To some degree, this is supported by newer survey studies and anthropological studies of ethnocentrism throughout the world which have shown significantly more positive evaluations of ingroup members than of outgroup members (e.g. Brewer, 1979: 77, 81). And, perhaps even more impressively, a range of socio-psychological experiments with so-called minimal groups starting with Tajfel, Flament, Billig and Bundy (1971) have invariably found some, albeit weaker, form of ethnocentrism to be present. In the minimal group experimental paradigm subjects are randomly classified as members of two non-overlapping groups thereby isolating the 'minimal' effect of social categorization from the influence of, for example, conflict of interests, previously existing hostilities, and social interaction. Measuring ethnocentrism mostly through the individual participant's distribution of money or points between anonymous ingroup (excluding self) and outgroup members, but also through more evaluative scales such as likable–unlikable and fair–unfair, some of the results of minimal group experiments are:

1. categorized subjects *favour* ingroup members over outgroup members (i.e. the outgroup is discriminated against as regards tangible goods); and
2. categorized subjects *prefer* ingroup members to outgroup members (i.e. the outgroup is evaluated lower than the ingroup).

(For a more comprehensive review of the results of minimal group experiments, see Brown, 1986: 543–51.)

However, the seeming universality of ethnocentrism should be treated with caution as ingroup attachments and outgroup attitudes show a considerable flexibility and diversity. First of all, both the empirically and the experimentally detected ethnocentrism obviously requires membership of one group or another to be salient. That is, the practical importance of ethnocentrism is restricted to cases involving *intergroup* interaction as opposed to *interpersonal* interaction. Intergroup interaction is defined as 'interactions which are largely determined by group memberships of the participants and very little – if at all – by their personal relations or individual characteristics', while interpersonal interaction is not influenced by the group membership of the agents (Tajfel, 1979: 401). As real life contains both interpersonal and intergroup interactions in varying degrees, it would be deterministic to suggest that ethnocentrism necessarily must be present in all dealings with members of another group.

Secondly, not all group members abide by the features of ethnocentrism. They can be disloyal to the group, reject the standards of the group, aspire to membership in another group, or accept the standards of another group. And even if they do display ethnocentric attitudes, this can be in varying degrees, as shown by Adorno et al. (1950: Ch. 4).

However, these first modifications of the universality of ethnocentrism, in so far as they remain exceptions to the general rule, do not influence our use of ethnocentrism as an intervening variable between the attitudes and behaviours of the individual and mass national movements. This is because the important aspect of ethnocentrism for our purposes is its overall level in the group taken as a whole.

More important for our purposes is the fact that the range of groups to which the individual can feel loyal is almost infinite. And even if we limit ourselves to the cultural groups indicated by the prefix of ethno-centrism, the possibilities for each individual can include tribal, regional, national, and continental identities. Which differences are emphasized and which identities are chosen appears to be dependent on the context and the purpose (Brewer, 1981: 350).

And finally, even if we consider our primary interest, namely the ethnocentrism of the group as a whole, not all groups actually evaluate themselves higher than other groups. That is, outside the minimal group experimental premises, belonging to a group is still not enough to produce ethnocentrism in the sense of ingroup preference and outgroup derogation. As one scholar summarizes the first studies on majority and minority children's identifications and preferences,

> [t]he conclusions of the earlier research have been that at a very early age children from underprivileged groups tended to reflect the social consensus about the status and the image of their group by adopting outgroup identifications and preferences, while the majority children clearly showed ethnocentric attitudes. (Tajfel, 1982: 9)

Thus, it seems that the surrounding 'social climate' of intergroup differentials and evaluations is important to whether a group displays ethnocentrism at all (pp. 9ff). This points to the importance of macrosociological phenomena in the formation of ethnocentrism and, with that, nationalism.

3 EXPLANATIONS OF ETHNOCENTRISM

To summarize, ethnocentrism is a pervasive, though not universal, phenomenon in human societies. In context-free groups, individuals seem to favour and prefer ingroup members to outgroup members, but this is not equal to the outgroup hostility and moral preference for ingroup dominance included in the pure form of ethnocentrism. What accounts for the outright hostility of some groups and the self-effacement of other groups is the historical and social context of the groups. This is the interest of the following chapter. But the individually based theories of ethnocentrism to be discussed in this chapter must be flexible enough to account for the variability of ethnocentrism.

3.1 Sociobiological Theories

Sociobiological theories cover a range of theories characterized by their common Darwinian heritage. As an example of this category of theories, we have chosen to discuss the much-debated sociobiological theory of van den Berghe (1978) who employs evolutionary arguments to explain the behaviour and attitudes of individuals towards ethnic groups.

3.1.1 The Theory of Kin Selection

Van den Berghe uses the Darwinian concept of natural selection as a point of departure. The more reproductively successful organisms have greater probability of replicating their genes in the population's next generation. The most well-known Darwinian conclusion from this statement is, of course, that the most adaptive organisms survive and get to reproduce themselves, or, in other words, 'survival of the fittest'. Van den Berghe's interest, however, is that this basic condition of life has implications for the *social* life of human beings (and other species as well).

If the meaning of life is to survive in order to replicate one's genes, there is nothing strange in the care and protection that parents give their offspring, for parents have to make sure that not only they but also their offspring attain the highest possible fitness. But what then accounts for the wider sociality of human beings – that is, for individuals' contribution to the fitness of individuals other than their children? The answer is that not only children but also other relatives are carriers of some of the same genes as the individual. Therefore, the biologically determined urge to replicate one's genes can be satisfied also by contributing to the fitness of relatives, thereby increasing the so-called *inclusive fitness* of the individual. Such genetically based cooperative behaviour to maximize inclusive fitness is termed *kin selection* (van den Berghe, 1978: 402). And, according to van den Berghe, to explain ethnicity and ethnocentrism only kin selection is needed (pp. 403ff).

Van den Berghe argues that ethnic and racial relations 'are, in fact, extensions of the idiom of kinship, and ... therefore, ethnic and race sentiments are to be understood as an extended and attenuated form of kin selection' (p. 403). Ethnicity and race are important because they help individuals to determine the probability of relatedness, and the ethnic and racial sentiments, such as ethnocentrism, can be traced back to the early evolutionary stages of humankind when ethnic groups were simply 'inbreeding superfamilies' (p. 404) that had to behave in solidarity against other competing groups.

3.1.2 Discussion

Van den Berghe developed his theory in an effort to give the 'primordialist' view on race and ethnicity a more solid theoretical basis (this view is elaborated in Chapter 3). However, the theory suffers from some major shortcomings both as regards internal consistency and in its ability to explain ethnocentrism.

The first problem arises when the relations in and between larger ethnic groups are considered as extensions of the idiom of kinship. Kin selection may be able to explain the loyalty of a small group such as a small tribe where everybody is obviously related (or it may not: this is ultimately an unfalsifiable hypothesis), but in large societies the interrelatedness is clearly a myth. Van den Berghe argues that the reality or not of common ancestry is not important to the derived feelings of ethnocentrism and nationalism (1978: 404), but this is hardly convincing, for the premise of his theory is the *biological* necessity of securing the reproduction of some of one's own genes. This is obviously not accomplished through myths alone, and the strictly genetically based concept of kin selection is therefore insufficient to explain ethnocentric feelings in large societies. Something other than partly identical genes, then, must account for ethnocentrism under these circumstances.

Secondly, if ethnocentrism is directly based on a common human biology, the theory has no way of explaining the diversity and flexibility of ethnocentrism in groups as described in Section 2.2. Indeed, as Reynolds (1980) points out, van den Berghe fails to provide any real evidence both regarding the supposed evolutionary basis of humankind in small, competing, and genetically distinct groups (p. 312) and regarding the relevance of kin selection to present-day examples of ethnic and racial relations (p. 314).

3.2 Psychodynamic Theories

Instead of resorting to genetical arguments, a great number of theorists have emphasized the functioning of the human psyche as the basis for ethnocentrism. Building on a common Freudian heritage, the common denominator for psychodynamic theories is the view that ethnocentrism is in some way or another a result of scapegoating – that is, blaming others for one's own hardships. In this section, we will present and discuss two such theories: the theory of the authoritarian personality and the frustration–aggression theory. Both take the individual's psyche as a point of departure, but they differ in two respects. Firstly, only the former theory goes on to explain the formation of the psyche, and secondly, the former attains relevance for the ethnocentrism of groups through *aggregation* of individual attitudes and behaviour, whereas the latter simply *extrapolates* the functioning of individuals to the functioning of groups.

3.2.1 The Theory of the Authoritarian Personality

Since its publication in 1950, the classic study by Adorno et al., *The Authoritarian Personality*, has deservedly received enormous attention, and it has formed the starting point for large numbers of followers and critics alike. *The Authoritarian Personality* raises a lot of both methodological and theoretical questions, but in the present context we shall focus primarily on theoretical aspects of relevance to ethnocentrism.

Originally, *The Authoritarian Personality* was intended to be a study of anti-Semitism involving the construction of an attitude scale in order to measure prejudice towards Jews (the A-S scale). The authors, however, proceeded to measure broader ingroup and outgroup attitudes through the construction of the E (ethnocentrism) scale. The varying degrees of ethnocentrism were then linked both statistically and theoretically to a certain personality type, namely the authoritarian. Theoretically, the attitudes revealed by high scorers on the E (and other) scales were seen as manifestations of an underlying authoritarian personality pattern (Adorno et al. 1950: 228). And statistically, the link was a high correlation of 0.73 between the E scale and the so-called F (fascism) scale developed to measure anti-democratic trends regarded as typical for authoritarian individuals but not involving direct questions about outgroups (p. 263). High correlations between authoritarianism on the one hand and scales measuring, for example, ethnocentrism and nationalism on the other have been reproduced in several other studies (see Eckhardt, 1991: 115).

In order to attain a comprehensive picture of the composition of the authoritarian personality, Adorno et al. also employed clinical interviews with high and low scorers on the above-mentioned attitude scales. According to the authors, some consistent patterns emerged during these interviews, especially regarding the family patterns of highly prejudiced people. These subjects generally reported a relatively harsh and more threatening type of home discipline which was experienced as arbitrary by the child. Their parents had been preoccupied with social status, tangible wealth, and above all social acceptability, and the goals in the upbringing of their children were, consequently, highly conventional. The clearly defined roles of dominance and submission in the family and the status-anxiety of the parents led to the adoption by the child of a rigid and externalized set of values and to a superficial identification with the parents, but also to an underlying resentment against them (Adorno et al., 1950: 384ff).

The correlation between the E and the F scale on the one hand and, on the other hand, the family pattern of high scorers on these scales became the basis of the theory of the authoritarian personality. The development of the authoritarian personality syndrome and, consequently, anti-Semitic, ethnocentric, and anti-democratic attitudes were seen as caused by the child–parent relationships of the subjects. Forced into a surface submission to parental authority, the child develops hostility and aggression which are poorly channelled. The repressed antagonism towards authority is then displaced onto legitimate targets, such as homosexuals and other outgroups.[2] And the socially unacceptable drives and faults of the authoritarian himself are projected onto powerless minority groups, fuelling the prejudice displayed towards them (Adorno et al., 1950: 482f). Thus, ethnocentrism is explained by reference to unsolved intra-psychic conflicts of some people due to their early childhood experiences.

3.2.2 Discussion

The Authoritarian Personality is an early indication of the potential usefulness of the concept of ethnocentrism in the study of intergroup relations, and the generalized prejudice identified by the authors has been documented by a range of other studies involving many different outgroups. Later studies have also documented the ingroup side of ethnocentrism through employment of, for example, different types of P (patriotism) scales (see Eckhardt, 1991; Fisher, 1990: 23).

Before turning to the criticism of *The Authoritarian Personality*, an initial problem in applying the theory of the authoritarian personality to our study must be mentioned. The principal aim of the theory is to explain the attitudes and behaviours of single individuals. It follows that in order to account for the ethnocentrism of groups as a whole, which is *our* main interest, sufficiently large numbers of individuals must have been subjected to harsh, punitive, and vindictive parents. In other words, the theory of the authoritarian personality can only become a theory of group ethnocentrism through aggregation of the individuals' repressed inner needs or impulses. Thus, no concepts apply to the group and intergroup level of analysis. This can be seen as a theoretical problem in itself, and it has a special bearing on our analysis of nationalism in Eastern Europe, as almost all available empirical evidence pertains to these levels of analysis.

Aside from this problem, both the methodological and the theoretical framework of *The Authoritarian Personality* have been legitimately criticized on their own premises.

Much effort has been devoted to a criticism of the statistical basis of *The Authoritarian Personality*. Among other things, the study has been accused of inaccurate statistics on the basis of non-representative samples and questionnaires which included ambiguous items and invited response bias (for a review of some of the critics, see Kirscht & Dillehay, 1966: 7ff). Further, the study failed to control for any other variables and, consequently, to examine alternative explanations. For example, a host of later studies have documented the influence of formal education on ethnocentric attitudes (for references and a critical assessment of these, see Jackman & Muha, 1984). And finally, it is questionable whether the content of psychological processes can be deduced at all from the content of attitude items and, thus, whether the responses can be said to reflect a well-articulated belief system.

The *theory* of the authoritarian personality might, of course, still be true, although the severe criticism of the statistical methods employed by Adorno et al. (1950) leaves only a thin foundation for their theoretical framework. The main problem in this respect, however, is the abovementioned failure to examine alternative explanations. This has been acknowledged also by theorists within the authoritarian personality research tradition. Thus, several different theories of the authoritarian personality are available today. They stress, for example, cognitive functioning through social learning theory, group orientation through social identity theory, and several *ad hoc* explanations rather than the psychodynamic theory of Adorno et al. (1950) in the explanation of authoritarianism and the involved ethnocentrism (for a review of recent trends in the study of authoritarianism, see Stone, 1993). The common ground for these theorists is the assumption that a consistent personality syndrome called authoritarianism exists. But they point in completely different directions from Adorno et al. (1950) in their explanations of this syndrome. In this context, we have concentrated on the original theory of the authoritarian personality as the recent developments in authoritarian theory are partly covered by the other theories in this and the following chapter. And the original theory is far from unequivocally supported.

3.2.3 The Frustration–Aggression Theory

Where the authors of *The Authoritarian Personality* focused on a personality syndrome as the basis of ethnocentric attitudes and explained this syndrome by the formation of the human psyche in early childhood, the frustration–aggression research tradition, starting with Dollard, Doob, Miller, Mowrer and Sears (1939), has focused on aggressive behaviour and viewed this as a stimulus–response phenomenon.

Aggression can relatively easily be defined as behaviour aimed at inflicting injury on some object or person (Berkowitz, 1962: xii; 1969: 3). However, the key explanatory term, frustration, is significantly more vague, and this leads both to disagreement on the proper definition of the term and to criticism of the frustration–aggression hypothesis as such. We shall not go into detail with the terminological discussion but confine ourselves to Berkowitz's definition (1969: 5f). According to Berkowitz, frustration is the external thwarting of a goal-directed activity as opposed to the resulting emotions in the human mind. Thus, frustration is distinguished firstly from the instigation to aggression, or anger, which frustration gives rise to, and secondly from deprivation, which implies that the individual is not engaged in (or, at least, gives up the) goal-directed activity. To become frustrated, in other words, an individual must have *expected* to achieve the goal he or she was aiming at but deprived of.

Dollard et al. hypothesized that '*aggression is always a consequence of frustration*' (1939: 1; emphasis in the original), thereby indicating a strict stimulus–response view of aggression. Later versions of the theory, however, recognize that not every aggression necessarily presupposes a frustration and that frustration does not always lead to aggression. Aggression can be both instrumental and learned and, thus, not the result of frustration (Berkowitz, 1962: 30f). Further, aggression resulting from frustration may be blocked by inhibitions such as power structures, fear of punishment, or social norms. Or it may not occur if the individual has learned to react non-aggressively or if the available target does not have appropriate stimulus qualities (Berkowitz, 1969: 12).

However, the above-mentioned inhibitions may be sufficient only to prevent aggression against the source of the frustration which, according to the theory, is the normal target of aggression. When the source of frustration cannot be attacked, the frustrated individual is likely to direct his or her aggression against a person (or an object) as similar as possible to the source of frustration but against whom the aggression is not connected with inhibitions to the same degree (Berkowitz, 1962: Ch. 5). This change of the target of aggression away from the instigating stimulus is called displacement. As the blocking of an impulse of aggression in the first place is a frustration in its own right, such displacement reactions are likely to be fuelled by an even greater impulse of aggression.

When applying the frustration–aggression theory to group ethnocentrism and intergroup conflict, displacement assumes a key role. Living in a community inevitably breeds frustrations as some level of self-restraint and, consequently, frustration is necessary for social life to function. This fact becomes even more pronounced in large societies where formal rules and sanctions become more important in the maintenance of social order. However, these very same sanctions inhibit the expression of aggression against ingroup authorities such as parents, teachers, and the state apparatus which are the immediate sources of frustration. Instead, according to the theory, aggression is displaced onto an outgroup similar enough to carry the same stimulus qualities as the instigator(s), but distant or powerless enough to allow unpunished aggression (Berkowitz, 1962: Ch. 6; LeVine & Campbell, 1972: 118ff). Further, groups institutionalize the displacement of hostility and aggression onto outgroups through socialization of young generations who learn which outgroups to express hostile attitudes and behaviour towards. The chosen outgroups often share certain qualities such as being visible, strange, and/or having been disliked in the past (Berkowitz, 1962: 149ff). The socialization even influences the perceptions of the source of frustration so that an outgroup can come to be perceived as the 'real' source of frustration (Berkowitz, 1962: 160ff; LeVine & Campbell, 1972: 123). Finally, the institutionalization of displacement of hostility onto outgroups often helps to control the otherwise disruptive effect of intragroup mutual frustration by portraying the outgroup as a threat necessitating ingroup solidarity (LeVine & Campbell, 1972: 123). In this way, the frustration– aggression–displacement relation explains both the outgroup hostility and the ingroup loyalty element of ethnocentrism.

Through employment of concepts such as socialization, frustration–aggression theorists acknowledge that not all aggressions against outgroups are the direct result of emotional tensions due to frustrations, but that social learning or, in other words, culture is also involved (e.g. Berkowitz, 1962: 135f). Yet, even with the modifications of inhibitions, displacements, and cultural factors, the basic relationship between frustration and aggression is held to be true though amendable to *ad hoc* hypotheses about situational factors inflicting on the strength (or even manifestation) of aggression.

3.2.4 Discussion

Compared to the psychodynamic theory of the authoritarian personality, the frustration–aggression theory addresses the problem of this chapter more directly because it is used to explain the ethnocentrism in a group as a whole. It does this by assuming that groups, just as individuals, can be frustrated, and that they are likely to displace the instigated aggressions onto other groups.

At first sight, the explanatory power of this theory appears to be considerable. Probably, everybody can relate to the feeling of anger following a frustration, and why should this not be true for groups as well? Members of groups may suffer frustrations in a lot of ways privately, culturally, economically, and politically, and in both interpersonal and intergroup interactions. And in all these instances, aggression is more easily expressed towards an outgroup than towards the ingroup.

However, even at the level of individual psychology several difficulties arise in connection with the frustration–aggression hypothesis. For example, theorists disagree about which and to what extent inhibitions and triggering stimuli intervene between the frustration and the aggression. Similarly, there is a variety of views in the literature on what actually constitutes a frustration – not to mention the fact that a frustration often depends on the cognition and interpretation by the individual rather than being completely objective.

Whereas the difficulties of the individual psychological concept of frustration do not directly disqualify the frustration–aggression hypothesis, there are more severe problems connected to a simple extrapolation of the concept to the group and intergroup level of analysis. As Dougherty and Pfaltzgraff point out, the time interval between a frustration and an eventual aggression is longer in large societies, thereby making the causal relationship between the frustration and the aggression less certain due to intervening inhibitions, displacements, etc. The time factor, the diverse interpretations of the same societal situations made by different individuals, and the broader variety of responses available to large groups also provide greater opportunity for groups to find other outlets of their aggressive impulses or simply to adjust to the existing conditions (1981: 269f). In other words, it is unclear how collectives actually experience frustrations which, presumably, have a different influence on each individual, and what determines whether or not, when, and against whom they will react aggressively upon such frustrations.

Thus, the power of the frustration–aggression theory is also its weakness. Because 'frustration' is such a widely used word with a lot of connotations, it is not surprising that it can be used to explain intergroup conflict. But when applied to group phenomena and intergroup conflict, the concept somehow loses its distinct meaning and becomes almost synonymous with the ordinary meaning of the word, namely 'dissatisfaction'. Dissatisfaction, of course, is not by itself an inexpedient variable, but frustration used in this way retains only little of the meaning attributed to the concept by frustration–aggression *theory* – that is, the interference with an ongoing goal-directed activity. It does, however, make it possible to retain the insight of the theory that the decisive point in frustrations is unfulfilled expectations. This insight, however, is not an exclusive property of frustration–aggression theory. That one of the important causes of social movements is frustrated expectations is a central premise to many political scientists (e.g. Davies, 1962, who develops a theory of revolutions on the basis of rising but frustrated expectations), and it has also been noted by other psychologists completely outside the frustration–aggression tradition (e.g. Brown, 1986: 575ff).

Later in this study we shall use the concept of frustrations at the intergroup level of analysis but with no reference to the original individual level concept included in the frustration–aggression *theory*, which we regard as at best problematic when extrapolated to the group and intergroup levels of analysis. We use 'frustration' simply to denote any economic, political, or cultural life conditions of a nation-group that are *perceived as unfair*, as opposed to an objective deprivation of a group. It is with reference to this 'dissatisfaction' in different spheres of collective life that we shall examine whether groups must be frustrated rather than just deprived to initiate a national revival.

3.3 Rational Choice Theory

Whereas both sociobiological and psychodynamic theories assume some kind of human predisposition as the basis of ethnocentrism, rational choice theory needs no such assumption. According to rational choice theory, people engage in groups and intergroup conflict because this activity is instrumental to their individual and selfish goals. The decision of whether or not to display ingroup solidarity and outgroup hostility is the result of each individual's cost-benefit analysis.

The relevance of rational choice theory to the ethnocentrism of groups lies in its examination of the conditions of collective action. The rational choice concept that most explicitly relates to ethnocentrism is the concept of group solidarity developed by Hechter (1987a). Before examining Hechter's theory of group solidarity, we shall give a short introduction to the assumptions of rational choice theory and to the problem of collective action.

Rational choice theory in its pure form is actually not a theory or even a family of theories, but rather an approach devoted to

> the study of nonmarket decisions and decision making, [and] based on the twin premises of *methodological individualism* and *rational utility maximation*, well known from economic theory. (Nannestad, 1992: 1; emphasis in the original)

The premise of methodological individualism claims that all explanations must ultimately be based on the motivations, interests, and behaviour of individuals. More controversial, however, is the premise of rational utility maximation which poses that these individuals, when faced with alternatives, choose the course of action that will produce maximum utility. To assess this, individuals must at a minimum be aware of their preferences, be able to order these preferences consistently, and not let them be influenced by the process of choice. Whether the preferences of individuals are characterized by pure self-interest, or whether altruistic behaviour is consistent with rational choice theory, is a matter of dispute (Opp, 1984: 3). But most textbooks on rational choice theory (e.g. Stevens, 1993: 20) and, importantly for our purposes, analysts applying rational choice theory to nationalism (e.g. Rogowski, 1985: 90; Hechter, 1987b: 417) assume self-interested individuals. Thus, rational choice theories of nationalism propose that *homo oeconomicus* and *homo ethnicus* are one and the same and should be approached from the same perspective.

However, individuals are not totally free to make choices. Institutions, understood as rules and structures of incentives, constrain individuals in a variety of ways and play a major role in the social outcome resulting from separately acting individuals.

In rational choice theory, as opposed to sociological theory, groups cannot be taken for granted because they have to be the result of utility maximizing individuals. Groups will only exist when they give each member greater net benefit than he or she could have gained by acting on an individual basis. Typically, this is the case when the individuals have a preference for a public good. A public good is characterized by nonrivalness (that is, the consumption of one individual does not influence the ability of others to consume) and non-excludability (that is, the good cannot be withheld from a potential consumer). Classical examples of public goods are national defence and lighthouses. If the production costs of a public good exceed the benefit gained by an individual, he will not produce it alone. But as groups can bear the costs collectively and enjoy the benefits individually, the way to produce public goods is to join a group. However, since nobody can be excluded from the consumption of a public good, everybody has an incentive to free-ride on the actions of others. Due to this free-riding, the group will not be formed at all, thereby creating the problem of collective action (Olson, 1965).

Olson's solution to the problem of collective action is that groups or organizations must provide selective incentives in the form of private goods to members or sanctions against non-members or defectors. But selective incentives do not really solve the problem of collective action because they presuppose an already existing organization with resources to provide these incentives. Indeed, selective incentives hardly even explain the continuance of groups providing public goods because one should think that such groups would be ousted by groups providing the selective incentive only, not wasting resources on the production of the public good.

3.3.1 The Theory of Group Solidarity

These considerations are the background of Hechter's *Principles of Group Solidarity* (1987a). The theory of group solidarity was developed in an effort to give his structural account of Celtic nationalism in Great Britain (Hechter, 1985: Ch. 2) a microsociological foundation, but it claims general relevance, and its application to nationalism appeared not in *Principles of Group Solidarity* but elsewhere (Hechter, 1987b; Levi & Hechter, 1985; Furtado & Hechter, 1992). At this point, however, our interest is confined to the general concept of group solidarity as this concept most clearly relates to ethnocentrism.

Hechter takes as his point of departure the problem of collective action. In his view, neither coercion, nor selective incentives, nor repeated interaction fully explains why groups providing public goods are formed. Instead, he proposes that groups exist in order to supply their members with some desired *collective* good. A collective good resembles a public good in that it must be jointly produced, but it has the quality of being excludable from non-contributors. Since non-contributors can be kept from consuming these goods, the threat of expulsion from the group is a selective incentive in itself which may be able to deter free-riders (1987a: 36f).

To be formed, however, the group still has to overcome some obstacles (1987a: 33f; 1987b: 416). Firstly, group members must congregate and come to appreciate their commonality of interest. Physical proximity and a common language is conducive to this process. Secondly, they must agree upon (or at least adopt) decision rules. Such constitutional procedures are likely to be facilitated by culturally homogeneous agents. Thirdly, they must obtain the necessary resources to produce the collective good. And finally, they must agree upon rules about coordination and allocation of the production.

Thus, Hechter's solution to the classical rational choice problem of collective action is that groups will form to produce collective goods if the above-mentioned conditions are met. But Hechter goes on to pose a new question which he also analyses using rational choice theory, namely: why do some groups display more solidarity than others? By a group's solidarity he means the extent of the influence it casts upon its members or, in other words, to what degree members will abide by the corporate obligations of the group. The greater the average proportion of each member's private resources contributed to collective ends without any compensation for this, for example through wages, the greater the solidarity of the group (1987a: 17f, 42f; 1987b: 416). This is the closest we come to a concept of ethnocentrism in rational choice theory. The concept of group solidarity captures the ingroup loyalty part of ethnocentrism while remaining silent as to the outgroup hostility displayed by group members. Conflict between the ingroup and the non-members, however, is inherent in the theory of group solidarity because the non-members necessarily must be excluded from the consumption of a valued good.

According to Hechter, a group's solidarity is a function of two independent factors: first, the extensiveness of its corporate obligations and, second, the degree to which individual members actually comply with these obligations (1987a: Ch. 3). The production costs of the collective good determine the minimum level of corporate obligations, but the greater the dependence of the members on the group, the more extensive are the obligations it can impose on them. Dependence in turn is a function of, among other things, the supply and knowledge of alternatives, the costs of moving, and the strength of personal ties.

However, dependence alone does not secure compliance with the corporate obligations because the collective good seen from the point of view of group members still has the non-excludable quality of a public good. Therefore, members will free-ride if the group does not establish a control capacity. This consists, firstly, of its sanctioning capacity – that is, its ability to punish or even exclude errant members – and, secondly, of its monitoring capacity – that is, its ability to observe whether members comply or not.

In sum, the solidarity of a group – or the ingroup loyalty element of ethnocentrism – is explained by the members' dependence on the group and the ability of the group to secure their compliance through different control mechanisms. If the members' behaviour can be fully controlled, solidarity will be a function of the members' dependence, but solidarity cannot be secured without a minimum of control. Thus, both the dependence of the members and the control capacity of the group are necessary conditions for group solidarity.

3.3.2 Discussion

At first glance, rational choice theory and the theory of group solidarity appear to contain a thorough examination of group dynamics based on assumptions about the individuals. However, both rational choice theory in general and the theory of group solidarity in particular suffer from some important liabilities.

Firstly, as mentioned, rational choice theory in its pure form is not a theory but an approach. Taken as a theory, it is at best empty, at worst tautological. This is because, in principle, the theory has nothing to say about the content of the preferences of individuals. It states that individuals must follow their preferences in certain ways, but it does not tell us what these preferences actually are. In this way, every social outcome can be explained retrospectively by postulating that the individuals desired it to happen. Or, in other words, the crucial individual cost-benefit analyses that are the cornerstone of rational choice theory are inferred tautologically from the actions that the theory is supposed to explain.

As an approach, on the other hand, rational choice theory is merely a language stating group dynamics in certain terms taken primarily from economic theory. This becomes clear when, for example, Hechter introduces so-called immanent goods to explain why members should contribute to a group without being compensated adequately through wages or selective incentives. The immanent goods of groups are defined as 'those that directly satisfy their members' utility (by increasing their sense pleasures, happiness, and so forth)' (1987a: 42). Thus, apparently, if there is no other reason why groups exist, then they exist because members feel good about them or because they feel that they should exist! In other words, the language is so general that it can be used to describe even the norm-guided behaviour that most rational choice theorists are eager to reject. And this possibility of including sociological explanations in the rational choice scheme is not merely hypothetical. Theoretically, Hechter implicitly points to the importance of sociological explanations by explicitly recognizing 'the primacy of institutional factors' in the theory of group solidarity (1987a: 53). Likewise, when applying his theory to nationalism, he is compelled to use terms such as 'norms of political conduct' (Furtado & Hechter, 1992: 178), 'status' (p. 181), and 'political and social atmosphere' (p. 182). In the same text, he acknowledges that membership of a group 'often leads to the adoption of its values and priorities', thereby violating the assumption of given preferences (p. 176).

To attain explanatory power, the preferences of individuals must be specified in advance. Fortunately, this is not so difficult as one might think given the formal emptiness of rational choice theory on this point. In reality, most rational choice theorists do have an – at least implicit – view of individuals as preoccupied with economic self-interest. The idea of wealth-seeking individuals is explicit also in some – if not most – rational choice writings on nationalism (e.g. Rogowski, 1985: 90; Hechter, 1987b: 417).

Now, some, mainly economic, scholars would insist that the assumption of economically self-interested individuals is an axiom to be judged solely by its ability to beget interesting and stimulating research questions (Lane, 1990: 71f). But if we are to *explain* and not merely predict a social outcome – in this case nationalism – this assumption should be liable to empirical testing. This task has been undertaken by Lewin (1991) who concludes that the hypothesis of self-interested voters, politicians, and bureaucrats does not get support in empirical studies in Western Europe. Unfortunately, however, we have no possibility of testing the hypothesis of wealth-seeking individuals in our case studies, but in Chapter 4 we do test whether a commonality of interest can be detected in the economic sphere.

To recapitulate, rational choice theory only has explanatory value when the preferences of the individuals are specified in advance. In the remaining part of this book, we treat rational choice theory as building on an assumption of economically self-interested individuals.

3.4 Integrative Theories

On the face of it, there seems to be a major chasm between predispositional and choice-related explanations of ethnocentrism. However, it is possible to fuse the two theoretical camps. Indeed, as we have hinted above, most of the predispositional explanations – at least in their newer and modified versions – have resorted to some kind of *ad hoc* explanations, thereby indicating that people act differently under different conditions. In our view, however, the most realistic and internally consistent attempt to provide an integrative theory of group ethnocentrism is offered by the social identity theory of Henri Tajfel and his colleagues.

3.4.1 Social Identity Theory

Social identity theory builds on the results of the minimal group experiments presented in Section 2.2. To the ingroup favouritism and preference mentioned there, we can now add the following results:

3. categorized subjects prefer *relative* ingroup advantage over the outgroup, even at the sacrifice of total ingroup rewards (i.e. social comparison is important); and
4. categorized subjects attain higher self-esteem than control subjects (i.e. the group membership has a direct influence on the psychological well-being of the individual).

(see Brown, 1986: 543–51; Fisher, 1990: 64)

Social comparison and especially self-esteem are the basic concepts of social identity theory as it tries to explain the intergroup discrimination revealed by the minimal group experiments.

As the minimal groups had no conflicting interests and no history, an explanation had to be sought in the influence of group membership on the individual. The categorization could be seen as having simply cognitive effects. Indeed, human beings do seem to have a tendency to perceive reality in categories and then exaggerate the differences between these categories (Tajfel 1981: Ch. 6; Grant, 1990: 45ff). But as the minimal ingroup was consistently *evaluated higher* than the outgroup, categorization must have had other than purely cognitive effects. More precisely, the theory assumes that social categories provide a system for *self*-reference in that they create and define the individual's place in society and thereby his or her self-image. Thus, groups provide their members with a social identity consisting of those aspects of an individual's self-image that derive from the social categories to which he or she belongs and from his or her evaluation of and emotional investment in such membership (Tajfel & Turner, 1979: 40; Tajfel, 1982: 2). Further, individuals' evaluations of their group membership and, consequently, their social identity rest primarily on comparisons with other groups. On this basis, the intergroup discrimination revealed by the minimal group experiments is seen as motivated by a desire for a positive social identity in order to increase the individual self-esteem. That is, the categorization not only had cognitive effects but it also initiated motivational processes in the individuals who are seen as predisposed to seek a high self-esteem by enhancing either their personal identity or, if possible, their social identity. What the categorization did was to provide such a possibility.

In short, the basic tenets of the theory can be spelled out as follows:

1. Individuals strive to maintain or enhance their self-esteem. This can be done by enhancing either the personal or the social identity of the individual.
2. Group membership contributes to an individual's social identity.
3. The evaluation of one's own group tends to be socially shared, and it is based primarily on social comparison with other groups.
4. Positive social identity is based to a large extent on favourable comparisons between the ingroup and relevant outgroups.

The theory then goes on to consider situations where social identity is unsatisfactory. In this case, individuals will strive either to leave their existing group and join some more positively evaluated group and/or to make their existing group more positively evaluated. In the words of Hirschman (1972), this is the choice between 'exit' and 'voice'. The first strategy involves individual action to increase self-esteem whereas the second involves social action, and it is, of course, the latter strategy that gives rise to group ethnocentrism. The choice between the two strategies – and, thus, the strength of group ethnocentrism – is dependent on at least three variables:

1. *Social mobility*, or, more precisely, the perceived possibility of individual movement between societal groups. When social mobility is high, individuals are more likely to choose to 'exit' and attempt to pass from a lower-status group to a higher-status group on an individual basis, and they are, consequently, less likely to contribute to the ethnocentrism of their initial groups (Tajfel & Turner, 1979: 43).
2. *Perceived system legitimacy*. When the existing, presumably hierarchical, system of group differences is perceived as legitimate, the 'voice' strategy is not likely to be chosen. However, when the apparently fixed state of affairs begins to be questioned and is shown to be inconsistent with general values, 'voice' is much more likely (p. 45).
3. *Perceived system security*. As with system legitimacy, the 'voice' strategy is not likely to be chosen when the existing group system is perceived as secure (p. 45). There are at least two ways in which a system of status differences can be perceived as secure. Firstly, the dominant group can have the power and the will to use it so as to dis-

courage other groups completely from taking any sort of social action. Secondly, the system security is closely connected to the existence of cognitive alternatives – that is, whether social outcomes other than the existing are at all conceivable. If subordinated groups cannot imagine things being different, they will not be likely to challenge the existing order of things. System security, of course, also pertains to the 'superior' group. If this group perceives its high status as threatened, social action to maintain it is likely.

As a consequence of these contingencies, it is possible to imagine societies with objective status differences and conflicting interests in which neither the subordinate group nor the dominant group shows much ethnocentrism. Members of the 'inferior' groups in such societies can either choose to exit or simply to remain silent in passive acceptance of the state of affairs.

In sum, social identity theory provides a general theory of ethnocentrism that can account for the variability of real-life ethnocentrism. The need for self-esteem will *ceteris paribus* lead social groups to attempt to differentiate themselves from each other and it will produce pressures to evaluate one's own group positively through ingroup/outgroup comparisons. Sometimes, however, historical and social contingencies will create negative social identities for the members of some groups and prevent them from attempting to enhance their social identities. This accounts for the self-effacement of some groups. But when one or more of the conditions change, an attempt to enhance social identity – and thus a rise in ethnocentrism – is likely. And as social identity is based on social comparison, attempts by an underprivileged group to enhance social identity are likely to spur a rise in the ethnocentrism of the dominant group as well in so far as it perceives its position to be threatened. It is easy to imagine that the further evolvement of ethnocentrism in the two groups can develop in a mutually reinforcing way.

3.4.2 Discussion

Apart from being able to account for the results of the minimal group experiments, social identity theory seems intuitively right. To name a Danish example, almost all Danes – football fans or not – followed the matches of the Danish football team in the European championship cup in 1992. Following the victory in the final, the streets of almost every city in Denmark were filled with happy and celebrating people. On the other hand, when Denmark in 1994 lost an important match to Spain in the qualification round for the next European championship, one student commented to us a few days later: 'It was so embarrassing to be a Dane.' These are clear-cut examples of the influence of a social identity on the psychological well-being of group members (and they are at the same time examples of human behaviour that is not guided by the economic self-interest of rational choice theory).

However, social identity theory does have some limitations. The ethnocentrism of the minimal groups included, at most, some outgroup derogation and it certainly never approached the ideal type of hostile ethnocentrism described by Adorno et al. (1950; see Section 2.1). Likewise, the social identity theory taken by itself does not provide any hints as to the causes of the outright hostility of some real-life groups. However, contrary to all the preceding theories, social identity theory does not claim to be complete in itself. Instead, it is explicitly conceived as complementary to the realistic theories of intergroup conflict which we shall discuss in Chapter 11 (Tajfel & Turner, 1979: 34). These theories emphasize the direct causal relationship between objective conflicting interests on the one hand and intergroup conflict and the ethnocentrism involved herein on the other. Thus, as an initial assumption, conflicting interests should promote group ethnocentrism and intergroup conflict. What social identity theory does is to add, first, the importance of the overall social climate determined by history and social structure and, second, the importance of perceptions. The quintessence of the three societal variables involved in the choice or not of social action to enhance social identity (social mobility and system legitimacy/security) is really that the existing group status system must be *perceived as unfair* by the group members. And, of course, objective status differences and conflicting interests are highly important – but not always decisive – variables in the formation of such a perception.

Thus, social identity theory itself insists that it should be combined with a macrosociological approach emphasizing real group differences. Such an approach is exactly what we present in the following chapter. Taken by itself, however, social identity theory still provides an integration of a predispositional and a choice-related view of ethnocentrism.

As mentioned, the decisive causal variable of social identity theory is the need for self-esteem, and this variable obviously has a predispositional nature. But the theory does not stop at this point. For, ideally, individuals have a choice between enhancing the personal or the social identity or even opting for a new social identity. And in a way not unlike the pure rational choice mechanism described above, the individuals choose the identity that is most likely to enhance their self-esteem. However, the behaviour of the social (in the sense of *social* identity theory) individual differs in several ways from the behaviour of the *rational* individual.

First of all, the goals of the social individual are not as tangible, restricted and cynical as the goals of the rational individual. As Turner (1975: 12) points out, intergroup conflict can be based not only on competition for scarce goods and resources in the economic sense of the words, but also on competition in which the scarce resources have no value outside the context of the competition itself. Such 'social competition' is present when groups compete for rank, status, prestige and other intangible goods for which value is determined by the norms of the social situation. And as the social identity is determined exactly by the overall status of the group, the social individual is likely to be interested not only in the economic well-being of the group but also in its political and cultural status. Furthermore, the overall status of the group is important to the individual irrespective of his or her own actual situation.

Secondly, social identity theory implies that the individuals have internalized their group membership to a considerable extent. It is part of their social identity and they most likely have an emotional investment in it. Consequently, it is a lot harder for the social individual than for the rational to drop or to shift his or her group membership. Thus, in contrast to rational choice theory, social identity theory expects a great deal of inertia in group formation and persistence.

And finally, the freedom of choice of group membership is limited by the social structure of the society which, in some instances, can produce insurmountable obstacles. Social structure is important also in rational choice theory, but social identity theory points to the overall climate of social mobility, social competition and comparison, and system legitimacy and security, rather than simply the decision problems of collective choice and the free-rider problems of collective action.

4 CONCLUSION

This chapter has examined the individual basis of the large-scale national movements which are the subject of this book. We regard the pervasive though flexible existence of ethnocentrism, understood as some level of ingroup preference and outgroup derogation or hostility, as the pivotal variable in the relation between individuals and nationalism. Ethnocentrism is a precondition for nationalism. The nationalism of specific nation-groups rests on exactly the ethnocentric preference for and loyalty towards co-nationals and the equally ethnocentric insistence on national sovereignty and refusal of outgroup dominance. However, it should be noted that nationalism is not just a specific instance of ethnocentrism. For ethnocentrism to become nationalism, it must be mobilized. In other words, the idea of a nation must be made a salient focus of identity for a sufficiently large part of the population, and the initiators of this mobilization will most often be found among the elites of the nation-group (Brass, 1985). The macrosociological conditions for this mobilization are the subject of Chapter 3 which concentrates on the societal level of analysis.

The theories discussed in this chapter offer different explanations of ethnocentrism. On the theoretical level, several of the theories suffer from problems regarding both internal consistency and empirical foundation. But, as noted, we do not have sufficient individual-level data concerning the ethnocentric and national thoughts, attitudes, and behaviours of the populations in Eastern Europe and, consequently, we cannot test any hypotheses about the motives and drives of the individuals that might be deduced from the theories. Some theories, however, are clearly more compatible with the flexibility and diversity of real-life ethnocentrism and with the above view that ethnocentrism must be combined with societal factors to produce national movements.

First of all, the deterministic quality of the sociobiological theory makes it totally unable to account for the variability of ethnocentrism described in Section 2.2. The problems with this approach only multiply when the transformation of the ethnocentrism of a group to a national movement adds yet another element of societal contingency.

Secondly, of the other theories, only rational choice theory and social identity theory actually embrace the problem of group formation and action as opposed to individual action to enhance either the material or psychological self-interest. The psychodynamic theories suffer from several problems in this respect. They fail to account for the process of group formation and the choice of group exactly because they are either aggregations or extrapolations of individual-level theories. In extending individual-level theories to group and intergroup relations, two things happen. Firstly, it becomes either difficult to allow structural and societal factors into the theoretical framework, as in the case of the theory of the authoritarian personality, or, as in the case of frustration–aggression theory, the original concepts lose their distinctiveness and become able to subsume almost any other thinkable explanation. And secondly, because the theories lack group-level concepts, they have to assume that a clear group identity and solidarity is already established. Therefore, the theories cannot explain the *processes* which lead to the group identity and solidarity. As psychological theories, they may carry some truth and explanatory power as to the functioning of the individual and they may even be able to account for the ethnocentrism of some individuals. But to explain the formation of group movements in general and national movements in particular something more is needed, and, in our opinion, this 'more' has to come from the group and intergroup levels of analysis.

Both rational choice theory and social identity theory allow for such an analysis. At first glance, this may not be apparent with respect to rational choice theory as it builds on an explicit methodological individualism. But through collective choice arguments, rational choice theorists integrate structural and societal elements in the theoretical framework. In the same way, social identity theory emphasizes the importance of the 'social climate' defined by, for example, the degree of social mobility and the legitimacy and security of the system.

As noted in Section 3.3.2, rational choice theory is only a theory when the preferences are specified in advance. In this context, we regard the rational preferences as determined primarily by economic self-interest. Whether the individual East European citizen was guided by economic self-interest, as in rational choice theory, or by concerns about his or her relative status as this inflicted on the self-esteem, as in social identity theory, is an empirical question. And unfortunately it is an empirical question that cannot be answered by means of the available data. What we *can* do, however, is to identify different commonalities of interest – both economic and non-economic – in the East European populations and then assess which theory seems most suitable. This assessment is made in the concluding chapter of Part One.

Anyway, the ability of rational choice theory and social identity theory to integrate the individual, group, and intergroup levels of analysis has two major advantages when applying them to our question about the causes of national revivals in Eastern Europe. Firstly, they allow for societal contingencies as the decisive causes of the national revivals, which is an absolute necessity taking into consideration the different strengths of the national revivals. The examination of these societal contingencies is undertaken theoretically in the following chapter and empirically in Chapters 5 to 8. Secondly, they both give some hints as to why groups form in the first place and, consequently, why some groups are preferred to other groups. This insight is exploited in Chapter 4 which provides a preliminary examination of the reasons why exactly the nation became the focus of group identity and formation in connection with the collapse of the communist regimes.

3 Explanations of National Revivals

1 INTRODUCTION

The microsociological theories presented in the preceding chapter offer different interpretations of the mechanisms that prompt the individual to join and remain loyal to ingroups while derogating outgroups. The ethnocentrism of groups, however, does not by itself generate national movements in those groups. For this to happen, the groups have to be mobilized, and mobilization is furthered significantly if certain structural conditions are present. The structural conditions for mobilization of national groups are the subject of this chapter on macrosociological explanations of national revivals.

However, there is a vast number of contending theories on the origins and causes of nationalism and, evidently, it is not possible to cover them all in this book. The focus here will be on some selected theories that represent the widely used distinction between primordial and instrumental explanations of nationalism.

Some of the theories that can be subsumed under these two headings have a slightly different aim from ours, but through a short discussion of each theory we nevertheless deduce hypotheses that are testable in the recent East European setting.

2 PRIMORDIAL EXPLANATIONS

Primordialists focus on the strong emotional attachments that accompany national revivals and they explain this fact as a consequence of the deep-rooted, almost 'natural' quality of ethnic belonging.

Primordialism is not a popular research direction. The established research society regards it as too deterministic and distances itself from it. Indeed, in a review article on recent developments in the study of ethnic political activity, Newman (1991) focuses only on the dominant modernization (that is, instrumental) strain within the literature. However, it seems that the critics of primordialism have concentrated primarily on calling attention to counter-examples (see Eller & Coughlan, 1993) and the mere reference to counter-examples does not, of course, *a priori* exclude some relevance of this kind of explanation to our specific cases.

One of the first to use primordialism as an analytical concept was Shils (1957), who applied it to ties of kinship. More relevant for our purposes, however, is Geertz's definition which applies to larger-scale groups, such as those based on common territory, religion, language, and customs:

> By a primordial attachment is meant one that stems from the 'givens' … of social existence: immediate contiguity and kin connection mainly, but beyond them the givenness that stems from being born into a particular religious community, speaking a particular language, or even a dialect of a language, and following particular social practices. (1973: 259)

We can detect two main ways in which this kind of attachment has been applied in explanations of national revivals. Primordialism 'in the strong sense' refers to the 'primeval' meaning of the word, which suggests something that has persisted from the beginning, whereas primordialism 'in the moderate sense' refers to something that is 'first created or developed' – that is, not necessarily natural or automatic in existence, but nevertheless historically deep-rooted.

2.1 Strong Primordialism

Primordialism in the strong sense is used in two ways to explain national revivals: either metaphysically or sociobiologically. Geertz himself provides an example of the former approach:

> These congruities of blood, speech, custom and so on, are seen to have an *ineffable*, and at times overpowering coerciveness *in and of themselves*. (1973: 259; emphasis added)[3]

When explaining national revivals, adherents of this metaphysical view often refer to Herder's notion of *Volksgeist* or *Nationalgeist* – a set of customs and a life style. It is a way of perceiving and behaving that is of value solely because it is special to the ethnic group in question. This *Volksgeist* cannot be dissolved by anything short of total extinction of the group; and it can only be repressed for so long. According to Isaiah Berlin, for example, 'a wounded *Volksgeist*, so to speak, is like a bent twig, forced down so severely that when released, it lashes back with fury' (Gardels, 1991: 20; see also Berlin, 1972).

The second way in which national revivals can be explained as a natural, inevitable phenomenon is by reference to sociobiological theory, such as the kin selection theory of van den Berghe which we discussed in Chapter 2. Van den Berghe argues that the relationships between ethnic and racial groups are irreducible as these relationships are based on a 'primordial identity'. The primordial sentiments of kinship are not based on shared group interests, but on the biological imperative of reproduction. And, in contrast to the calculating nature of non-primordial relations between interest groups, primordial sentiments can easily lead to 'blind ferocity' and 'orgies of passion' (van den Berghe, 1978: 404f).

2.2 Moderate Primordialism

An argument along the lines of primordialism in the moderate sense has been presented by Smith (1986; 1991; 1992). Although explicitly dissociating himself from a primordial stance (1991: 20), he nevertheless holds that nationalism can be fully explained only by reference to the ethnic foundation of the nation-group, i.e. the *ethnie*. As an ideal type, an *ethnie* is defined as

a unit of population sharing:

1. A common proper name
2. Myths of common ancestry
3. Historical memories
4. One or more distinctive elements of culture
5. An association with a given territory
6. A sense of social solidarity (Smith, 1992: 50)

In contrast to the sociobiological view, an *ethnie* is not naturally given, but historically and culturally developed. However, it has roots far back in time, and once in existence it acts as a powerful focus of identity for individuals and groups.

But how does an ethnic identity convert itself to nationalism? This is done mainly with the aid of secularized, and therefore alienated, intellectuals who, in the image of nationalism as a form of historicist culture, see a solution to their identity problem (pp. 93ff). Later on, this solution is also accepted by the large masses because it fulfils important functions in the modern world, especially in that nationalism transcends oblivion, restores collective dignity, and realizes fraternity (pp. 160ff).[4] The resulting conception of a nation-group differs from the notion of an *ethnie* primarily in that the link between the nation-group and the territory is physical and actual in contrast to the historical and symbolic association of an *ethnie* with a 'homeland' (p. 40).

According to Smith, however, the functions that national identity and nationalism perform are not enough to explain the historical appearance and development of nationalism. Smith suggests that the explanation should be found 'in the different kinds of *ethnic base* and *political process* in late medieval and early modern Europe, as well as in *the wider sense of cultural community* persisting in varying degrees in different parts of the world' (p. 97; emphasis added).

Firstly, the existence of an *ethnie* is the basis, and thus the precondition, of any national revival. Smith then outlines two main types of *ethnie* – lateral and vertical – from which modern nation-groups were formed. The lateral type of *ethnie* was socially confined to the upper strata and geographically spread out, whereas the vertical type was more compact and popular (Smith, 1991: 53).

Secondly, to become nation-groups, the two types of *ethnie* went through different political processes (pp. 54ff). Nation-groups built on lateral *ethnies* came into being by bureaucratic incorporation of lower social strata. Through the military, administrative, fiscal, and judicial apparatus of a bureaucratic state, the dominant aristocratic ethnic core was able to regulate and disseminate values, symbols, myths, traditions, and memories from their own cultural heritage, thereby defining a new and broader cultural identity for the population as a whole. In contrast, nation-groups built on vertical *ethnies* were the result of a vernacular mobilization of 'the people' by small circles of educator–intellectuals through an appeal to the community's alleged ethnic past. The reason why the bureaucratic state played a minor role in these cases was that vertical *ethnies* were usually subject communities.

Finally, the wider sense of cultural community in the world is important because it accounts for the spread of the idea of a nation and the ideology of nationalism when first conceived (pp. 84ff).

2.3 Discussion and Deduction of Hypotheses

Let us begin with a closer look at the problems of primordialism in the strong sense. We have already noted several objections to van den Berghe's sociobiological version of primordialism (see Section 3.1.2 of Chapter 2). As regards the metaphysical version of primordialism in the strong sense, a convincing criticism has been presented by Eller and Coughlan (1993) who attack the concept of primordialism as used by Geertz and his followers. Eller and Coughlan contend that the fact that primordial attachments are 'given', *a priori*, makes the concept inflexible and therefore vulnerable to the host of studies which have shown that ethnicity rests on a variable definition of self and others (1993: 188f). Combined with the notion of 'ineffability' – that is, the failure to analyse the functioning of primordial attachments – this makes the concept of primordialism unsociological, unanalytical, and vacuous (pp. 189ff).

As far as primordialism in the strong sense is concerned, we agree with Eller and Coughlan. And we might add the epistemological argument that there is no way that this theory can generate a testable hypothesis about national revivals.

However, these arguments are not fatal to the same extent with regard to Smith's version of primordialism in the moderate sense, because Smith is careful to note the changeableness of identity through history. Yet, when trying to formulate hypotheses about the present national revivals on the basis of Smith's theory, we encounter at least two other problems.

The first problem concerns Smith's conception of the attributes of an *ethnie* which combine to create an ethnic identity. We feel that the focus on the static, though historically developed, attributes of an *ethnie* misses the point that the ethnic – and later national – identity of a group is highly influenced by the dynamic interplay between the ethnic group in question and other significant groups.[5] Thus, to describe the ethnic base fully we must include a description of the historical relationship between the significant ethnic groups.

Secondly, the question that Smith tries to answer is partly different from ours. Smith traces the origins of nationalism as a phenomenon in an analysis covering millennia in time and the whole globe in space. Once nationalism is there, however, Smith offers only a few clues as to the waxes and wanes of nationalism, and this is exactly the type of question that we have set out to answer. This has two consequences. Firstly, Smith's historical distinction between lateral and vertical *ethnies* is of more relevance to the discussion of types of nationalism carried through in Chapter 11 than to the causes of national revivals in the present world. Secondly, given the fundamentality of nationalism in the modern world, what needs to be explained is the wanes rather than the waxes. In other words, to explain national revivals fully, Smith's theory on the origins of nationalism must be supplemented with an explanation of the temporary quiescence of otherwise virile national movements.

Such a supplement has been presented by Kellas (1991).[6] Kellas distinguishes between two complementary types of explanation of the politics of nationalism and ethnicity: a 'bottom-up' and a 'top-down' view. The former focuses on the resources generated by the nationalists themselves, whereas the latter, which is of interest here, focuses on the political context which 'ultimately determines [the nationalists'] success or failure' (p. 85). In a more specific analysis of nationalism in the 'second world', he points to the importance of 'top-down' factors in both the USSR and Yugoslavia, such as regime change and the existence within the federations of territorial political units and constitutional rights of self-determination that served as a resource for nationalism (pp. 106ff).

We are now prepared to formulate primordial hypotheses to be tested in our cases. We do this by rejecting primordialism in the strong sense, and then by deducing two complementary hypotheses from the moderate version: one that accounts for the ethnic base of national revivals (the perennial part), and one that points to the triggering, or contextual, factors (the temporal part). The hypotheses are:

$H_{1.1}$ National revivals are based on a common identity in nation-groups provided by 1) the *ethnie* and 2) the historical interplay between the *ethnie* and the other significant *ethnie(s).*

$H_{1.2}$ National revivals can be triggered by liberal policies adopted by former repressive regimes and eased by already existing republican political units and constitutional rights.

As mentioned, the distinctly primordial hypothesis, $H_{1.1}$, cannot stand by itself, but needs some kind of temporal supplement. This does not, of course, mean that a confirmation of the temporal hypothesis, $H_{1.2}$, is tantamount to a confirmation of the primordial explanation as such.[7] The demonstration of triggering factors could just as well be combined with explanations emphasizing naked interests, and it is to this kind of explanation that we now turn.

3 INSTRUMENTAL EXPLANATIONS

Instrumentalists view ethnic and national identity not as a primordial constant, but as a social construct. Further, most instrumentalists see this social construct as an epiphenomenon of modernization. Thus, national identities and institutions are seen as phenomena that, in the course of the still evolving modernization, can be repeatedly created and recreated (Newman, 1991: 452ff).

The primary assertion of instrumentalists is that national identity is instrumental in terms of achieving desired ends because it can serve as a basis for mobilization in the competition between groups and elites for control over scarce resources. Nationalism is viewed as an ideology, but its content is based on material interests rather than ideal values about the good society. Thus, the politics of ethnicity and nationalism is just another kind of politics (Sampson, 1992: 394). According to the instrumental perspective, a national revival is therefore not an awakening of an age-old, latent, and dormant force (Gellner, 1983: 48f). On the contrary, there need not necessarily be a strong ethnic past to build on because such a past, if need be, is invented and then propagated. The result of this process is the building of a nation-group which essentially is an imagined political community (Anderson, 1991: 6). However, the basic goal of a national revival is still to fulfil the nationalist principle of one nation-group, one state (Gellner, 1983: 1).

In the following sections some of the instrumental explanations of national revivals will be presented. Although theories based on economic interests are most clearly associated with an instrumentalist stance, we shall argue that national revivals can be based also on political and cultural interests. Following a short discussion we will then deduce hypotheses from the theories.

3.1 Economic Explanations

One of the most famous theories of nationalism is Hechter's theory of internal colonialism. According to this theory, the uneven spread of modernization in a state territory results in relatively advanced and less advanced groups (Hechter, 1975: 38). The superordinate or core group institutionalizes its relative advantage through a stratification system, which allocates high prestige positions and economic privileges solely to core-group members. The result is a cultural division of labour, and this encourages distinctive ethnic or national identifications in the two groups (p. 39).

The stability of the system depends on how the periphery group evaluates its situation. Basically, the situation of the periphery group is marked by relative deprivation and alienation, but the mobilization of this group depends on changes which can occur in two ways (p. 20). Firstly, the economic and social imbalance between the two groups can be tipped so that the suppression of the periphery group gets even worse. Secondly, the expectations of the periphery group concerning correction of the imbalance can rise. In this way, the contemporary and triggering factors of $H_{1.2}$ are also of importance to the instrumental perspective. The ultimate goal of the resulting national revival is then to create an independent state in order to escape the colonialism.

In sum, Hechter's theory is that internal colonialism leads to a cultural division of labour, which implies that 'objective cultural differences are superimposed upon economic inequalities' (p. 43). And it is this cultural division of labour that makes a national revival in the disadvantaged group likely.

3.2 Political Explanations

Hechter's theory was originally developed to explain national revivals by reference to economic or social inequalities between cultural groups. However, as Kellas (1991: 56), for example, points out, the concept of internal colonialism can easily be extended to include political and cultural inequalities.

An example of a theory that stresses political inequalities is Laitin's (1991) elite incorporation model. According to this theory the decisive question is whether the elite in the centre has incorporated the peripheral elite or not. If the peripheral elite has been incorporated, it enjoys a status of 'most-favoured-lords', which means that it has rights and privileges equal to those of the centre elite (pp. 143ff). In this case, the elite of the regional territory will be co-opted in the power establishment of the centre. And over generations, this situation leads to the assimilation of the lower periphery strata into the dominant culture.

If, on the contrary, the local elite has not been privileged with a most-favoured-lords status, only a lesser part of the elite will seek co-optation in the centre (p. 146ff). They then serve as mediators so that the centre retains control over the periphery, but they are not able to translate their primarily economic rewards into social status in the centre. This situation paves the way for a national revival because the new generations in the periphery find that they face barriers to mobility. The opportunities in the centre are constrained and the local mediator-elite is also unwilling to make way for the 'new men'. This means that the idea of full political independence is attractive to the aspiring local elites because they would then gain access to powerful jobs in a new state.[8]

Laitin's theory suggests that we should search for power inequalities between different ethnic groups in order to explain national revivals. In contrast with Hechter, Laitin focuses more specifically on a special group of actors, namely the elite. But as the elite encompasses those individuals who have or aspire to attain power, the elite focus is only natural when applying the concept of internal colonialism to political inequalities.

3.3 Cultural Explanations

As Taylor points out,

> our identity is partly shaped by recognition or its absence, often by the *mis*recognition of others, and so a person or group of people can suffer real damage, real distortion, if the people or society around them mirror back to them a confining or demeaning or contemptible picture of themselves. Non-recognition or misrecognition can inflict harm, can be a form of oppression, imprisoning someone in a false, distorted, and reduced mode of being. (1992: 25)

The cultural version of internal colonialism would see national revivals as a result of cultural inequalities, or, in Taylor's terminology, of non-recognition or misrecognition of the nation-group. The national revival is instrumental in so far as it is used by elites or groups to mobilize the nation-group in order to correct the inequalities. However, the aspiration of these elites or groups, namely cultural recognition, is a less concrete good than the more tangible goods desired by elites or groups initiating national revivals on economic or political grounds.

So, according to this view, national revivals are a result of '[c]ultural deprivation [which] is experienced when discrimination or insult takes place on account of a person's national identity, language (including accent), religion, habits, tastes, and so on' (Kellas, 1991: 69). As Kellas notes, such discrimination operates in two ways. Most frequently, it takes place in face-to-face encounters between members of dominant and dominated nation-groups. But just as importantly, discrimination, or misrecognition, is also experienced collectively, and at a distance, as when linguistic or educational usages are imposed officially on all citizens by the state (*ibid.*).

3.4 Discussion and Deduction of Hypotheses

The concept of internal colonialism and its consequences for the economic, the political, and the cultural sphere provide a solid basis for the deduction of testable hypotheses. However, before turning to these hypotheses, a few comments should be made.

Firstly, we must stress the inherent interdependence between the three spheres. For instance, political power is often due to economic power, and vice versa. Further, as national revivals in the instrumental view are mobilizations around ethnic or cultural symbols, a discrimination against these symbols of 'the national culture' can only strengthen the persuasive powers of nationalist mobilizers.

Secondly, we should bear in mind that structural inequalities in the spheres of economy, politics, and culture achieve political significance only through the perceptions and actions of individuals. That is, the individuals must perceive the inequalities to be unfair, and they must decide to act upon this perception by initiating or joining a nationalist movement. This is why the macrosociological theories of this chapter cannot stand alone; they must be combined with microsociological theories such as those presented in Chapter 2 in order to achieve a complete picture of the causes of national revivals. A discussion of the relationship between the microsociological and macrosociological theories is carried through in Chapter 9. For the present purposes, we will point to just one illustrative example of the importance of perceptions also to macrosociological explanations of national revivals. This example is provided by the difficulties of applying Hechter's theory to the occurrence of national revivals in situations where the modernization process has made the average per-capita income in the periphery higher than in the centre (Douglass, 1988: 193; Horowitz, 1992: 14f).[9] A national revival under these circumstances could be explained by political or cultural internal colonialism. But it might as well arise because the regional group *perceives* that it could have done better without the centre which allegedly derives more revenue from the region than it returns. Wallerstein (1961) argues that this kind of national revival is in fact the most common because the richest groups in the periphery get tired of supporting their poorer fellow citizens and start looking for greener pastures in a nation-state of their own. To distinguish these two variants of Hechter's original theory we shall employ Berkowitz's distinction between deprivation and frustration (see Section 3.2.3 of Chapter 2). We use the word 'deprivation' when referring to objective inequalities and 'frustration' when referring to perceived unfair inequalities.

Thirdly, we must add a comment to the notion of 'cultural internal colonialism'. As mentioned, the national revival is instrumental in so far as it is used by elites or groups to mobilize the nation-group in order to correct inequalities, in this case cultural deprivation. For this reason, and because cultural discrimination by a centre fits the general picture of colonialism, this subject is treated under the heading of instrumental explanations. But there seems to be a prior question to this instrumentality, namely: why is cultural (or national) recognition important to people? Obviously, by posing this question we are approaching the primordial emphasis on the emotional strength of cultural ties. And, indeed, in our deduction of hypotheses about the consequences of nationalism in Part Two, the need for recognition of the group's culture and the following resistance to non-recognition and misrecognition is treated as a 'primordial interest'.

Bearing these remarks in mind, we can now formulate the following hypotheses:

H_2 National revivals are caused by internal colonization of nation-groups leading to:

- **$H_{2.1}$** economic deprivation or frustration through a cultural division of labour,
- **$H_{2.2}$** political deprivation or frustration through assignment of non-most-favoured-lords status to local elites, and/or
- **$H_{2.3}$** cultural deprivation or frustration through non-recognition or misrecognition.

4 CONCLUSION

At this point, we have a lot of unanswered questions. On the microsociological level of analysis, the quarrel is between the rational choice view of individuals as motivated by economic self-interest and restricted by the problem of collective action on the one hand, and the social identity view of individuals as motivated by a need for self-esteem and restricted by social norms and structures on the other. The available empirical evidence does not make these theories directly testable, and this is why we have not deduced hypotheses in Chapter 2. On the macrosociological level of analysis, the quarrel is between the primordial view of nationalism as based on ethnic groups with a long history and liable only to external suppression on the one hand, and the instrumental view of nationalism as strategic action to correct imposed inequalities on the other. Contrary to the microsociological theories, it is possible to test hypotheses from the macrosociological theories. However, we have argued that some important modifications are necessary in order to formulate realistic hypotheses from the often very general macrosociological theories.

Firstly, to avoid the inherent tendency of metaphysical and sociobiological primordialism to generate tautological explanations, these 'strong' primordial explanations must be rejected. However, recognizing reality partly as a construct of human beings does not automatically lead to an instrumental view of national revivals as based purely on strategic considerations. Primordialism in the moderate sense builds on a view that human beings are as much engineers of culture as they are captives of culture.

Therefore, it focuses on the historical existence of an *ethnie* as the origin of nationalism. In the explanation of the present national revivals, however, the existence of an *ethnie* can only be a necessary condition, and, consequently, primordialism in the moderate sense must be supplemented with an account of the contemporary developments which were conducive to each specific instance of national revival. Further, in our view, the historical interplay between an *ethnie* and other *ethnies* plays a significant role in the development and self-concept of an *ethnie*. Therefore, an account of the historical relationship between *ethnies* must be included in the examination of the ethnic base of national revivals.

Secondly, the instrumental view of national revivals as mobilizations to correct inequalities should recognize that such distressing inequalities can be found in the economic, the political, and the cultural sphere. Further, what is important is whether or not these inequalities are perceived as unfair or not. Perceptions are not easy to operationalize on a macrosociological level of analysis and, when introduced as a theoretical concept, they compound the risk that the subjective evaluations of the observers will influence the result of the analysis. On the other hand, it would be even more wrong simply to ignore the obvious fact that perceptions *do* matter.

At the end of the theoretical chapters of Part One, two theoretical questions are left unanswered. The first question is whether the primordial and the instrumental views should be combined or whether they are at all combinable. In order to generate clear hypotheses about the empirical cases, we have so far maintained a clear distinction between the theories and their derived sub-hypotheses although we have noted the connection between primordial and cultural instrumental explanations. Our view on the appropriateness of a theoretical synthesis will become clear in the conclusion of Part One. At that point of the analysis we can also add some empirical arguments to the discussion.

The second question concerns the relationship between the microsociological theories presented in the preceding chapter and the macrosociological theories of this chapter. Our decision to assign theoretical importance to perceptions is a first indication of our view that the two levels of analysis must be combined. Microsociological theories alone cannot explain the rise and fall of specific national movements. Macrosociological theories, on the other hand, can only detect similarities and differences in the conditions of groups of individuals, and they specify neither why nor how the single individual should act upon these conditions. A more detailed discussion of the relationship between the theories is presented in the conclusion of Part One where we also propose an integrative theoretical model of the causes of national revivals.

Now, however, is the time to give our discussions of ethnocentrism and nationalism an empirical foundation. In Chapter 4 we describe some general characteristics of national movements and the East European societies in late-20th-century in order to explore whether any of these environmental characteristics can account for the overwhelming popularity of national movements in late-20th-century Eastern Europe. In Chapters 5 to 8, this is followed by a detailed search for the explanations of each of the national revivals in turn based on the hypotheses deduced in this chapter. Finally, in Chapter 9, we compare the results of the analyses and go more thoroughly into the above-mentioned theoretical questions.

4 Why Nationalism in Eastern Europe?

1 INTRODUCTION

Although microsociological theories are not directly testable with the empirical evidence at our disposal, there are other ways to take advantage of their insights. Their assertion is that social action must in some way lead to individual satisfaction. In this chapter, we pose the question of why the thought of joining or supporting exactly a *national* movement should be appealing exactly to the *East European* citizen of the late 20th century, and we answer it in terms of the individual's situation and considerations as theorized in Chapter 2.

It should be emphasized, however, that this chapter does not by itself bring any answers to the main question of our Part One, namely the *causes* of the national revivals. At this point, we merely use the microsociological theories to explore whether the general properties and environments of nationalism in Eastern Europe could be seen as conducive to the individual's decision to join or support a national movement. The detailed examination of the causes of the national revivals, however, will have to await the test of the hypotheses deduced in Chapter 3.

The title question of this chapter is actually composed of two subquestions. First, we examine which general properties of 20th-century *national* movements and their environments make them a likely outcome of the processes and conditions of group formation outlined by rational choice theory and social identity theory. The second question is whether there are any general properties of the 20th-century *East European* societies that would facilitate the choice of national movements as opposed to other group movements.

2 CHARACTERISTICS OF LATE-20TH-CENTURY NATIONAL MOVEMENTS

Why should one choose to be loyal to a *nation-group* rather than a regional group, a class, or some third group? Actually, the widespread choice of a nation-group as the relevant basis of group formation runs counter to the expectancies of the two most prominent theoretical and ideological directions of the 19th and 20th centuries, liberalism and Marxism. The liberal expectancy was that ethnic divisions would inevitably lose their weight and sharpness in modern and modernizing societies because of the unifying effects of education, communication, and integrated economic and political systems. The slightly different Marxist expectation was that the salience of ethnic divisions would decrease, but only to make room for the primacy of class divisions which for their part would eventually disappear after a revolution (Glazer & Moynihan, 1975: 6f). Contrary to these expectancies, however, ethnic and national loyalties have retained their importance, and ethnic and national conflicts have increased both in number and intensity almost constantly throughout the 20th century (Connor, 1973).

Numerous books have been written to explain this unexpected persistence of nation-groups and nationalism.[10] In this chapter, however, we do not attempt to give a full examination of the complex interplay of economic, political, and ideological factors that might explain the phenomenon. Instead, we apply the insights of rational choice theory and social identity theory to give a preliminary account of factors that could have been conducive to the persistence of national movements in the late 20th century. In Chapter 2 we were primarily interested in that part of the theories that explains ingroup cohesion and outgroup relations. In this context, however, we focus on what they have to say about the conditions and processes of group *formation* to detect what properties and environments of national movements make them a likely choice of the individual.

2.1 A Group Solidarity Analysis

Hechter sees groups as forming to produce collective goods (see Section 3.3.1 of Chapter 2). To overcome the problem of collective action, however, at least three further conditions must be met. And, according to Hechter, each of these conditions gives national groups a comparative advantage as opposed to other bases of group formation.

Firstly, group members must congregate and come to appreciate their commonality of interest. There are many ways in which this might happen, but there is no doubt that physical proximity and a common language are conducive to this process. And physical proximity and especially common language are two of the most central characteristics of nation-groups. Further, in contrast to the environment of the 19th-century wave of national revivals, modern national movements can draw on extensive communication and transportation networks, in particular the modern mass media.[11] Of course, to a large degree, the interest articulation of nation-groups, as well as any other groups, depends on whether the individual group members are allowed to associate freely with one another at all.

Secondly, group members must agree upon – or at least adopt – decision-making rules. According to Hechter, such constitutional procedures are likely to be facilitated by culturally homogeneous agents (1987b: 416). Thus, in contrast to those groups whose potential members are culturally heterogeneous, such as interest groups, the obstacles to constitutional choice among national movements are likely to be less severe.

Thirdly, prospective group members must obtain the necessary resources to produce the collective good and they must coordinate and allocate this production. The necessary resources are obtained by obligating all members to contribute a certain amount of their private resources towards the corporate project. But as the goal of national movements is to attain or maintain autonomy – or, more specifically, to gain control of a state apparatus – the potential resources obtainable by national movements are far greater than the prospects for most other groups. In a way, they opt not only for a greater share of the cake, or for influence on its content as interest groups do, but for control of the content and allocation of the whole cake. And in opting for control of the state bureaucracy and the concomitant jobs, offices, and other spoils, the national movement at the same time potentially gains access to some weighty selective incentives for the most active members. The formidable growth of the power of the state since the Second World War has significantly heightened the potential benefit of joining a national movement to gain access to or control over a state, and, consequently, has made such a decision more lucrative to the individual.

2.2 A Social Identity Analysis

According to social identity theory, the three variables of social mobility, system legitimacy, and system security play a decisive role in the individuals' choice between individual and social action to increase their self-esteem (see Section 3.4.1 of Chapter 2). Slightly reformulated, these variables can be seen as conditions of group formation.

The first condition of group formation is *low levels of social mobility* – that is, perceptions of little possibility of individual movement between societal groups. At first glance, the social mobility of modern societies does not seem to further the formation of a nation-group as increasing social mobility is one of the most prominent elements in the transition from traditional to modern societies. There is no doubt that the inhabitants of developed countries today have far greater opportunities for individual movements compared to just one century ago. It is also true that belonging to a nation-group is by no means an unchangeable fact. Individuals and even groups of individuals do from time to time change their nationality, and children of mixed marriages are just one kind of numerous borderline cases.

However, it is our contention that while social mobility in general, such as between regions or occupations, has increased enormously during the 20th century, this is not so with regard to movements between nation-groups. Today, the nationality of a person has become an extremely important piece of information to most states, both with regard to general considerations about the composition of its population and with regard to more specific matters, such as granting or refusing to grant asylum, residence permit, citizenship, and other rights. And, in order to procure a basis for decision-making in these matters, the state holds people to their established nationality. In some multinational states, such as the former Soviet Union and the former Yugoslavia, this happened (or happens) by, for example, including the nationality in each citizen's passport.[12] To these real obstacles to individual shifts between nation-groups, one should add the psychological aversion to violating values central to self-esteem. Often, people have an emotional investment in their nationality large enough to prevent them from changing it. And if some people shift allegiance anyway, the consequences, especially in times of conflict, are most often accusations of treason and renegading, and this condemnation in turn has a deterrent effect on the remaining members of a nation-group.

To sum up the argument, if unfair status differences between *nation-groups* become a salient belief to an inhabitant of a late-20th-century modern society, the probability that he or she will participate in the formation of a group – in this case by supporting or joining a national movement – is higher than if the same status differences were perceived between, for example, occupational groups, because in the latter case he or she will have greater chances of improving status and self-esteem on an individual basis.

Secondly, a perception that the existing system of status differences is *illegitimate* is conducive to the individual's decision to join a group. It is beyond the scope of this book to discuss which kinds of status differences have become more or less legitimate in modern societies. In relation to the legitimacy of status differences between *nation-groups*, however, Connor's description of the inherent legitimacy of national self-determination in modern societies is informative:

> Ever since the abstract philosophical notion that the right to rule is vested in *the people* was first linked in popular fancy to a particular,

> ethnically defined people – a development which first occurred at the time of the French Revolution – the conviction that one's own people should *not*, by the very nature of things, be ruled by those deemed aliens has proved a potent challenger to the legitimacy of multinational structures. (Connor, 1977: 25; emphasis in the original)

The strong legitimizing powers of national self-determination are reflected in the configuration and functioning of the present international system. The political principle of the sovereign state has been successful to the point that, today, almost every part of the world is divided into bureaucratic states which are normally very free to handle internal affairs without interference from other countries. That the principles of sovereignty and non-interference derive their legitimacy from the ideology of nationalism is clear already from the somewhat misleading terms 'international system' and 'nation-states'. Thus, given the widespread and potent philosophical idea of national self-determination and the actual power and discretion of the late-20th-century states deriving from the – often false – premise that they are 'nation-states', multinational social systems involving status differences between the constituent nation-groups face high chances of being perceived as illegitimate by members of the suppressed nation-group(s).[13]

The third condition of social action emphasized by social identity theory is that the system must be perceived as *insecure* either through the rulers' lacking ability or will to suppress challenges to the existing system, or through appearance of cognitive alternatives among the dominated groups. The power balance and the will to use power for suppressive purposes are, of course, highly contingent variables, and it is an open question whether the late-20th-century world situation in this respect has any general bearing on the possibility of forming national movements. It is, however, safe to say that in the late-20th-century modern world, basic liberal and democratic rights have gained prominence and respect to the degree that open suppression of the freedom of expression and association has become much more suspect. Thus, although the sovereignty of the state is still the dominant principle in international relations, states which today severely suppress national minorities are more likely to be put under international pressure. In general, therefore, the modern individual should be less afraid of challenging the existing system through association with a national movement because modern states should be expected to care about their international reputation. Still, this is, of course, highly dependent on the particular intentions and actions of the rulers of the state.

As for the cognitive alternatives, their existence is significant in the realm of national movements. All over the world, the above-mentioned idea of national self-determination has led to numerous national revivals, often with successful results. Combined with the explosive increase in formal education and world-wide communication networks, this development provides a host of cognitive alternatives to members of suppressed nation-groups. All in all, in the late 20th century, systems of status differences between nation-groups are not likely to be perceived as secure as they were before, and, in general, the individuals thus face fewer obstacles to formation of national movements than before.

2.3 Summary of the General Late-20th-Century Environment

Contrary to the predictions of some long-established traditions in sociological and political thought, national resurgences and identities have persisted even in advanced countries. From the perspectives of Marxist and liberal theories, national movements in modern societies are basically *anomies*. Contemporary political scientists, however, generally agree that the view of national movements as anomies is unsatisfying, and it can be shown in a lot of ways that modernization is perhaps even conducive to the politicization of national identities (see e.g. Nielsen, 1985, and Newman, 1991, for overviews). The perspective chosen here is to analyse the politicization of ethnic identity as opposed to other bases of group formation from the point of view of the individual's decision to join or support a national movement.

Both rational choice theory and social identity theory highlight some important advantages of nation-groups over competing groups in this respect. Rational choice theory points to the inherent cultural homogeneity of nation-groups that allows them to congregate and appreciate their common interests and to adopt decision-making rules more easily than most other groups. However, the strongest argument made by rational choice theory in relation to national movements in the *modern* world is the perspective of nation-groups of gaining access to or even control over the state apparatus with all its contemporary power and spoils.

Social identity theory emphasizes the few possibilities of individual movements out of nation-groups partly as a result of political and normative limitations and partly because of the individual's own emotional investment in his or her identity. On a more general level social identity theory points, firstly, to the illegitimacy of discriminating systems in a world of proclaimed nation-states that adhere to the principle of national self-determination and, secondly, to the insecurity of such systems in a world dominated by democratic *Rechtsstaats* and with populations well informed about alternatives to discrimination and suppression.

3 CHARACTERISTICS OF LATE-20TH-CENTURY EAST EUROPEAN SOCIETIES

In Eastern Europe, however, the above-mentioned benign conditions for formation of national movements have for a long time been restricted by factors attributable to the general prevalence of communist regimes. And the fact that the recent national revivals in Eastern Europe started almost simultaneously also indicates that some general developments in Eastern Europe have favoured the formation of national movements as opposed to other kinds of groups. Of course, few would disagree that this has something to do with the effects both in the Soviet Union and in Eastern Europe of the democratization (*demokratizatsiya*) and openness (*glasnost'*) initiatives included in Gorbachev's policy of reconstruction (*perestroyka*). A more detailed discussion of this assertion is provided in the tests of $H_{1.2}$, but some general points can be made on the basis of rational choice theory and social identity theory, although the two theories give slightly different interpretations of *perestroyka*'s effect on the formation of national movements.

3.1 A Group Solidarity Analysis

First of all, the theory of group solidarity would point to the fact that before *perestroyka* the repressive communist regimes of the Soviet Union and Eastern Europe did not allow articulation of interests and demands outside the state and party controlled associations. And demands within these associations on behalf of nation-groups were mostly considered politically unacceptable. When such demands were forwarded to any significant extent, they were consistently suppressed, as in the cases of Prague in 1968 and Zagreb in 1971. Thus, to a large degree, repression removed the first and most basic condition for group formation: the ability to congregate and appreciate a commonality of interest, whereas *perestroyka* reintroduced this ability.

The introduction of *perestroyka* also had an indirect effect on the possibility of forming autonomous groups in that it lowered the solidarity of the most important existing groups, namely the communist parties. Before the repeal of the constitutionally provided monopoly of political power of the communist parties, the parties exercised this monopoly partly through the *nomenklatura* system – that is, the party's right to approve appointments to key political, economic, military, and social posts. The abandonment of the *nomenklatura* system significantly lowered the dependence of both party members and non-members on the party. At the same time, *perestroyka* implied less willingness to make use of the formidable monitoring and sanctioning capacity maintained primarily through organizations such as the KGB in the Soviet Union and similar – and to a large extent subordinated – security organs in the East European states. According to the theory of group solidarity, lower dependence and lower control capacity lead to lower group solidarity (see Section 3.3.1 of Chapter 2), and this fact made the prospects of alternative groups brighter than at any other time since the communist parties' acquisition of power.

These arguments account for the heightened probability that alternative groups would be formed in the Soviet Union and Eastern Europe in the late 1980s. In terms of why specifically *national* movements were predominantly chosen, the theory of group solidarity does not point to any general properties of the East European societies. The point is that national movements are seen as just another kind of political group that, admittedly, have the advantages described in Section 2.1 above. Their success or failure, however, depends exclusively on their ability to provide collective goods to their members. This ability, in turn, is dependent on the specific environments of the national movement and not on the general environments of Eastern Europe.

3.2 A Social Identity Analysis

Whereas the theory of group solidarity emphasizes the effects of *perestroyka* on the solidarity of the communist parties and the opportunities of alternative groups to work for the provision of their preferred collective goods, the focus of social identity theory is on the effects of *perestroyka* on the general social climate. In particular, *perestroyka* can be said to have influenced perceptions of system legitimacy and security, but the unintended consequences of *perestroyka* for social identity also hit the core of the East European citizen's self-image.

Paradoxically, the policy of *perestroyka* that was meant to add legitimacy to the communist regimes had the opposite effect. Although the new freedom of speech was initially still somewhat restricted, central control of *glasnost'* could not be upheld in the long run. Soon, critics were allowed to express themselves, and the major faults of the communist systems were quickly exposed in public. As a consequence, legitimacy decreased and the way for 'voice' strategies to change the systems was open. Especially, the Soviet control over the formally independent states in the rest of Eastern Europe was perceived to be inconsistent with the general value of national self-determination.

At the same time, system security was declining rapidly. Firstly, the willingness to suppress alternative groups violently was obviously lower than before. And secondly, when in 1988 the Popular Fronts of Estonia and Latvia and Sajudis in Lithuania were allowed to be formed and the Estonian Supreme Soviet, as the first among the Soviet republics, adopted a declaration of sovereignty, the former belief – both in the Soviet Union and in the rest of Eastern Europe – that nothing could change was immediately replaced by vivid cognitive alternatives which were soon to be followed by many others.

As in the case of the theory of group solidarity, these general observations of the changing East European environment primarily account for the probability that alternative groups of *some kind* would be formed in Eastern Europe in the late 1980s. However, social identity theory can point to one further general East European consequence of *perestroyka* which at least narrowed the spectrum of probable bases for group formation. During about 70 years of communist rule in the Soviet Union and 40 years in the rest of Eastern Europe, people were taught the Marxist–Leninist ideology of class struggle and capitalist imperialism. This ideology provided a clear-cut set of values and asserted that the inhabitants of Eastern Europe were part of the vanguard of humanity in the search for a better world. Further, as one of the victors of the Second World War and later a nuclear superpower, the Soviet Union and – with the establishment of the Warsaw Pact – the rest of Eastern Europe could pride themselves on being one of the world's most powerful blocs. That the official ideology and international position had the effect on the bulk of the populations of providing them with a positive social identity is highly likely. And it is equally clear that the collapse of the communist regimes and the exposition of their hollowness almost overnight negated that positive social identity, leaving a vacuum in the realm of values and meanings. Given this vacuum, the more probable groups to be formed would be groups building not only on simple interest calculations but groups that could provide a new ideology and sense of meaning. And nation-groups did just this.

3.3 Summary of the Late-20th-Century East European Environment

Thus, both rational choice theory and social identity theory point to some important effects of *perestroyka* on the probability that alternative groups would be formed in late-20th-century Eastern Europe. Rational choice theory argues that *perestroyka* made congregation possible where it had earlier been very difficult due to repression. At the same time, both the abandonment of the *nomenklatura* system and the less extensive use of security forces served to lower the solidarity of the communist parties, thus making it possible for alternative groups to be formed.

With the same conclusion, social identity theory argues that *perestroyka* had the complete opposite of its intended effects in that it lowered both the legitimacy and the security of the communist regimes. Legitimacy decreased as a result of the exposition of the misgovernment of the regimes, and security decreased because of their unwillingness to suppress autonomous groups and their inability to prevent the diffusion of cognitive alternatives.

The best argument, however, that *national* movements in particular should be chosen among the many possible alternative groups in the turmoil of East European *perestroyka* is delivered by social identity theory. Because of this theory's assumption of self-esteem as the motivational basis of human beings and its acknowledgement that such self-esteem can be derived not only from individual achievements but also from qualities that only exist among collectives of individuals, it captures the identity crisis of those East Europeans who, before *perestroyka*, took pride in the allegedly supreme communist model of society and the powerful international position of the communist bloc. With the atomistic and utility maximizing individuals assumed in rational choice theory, such insight is impossible.

4 CONCLUSION

An understanding of the drives and motives of individuals is essential to an understanding of the behaviour of individuals acting together in groups. Microsociological theories provide concepts that further this understanding. Some microsociological theories, however, are more explicit than others about the importance of events and properties of the individuals' social environment. Rational choice theory and social identity theory are examples of such theories.

Due to their additional ability of accounting for group *formation*, rational choice theory and social identity theory are excellent bases for an exploratory analysis of the reasons why some groups tend to be chosen by individuals instead of others. Of relevance for our purposes, both theories capture the special appeal that national movements have to individuals both in modern societies in general and in late-20th-century Eastern Europe in particular. Their explanations of this appeal, however, are somewhat different.

With its assumption that groups form to produce collective goods, Hechter's group solidarity theory is bound to seek its explanations in the practical and material potentials and obstacles of this production. This leads to a very concrete view of the relevant properties and environments of nationalism. National movements in modern societies are seen as privileged due to the practical advantages that cultural homogeneity and common language have for group formation as well as to the potential that modern states have to produce collective goods and selective incentives. In late-20th-century Eastern Europe, national movements could take advantage of the renewed possibility to form groups outside communist control as well as a lower group solidarity within the communist organizations.

In contrast, social identity theory's focus on the wider social climate brings it to identify the socially shaped conceptions and ideas of human beings as the foundation of the appeal of national movements. Thus, the relevant properties and environments of nationalism are those that enhance positive identity and self-esteem rather than those that lead to material production. In this view, national movements in modern societies profit from the illegitimacy of discriminating multinational states and from the insecurity of modern states which have to observe human rights to some degree and whose populations know sufficiently well that things could be different. Furthermore, individuals are often prevented from giving up their nationality due to political norms and rules as well as to their own emotional investment in the group membership. In late-20th-century Eastern Europe, national movements had the additional advantage of providing a new and unifying ideology at a time when the legitimacy, the security, and, most importantly, the perceived positive qualities of the communist regimes had become tarnished.

Through rational choice theory and social identity theory, we have answered the question of why nationalism was chosen as the basis for group formation in late-20th-century Eastern Europe by pointing to the potential of national movements as well as the functions they perform for the individuals. Of course, such an analysis of potentials and functions can only be a preliminary answer, and it cannot amount to a causal explanation of the national revivals. It is to this explanation that we now turn.

In the following four chapters we examine the development of and the macrosociological conditions of the national revivals in Estonia, Moldova, Croatia, and Czechoslovakia. Each chapter begins with a description of our dependent variable, the national revivals. The descriptions focus on political decisions and mass public actions which reflect the pace and support of the revivals from the rise of the national revivals in the second half of the 1980s until the declarations of independence and the subsequent international recognitions in the 1991–93 period. Then we turn to the task of explaining the national revivals, firstly as seen from a primordial perspective and then as seen from an instrumental perspective.

5 The National Revivals in Estonia

1 INTRODUCTION

In the Soviet Socialist Republic of Estonia, some of the first organizations in the USSR aiming explicitly at achieving national autonomy or independence were formed. Eventually, the formation and subsequent actions of the Estonian and the numerous other national movements led to the dissolution of the USSR.

Actually, the appearance of the Estonian national movement was one of the first signs indicating that the nationality problem had never been solved in the USSR – despite the comprehensive efforts of the Soviet regime to realize the tenets of Marxism–Leninism and to create a united socialist or communist society in which nationality would gradually lose importance. Yet, influenced by the propaganda of the communist regimes, the perception that nationalism was not an issue in Eastern Europe and the USSR was commonplace in Western societies.[14] Therefore, it was surprising to the Western public to hear about the evolving national revival among the Estonians and, subsequently, among numerous other nation-groups in Eastern Europe and the USSR.

But what were the reasons why the Estonians initiated a national revival that set off an avalanche of other national movements? This chapter seeks an explanation of the Estonian national revival as well as the response of the Russian minority in Estonia.

2 THE NATIONAL REVIVALS

2.1 The Estonian National Revival

Following large demonstrations against plans to increase phosphorite mining in the north-eastern part of the republic and against the Molotov–Ribbentrop Pact (Uibopuu, 1990: 30ff), the first Estonian opposition parties were formed in 1988 (Kaplan, 1993: 212f). The most important of these was the Popular Front of Estonia (PFE), initially founded as a mass movement in support of Gorbachev's policies of *perestroyka* and *glasnost*'. Originally, the PFE supported the autonomy option inside a confederate Soviet Union. However, other parties with programmes demanding an independent Estonia outside the Union also appeared on the political scene. In order not to lose political and potential electoral ground to these parties, the PFE soon switched to the independence option. The opposition parties and the huge demonstrations arranged by them strongly influenced the ruling Communist Party of Estonia (CPE). Thus, in mid-June 1988, some 100 000–150 000 Estonians celebrated the replacement of the conservative Russian–Estonian[15] first secretary of the CPE with a reformist Estonian. In September 1988, the numerous mass events culminated with the Estonian song festival which drew an estimated 250 000–300 000 people from all over Estonia, approximately 30 per cent of the population (Taagepera, 1993: 136ff).[16] This development led to the adoption by the parliament, the Estonian Supreme Soviet, of a declaration of sovereignty as early as in November 1988.

In the following year, the Supreme Soviet passed laws declaring Estonian the official state language and the Estonian national flag the official state flag. At the elections to the all-Union Congress of People's Deputies in March the same year, the mass public showed its national stance when the PFE won 27 out of the 36 seats allocated to Estonia (Hosking, 1992: 192).

In 1990, political pluralism was officially recognized when the Estonian Supreme Soviet abolished article 6 in the constitution which guaranteed monopolized political power for the communist party. This act, together with the passing of a new electoral law, paved the way for largely free elections to the Supreme Soviet in March 1990. In the elections, party or group affiliations of the candidates did not appear on the ballot – at the insistence of the CPE leaders whose personal reputations surpassed the popularity of their party (Taagepera, 1993: 176f). Yet, as the numerous independents chose sides, the PFE consisted of 45 of 105 deputies (43 per cent). Free Estonia (the reformed communist party) had 29 deputies, and some of the remaining ten independent deputies were more nationalist oriented than the PFE members. The result of these elections further accelerated the development of the national revival. As one of its first acts, the new and renamed parliament, the Supreme Council, adopted a declaration which announced the beginning of a transitional period towards full independence. Also, an immigration law was passed, according to which the annual immigration was not to exceed a quota of 1 per cent of the population living in Estonia (Andersen, 1991: 24).

During the second half of 1990 and the first of 1991, negotiations between Estonia and the Union regarding terms of secession were held

(Kionka, 1992a: 65). They turned out, however, to be *pro forma* negotiations since the Soviet authorities were not really interested in making any progress in this direction. The mass public in Estonia, on the contrary, expected progress. In a referendum on the issue of independence conducted by the Estonian authorities in March 1991, 78 per cent of the inhabitants voted for independence (Geron, 1991: 136).

The deadlocked situation found its unexpected solution in the failed *coup d'état* in Moscow in August 1991 (Kionka, 1992a: 66). During the coup, the Supreme Council adopted a resolution declaring full and immediate independence. As the coup failed, the government soon asserted full authority in the republic. In the following weeks, most major states, including the USSR, recognized the independence of Estonia.

2.2 The Russian National Revival

According to the 1989 census, the Russians in Estonia accounted for 30.1 per cent (471 000) of the republic's population (Kaplan, 1993: 208). Paralleling the Estonian national revival, a revival among these Russians also saw the light of the day, though it turned out to be a rather weak version.

In response to the formation of Estonian opposition parties, the so-called Intermovement (*Interdvizhenie*) which represented the interests of the Russians was established in July 1988 (Ilves, 1991: 72).[17] Initially, Intermovement seemed to gather a rather large following among the Russians. Thus, in the elections in March 1989, the party won five of the 36 Estonian seats in the all-Union Congress of People's Deputies. In August 1989, following the proposal of the new electoral law, the Intermovement organized protest rallies and strikes (*CIS*, 1992: 532). On this occasion some 30 000 Russians participated.

But the scale of these actions was somewhat deceptive as to the intensity of the Russians' national attitudes. Surveys conducted in May 1989 showed that approximately one third of the non-Estonians supported an independent Estonia, another third supported the preservation of the status quo, while the remaining third were indifferent (Ilves, 1991: 80f). The passivity of the Russians was also revealed when, in May 1990, the Intermovement attracted only some 2000 participants to demonstrations against the parliament's declaration of a transition period towards independence (*CIS*, 1992: 533). Later, as the Estonian revival became even more comprehensive, the Russians' attitude did not change. A poll carried out two weeks before the referendum on independence in March 1991 showed that 36 per cent intended to vote for independence (Taagepera, 1992: 125f).

Furthermore, the majority of the Russians also remained passive after the Estonians actually achieved independence. Although the Estonian government adopted several laws which were clearly discriminatory against non-Estonians, in particular regarding citizenship and electoral rights (Sheehy, 1993: 8f), only a few small demonstrations occurred (Kionka, 1993: 90f). However, when a law on aliens, which classified non-citizens as aliens and obliged them to seek residency permits, was adopted in June 1993, the patience of some of the Russians finally ran out. In July 1993 the local authorities in Narva, a town located on the Estonian–Russian border and populated by 90 per cent non-Estonians, arranged a referendum on territorial autonomy of the north-eastern part of Estonia (Stepan, 1994: 137). Only about half of Narva's residents voted in the referendum, yet of these over 97 per cent were reported to be in favour of autonomy. Although the Estonian authorities did not attempt to block the referendum, the Supreme Court consequently ruled it unconstitutional. Nevertheless, the issue of autonomy subsequently faded away as the Narva authorities accepted the ruling and did not proceed to take action towards autonomy.

Thus, the efforts of the Estonians to achieve independence did result in a national revival among the Russians in Estonia. This revival, however, never gained widespread support.

3 THE NATIONAL REVIVALS IN A PRIMORDIAL PERSPECTIVE

According to H_1, we should expect that the strong national revival among the Estonians was based on a common group identity provided by the *ethnie* and the historical interplay between the Estonians and the Russians, and that the revivals were triggered by liberal policies adopted by the formerly repressive Soviet regime and eased by an already existing republican unit and constitutional rights. In contrast, the absence of a strong Russian national revival could be explained if the Russians lacked a distinct *ethnie* or if no triggering factors applied to the Russian nation-group.

3.1 The Ethnic Base

3.1.1 The Estonian Ethnie

Smith defines an *ethnie* as a unit of population which shares six characteristics (see Section 2.2 of Chapter 3). First of all, the Estonians obviously share a common name. Concerning myths of common ancestry and historical memories, the Estonians have a rich collection of peasant folk-songs and fairytales which communicate such myths and memories (Lieven,

1993: 110ff). These songs have played an important role in creating, preserving, and confirming the Estonian ethnic base, not least because of the popular song festivals which have been held continually since the 1860s. Thus, in the period between the 1860s and the 1880s, Estonian intellectuals made big efforts to assemble Estonian songs, legends, and folklore (Raun, 1987: 57ff). Furthermore, these intellectuals sought to convince the Estonians of the merits of a modern Estonian nation-group, thereby turning the ethnic identity into a national identity. Consequently, in the words of Smith, the Estonian nation-group was built on a vertical *ethnie* because of the vernacular mobilization by the intellectuals. In 1920 this first national revival among the Estonians led to the establishment of an independent republic of Estonia in the wake of the First World War and the Russian Revolution.

Continuing with Smith's attributes of an *ethnie*, the most important distinctive element of the Estonian culture is the Estonian language which belongs to the Finno-Ugric language group (Taagepera, 1993: 13). Among the neighbouring ethnic groups, only the Finns are able to communicate with the Estonians. The language is also one of the most important factors behind the Estonians' feeling of association with their 'motherland'. According to Taagepera, the Estonians live on ancestral grounds where their language can be traced back for perhaps 5000 years (*ibid.*). Finally, Smith contends that an *ethnie* also has a sense of social solidarity. This factor is not easy to operationalize, but an opinion poll conducted in 1988 nevertheless hints that the Estonians also score high on this factor: respectively 80 and 82 per cent of the Estonians believed that the nationality of co-workers and neighbours is important (Ilves, 1991: 76).

On this background we can conclude that the Estonians have a strong ethnic base since they share all of the characteristics of an *ethnie*. Moreover, the Estonian *ethnie* had already developed into a national identity during the last decades of the 19th century.

3.1.2 The Russian Ethnie

However, when we turn to the Russians living in Estonia, we find that they lack a distinct ethnic base and national identity. This is primarily due to the fact that the majority of the Russians immigrated to Estonia after the Second World War. Thus, Russians made up only 8 per cent of the population in independent Estonia in the interwar period, whereas this number rose steadily to 30 per cent (by 1989) during the postwar period (Kirch, 1992: 206). In 1990, 57 per cent of the Russians living in Estonia were first-generation immigrants (Kaplan, 1993: 209). The Russians immigrated to Estonia mainly because of the expanding Soviet industrial enterprises and military bases. Furthermore, the majority of the Russians associated with the Soviet culture and state, not with the Russian. Thus, an opinion poll carried out in 1988 showed that 78 per cent identified themselves as citizens of the USSR, whereas only 15 per cent identified as members of a nation-group (Ilves, 1991: 76). When the legitimacy of the Soviet system fell drastically in the late 1980s, the Russians in Estonia were suddenly faced with an identity problem. At first glance, the rise of Russian nationalism, led by the president of the Russian Federation Boris Yeltsin, might seem to have been a solution. But Yeltsin actually supported the independence of the Baltic republics (Kionka, 1992a: 65) and did not, therefore, really solve the identity problem of the Russians. Furthermore, most Russians in Estonia seemed to be prepared to shift allegiance towards the republic of Estonia rather than Russia. Thus, a survey conducted in June/August 1990 showed that 77 per cent of the Russians in Estonia took pride in being a resident of Estonia. Even after independence had been established, 49 per cent of the Russians preferred to receive Estonian citizenship while 38 per cent preferred Russian citizenship (Stepan, 1994: 131f).

Thus, the Russians in Estonia lacked a distinctive ethnic base. Certainly, they had a common name, but they were hard pressed to point to any positive distinctive elements of culture because of the retreat of the *Homo Sovieticus*. Concerning demography, the Russians made up a majority in the cities of Narva, Kohtla-Järve, and Sillamäe in the north-eastern part of Estonia, but many Russians had also settled in Tallinn (Saar & Titma, 1992: 49; see Map 1). And even in these majority areas, the Russians' association with the Estonian territory was not particularly old.

3.1.3 The Historical Interplay between Estonians and Russians

Since the Estonians have been dominated by foreign powers ever since the 13th century, except for the interwar period of independence, fear of assimilation has been an important and enduring aspect of Estonian identity (Kionka, 1990: 40). The Russian dominance in particular has long contributed to this fear. As early as 1710, the Russian empire conquered Estonia (Taagepera, 1993: 26ff). However, the Russian tsars agreed to generous terms of internal autonomy, essentially letting the ruling German nobility keep its power in exchange for political acceptance of the Russian supremacy. So, the Russian empire did not colonize the Estonians on any larger scale until the 1880s, when russification was employed in response to the first wave of Estonian nationalism. The russification campaign provided the basis for an anti-Russian attitude as a part of the Estonian identity. During the Second World War and the postwar period, this attitude was reinforced. The Soviet army occupied Estonia twice, and in the Stalinist period thousands of Estonians were deported to labour camps in Siberia from which many never returned (Kionka, 1990: 44f).[18] Later, when a large number of Russians immigrated to Estonia, these Russians unwillingly came to symbolize the repressive Soviet regime from an Estonian point of view.

According to Taagepera, some of the Russians had a *Herrenrasse* attitude which had been supported by Soviet propaganda, according to which the Russians had come to help the Estonians overcome their backwardness (1992: 124). Nevertheless, the Russians' attitude towards the Estonians was not marked by the same degree of animosity as the Estonians felt towards the Russians primarily because the Russians never were nor felt suppressed by the Estonians. At the only time in history when the Estonians were in a position to suppress the Russians in Estonia, in the interwar independent Estonia, they refrained from doing so. On the contrary, the Russian (and the German and Swedish) nation-groups enjoyed extensive minority rights (Coakley, 1990: 444f). These rights were guaranteed by the Estonian constitution of 1920 and implemented with the passage of the law on cultural autonomy in 1925. According to this, the minorities were authorized to elect a council which was empowered to enact by-laws, adopt a budget, and raise taxes to finance its responsibilities in the areas of education, culture, and welfare.

3.2 The Triggering Factors: Recent Developments in the Soviet Legal–Political Setting

Following the rise of Mikhail Gorbachev to the pinnacle of the Soviet hierarchy in 1985, the Soviet regime implemented profound economic and political reforms. Gorbachev's programme of *perestroyka* had at its centre a campaign for *glasnost'*. This campaign led to a recognition of individuals' right to freedom of speech and of the right of citizens to organize collectively. And it also meant that nationalist opinions could be set forth and that prior obstacles to the founding of nationalist movements were removed.

The Estonians did not wait long after the green light had been given. At a demonstration in Tallinn in August 1987 former dissidents were for the first time able to demand Estonian self-determination publicly without being harassed (Taagepera, 1993: 125). And soon afterwards, in 1988, the first Estonian nationalist parties were formed (see Section 2.1). Nor did the Russians in Estonia hesitate long before they took advantage of the liberalization. However, the first organization committed to resist the

Estonian revival, the United Council of Work Collectives (UCWC), founded in the summer of 1988, characteristically of the weak Russian revival, was a movement which defended economic rather than ethnic interests (Hosking, 1992: 188).

The democratization entailed, furthermore, the introduction of competitive elections for party and state positions, thus allowing non-communist party candidates, including candidates with nationalist programmes, to participate (Furtado & Hechter, 1992: 174ff). When article 6 in the USSR constitution, which guaranteed the communist party its monopoly on political power, was repealed in January 1990, the way was open for these candidates to form opposition parties. Thus, in the spring of 1990, both Estonian and Russian nationalist parties won seats in the elections to the Estonian Supreme Soviet (Taagepera, 1993: 176). Even at this point, the Soviet regime did not try to restrain the evolving national revivals. On the contrary, general secretary Gorbachev called upon the communist party officials, who had been rejected by the electorate, to resign from their positions (Furtado & Hechter, 1992: 177). Later on, when the Soviet regime tried to block the revivals, they had already gained so much momentum that it was impossible to stop them without resorting to large-scale violent suppression – an option the Soviet regime chose not to employ.

The Estonians not only took advantage of the new opportunities offered by the reforms but also made use of the federal structure of the USSR. According to the latest USSR constitution from 1977, a host of nationalities were officially recognized, 15 of which were assigned a republic (CUSSR, 1987: arts. 71, 85, 87). These territorial political units provided a formal structure of government consisting of a republican parliament and ministries which the new Estonian national elite used as a platform for initiating the revival. Evidently, the Russian minority could not use such a resource.

Furthermore, according to article 72 in the USSR constitution, each republic had the right to secession (CUSSR, 1987: art. 72). In November 1988 the Estonian Supreme Soviet adopted a declaration of sovereignty referring to this article (Taagepera, 1993: 145ff). However, soon afterwards the USSR Supreme Soviet declared this act unconstitutional, referring to other articles in the constitution. In the ensuing debate about the interpretation of the constitution, however, the Estonian politicians came up with another argument. They rejected the legitimacy of the USSR constitution, arguing that the Soviet annexation of Estonia in 1940 was illegal (Meissner, 1990: 192ff). Therefore, the Estonians contended that the Tartu peace treaty of 1920, when the Soviet regime recognized Estonia as an independent state, was the only legal foundation of the Estonian–Soviet interstate relations. As the Soviet authorities rejected this standpoint, the constitutional debate ended in a stalemate and the constitutional rights of the USSR thus proved of limited use to the Estonians.

4 THE NATIONAL REVIVALS IN AN INSTRUMENTAL PERSPECTIVE

Before we draw any final conclusions about the explanatory power of H_1, we turn now to a test of the sub-hypotheses of H_2.

4.1 Internal Colonization of the Estonians

In the USSR, political and economic power was centralized in Moscow in the all-Union party and state bodies. Thus, Moscow and the largest republic, the Russian Soviet Federated Socialist Republic (RSFSR) (mainly inhabited by Russians), constituted the centre, while Estonia belonged to the periphery.

4.1.1 Economic Colonization

According to $H_{2.1}$, the Estonian national revival could be explained if the Estonians were economically deprived and underdeveloped because of the internal colonialism established by the centre. However, this was not the case. On the contrary, the standard of living in Estonia was among the highest compared to the other republics. In 1989 the monthly average per-capita income in Estonia was 270 rubles, while the average all-Union level was 240 rubles. In the same vein, only 1.9 per cent of the population in Estonia had a monthly income beneath the poverty level (75 rubles), while the average for the all-Union population was 11 per cent (Götz & Halbach 1991: 11). The relatively high standard of living was due to a comprehensive all-Union-led industrialization which took place in the postwar period (Raun, 1987: 198ff). Furthermore, the Estonian economy profited because of the access to the huge all-Union market. This meant that energy and other raw materials could be imported at prices below the world market level, while otherwise non-competitive manufactured products of the food and light industry were exported to the other republics (Steele, 1992).

On this background we can conclude that Estonia was not subject to economic internal colonialism. However, as discussed in Section 3.4 of Chapter 3, empirical facts are one thing, another is the way these facts are interpreted and perceived. Thus the Estonians argued that the level of economic development in interwar independent Estonia was comparable to small Western countries like Denmark, while in the 1980s Soviet Estonia lagged far behind these economies (Taagepera, 1991: 480). The involuntary integration of the Estonian economy into the Soviet was blamed for this development. Thus, the benefits foregone and the opportunities missed were a frequent complaint addressed by Estonian economists with respect to the country's economic links with the USSR (Stålvant, 1993: 127). Furthermore, the Estonians complained that almost all of the Estonian industry was controlled by the all-Union ministries in Moscow (Kaplan, 1993: 208).[19] Finally, the Estonians blamed these ministries for the large environmental problems in the republic (Karlsson, 1992: 71ff). In particular, protests were directed against the centrally controlled large-scale extraction of Estonian raw materials, primarily oil-shale and phosphorite. And in independence the Estonians saw an opportunity of substituting a market economy for the Soviet planned economy. Thus, economic issues were a part of the Estonian national revival in spite of the relatively advantageous situation of Estonia.

In conclusion, the above analysis shows that $H_{2.1}$, when based on deprivation alone, must be rejected in the Estonian case as the Estonians were not economically deprived or subject to economic internal colonialism. However, when based on frustrations, $H_{2.1}$ is able to contribute to an explanation of the revival because the Estonians felt that their economy would fare better outside the USSR.

4.1.2 Political Colonization

According to $H_{2.2}$, another explanation of the Estonian revival is to be found in the *political* deprivation or frustration of the Estonian elite. As for the distribution of political power among the nation-groups in the USSR, the Slavic nation-groups always dominated the upper reaches of the Communist Party of the Soviet Union (CPSU), while the Estonians, like other periphery nation-groups, found it difficult to rise to positions within the central party apparatus (Furtado & Hechter, 1992: 190, 202). So, the Estonian elite was not granted most-favoured-lords status. Even at the Estonian republican level, the Estonians' progress to top positions was often barred. Instead, the CPSU often preferred to promote Russian–Estonians who were considered to be politically more reliable (Raun, 1987: 190ff). Thus, in the two most powerful bodies, the Politbureau and the Central Committee, ethnic Estonians were a minority during most of the Soviet era. And the top post of first secretary was filled exclusively by Russian–Estonians until June 1988 (Taagepera, 1993: 136). Furthermore, the Estonians were underrepresented in membership of the CPE, the main gateway to a career. In 1981 they constituted only 51 per cent of the membership, while making up 61 per cent of the population (Raun, 1987: 190).

This political deprivation was an important factor behind the national revival as the Estonians – or in any case the Estonian elite – indeed perceived themselves to be deprived of political power. Thus, when the political liberalization made it possible, Estonian activists set forth policy proposals aiming at independence because it would give them political power. They also offered policies which would one-sidedly favour the Estonians, such as a proposal on a new law on citizenship which would exclude non-Estonians from automatically obtaining citizenship (Uibopuu, 1992: 111). With the electorate given real power, the Estonian politicians were soon elected to the new *locus* of political power, the Supreme Soviet, from which they could add further momentum to the revival. Thus, $H_{2.2}$ offers a convincing explanation of the Estonian national revival.

4.1.3 Cultural Colonization

According to $H_{2.3}$, internal colonialism also involves *cultural* deprivation or frustration of the periphery group. Because of the large immigration of Russians into Estonia in the postwar period,[20] the Estonians perceived that their culture and language were threatened (Taagepera, 1992: 123). The Estonians felt that they were exposed to russification policies, and they complained in particular about the apparent unwillingness of the Russian immigrants to become acquainted with their language. Thus, a poll conducted in 1988 revealed that only 38 per cent of the Russians spoke Estonian fluently or adequately for everyday needs, while 92 per cent of the Estonians spoke Russian (Ilves, 1991: 77). This situation meant that the Estonians often could not use their mother tongue when addressing public authorities. This was especially relevant in public services such as police and medicine which were dominated by Russian-speakers (p. 78).

The Estonians' feeling of being culturally deprived and discriminated against was fertile ground for a national revival which would also include a correction of the cultural inequalities. For example, the importance of cultural issues was reflected in the Supreme Soviet's adoption in 1989 of a language law which demanded that all employed in the state bureaucracy should be able to speak Estonian within four years (Andersen, 1991: 24). Consequently, we conclude that $H_{2.3}$ also offers an explanation of the Estonian national revival.

4.2 Internal Colonization of the Russians

In this section we will test whether H_2 is able to explain the relative weakness of the Russian national revival. H_2 points to the importance of a colonizing centre. However, in the Soviet period, the constituent republics had very little influence in relation to the Moscow centre. But as the Estonians achieved still more power on the republican level, Tallinn became the potential colonizing centre from the point of view of the Russian minority.

4.2.1 Economic Colonization

In Estonia, a cultural division of labour existed in so far as the Russians mainly worked in industry, while the Estonians were employed in light industry, agriculture, or white-collar jobs (Kaplan, 1993: 208f). This, however, did not mean that the Russians were economically deprived. On the contrary, a research on the income levels of Estonians and Russians carried out in September 1991 showed that 65 per cent of the Russians had a monthly income above 300 rubles, while the figure for the Estonians was only 52 per cent. The percentage of the two groups at lower income intervals did not differ significantly (Kirch, 1992: 207). The Russians had also benefited from social welfare policies which favoured the immigrant labour force. For example, the Russians often jumped the waiting-lists to get a flat (*ibid.*).

Thus, in accordance with $H_{2.1}$, the absence of economic deprivation among the Russians explains the weak support behind the Russian revival. However, as the Estonian national revival evolved, the economic prospects of the Russians worsened. The *de facto* political disenfranchisement of the Russians (see below) made them vulnerable to attempts by possible future radical governments to use economic pressure to force them to leave. Even more important was the fact that the lack of political representation left the economic interests of the Russians unprotected in a time when market economy reforms threatened to close down many of the large, unprofitable, and ineffective enterprises (Lieven, 1993: 313f). On the other hand, the Russians still believed that they would fare economically better in an independent Estonia than in Russia. Thus, according to a survey conducted in September 1993 – when some economic hardships due to the economic reforms had already occurred – 82 per cent of the Russians in Estonia agreed that Estonia offered a better chance to improve living standards than Russia (Maley, 1995: 5). This was probably the most important reason why close to 40 per cent of the Russians had voted for independence at the referendum in March 1991 (Taagepera, 1992: 126). However, although the Russians apparently envisioned better chances of economic prosperity in an independent Estonia with a market economy, this was not tantamount to a perception of their future economic position in Estonia as completely unproblematic. They did fear future economic and social discrimination from the Estonian authorities, which they were very well aware did not like the large Russian presence in their country (Lieven, 1993: 315).

4.2.2 Political Colonization

As for political internal colonialism, the Russians in Soviet Estonia were far from being politically deprived. However, as the Estonian national revival evolved, the Estonian policies of nationalism threatened to and later actually did deprive the Russians of their former favourable political status. The activity of the Estonian citizens' committees provides an illustrative example in this regard (Taagepera, 1993: 170ff). During the winter of 1989, these committees registered all citizens of the interwar republic of Estonia and their descendants. In February 1990, just before the elections to the official Supreme Soviet, the committees then arranged elections for a parallel Estonian Congress in which only the registered Estonians could take part. This event turned out to be a forerunner of later official policies. In February 1992, after independence was gained, the renamed parliament, the *Riigikogu*, adopted a law on citizenship which barred all Soviet-era immigrants from automatic citizenship, thereby also depriving them of their suffrage (Pettai, 1993: 118). As for the former Russian elite members, they lost their suffrage as well as their eligibility.

Thus, as the Estonian centre attained still more power *vis-à-vis* the centre of the USSR, policies of nationalism were enacted that deprived the Russian minority of its former privileged status, and the Russian elite was granted non-most-favoured-lords status. Apparently, however, this political deprivation did not lead to any strong frustrations, and it was not sufficient to cause a strong national revival.

4.2.3 Cultural Colonization

This is also the case regarding $H_{2.3}$. On the street level, Russians were probably often exposed to small episodes which revealed some Estonians' aversion against them. As an example, Taagepera reports an episode when a Russian-speaking taxi-driver had to ask ten times for an address before he got an answer in Russian (1991: 479). However, such episodes were not tantamount to cultural deprivation of the Russians as long as they could identify with the countervailing dominant Soviet culture. But when the Estonians began to launch official policies of nationalism directed against the Russians, at the same time as the Soviet culture began to lose prestige, the Russians were subject to cultural deprivation through official as well as unofficial misrecognition. For example, the importance and prestige of the Russian language decreased considerably when, in January 1989, the Estonian Supreme Soviet adopted a language law that raised the status of Estonian to state language (Raun, 1994: 166ff). One consequence of the law was that Russians in public service positions requiring interaction with clients had to acquire a working knowledge of Estonian.

How severe the cultural deprivation was felt is, however, difficult to say as many Russians lived and worked with little contact with Estonians.

5 CONCLUSION

The description of the national revivals showed that the Estonian revival was intense and widely supported while the Russian one was relatively weak.

This corresponds with the fact that only the Estonians scored high on the characteristics of an *ethnie*. Furthermore, the common identity of the Estonians was marked by historically based antagonistic relations with the Russians, while the Russians had never experienced Estonian persecution. Thus, a well-developed ethnic base, which according to $H_{1.1}$ is a necessary condition of a national revival, was present among the Estonians only. Therefore, $H_{1.1}$ is able to explain the differing strength of the two national revivals and is confirmed in both cases.

However, as explained in Section 2.3 of Chapter 3, this primordial hypothesis cannot stand alone as it is only able to explain whether the conditions for a national revival are present or not. When complemented with the other primordial hypothesis, $H_{1.2}$, the moderate version of the primordial perspective also aspires to explain *when* national revivals occur. In the USSR, liberalizing reforms launched by the centre from 1985 onwards removed previous obstacles to the formation of national movements. Subsequently, an Estonian and a much weaker Russian revival saw the light of day. Moreover, the Estonian revival was eased by the already existing republican political unit and, finally, the Estonians tried to legitimize their secessionist policies by referring to constitutional rights formally granted by the USSR constitution. However, as the Soviet authorities interpreted the constitution differently, these rights were of limited use to the Estonians. All in all, though, $H_{1.2}$ is able to explain why the revivals occurred in the second half of the 1980s, and it is therefore confirmed.

As for the three-dimensional instrumental hypothesis H_2, it was confirmed in the Estonian case. The political and cultural deprivation of the Estonians caused by the internal colonization of the Soviet centre, in combination with the Estonians' perception that they could have been economically better off had they not been incorporated into the Soviet centrally planned economy by force, meant that the Estonians *felt* economically, politically, and culturally deprived although, strictly speaking, they were in fact only politically and culturally deprived. This explains the strength of the Estonian revival.

With respect to the Russians, however, H_2 fares less well. True, the Russians were not deprived regarding any of the three spheres during the Soviet era. But as the Estonian revival evolved, they increasingly became subject to political and cultural deprivation. Apart from some political and cultural frustrations, another consequence of the political deprivation was a certain level of economic frustration as the Russians feared for their jobs and social welfare in a future liberal Estonian market economy in which they had no political rights, even if their prospects in this economy looked better than in Russia. But because the Russians remained passive despite the deprivations and the frustrations, H_2 has difficulties in accounting for the Russian case.

6 The National Revivals in Moldova

1 INTRODUCTION

The appearance of national revivals all over the USSR made many Western laypeople as well as scholars aware of the existence of nation-groups which they had never heard of before. The Gagauz of southern Moldova was one such example. Thus, the case of Moldova provides a relatively rare instance of no less than three simultaneous national revivals in a rather small territory. Yet, although Moldovans, Slavs, and Gagauz initiated national revivals, and although these revivals led not only to a separation of the Moldavian SSR from the USSR but also to a *de facto* partition into three political–territorial units and violent conflict between the Moldovans and the Slavs, the Western media did not pay any particular attention to these events. The national revivals among the Baltic nation-groups and among the nation-groups in the Balkans received much more attention. Nevertheless, due to the afore-mentioned characteristics of the case of the national revivals in Moldova, we think these national revivals and their causes deserve a closer examination.

2 THE NATIONAL REVIVALS[21]

2.1 The Moldovan National Revival

The first signs of a Moldovan national revival appeared in 1987 when intellectuals began publicly to espouse the reforms of *perestroyka* and *glasnost'* and at the same time criticize the prevalent economic, social, and political conditions in the republic (Crowther, 1991: 188ff). The criticism was fuelled by the resistance of the Communist Party of Moldavia (CPM) to implementing the reforms launched by the centre. In 1988, the criticism became organized with the formation of the Democratic Movement in Support of Perestroyka (DM) (Fane, 1993: 134).

However, the Moldovan intellectuals did not succeed in initiating a large-scale popular mobilization until they began to make more clear-cut nationalist demands. Among these, demands regarding language policies soon came to dominate. Led by the DM and the Aleksei Mateevici Literary–Musical Circle, also founded in 1988, the opposition argued that Moldovan should be made the state language, that the Latin script should replace the Cyrillic, and, finally, that Moldovan should be recognized as identical to Romanian (Socor, 1989a: 1). In order to back up these demands, the opposition repeatedly arranged demonstrations in the capital, Chisinau, during the 1989 spring and summer months (Socor, 1989b: 2f). Due to the massive support behind the demands,[22] the CPM finally gave up the resistance in August 1989 and the Supreme Soviet adopted a language law which, on the whole, fulfilled the demands of the Moldovan opposition (Fane, 1993: 136).

In May 1989 the opposition grew stronger when several opposition groups, including those already mentioned, united in the Popular Front of Moldova (PFM) (Socor, 1989c: 2). Demanding a range of democratic and national rights, including the right of Moldovans to seek reunification with Romania, the PFM soon became popular among the Moldovans. This was reflected in the elections to the Supreme Soviet in March 1990. As in Estonia, the constitutionally guaranteed leading role of the communist party had been abolished, and this paved the way for other parties to participate. The PFM won 40 per cent of the seats (Socor, 1991a: 25).

Thereafter, expressions of Moldovan nationalism became ever more dominant in the parliamentary outputs. Moldovan national symbols such as a national flag – the Romanian tricolour with a Moldovan coat of arms added in order to highlight the Moldovan distinctiveness – were adopted (Socor, 1991d: 19ff). Although some politicians in the PFM preferred reunification with Romania, the second congress of the PFM held in June 1990 voted overwhelmingly in favour of setting as its chief goal the formation of an independent republic of Moldova (Socor, 1991a: 24).[23] This was reflected later in the same month when the new parliament declared Moldova sovereign and established the precedence of Moldovan law over USSR law. In the ensuing period more steps were taken in order to extricate Moldova from the political, economic, and military mechanisms that had tied it to the USSR. In December 1990 the Supreme Soviet, which was then fully dominated by the PFM because several communist deputies had switched to the opposition, rejected Gorbachev's proposal for a renewed Soviet Union (Socor, 1991b: 12f). This decision was taken following one of the highlights of the Moldovan national revival, a so-called Grand National Assembly held in central Chisinau which attracted as many as 800 000, according to the official news agency *Moldovapres* (*ibid.*). In March 1991 the Supreme Soviet also decided to boycott the all-Union referendum on the Union treaty (Socor, 1991c: 9f).

As in Estonia, the demands of the Moldovan politicians were rejected by the central Soviet authorities. Therefore, the declaration of full independence, proclaimed on 27 August 1991, was not made possible until the Soviet hard liners' *coup d'état* was defeated (Socor, 1991d: 19ff). Exploiting the paralysis of the all-Union and local communist and security structures, the Moldovan parliament then took the necessary steps to secure independent statehood. Unlike Estonia, however, Moldova did not receive full international recognition until early 1992 (Socor, 1993: 12). The hesitation of the international community was caused by the fact that the incorporation of Moldova into the Soviet Union, in contrast to the annexation of the Baltic states, had actually been recognized by the international community in the immediate postwar period.

However, in spite of the fact that the national revival was crowned with the achievement of independent statehood, Moldova did not control roughly one quarter of the former republic's territory and population because of competing national revivals.

2.2 The Russian National Revival

The Moldovan revival was matched by a Russian counter-revival with almost the same degree of support and intensity. According to the 1989 Soviet census, Russians and Ukrainians made up 13 per cent (560 000) and 14 per cent (600 000) respectively of the population of Moldova (Fane, 1993: 137). At first glance, a national revival supported by members of two different nation-groups might seem odd, but as the heavily russified Ukrainian minority in Moldova to a large extent supported the Russian national revival rather than initiating their own, it is appropriate to include the Ukrainians in the demographic basis of the Russian national revival. To avoid any misunderstandings we have chosen to use the word 'Slavs' when referring to the supporters of this revival while using 'Russian' as the most appropriate description of the content and aim of the national revival. The Slavs lived primarily in the capital Chisinau or in the so-called Dnestr area (see Map 2).[24] In the Dnestr area, the concentration of Slavs was 54 per cent in 1989 (Crow, 1992: 9) and this area became the prime locus of the Russian national revival.

During 1988, Slavic protests against Moldovan demands, especially those pertaining to language policies, appeared in the Russian-language press (Crowther, 1991: 194). In the spring of 1989 the two main movements leading the Russian national revival, the Intermovement, also named *Yedinstvo* (Unity), and the United Council of Work Collectives, had been formed in order to protect the interests of Slavs (Socor, 1991a:

24f). The formation of these movements was inspired by the existence of similar ones among the Russians in the Baltic republics (see Section 2.2 of Chapter 5). Initially, the demonstrations arranged by these movements attracted only relatively few Slavs, but in connection with the adoption of the language law in August 1989 some 80 000 Slavic workers in 150 factories, primarily situated in the Dnestr area, went on strike for a whole month in protest (Fane, 1993: 138f).

Following the victory of the PFM in the republican elections in March 1990, the Russian national revival manifested itself on the local level as nationalist politicians won a series of local elections in the spring of 1990, especially in the Dnestr region (Crowther, 1991: 200). Having won control over a number of local Soviets, the Slavs soon took advantage of the newly gained institutional platforms. Firstly, they decided to invalidate all the reform legislation adopted in Chisinau during the preceding months (Socor, 1991a: 27f). Secondly, on 2 September 1990, following the Moldovan declaration of sovereignty, they declared the Dnestr area a separate SSR named the Dnestrian Moldavian Republic (Pridnestrovskaya Moldavskaya Respublika – hereafter referred to as the Dnestr republic).

In late November 1990 elections to a newly formed parliament of the Dnestr republic were held in which the Slavs won 43 out of 60 seats (Fane, 1993: 139f). In contrast to Moldova, the Dnestr republic took part in the March 1991 all-Union referendum, and the Slavs voted almost unanimously in favour of the proposal for a renewed Soviet Union while most local Moldovans boycotted the referendum (Socor, 1992a: 43ff). Later, the Slavic leaders welcomed the attempted *coup d'état*, and as the Soviet Union came to an end in December 1991 they arranged a local referendum on joining the newly established Commonwealth of Independent States (CIS). At the same time, elections for a president of the Dnestr republic were held. The Dnestr authorities reported landslide returns in favour of both the CIS and the leader of the Dnestr republic, Igor Smirnov.

Thus, the national revival of the Dnestr Slavs resulted in the de facto establishment of an independent state-like unit although, so far, it has not attained international recognition.

2.3 The Gagauz National Revival

Besides Moldovans, Russians, and Ukrainians, the Gagauz, a Turkish-speaking but orthodox Christian nation-group also inhabited the territory of the Moldavian SSR. According to the 1989 census, the Gagauz made up only 3.5 per cent (153 000) of the population (Fane, 1993: 137f). However, 92 per cent of the Gagauz resided in Moldova's five southernmost regions (see Map 2) in which they constituted 47 per cent of the population. In response to the Moldovan revival, the Gagauz also initiated a national revival which was similar to the Russian national revival in many ways.

From 1986 onwards, the liberalizing reforms made possible a revival of the Gagauz cultural life and language (Socor, 1990a: 9). In this phase, the Gagauz moved rather cautiously and focused primarily on culture-related demands. In 1989 two national organizations were formed and the seeds to a continued split in the Gagauz national revival were sown. On the one hand appeared the Gagauz People (GP) which was led by russified members of the CPM and bureaucrats from the agricultural complex (Cavanaugh, 1992: 12). On the other hand, the Cooperation Movement (CM) was led by anti-communist former political prisoners and did not include any officials of the CPM or Soviet apparatus. However, GP managed from the outset to outmanoeuvre CM into a subordinate position.

Nevertheless, both movements were formed in opposition to the evolving Moldovan revival. When the Moldovan language law was adopted, the simmering Gagauz frustrations came out into the open. Thus, as early as November 1989, following large demonstrations in Komrat, the main town of the Gagauz area, the GP proclaimed a Gagauz Autonomous Soviet Socialist Republic (ASSR) (Fane, 1993: 143f). However, the Moldovan authorities promptly rejected the idea of an autonomous entity.

On 19 August 1990, following the Moldovan declaration of sovereignty and a Moldovan parliamentary report which concluded that the Gagauz were not indigenous and, therefore, were to be viewed as an ethnic group and not a nation-group with rights to its own territory, a congress of Gagauz announced the secession of the Gagauz inhabited territory from Moldova and the formation of a Gagauz Soviet Socialist Republic (*ibid.*). The Slavic leaders made a similar declaration two weeks later (see Section 2.2) which reflected the common interest of the Slavs and Gagauz in opposing the Moldovan revival. In connection with the declaration, the Gagauz leaders also adopted symbols of the new republic, such as a Gagauz national flag, a coat of arms, and an anthem (Socor, 1990a: 11).

In the ensuing period, the Gagauz leaders established separate state institutions while seeking to obtain a status of the Gagauz region as a federal subject of the USSR. In October 1990 elections were held to the newly created Gagauz national parliament (Cavanaugh, 1992: 13). In March 1991 the Gagauz republic participated in the all-Union referendum on the proposal for a renewed USSR (p. 14). During the autumn and winter of 1991 the GP leaders strengthened the legitimacy of their rule as 98 per cent of the voters in the Gagauz area were reported to have voted for the GP leader, Stefan Topal, as president while 90 per cent supported an independent Gagauz republic as a constituent part of the USSR 83 per cent of the electorate was reported to have participated (p. 16).

Thus, paralleling the Russian national revival, the result of the Gagauz national revival was the formation of a separate state-like unit.

3 THE NATIONAL REVIVALS IN A PRIMORDIAL PERSPECTIVE

According to H_1, the strong national revivals among the Moldovans, Slavs, and Gagauz could be explained if the three nation-groups had well-developed ethnic bases provided by the *ethnies* and the historical interplay between them, and the occurrence of the national revivals in the late 1980s could be explained by liberal policies adopted by the formerly repressive Soviet regime, and eased by already existing republican units and constitutional rights.

3.1 The Ethnic Base

3.1.1 The Moldovan Ethnie

The common name of the Moldovans as well as their association with a territory is rooted in the formation of a medieval principality in 1359 between the Eastern Carpathians, the rivers Danube and Dnestr, and the Black Sea (see Map 3) (Spinei, 1986: 33ff). The principality came to be known as Tara Moldovei, the Land of Moldova. According to Moldovan myths of common ancestry, the forefathers of the Moldovans were the Geto-Dacians who settled in the Moldovan lands long before the establishment of the medieval principality (Nedelciuc, 1992: 8). The historical memories of the Moldovans are found in chronicles, legends, and folksongs, many of which celebrate the golden age of the medieval principality (Spinei, 1986: 13ff). A favourite theme of these legends is Prince Dragos who came from his exile in Hungary with a glorious army and saved the Moldovans from the barbaric Mongols. Furthermore, the legend has it that Dragos and his followers were not only chasing the Mongols but also an aurochs which they finally killed by the river Moldova.[25] Another national hero whose exploits have been handed down by folklore is Stephen the Great who successfully defended the Moldovan principality against the Ottoman Turks (Kolstø et al., 1993: 976).[26]

Thus, the ethnic base of the Moldovans is without doubt strong. However, the sense of Moldovan-ness coexists with a sense of Romanianness because nearly all cultural elements are shared with the Romanians.

Most importantly, the Moldovan language is almost identical with the Romanian (Dima, 1975: 38).[27] These cultural similarities were furthered by Romanian and Moldovan intellectuals and leaders who, prior to the formation of an independent Romanian state in 1878,[28] initiated a national revival to gain control of all territory deemed to be Romanian (Dima, 1991: 7ff). One part of this territory was the eastern part of the former Moldovan principality, Bessarabia,[29] which the Russian empire had occupied in 1812. The national revival also spread to this area although the Russian authorities tried their best to prevent it. During the interwar period, when Moldova was a part of Romania, this obstacle was absent and the intellectuals had free hands to promote the pan-Romanian features. Following the Soviet annexation of Bessarabia in 1940, the Soviet authorities propagated the idea of a separate Slav-related Moldovan nation in order to legitimize the occupation (pp. 43ff). However, this idea was never accepted by the Moldovans.

The question of whether the Moldovans were a distinct nation-group or whether they were Romanians was echoed in the Moldovan national revival in the late 1980s. On the one hand, the Moldovan politicians adopted the Romanian national anthem, 'Romanians Awake', as the national anthem of Moldova (Socor, 1991d: 23). On the other hand, when the Moldovans chose a new national flag, they added the Moldovan coat of arms, an eagle and an aurochs, to the Romanian tricolour. These seemingly contradictory events reflect the continued coexistence of feelings of both Moldovan-ness and Romanian-ness. The Moldovan-ness is rooted in the still strong and distinct Moldovan *ethnie* while the Romanian-ness is a kind of overlay which the modern intellectuals have sought to promote since the second half of the 19th century. The leading Moldovan politicians of the late 1980s took advantage of these two currents and tried to make them compatible.

In conclusion, although the feelings of Romanian-ness and Moldovanness coexist among the Moldovans, their common identity is not weakened by this duality. On the contrary, these two strains have merged into a symbiosis which have created a strong common identity. As will become apparent in the ensuing sections, this identity is furthermore clearly distinct from that of neighbouring groups.

The theory of moderate primordialism is thus able to explain the strength of the Moldovan revival. Yet because of the dual identity of the Moldovans, it could not have predicted whether they would have opted for an independent Moldova or for a reunification with Romania.

3.1.2 The Slavic Ethnie

The Slavic population in Moldova consisted of approximately the same number of Russians and Ukrainians (see Section 2.2). Due to the russification policies of the tsarist and Soviet empires, a remarkably large share of the Ukrainians in Moldova had been russified and sovietized. Therefore, a majority of the Ukrainians, like almost all of the Russians in Estonia and Moldova, associated with the Soviet culture and state. Thus, by 1989, only 9 per cent of these 600 000 Ukrainians were fluent in Ukrainian while 37 per cent were unable to speak the language of their professed nationality (Nahaylo, 1992: 42). And in 1990 as many as 80 per cent reported complete fluency in Russian (Odling-Smee, 1992: 51).

Concerning a common name, the Slavs referred to themselves as Slavs or Russians, which also reflected the continued domination of the Russians *vis-à-vis* the Ukrainians. To our knowledge, myths of a local age-old common ancestry did not make up a part of the arsenal used by the mobilizing Slavic leaders. This would also entail a somewhat far-fetched reconstruction of the past, but still the historical memories of the Moldovan Slavs do date back several centuries. Thus, the first Ukrainians settled in the area along the Dnestr river as early as in the 17th and 18th centuries (Kolstø et al., 1993: 977ff). Later, from 1791, when the Russian empire conquered the Dnestr area, and from 1812, when it conquered Bessarabia, Russian colonists followed and settled in the fertile lands along the river Dnestr. They saw themselves as those who opened up a New Russia (*Novorossiya*) (Nahaylo, 1992: 40). This 19th-century Russian colonization wave was bigger in Moldova than, for example, in Estonia. Thus, the number of Russians in Moldova prior to the Soviet period was larger than in Estonia, both relatively and absolutely.[30]

In this process, the Slavs came to associate with the territory along the Dnestr. This was especially so regarding the left bank or eastern part of the Dnestr region which constitutes the present-day territory of the Dnestr republic. In this area, which had never been part of any Moldovan entity until 1940,[31] when Stalin redrew the borders and incorporated it in the Moldavian SSR, emigrant Ukrainians and Russians had developed a local Slavic culture from the 17th century onwards. This meant that when the massive Russian immigration took place following the Second World War, those Russians who arrived in the Dnestr area were grafted into an older Slavic culture, while to a larger extent constituting a new cultural element in the rest of Moldova (Kolstø et al., 1993: 979).

Finally, the Slavs successfully appealed to the Great Russian sense of social solidarity. While the Yeltsin-led Russian government kept a more or less neutral position towards the Moldovan Slavs, several leading Russian nationalists, including Rutskoy and Zhirinovsky, repeatedly visited the Dnestr republic and voiced fervent support of their cause (Crow, 1992: 11). Also, several hundred Russian Cossacks, descendants of Russia's legendary imperial warriors who contributed heavily to the conquest of, for example, Bessarabian Moldova, arrived as volunteers and were cordially welcomed by the local Slavs.

In conclusion, while the Slavs in Bessarabian Moldova (i.e. outside the Dnestr area), like the Russians in Estonia, stuck to the Soviet identity as long as possible, the Dnestr Slavs had the advantage of an older local Slavic culture to which they could turn when the Soviet project failed. In this way, H_1 is able to explain why the strong Russian national revival occurred in the Dnestr area and not among the Russians living in the rest of the Moldavian SSR.

3.1.3 The Gagauz Ethnie

Besides their common proper name, the Gagauz could rely on myths of common ancestry and collective historical memories. The Gagauz are the descendants of Turkish tribes which moved into eastern Bulgaria in the middle ages (Nedelciuc, 1992: 23f). In Bulgaria they adopted orthodox Christianity – the main reason why they later fled to Bessarabian Moldova during the Russian–Turkish wars in 1768–74 and 1806–12. The Gagauz were attracted by special privileges which they were accorded by the Russian tsar. These included substantial land allotments and release from taxes and military service.

The Gagauz language, which became a written language during the first Gagauz national revival at the end of the 19th century, belongs to the group of Turkish languages and is the most distinctive element of the Gagauz culture (Bruchis, 1984: 8ff; Socor, 1990a: 8f). While completely incomprehensible to the neighbouring Slavs and Moldovans, the Gagauz still converse easily with visitors from Turkey. That the language is a crucial part of the Gagauz ethnie is reflected in the fact that 90 per cent of the Gagauz, despite the harsh russification policies (see Section 3.3), considered Gagauz their native language in 1989 (Fane, 1993: 142).

Even today, an overwhelming majority of the Gagauz are farmers and live in villages and small towns. The Gagauz farmers cultivate the relatively fertile land which was allocated to their forefathers by the tsar some two hundred years ago. For that reason, the association of the Gagauz with the southern part of present-day Moldova is strong. Also, the fact that only few Gagauz have been urbanized most probably contributed to the preservation of a sense of social solidarity among the predominantly rural Gagauz.

In conclusion, this factor, together with the other *ethnie* features already mentioned, leaves a picture of a strong Gagauz ethnic base and national identity.

3.1.4 The Historical Interplay between Moldovans and Slavs

In many respects the Moldovans had an anti-Slavic attitude similar to the Estonians' anti-Russian attitude. The roots of the Moldovan attitude towards the Slavs are to be found in the incorporation of Moldova into the Russian empire in the 1812–1918 period (Nedelciuc, 1992: 5f, 9). The semi-autonomy which Moldova had retained under Ottoman supremacy was replaced by the status of a province (Guberniya Besarabiya), and harsh russification policies were directed against the local administration, church, and school system (Siupur, 1993: 154ff; Dima, 1975: 33). These policies were especially intensive from the 1870s and onwards in the face of the first Romanian/Moldovan national revival. For example, from 1871 teaching in Moldovan was forbidden in the entire school system. Furthermore, the anti-Slavic attitude was reinforced as the Soviet Union, following the conclusion of the Molotov–Ribbentrop pact including the secret protocols, occupied Moldova twice during the Second World War (Crowther, 1991: 186f). In the periods 1940–41 and 1944–53, the Stalinist regime deported many thousand Moldovans, mostly intellectuals, politicians, civil servants, students, and so-called kulaks, to camps in Siberia and Central Asia. Furthermore, compulsory grain collections and a forced collectivization of the farmland was carried through, leading to widespread famine. Finally, the territory of Moldova was diminished once again as the southern and northern parts of Bessarabian Moldova were joined to the Ukrainian SSR.

In contrast to the attitude of the Russians in Estonia towards the titular nation-group, the Slavic *ethnie* was characterized by an anti-Moldovan/Romanian attitude. The foundation of the so-called romanophobia among the Slavs, who made little if any distinction between Moldovans and Romanians, was laid during the interwar period when Moldova was a part of Romania (Nahaylo, 1992: 44f). The Slavic minority, like, for example, the Hungarian minority, was granted no minority rights whatsoever. During the Second World War, the oppression of the Slavs, which most probably carried elements of revenge due to the Russian annexation of the Bessarabian part of Moldova, was pursued more directly and on a much larger scale. The Nazi-German military campaign against the Soviet Union made possible the establishment of Romanian authority in 1941–44 not only over the whole of Moldova but also over the left-bank Dnestr area and the eastern part of Ukraine (Kolstø et al., 1993: 979). In this way Hitler rewarded the Romanian fascists and Romania's siding with Germany against the Soviet Union. Backed up by the German army, the Romanians and Moldovans were given free hands to persecute the local Slavs, and this resulted in the death of an unknown number of Slavs in Romanian and German labour and concentration camps.

Today, these and the aforementioned events are still a vivid part of the memory of many Moldovans and Slavs who have also told the younger generations about their experiences. For that reason the Moldovan and Slavic *ethnies* were, by the 1980s, still marked by enough mutual animosity to create a fertile ground for mobilizing nationalists.

3.1.5 The Historical Interplay between Moldovans and Gagauz

Unlike the Moldovan–Slavic relations, the historical record of Moldovan–Gagauz relations does not contain significant atrocities or large-scale oppression.

Although the Moldovans most likely did not welcome the early 19th century Gagauz immigration and the privileges accorded especially to the Gagauz by the tsar, the Gagauz were not repressed to the same extent as the Slavs (or Hungarians) during the interwar and war periods because the Romanians and Moldovans did not see them as representatives of an 'evil empire' (Cavanaugh, 1992: 11f). On the contrary, the Moldovans never really had any reasons to feel threatened by the Gagauz because the Gagauz never sided with the Slavs against them (that is, until the present national revivals). Just as importantly, there were relatively few Gagauz, and they had no significant resources and no potential support of a mother-nation.

On this background, the Moldovan mobilizers of the 1980s neither could nor tried to rely on a Gagauz-hostile attitude (Fane, 1993: 142). The pro-Soviet or -Russian wing of the Gagauz mobilizers did try to evoke some degree of romanophobia, but they were balanced by the oppositional mobilizers who accentuated the peaceful historical cohabitation of the two groups.

3.2 The Triggering Factors: Recent Developments in the Soviet Legal–Political Setting

Like the Estonians and the Russians in Estonia, the nation-groups in Moldova also took advantage of the right to freedom of speech and the right to organize collectively which were realized following the *perestroyka* reforms launched by the Soviet centre.

The Baltic nation-groups were among the first groups in the USSR to initiate national revivals. And once in existence, these revivals had an important spill-over effect. Thus, leading representatives of the PFM openly admitted that the progress of the national movements in the Baltics (and in the rest of Eastern Europe) had helped to broaden their sense of what was possible (Socor, 1989c: 2). The spill-over effect was evident in so far as the content and timing of the demands of the Moldovans to a large extent followed the same pattern as, for example, the Estonian demands, but with a certain delay. For example, the Estonian parliament adopted a language law in January 1989 (see Section 2.1 of Chapter 5), while the Moldovan parliament adopted a similar language law in August 1989 (see Section 2.1). Another cause of the delay of the Moldovan national revival was the more conservative attitude of the incumbent communists in Moldova. However, the leeway of the republican communists to resist implementation of the liberalizing reforms was strongly circumscribed by the Soviet centre and it was, therefore, mainly a matter of time before the Moldovan nationalists had their way.

Thus, the regime change in Moscow triggered national revivals and eventually also regime change in Moldova. As the Moldovan nationalists took over the parliamentary power in the spring of 1990, they also came to control the republican ministries and other governmental institutions which were a ready-made platform from which national demands could be promoted more radically. However, although the Moldovan nationalists' possibility of rising to power initially was due to the liberal reforms introduced by the centre, the Moldovan politicians that seized the reins of power were not ready to accord the same liberties to the Slavs and Gagauz. As these groups also began to pursue nationalist goals of sovereignty, the Moldovan authorities tried their best to curb these revivals (see Sections 2.2 and 2.3). For example, the Gagauz were deprived of the right to organize collectively when the leading movement, GP, was banned.

Thus, as for the possibility of using institutional resources, the Moldovans were in a relatively favourable situation, being a titular nation-group in one of the 15 republics of the USSR (CUSSR, 1987: arts. 71, 85, 87). Although the Slavs and Gagauz made some use of the local administrative units, these were far from comparable with the republican institutions. In this respect, especially the Gagauz had reasons to feel discriminated against by the Soviet authorities since they, unlike other nation-groups of similar or even smaller size (e.g. the Karelians), were never granted any form of autonomy (Sheehy, 1987: 1).[32]

Concerning constitutional rights, the Moldovans were the only group in Moldova which could and did try to pursue their national cause in that way. Like the PFE, the Moldovan counterpart sought to legitimize the demand for independence by referring to the formal rights of republican sovereignty and secession given by both the USSR and Moldovan constitutions (Socor, 1989c: 5f; CUSSR, 1987: arts. 72, 76). As in the Estonian case, the tolerance of the Soviet authorities was depleted, and the USSR Supreme Soviet declared the Moldovan proclamation of sovereignty unconstitutional, referring primarily to article 73 in the USSR constitution which placed the final authority in all vital matters at the all-Union level. However, in contrast to the Estonian politicians, only very few Moldovan leaders emphasized the illegality of the Soviet annexation in 1940 because the logic of that argument would lead to the conclusion that, *de jure*, Moldova was still a part of Romania and that the Dnestr area was not a part of Moldova (Gabanyi, 1993: 166ff).

In conclusion, the liberalizing reforms made three national revivals possible in Moldova in the second half of the 1980s and, furthermore, the Moldovans were relatively privileged in their ability to use republican structures and constitutional rights, although the latter turned out to be of little avail in the world of *Realpolitik*.

4 THE NATIONAL REVIVALS IN AN INSTRUMENTAL PERSPECTIVE

According to H_2, the strong national revivals among the Moldovans, Slavs, and Gagauz could be explained if these nation-groups were subject to economic, political, and cultural deprivation or frustration due to internal colonization.

4.1 Internal Colonization of the Moldovans

In the USSR, power was centralized in Moscow in the all-Union party and state bodies. Moscow and the largest republic, the RSFSR, which was mainly inhabited by Russians, thus constituted the centre, while Moldova belonged to the periphery.

4.1.1 Economic Colonization

Eighty per cent of the land in Moldova is arable, and the Moldovan economy was almost completely agricultural before the Soviet period (Krausing, 1992: 19). And it very much remained so throughout the Soviet period. Although the forced incorporation into the Soviet economy led to some industrialization, Moldova had the lowest rates of productivity, capital investment, and industrial employment of all the Union republics as late as in the mid-1960s (Schroeder, 1986: 298ff). Later, in 1980, Moldova still produced less national income per capita than any other republic except for Azerbaijan and the republics in Central Asia – that is, considerably below the all-Union average. Thus, the Soviet authorities kept the Moldovan economy predominantly agricultural. Moreover, in

1990 as many as 95 per cent of the enterprises were still controlled directly from the ministries in Moscow (Kolstø et al., 1993: 980). In the agricultural sector, output rose as modern Soviet production methods were introduced, but the careless use of huge amounts of pesticides led to serious pollution of the environment. Many Moldovans pointed to this problem as the explanation of the decline in average life expectancy among Moldovans. In 1980, the Moldovans had the lowest average life expectancy (64.7 years) of any of the major Soviet nationalities (Crowther, 1991: 185).

In addition, most of the Moldovan agricultural products were processed in other republics, primarily in the RSFSR, because very few processing factories were located in Moldova (Socor, 1991a: 25). Instead, many of the enterprises belonged to heavy industry and the military–industrial complex (Crowther, 1993: 185ff). These enterprises preferred in particular to employ Russians who were better educated than the local Moldovans, and therefore many Russians immigrated to Moldova in the postwar period. Consequently, in 1959 only 33 per cent of the specialists with higher education in Moldova were Moldovan. By 1989, although ever more Moldovans had been enrolled in institutions of higher education in the previous years, they still only comprised 48 per cent of the industrial work force, 51 per cent of those employed in leadership, and 37 per cent of those in scientific work. At that time, 64 per cent of the population was Moldovan (*ibid.*).

Thus, the cultural division of labour in the Soviet economy was displayed very clearly in the Moldovan case. Therefore, the Moldovans, in contrast to the much more favourable economic situation of the Estonians, had good reasons to complain about the structural economic inequalities caused by the Soviet system. As the economic crisis of this system worsened during the 1980s, the Moldovans did indeed perceive themselves to be economically exploited. One of the recurring themes of the huge demonstrations in Chisinau was 'Down with Colonization', referring in particular to the exploitation of the republic's agricultural resources (Socor, 1989b: 2). The Moldovan politicians also rejected the proposed new Union treaty, arguing that Moldova had always transferred more resources to the centre than it had received and that its relationship with the centre had not enabled it to overcome its backwardness (Socor, 1991b: 13). Instead, the new Moldovan government favoured economic autonomy and market economy reforms, including privatization of state-owned enterprises.

The importance accorded to economic arguments by the Moldovans was also one of the reasons for their reluctance to seek reunification with

Romania. The Moldovans lacked economic incentives to do this because the Romanian economy fared even worse (Socor, 1992c: 28f). Instead, Moldova started to look around for development partners in the West.

In conclusion, although the incorporation into the USSR took the Moldovan economy some way along the road of modernization, a cultural division of labour was established that kept the Moldovans economically deprived. This is consistent with $H_{2.1}$ which is therefore confirmed in the case of the Moldovan national revival.

4.1.2 Political Colonization

During and after the Second World War, almost all of the former Moldovan political elite disappeared because of emigration and the Stalinist purges (Bruchis, 1984: 4ff). Many of the remaining Moldovans, even the former members of the Communist Party of Romania, were considered politically unreliable by the Soviet authorities, and the postwar Moldovan peripheral elite was therefore not granted most-favoured-lords status. Furthermore, throughout the Soviet period, the Moldovan elite never managed to achieve this status as it remained underrepresented in the power organs of the centre.

The Soviet centre, however, wanted to establish a republican elite of loyal mediators in order to secure some degree of indigenous support of the regime. While in 1946 only 14 per cent of the members of the Central Committee of the CPM was Moldovan, from 1949 onwards the CPSU increasingly allowed recruitment of Moldovans into the ranks of the CPM. By 1967, 37 per cent of the members of the CPM were Moldovans, while the figure rose to 48 per cent in 1988 (Bruchis, 1984: 78; Crowther, 1991: 186f). But still the Moldovans were heavily underrepresented in relation to their share of the population (64 per cent) by 1989. This pattern was repeated on the all-Union level where, in 1976, the Moldovans composed 1.1 per cent of the population but only 0.4 per cent of the CPSU membership (Bruchis, 1984: 54). Moreover, it was one thing to gain entrance into the CPM, and quite another to climb the ladder of the hierarchy. Not until 1961 did a Moldovan become a member of the Politbureau of the CPM (p. 76). Being russified to the extent that he could hardly speak Moldovan and a trusted ally of Brezhnev, Ivan Ivanovich Bodyul became secretary of the CPM in 1962. Still, by 1981 only five out of 13 members of the Politbureau were Moldovans (p. 56). The only republican organ in which the Moldovans were allowed to be proportionally represented was the parliament, the Supreme Soviet. For example, in 1970, 70 per cent of the delegates were Moldovans. However, the parliament played a merely symbolic role as it always adopted the resolutions prepared by the CPM. Thus, paralleling the situation in Estonia, the Moldovan elite was not even granted most-favoured-lords status on the republican level.

Consequently, the Moldovan masses remained politically alienated and the majority of the local elite frustrated. But as the barriers to upward mobility were removed, beginning with the first free elections to the parliament in 1990, the aspirations of the new nationalist elite were soon realized. Arguments of political degradation were very powerful in mobilizing the slumbering Moldovans, and when the Moldovan politicians had reached the powerful positions, they consolidated their new status by declaring independence as soon as it became possible. Thus, the explanatory power of $H_{2.2}$ is significant in the case of the Moldovan national revival.

4.1.3 Cultural Colonization

The Moldovans felt strongly misrecognized by the Soviet regime not least because of the Soviet contention that the Moldovan language, as opposed to Romanian, had Slavic roots (Heitmann, 1989: 29ff). Furthermore, they felt culturally discriminated against because of the Soviet language policies which apparently aimed at linguistic assimilation of the Moldovans by promoting Russian at the expense of Moldovan. This policy was pursued in numerous ways, for example by the forced substitution of the Cyrillic for the Latin alphabet, by giving many locations and institutions Russian and not Moldovan denominations, and by making Russian the dominant language of instruction, especially in institutions of higher education. Consequently, Russian became the most widely spoken language in the spheres of public administration, industry, and trade, and knowledge of Russian became a precondition of upward mobility. The republican media were also relatively strongly influenced by the Russian language. In 1978, 43 per cent of all the republican and local newspapers were published in Russian (Crowther, 1991: 189). Many Moldovans took offence because they had learned Russian, while very few Slavs became familiar with Moldovan. By 1979, 47 per cent of the Moldovans spoke Russian fluently, while in the same year only 11 per cent of the Russians spoke Moldovan (Bruchis, 1984: 23). As a result of this imbalance, Moldovans who spoke their mother tongue at public gatherings and meetings were branded as nationalists, a very contemptuous term in the Soviet ideology. Those who spoke Russian, on the other hand, were termed Soviet internationalists and socialist patriots (Heitmann, 1989: 39f).

As examples of cultural colonization, the Moldovans could also point to the immigration of Slavs, especially Russians, which increased heavily in the postwar period (Nedelciuc, 1992: 57). Thus, in 1991 only 52 per cent of the Russians were born in Moldova. Furthermore, since the 1950s the celebration of the traditional holidays and the folkloristic ceremonies performed in connection with these had been banned (Dima, 1975: 54). Priests, for their part, regretted that the Moldovan Orthodox Church, previously under the authority of the patriarch of Romania, had been transferred to the jurisdiction of the patriarch in Moscow.

Thus, cultural colonization was also a driving force behind the national revival of the Moldovans.

4.2 Internal Colonization of the Slavs

Throughout the Soviet era, the constituent republics had very little influence in relation to the Moscow centre. However, as the Moldovans achieved still more power on the republican level, Chisinau became the potential colonizing centre from the point of view of the Slavic minority.

4.2.1 Economic Colonization

Forty per cent of the industry in Moldova was located in the Dnestr region which accounted for 33 per cent of all industrial goods and 56 per cent of all consumer goods produced in the Moldavian SSR (Kolstø et al., 1993: 980). The industry in this region employed primarily Slavs, and as the industrial workers in the Soviet economy received relatively high wages, the living standard of the Dnestr Slavs was above the average in Moldova. For example, in 1991, 75 private cars per 1000 inhabitants were registered in the Dnestr region while the average number for the whole of Moldova was 48 per 1000 (Nedelciuc, 1992: 61). Furthermore, as in the rest of the USSR, military personnel and their families enjoyed substantial housing and employment privileges. This had a special bearing on the Dnestr Slavs as both the Soviet 14th Army and some defence industries were located in the Dnestr area and as the majority of personnel, army reservists, and employees of the local defence industry were Slavs (Socor, 1992f: 40f). Thus, the Slavs were not economically deprived and had no reasons to feel economically colonized by the republican centre.

However, as the political influence of the Moldovan nationalists rose in the late 1980s, they demanded introduction of market economy reforms, including privatization of industry and an end to government subsidies (Radu, 1992: 146f). Therefore, the Slavs who were mainly employed in the industry feared losing their jobs, and the Slavic factory directors and technocrats were anxious about losing their influential positions. The Slavs expected that the continuation of their relatively privileged position depended on the Moldovan economy remaining an integrated part of the

Soviet socialist economy. Also, the prospects of economic prosperity of the relatively backward Moldovan economy in an independent state, or fused with the even poorer Romanian economy, seemed much worse than in Estonia where the economy was more modern and connections with the West were better. Therefore, unlike the Russians in Estonia, the Slavs had no reason to trust that their economic welfare would be preserved or even improved in an independent state.

In this way, economic issues played a prominent part in the Slavic national revival. At the popular rallies held in Tiraspol, the main city in the Dnestr region, the Slavs cheered their leaders' speeches in favour of socialist ownership of industry (Socor, 1992b: 9). When the Moldovan government moved to abolish the privileges of the military personnel in 1990, the Dnestr authorities guaranteed their continuation (Socor, 1992f: 41). And economic motives were probably important when most of the Dnestr population voted in favour of the proposal on a renewed Soviet Union (Socor, 1991c: 12). When the new Moldovan government introduced a coupon system in February 1991 as a first step towards leaving the ruble zone, the Dnestr authorities repealed it and instead declared that henceforth all Dnestr enterprises would cease to make contributions to the Moldovan state budget and that the Dnestr republic would establish its own state bank (Fane, 1993: 140).

In conclusion, the Dnestr Slavs were not at all economically deprived and they were most probably very well aware of their privileged position in the Moldavian SSR. However, as the Moldovan national revival evolved and as the prospects of a relatively underdeveloped Moldovan economy separated from the Soviet centre came closer, they had reasons to believe that their economic welfare would be in danger. Thus, if the frustration aspect of $H_{2.1}$ is widened to include fear of *future* economic colonization, the hypothesis provides an explanation of the Russian national revival in Moldova. The perceptions of the Slavs were the opposite of those of the Estonians and the Moldovans in the sense that the Slavs feared future economic colonization in an *independent* state while the other two groups feared future economic deprivation in the Soviet federation.

4.2.2 Political Colonization

Throughout the Soviet period, the Slavs were far from being politically deprived (see Section 4.1.2). In the immediate postwar years, the leadership of the new republic was almost totally dominated by Slavs.[33] Although loyal Moldovans were gradually allowed to rise to more important positions, the Slavs still dominated the CPM. Thus, by 1988 the Slavs made up 43 per cent of the membership of the CPM while constituting only 27 per cent of the population (Crowther, 1991: 187).

Therefore, the Slavs did not welcome the demands of the rising Moldovan nationalists to break the power of the CPM and to replace the Soviet political system with independence and liberal democracy (Socor, 1991a: 25). Following the elections in 1990, the new Moldovan-dominated government[34] adopted a law on political and state power which, for example, mandated the separation of CPM organs and state institutions at all levels, required officials and managers above certain levels to give up their CPM membership, and ended the control of the CPM over the media of the republic. And though it was not officially endorsed, the personnel policy of the new government meant a gradual replacement of Slavs with Moldovans (Socor, 1990b: 13).

Another important element of the Russian national revival was romanophobia (Socor, 1992c: 30ff). Especially after the fall of the Ceauşescu regime in December 1989 and in connection with the rising national euphoria following the spring 1990 electoral victory, many Moldovan intellectuals and politicians openly supported the idea of a speedy reunification. Fervently opposing this idea, the Slavic mobilizers argued that the Slavs would have no political rights in a Great Romania. They substantiated this argument by pointing to the fate of the Hungarian minority.[35]

Consequently, the Slavic politicians boycotted the sessions of the Moldovan parliament, proclaimed the Dnestr republic, and arranged elections to a new Dnestr parliament (Socor, 1990b: 13; 1991a: 27f). Following the elections, the Slavic leaders could claim overwhelming support of the Dnestr population and they proceeded to establish a new state structure, the positions of which were filled with the Slavs who had been degraded or dismissed during the Moldovan regime change. In this way, the Slavic elite escaped the looming political deprivation which they perceived to be the goal of the new Moldovan (or Romanian) centre. But the Slavs had no intention of creating a fully independent state, which would probably also be difficult, given the size of the region. On the contrary, in September 1991, following the *coup d'état* which, to the regret of the Dnestr leaders, failed, the Dnestr parliament voted unanimously to reaffirm the wish of the Dnestr republic to join the USSR. And as the USSR ceased to exist in December 1991, the Dnestr leaders sought to achieve incorporation of the republic into the Russian Federation (Socor, 1992b: 9). However, the Russian government did not take steps to accommodate that idea. Therefore, *de facto*, the Dnestr republic remained an independent unit.

Thus, the Slavs' fear of future political colonization was an important driving force behind the Slavic national revival.

4.2.3 Cultural Colonization

Like the Estonian, the Moldovan national revival led to the degradation of the earlier dominant Soviet culture and of the Russian language. The symbols of the Soviet era were replaced with Moldovan ones, the Soviet denominations of places were changed into entirely new or into the original Moldovan names, and the Soviet holidays were abolished while Moldovan holidays were restored (Fane, 1993: 136). The Slavs, whose identity was closely connected to the Soviet culture, felt humiliated by these changes. Furthermore, the introduction of Moldovan as the new state language and the concomitant linguistic demands were a real threat to the Slavs because only rather few spoke Moldovan (Furtado & Chandler, 1992: 271ff). Apart from the degradation of Russian from state to interethnic language, the language law introduced the principle that the citizens of Moldova could choose which language to use when communicating with public employees. Therefore, most Slavic public employees had to learn Moldovan to secure their jobs. Another consequence of the language law was the introduction in the universities of a Moldovan language test as a part of the entrance examinations (Fane, 1993: 148). This was a barrier to many Slavic students. In addition, many primary schools downgraded or simply dropped education in Russian, thereby forcing the Slavic pupils to shift to 'pure' Russian-language schools (Kolstø et al., 1993: 982).

The accusations of the Slavic leaders that the Moldovan nationalists were to blame for the perceived humiliation of Soviet values and culture were, therefore, not unfounded. This, in turn, explains why the Slavic leaders took action to prevent the removal of the symbols of Soviet communism and the implementation of the language law in the Dnestr region (Socor, 1991a: 25). Later, when the Dnestr republic had been established, the Dnestr parliament resolved to adopt as symbols of the new republic the flags, coats of arms, and anthems of both the USSR and the former Moldavian SSR (Socor, 1992b: 9). However, as the USSR eventually dissolved, the Slavs increasingly turned to their older and preserved local Slavic culture.

Thus, fear of cultural misrecognition was another factor behind the Russian national revival that led to the establishment of the Dnestr republic.

4.3 Internal Colonization of the Gagauz

The problems of identifying the relevant centre seen from the point of view of a nation-group in the periphery of the periphery has a special relevance in the Gagauz case. As will become clear, the Gagauz disagreed about whether the colonizing centre was to be found in Moscow or Chisinau.

4.3.1 Economic Colonization

In contrast to the Slavs, a majority of the Gagauz were farmers who worked at the collective farms (*kolkhozy* and *sovkhozy*), and their average standard of living was below the Moldovan average (King, 1993: 137f). Furthermore, the Gagauz-populated southern region of Moldova suffered from a level of investments below the republican average. The numbers of hard-surface roads, modern irrigation systems,[36] and doctors and nurses relative to the region's population were less than half the total republican average. Thus, the backwardness of the Moldovan economy as such was particularly acute in the southern region. Structurally, the Gagauz were, therefore, economically deprived. But it is questionable whether this deprivation can be accorded to the Moldovan centre as the leeway for independent economic policies of that centre was very much circumscribed throughout the Soviet period.

The perceptions of this issue among the Gagauz differed (Cavanaugh, 1992: 12f). The separatists in the dominant GP blamed the Moldovans for the lack of development, while the autonomists in the oppositional and smaller CM blamed the Soviet centre. Accordingly, the opinions also differed regarding the policies and intentions of the new nationalist Moldovan government (Socor, 1990a: 12f). While both wings insisted that the republican authorities should redress the conditions that had led to the underdevelopment, the CM stressed that the Moldovan government had offered economic assistance to the region, while the GP argued that the negotiations on that subject had not resulted in any concrete Moldovan steps. In the same vein, the CM supported the Moldovan demands for market economy reforms and went even further than the Moldovans by demanding break-up of the *kolkhozy* and introduction of private ownership of the land.[37] In contrast, the GP strongly opposed such policies and supported Soviet economics instead. As this movement took the lead in the Gagauz revival, the official policies of the Gagauz republic, adopted in August 1990 by the newly created Gagauz parliament, aimed at securing the independent functioning of the Gagauz economy *vis-à-vis* the Moldovan, including a separate financial and banking system (Furtado & Chandler, 1992: 297).

Thus, as regards the economic sphere, the views and practical measures taken by the dominating wing of the Gagauz resembled those of the Slavs.

In conclusion, there is no doubt that the Gagauz were economically deprived in comparison with both the Moldovans and the Slavs. However, it is difficult to determine whether the Gagauz perceived that this deprivation was caused by the Moldovan or the Soviet centre. What we can conclude is that the Gagauz leaders, who blamed Chisinau for the deprivation and argued that this deprivation could only worsen in an independent Moldova, received widespread support. Consequently, $H_{2.1}$ contributes to some extent to the explanation of the Gagauz revival.

4.3.2 Political Colonization

The Gagauz never played any significant role in the CPM because they were favoured by neither the federal nor the republican centre. The political deprivation of the Gagauz was reflected in the fact that they were never assigned a separate administrative unit (Bruchis, 1984: 36). The failure of the Gagauz elite to achieve the status of most-favoured-lords was also reflected in the underrepresentation in, for example, the *nomenklatura* of the Central Committee of the CPM. In 1987 only 2.3 per cent of the posts were occupied by Gagauz, while the Gagauz nation-group constituted 3.5 per cent of the population (Sheehy, 1987: 2). Nevertheless, a small russified mediator-elite did exist.

As the Moldovan national revival evolved, both Gagauz elite wings feared moldovanization and feared romanization even more (Socor, 1992c: 30). This fear was reinforced in so far as the Moldovan nationalists agreed only to the idea of cultural autonomy, not to the idea of administrative or territorial autonomy.[38] Following the adoption of the language law, the Gagauz especially feared that Moldovan bureaucrats would replace the Gagauz in the local administrative units (Socor, 1990a: 10). As this law demanded knowledge of Moldovan for all public employees, it was a real threat to the Gagauz since, in 1989, only 4.4 per cent said that they spoke Moldovan (Fane, 1993: 142).

All in all then, the Gagauz were politically colonized in the Soviet period. Furthermore, they had reasons to fear continued political deprivation in an independent Moldova or in a Great Romania. Thus, political factors add to the economic ones in explaining the occurrence of the relatively strong Gagauz revival.

4.3.3 Cultural Colonization

The Gagauz were subject to russification and sovietization policies which were even more thoroughgoing than those which the Moldovans and Ukrainians experienced. Thus, whereas 58 per cent of the Moldovans in 1989 claimed that they spoke Russian as either their native or second language, the corresponding number for the Gagauz was 80 per cent (Fane, 1993: 134). Gagauz was not taught in the schools and no newspapers were published in Gagauz until the reforms of the second half of the 1980s (Sheehy, 1987: 2). This meant that in the Soviet period the Gagauz language was only used in unofficial spheres and the Gagauz were forced to learn Russian to cope in the official sphere. Even after the onset of *perestroyka*, there was not much room left for the Gagauz culture and language in the official media of the Moldovan republic. Thus, by 1990 only three Gagauz magazines and not a single Gagauz newspaper were being published and, in addition, the Moldovan television and radio broadcasted no more than three hours and one hour per month respectively in Gagauz (Nedelciuc, 1992: 66).

However, as with economic and political colonization, the opinions of the Gagauz differed as to whether the cultural deprivation was caused by the Moldovan or the Soviet centre. The assimilation of some Gagauz had been so successful that they did not perceive themselves as culturally colonized by the Soviet regime. This stance was represented by the dominating separatist wing of the nationalist mobilizers, and it was revealed when the Gagauz parliament adopted *Russian* as the official language of the newly proclaimed Gagauz SSR (Cavanaugh, 1992: 11). Instead, the Gagauz separatists, like the Slavs, focused on the danger of future cultural deprivation in an independent Moldova or in a Great Romania (Nahaylo, 1992: 41). Thus, they succeeded in arranging protest rallies against the Moldovan language law (Fane, 1993: 135f).

However, the best argument against the language law was political in that it reduced the possibilities for Gagauz to be employed in the public sector (see Section 4.3.2). Culturally, the law accepted the legitimate wish of the Gagauz to use their language in the public spheres. Thus, the law stated that Russian or Gagauz would be the official language in areas with a compact population of Gagauz (Furtado & Chandler, 1992: 272). The conciliatory attitude of the Moldovans regarding cultural issues was reflected also in the persistent Moldovan offer of Gagauz cultural autonomy – an offer never made to the Slavs. Thus, from its inception, the PFM supported Gagauz *cultural* demands in order to win the Gagauz as an ally in the struggle against russification (Socor, 1990a: 12f). More importantly, when the nationalist Moldovan government had been formed, this position resulted in official measures such as offering to support Gagauz folk festivals, importing of Turkish textbooks for Gagauz schools, and expanding Gagauz language programmes on radio and television.

The diagnosis of the Gagauz opposition was somewhat closer to reality. They blamed the Soviet centre for the deprivation of Gagauz culture. Thus, Gagauz intellectuals, many of whom later joined the CM, originally initiated the Gagauz revival in 1987 by demanding better conditions for the Gagauz culture and for the language in particular (Sheehy, 1987: 2ff; see Section 2.3). These mobilizers supported a shift to Gagauz as the language of instruction and administration in an autonomous Gagauz region (Cavanaugh, 1992: 12) – demands that the Moldovan government to a large extent was ready to accommodate.

The conclusion to be drawn is, therefore, that the Gagauz were culturally deprived in the Soviet period. This cultural deprivation was an important element in the national revival initiated by Gagauz intellectuals and later organized in the GP and the CM. The dominant GP, however, did not perceive the cultural deprivation as important. While the GP feared the *political* consequences of, for example, the language law, the Gagauz nation-group had no reasons to fear future *cultural* colonization from the Moldovan side. Thus, $H_{2.3}$ only provides an explanation of why the Gagauz national revival was initiated when the Soviet regime loosened its grip on the constituent nation-groups, not why it continued as the Moldovan national revival evolved.

5 CONCLUSION

In the late 1980s and early 1990s, strong national revivals took place among the Moldovans, the Slavs, and the Gagauz.

The test of the explanatory power of the hypothesis of moderate primordialism led to equivocal results in some respects. Thus, although the ethnic base of the Moldovans contains distinct Moldovan elements, their national identity is at the same time a blend of Moldovan-ness and Romanian-ness. Nevertheless, this identity is characterized by an anti-Russian attitude due to the historical interplay with that nation-group, and this can explain the strength of the Moldovan national revival *vis-à-vis* the Soviet regime. But due to the dual identity of the Moldovans, $H_{1.1}$ could not have predicted whether they would strive for an independent state or for unification with the Romanians.

As for the Dnestr Slavs, they have preserved a distinct ethnic base which, furthermore, is marked by the historically antagonistic relations with the Moldovans and the Romanians. Therefore, $H_{1.1}$ offers an explanation of the strong national revival among the Slavs in the Dnestr region. And finally, the strong Gagauz national revival can be explained by reference to the fact that although their historical relations with the Moldovans is not characterized by animosity, they score high on all the characteristics of an *ethnie*.

With respect to the temporal location of the revivals, the liberal policies initiated in the second half of the 1980s by the Soviet regime can explain the reasons why the revivals occurred in that period. Moreover, the Moldovans had the advantage of being able to use existing republican structures while the rights granted by the USSR constitution turned out to be merely formal.

The test of the instrumental hypothesis points to different explanations of the revivals. Thus, the Moldovans were subject to economic, political, and cultural colonization by the Soviet centre, and the resulting frustrations led to a strong national revival in order to escape this internal colonization. In contrast, the Slavs were not deprived as regards any of the aforementioned spheres during the Soviet era. But as the Moldovan national revival evolved, they feared future internal colonization in an independent Moldova or in a Great Romania. This can explain the Slavic counter-revival. Finally, the Gagauz were colonized to an even larger extent than the Moldovans. Yet, paralleling the Slavs, the majority of the Gagauz feared that their situation was not going to improve in an independent Moldova – although they were offered cultural autonomy by the Moldovans.

7 The National Revivals in Croatia

1 INTRODUCTION

The national revivals among the Croats and the Serbian minority in Croatia constituted one of the decisive factors of the dissolution of Yugoslavia and led to a bloody and violent civil war in Croatia. The events in Croatia and in the rest of Yugoslavia were covered intensively by the Western media. One of the most common explanations offered by journalists was that the end of communist rule took the lid off national aspirations and old hatreds. This chapter puts the popular imagery of 'tribalism' and 'irrationality' to the test and examines whether the national upheavals can be seen as the result of more rationally based strategies.

2 THE NATIONAL REVIVALS

2.1 The Croatian National Revival

Compared with the national revivals of the Estonians and Moldovans which were also titular nation-groups, the Croatian revival was similar in many respects, but it covered a shorter time span before full independence was achieved. Thus, the first opposition parties were not formed until the autumn of 1989 (Križan, 1992: 124ff). Among these, the Croatian Democratic Community (CDC) soon gathered the largest following.[39] The programme of the CDC insisted on the sovereignty of Croatia within or outside a Yugoslavian state.

As in Estonia and Moldova, the ruling communists gave way to the nationalist pressures, first by accepting the formation of opposition parties, and then by agreeing to hold democratic multiparty elections in April/May 1990 (Andrejevich, 1990a: 34ff). These elections gave the national revival further momentum and clearly reflected the popularity of the CDC. Led by the charismatic nationalist Franjo Tudjman – himself a former communist – the party won a landslide victory of 43 per cent of the vote and, in coalition with other nationalist parties, secured 59 per cent of the seats in the parliament, the *Sabor*. With this electoral backup, the new CDC-led *Sabor* adopted a range of policies of nationalism in the following period.

In July 1990, the *Sabor* declared Croatia sovereign and at the same time reinstated national symbols associated with the Croatian history, such as the Croatian coat of arms, the *Šahovnica* (Košuta, 1993: 135f). In October the *Sabor* proposed to change the Yugoslavian state into a confederation of independent states.

At the beginning of 1991 the *Sabor* passed a resolution calling for a peaceful negotiated secession, in case the other republics would not accept the proposal on a confederation (Andrejevich, 1991: 34). However, the negotiations between the republics on the future of Yugoslavia did not progress, mainly because Serbia and Montenegro refused to accept a confederation. Therefore, Croatia took further steps towards the ultimate goal of independence. In May 1991 the Croatian authorities arranged a referendum on independence (Križan, 1992: 126). Though boycotted by most Serbs, 84 per cent of the eligible citizens voted and 94 per cent of those declared themselves for independence.

Frustrated with the deadlocked negotiations on the future of Yugoslavia and referring to the referendum, the *Sabor* took a decisive step on 25 June 1991 and unilaterally declared the republic an independent state (Andrejevich et al., 1991: 24f). However, this move was not accepted by either the Krajina Serbs or the federal authorities. As a result of the civil war between Croatian forces and Serbian irregulars, backed up by the Yugoslavian People's Army (YPA), one third of Croatia's territory came under Serbian control. Nevertheless, Croatia managed to establish itself as an independent state. In early 1992, following a period of stable ceasefire and the decision to send in a UN peacekeeping force, the European Community and, soon afterwards, other major states recognized Croatia as an independent state (Mastnak, 1992: 10f). Thus, the Croatian national revival resulted in the founding of a new independent state, but, paralleling the Moldovan revival, the new state-bearing nation-group controlled only a part of the territory of the former republic.

2.2 The Serbian National Revival

According to the 1991 census, the Serbs made up 12.2 per cent (581 000) of the population in Croatia (Karger, 1992: 141). These Serbs lived primarily in the capital, Zagreb, and in the Krajina area (see Map 4). Paralleling the development in Estonia and Moldova, this minority also founded a political party, the Serbian Democratic Party (SDP), in order to counter the newly formed Croatian opposition parties which one-sidedly and explicitly sought to forward the interests of the titular nation-group (Irvine, 1993: 281f). Following the victory of the Croatian nationalist parties in the elections in

May 1990, many Serbs feared that their position was now less secure. In line with this, the SDP called upon the new Croatian government to grant autonomous political status to regions with a Serbian majority. A rally held on 25 July 1990 hinted at the degree of support behind the demand for autonomy when as many as 120 000 Serbs gathered in the town of Srb (Andrejevich, 1990c: 39). As the government did not take decisive actions even towards *cultural* autonomy, the SDP organized a referendum in August 1990 on independence for the mainly Serb-populated border area, Krajina (Andrejevich, 1990b: 38ff). According to SDP leaders, the Serbs voted overwhelmingly in favour of this proposal.[40]

The interests of the Serbs were defended not only by the SDP, but also by the Serbian National Council, an unofficial 'parliament' composed of Serbs only (Thompson, 1992: 260ff). Following the Croatian proposal for a confederation in October 1990, this council issued a declaration of autonomy and, a few days before the promulgation of the new Croatian constitution in December 1990, the Serbian leaders went one step further and announced the separation of the so-called Serbian Autonomous Region Krajina (SARK) from Croatia. Later, the Serbian leaders renamed the area the Republic of Serbian Krajina (RSK).

Following the Croatian declaration of independence in June 1991, large-scale civil war broke out and the Serbian minority secured control over the Krajina region. Yet, the RSK was only recognized by the Dnestr republic which was also caught in a situation of *de facto* but not internationally recognized independence (see Section 2.2 of Chapter 6).

3 THE NATIONAL REVIVALS IN A PRIMORDIAL PERSPECTIVE

H_1 offers an explanation of the national revivals among Croats and Serbs in Croatia if both nation-groups had a strong common identity based on the *ethnies* and the historical interplay between them. The fact that the national revivals took place in the late 1980s and early 1990s could be explained if the formerly repressive regime of Yugoslavia adopted liberal policies. Finally, the national revivals could have been eased by already existing republican units and constitutional rights.

3.1 The Ethnic Base

3.1.1 The Croatian Ethnie

The Croats possess a host of historical memories and myths of common ancestry which make up the foundation of a strong ethnic identity. According to these myths, the present Croatian people are the descendants of the first Croats who came from 'beyond Bavaria' and, under the leadership of five brothers and two sisters, settled on the eastern shores of the Adriatic Sea some time in the 6th century (Banac, 1984: 33). Most of the historical memories focus on the Croats' glorious medieval kingdom established in the 9th and 10th centuries (Čuvalo, 1990: 5). The Croats' association with their present territory is based on these memories.

Regarding distinctive elements of culture, the Croatian culture is rather close to other south Slavic cultures. For example, the Croatian language is merely the western dialect of the common Serbo-Croatian language. However, this has not prevented Croatian intellectuals from emphasizing the distinctiveness of the Croatian language (Schaller, 1987: 27). Finally, the Croats (together with the Slovenes) differ from the other south Slavic groups in that they belong to the Catholic Church and use the Latin alphabet.

We can therefore conclude that the Croats have a strong common identity. This is mainly due to the tireless efforts of Croatian intellectuals. As in most other cases in Eastern Europe, intellectuals initiated a vernacular mobilization focusing on the Croats' identity in the second half of the 19th century (Čuvalo, 1990: 9ff; see also Section 2.2 of Chapter 3). In the same period, the idea of a Croatian nation-state as distinct from the multinational Austro-Hungarian empire and the concept of a Yugoslavian multiethnic conglomerate was developed. The idea was originally formulated by intellectuals who, in 1861, founded the Croatian Party of Historical Rights (Jelavich, 1967: 85f). In this way, the Croatian ethnic base was reinforced and turned into a national identity which intellectuals have continued to nurture.

3.1.2 The Serbian Ethnie

The Serbs living in Croatia share their common name with the Serbs in Serbia proper, just as the Russians in Estonia and Moldova share their name with other Russians. Yet, in parallel with the Dnestr Slavs, the Serbs in Croatia pride themselves upon a unique identity (Banac, 1984: 170f). This identity is based on the peculiar background of the Serbian presence in Croatia. In the early 16th century the Habsburgs established a military buffer zone against the Ottoman empire in the crescent-shaped area along the borders with Serbia and Bosnia (Irvine, 1993: 18f; see Map 5). The Serbs, who fled northwards from Turkish rule, were given grants of land in this military border area (in Serbo-Croatian: *Vojna Krajina*) in exchange for military service. They were simply to defend the border against Ottoman intrusions. Thus, both as soldiers and as farmers, the Serbs have a long history of close association with the Krajina area. In addition to grants of land, the Serbs were given tax privileges, religious freedom, and the right to elect their own leaders (Thompson, 1992: 236). The Serbs therefore not only emphasize their historical status as frontier-men (*graničari*) with a distinct warrior culture, but also underline the cultural importance of the Orthodox Church and their traditional semi-independent status.

Thus, contrary to the Russians in Estonia, but paralleling the Slavs in Moldova, the Serbs in Croatia have a well-developed and distinct ethnic base which their identity relies on. However, both the Croatian and the Serbian identities are also influenced by the historical interplay between them.

3.1.3 The Historical Interplay between Croats and Serbs

As a part of the Austro-Hungarian empire, Croatia had a semi-autonomous status. Yet, the Croatian authorities, led by the viceroy or *ban*, had no jurisdiction over the *Vojna Krajina* area although they repeatedly tried to obtain this, arguing that the area belonged to the historical Croatian lands (Irvine, 1993: 20). On the other hand, the Serbs wanted to retain their autonomous status. The dispute over the status of the Serb-inhabited region has carried on ever since and has thereby created a conflicting Croatian–Serbian interrelation. The Croats have always feared that the Krajina Serbs would unite with the other Serbs in a Great Serbia. According to the Croats, this scenario was practically realized in the inter-war Yugoslavian state (Schöpflin, 1973: 123f). Although the Croats voluntarily supported the formation of the Kingdom of Serbs, Croats and Slovenes in 1918, they came to perceive that they were as much dominated by Belgrade and the Serbs as they had been earlier by Budapest and the Hungarians. This perception was reinforced when the Serbian king Alexander invalidated the constitution and introduced dictatorship in 1929.[41]

The Croatian fear of Serbian hegemony led to the extremist policy of literally trying to eradicate the Serbs in Croatia during the Second World War. During the war, Croatia, like Romania and Slovakia, was a pseudo-independent state led by the fascist Ustasha movement which cooperated with the Nazi occupiers (Thompson, 1992: 266f). Although the Croats did not fully succeed, they nevertheless managed to exterminate several hundred thousand Serbs (as well as Muslims and Gypsies) in KZ-camps.[42] These events resulted in an enduring anti-Croatian attitude among the Serbs in Croatia.

3.2 The Triggering Factors: Recent Developments in the Yugoslavian Legal–Political Setting

After the Second World War, the Tito-led Communist Party of Yugoslavia (in 1952 renamed the Yugoslavian League of Communists – YLC), established the second Yugoslavia as a federal state, consisting of six republics and two autonomous provinces (Irvine, 1993: 3f). However, in the first decades after the war, the federal system in practice meant strict centralization of the party and the state. But as early as the 1960s, the federal authorities introduced economic and political reforms which meant a higher degree of decentralization towards the republics. These reforms led to the adoption of the 1974 constitution. According to the preamble of this constitution, Yugoslavia was a federal republic of six free and equal 'nations' (i.e., in our terminology, nation-groups). Among these were 'Croats' and 'Serbs' and each nation-group had a 'home' republic (Englefield, 1992: 7). The constitution also guaranteed each nation-group the right to self-determination, including the right to secession, although borders could only be changed by mutual agreement. Furthermore, the constitution established a new federal body, the collective state presidency, which was to serve as the executive head of the federal political apparatus (Ramet, 1992: 69). The state presidency consisted of one delegate from each of the six republics and the two provinces with each delegate having the right to veto federal decision-making. Thus, the creation of this body was an attempt to maintain the delicate balance between the nation-groups of Yugoslavia.

However, the state presidency never really began to function until the charismatic Tito died in 1980. Nor did the institutional decentralizations carried through in the late 1960s and early 1970s mean that decentralization proceeded further than the Tito-controlled federal authorities wanted. Thus, when Croatian communists, during 'the Croatian Spring' in 1971, agitated for Croatian sovereignty, Tito simply removed them from power (Irvine, 1993: 258ff). But when Tito died, the most important enforcer of party discipline and the ultimate arbiter of interrepublican conflicts disappeared from the scene. Consequently, it became possible for the republics to make full use of the earlier reforms and transfer real political and economic power from the federal to the republican level.

Thus, like the Estonians and the Moldovans, the Croats made use of the republican political structures, primarily the republican parliament and government, as a platform from which interests that served the republic could be advanced. At the same time, the power of the federal authorities became gradually weaker, not least because the republics frequently used their right to veto, and this often prevented efficient federal decision-making (Irvine, 1993: 272ff). Rising economic problems during the 1980s and the malfunctioning of the federal authorities led to a debate about the constitutional arrangement of Yugoslavia. The Croatian communists argued in favour of a confederate solution, but this was blocked by the Serbian elite.

The withering away of the power of the federal centre meant that the republican elites could now go on unhindered to make concessions to aspiring nationalists. Thus, a national revival in Serbia proper was initiated by the leader of the Serbian League of Communists (SLC), Slobodan Milošević, who, like Tudjman, traded the ideology of communism for that of nationalism and organized a series of large-scale demonstrations in Serbia, Kosovo, and Vojvodina from 1987 onwards (Glenny, 1992: 32f).

Thus, apart from the liberalization of the Yugoslavian regime, the temporal location of the revivals in Croatia was also influenced by the wave of national revivals in the rest of Eastern Europe in the late 1980s and by the Serbian national revival in particular. This led to the formation of new nationalist parties in 1989, and in 1990 multiparty elections became possible (see Section 2.1). From a Croatian point of view, however, an unintended side-effect of this liberalization was that the Serbian minority also used it to form a nationalist party.

In July 1990, paralleling the Estonian and the Moldovan Supreme Soviets, the new nationalist Croatian government tried to test the validity of the right of the nation-groups to secede, accorded by the 1974 Yugoslavian constitution, by declaring Croatia a sovereign republic (Košuta, 1993: 135f). The federal constitutional court then declared this act unconstitutional, but the Croatian government simply ignored the verdict (Cohen, 1993: 177). At that time, the authority of the federal institutions was already so depleted that they were unable to enforce decisions.

In contrast with the Russians in Estonia and the Slavs and Gagauz in Moldova, the Serbs in Croatia could refer to the constitutional right of nation-groups to self-determination. However, in this respect, the 1974 constitution contained contradictory clauses as article 5 stated that the territory of a republic could not be altered without the consent of that republic (Englefield, 1992: 7). Therefore, the Croatian authorities naturally rejected the Serbian declaration of autonomy referring to this article. In this way, the constitution was invoked by federal authorities, Croats, and Serbs as all three sides sought to legitimize their one-sided acts. Like the cases in the USSR, the Yugoslavian constitutional rights were therefore of equally limited use in the efforts of the nation-groups to obtain independence.

4 THE NATIONAL REVIVALS IN AN INSTRUMENTAL PERSPECTIVE

According to H_2, the strong national revivals among the Croats and Serbs in Croatia could be explained if these nation-groups were subject to economic, political, and cultural deprivation or frustration due to internal colonization.

4.1 Internal Colonization of the Croats

From a Croatian point of view, Serbia and Belgrade were the colonizing centre, while Croatia and the other non-Serbian republics belonged to the periphery.

4.1.1 Economic Colonization

According to $H_{2.1}$, the Croatian revival could be explained by the economic deprivation among the Croats caused by the federal centre's policies of internal colonization. However, like Estonia, Croatia was not an underdeveloped periphery. On the contrary, in 1986 the GDP per capita was 25 per cent above the Yugoslavian average due to the relatively well-developed industrial and tourist sectors (Gapinski et al., 1989: 26). In addition, compared with the Estonians and the Moldovans, the Croats had considerably more control over the republican economy in relation to the federal centre. This was due to the economic reforms in the late 1960s and early 1970s which meant that significant responsibility for the administration of the economy was transferred to the republics (Irvine, 1993: 255).

Croatia retained the relatively high level of economic autonomy through the 1970s. But as a prolonged economic crisis hit Yugoslavia in the 1980s, the federal authorities urged that they should be given more power over economic policy and planning, and they adopted a so-called stabilization programme to achieve this goal (Flakierski, 1989: 17). As the Croats stood to lose the earlier gained economic influence, they fiercely (and successfully) resisted the implementation of the programme. In the same vein, the Croats also complained that they still had to transfer, albeit rather small,[43] economic means to a federal fund which was meant to further the development of the poorer southern republics (Ramet, 1992: 155).

So, although the empirical evidence does not indicate any significant economic colonization, the Croats nevertheless focused on the above-mentioned federal policies to such an extent that perceived economic grievances became one of the driving forces behind the national revival. Fuelled by the fact that the economic situation in Yugoslavia worsened drastically during the 1980s, the Croats, like the Estonians, perceived that they would do much better outside the federation. This stand was reflected in the new nationalist party programmes which emphasized private ownership, a free market economy, and Croatia's integration into the EC (Andrejevich, 1990a: 34). As another example pointing in the same direction, in July 1990 the newly elected Croatian government simply announced that henceforth Croatia was no longer going to transfer money to the federal development fund (Ramet, 1992: 161).

Therefore, the conclusion regarding $H_{2.1}$ parallels the one drawn in the Estonian case. When based on economic deprivation alone, $H_{2.1}$ must be rejected. In contrast, if we focus on the frustrations of the Croats, $H_{2.1}$ can explain the national revival by pointing to the Croats' 'we would have done and will do better on our own' perception.

4.1.2 Political Colonization

In the late 1960s, the federal authorities also carried out reforms which increased the political influence of the republics (Irvine, 1993: 256ff). Although the federal authorities purged the Croatian elite in 1971 because it had taken advantage of the political liberalization and forwarded demands for even more autonomy, these events did not mean that the reforms were rolled back. On the contrary, the decentralizing reforms were incorporated in the 1974 constitution. The consociational features of the new federal political system actually implied that all the republican elites were granted most-favoured-lords status. Thus, each republic elected a representative to the federal state presidency, the apex of the political system. The chairmanship was to rotate annually, and each representative had a right to veto. Furthermore, such principles of 'ethnic arithmetic' were also to be applied in other bodies of the federal government and administration (Cohen, 1993: 51ff).

Consequently, the Croats were apparently not politically deprived. However, the state presidency never really began to function until Tito died in 1980. Then, in the 1980s, the functioning of the body was often blocked due to frequent use of the right to veto. Furthermore, the Serbs dominated the presidency since they controlled half the votes.[44] In addition, the Serbs proposed a recentralization of Yugoslavia which the Croats strongly opposed (Križan, 1992: 123).

The Serbs dominated not only the federal decision-making but also the repressive organs in the federation. Thus in 1990 only 13 per cent of the officers in the YPA were Croats, while 54 per cent were Serbs. The two groups constituted respectively 20 and 37 per cent of the Yugoslavian population (Cohen, 1993: 182f). In addition, the Croats complained that the Serbs, throughout the postwar period, had made up approximately 25 per cent of the membership of the Croatian League of Communists (CLC), while the Serbian minority only accounted for 12 per cent of the population in Croatia. Finally, the Serbs dominated the police force in Croatia as 67 per cent of the police officers were Serbian (Markotich, 1993: 29).

In conclusion, $H_{2.2}$ must be rejected in so far as the Croats in some respects enjoyed a most-favoured-lords status. However, although the Croats gained still more political influence in concurrence with the crumbling of federal power during the 1980s, they nevertheless perceived that they did not have most-favoured-lords status. Thus, they focused on the Serbian domination of the state presidency and of the repressive organs in Yugoslavia. The demands of the leaders of the Serbian republic that Yugoslavia should be recentralized only added to the fears of the Croats. Therefore, $H_{2.2}$ offers an explanation of the Croatian revival in that the Croats were politically deprived to some extent and in that *perceived* political inequalities were one of the factors that led to the revival. Thus, the Yugoslavian centre's earlier attempt to integrate the Croatian elite by officially granting it a most-favoured-lords status was overshadowed by these perceptions.

4.1.3 Cultural Colonization

During the so-called Croatian Spring in 1971, Croatian leaders complained that Croatian language, culture, and history had been ignored and denigrated in the socialist Yugoslavia (Irvine, 1993: 259, 262). After the purges it was prohibited to make such statements in public. Only the Croatian Catholic Church continued to declare that the Catholic religion was being discriminated against (Ramet, 1992b: 165). Against this backdrop, the rising Croatian opposition politicians of the late 1980s mobilized the Croats by criticizing the federal authorities' neglect of the Croatian culture. Thus, during the election campaign in April 1990, the future president of Croatia, Franjo Tudjman, repeatedly complained that for decades everything Croatian had been enslaved by the Yugoslavian unitarism, thereby preventing Croatian culture from affirming itself (Petković, 1991: 18).

In conclusion, issues of cultural deprivation were part of the efforts of the nationalists to mobilize the masses. However, the extent to which the Croats as a whole experienced real cultural deprivation is difficult to assess, given the available empirical evidence. Probably, some level of cultural deprivation was felt due to the unitary cultural policies of socialist Yugoslavia, but the cultural deprivation suffered by the Croats was not comparable to that of the Estonians, Moldovans, and Gagauz in the USSR.

For example, the Croatian language was part of the state language just as some level of religious freedom was allowed.

4.2 Internal Colonization of the Serbs

From the point of view of the Serbian minority in Croatia, Zagreb was the relevant centre. This is so, firstly, because the Croatian republic in the Yugoslavian federation had a relatively high level of self-determination and, secondly, because after their seizure of power in the spring of 1990 Croatian nationalists began to act even more independently *vis-à-vis* the federal centre.

4.2.1 Economic Colonization

The rural Serbian population in Croatia was predominantly employed in the agricultural sector. However, due to the geographic conditions in the Krajina area where hilly woodlands dominate, farming was never well developed. Furthermore, the Serbs complained that the Croatian authorities had given the Krajina area low priority regarding capital investments and infrastructure (Ramet, 1992: 205f). Thus, in contrast to the relatively well-off economic situation of the Russians in Estonia and Moldova, the Serbs in Croatia had reasons to blame the titular nation-group for the relative underdevelopment of their region. Although we lack statistical evidence concerning, for example, the relative income level of the rural Croatian Serbs, our experiences as UN peacekeepers in the Krajina area confirm the picture that the industrial development and standard of living of the region lagged behind that of other parts of Croatia. This is also consistent with a survey conducted in early 1990 which demonstrated that a large segment of the Serbian minority believed that they were discriminated against by the Croatian majority (Cohen, 1993: 99).[45]

Furthermore, the Serbs had no reason to expect that their economic welfare would increase in an independent Croatia. On the contrary, in the wake of the Croatian national revival many Serbs lost their jobs simply because they were Serbs (Nativi, 1991: 94). Thus, the Serbs *felt* economically deprived and feared a worsening of this deprivation in the future. Therefore, we conclude that $H_{2.1}$ is confirmed in the Serbian case because it provides an explanation of the national revival by referring both to economic deprivation and to economic frustration.

4.2.2 Political Colonization

Owing to the disproportionately high participation of Krajina Serbs in the ranks of Tito's partisan army, the Serbs in Croatia were accorded a relatively privileged political status in the postwar socialist republic of Croatia (Cohen, 1993: 126ff). Thus, the Serbs were overrepresented in the membership of the CLC as well as in Croatia's political elite and state administration (see also Section 4.1.2). In this way, the federal centre granted the elite of the Serbian minority a most-favoured-lords status.

When the Croatian opposition took over governmental power in the spring of 1990, the Serbs officially kept their privileged status. Thus, according to the new Croatian constitution adopted in December 1990, the Serbs formally enjoyed all legal and civil rights and were accorded the status of an official national minority (CC, 1990). At the same time, however, the Croatian nationalist politicians used their newly gained political power to dismiss Serbs from prestigious and influential positions on both the republican and local levels (Irvine, 1993: 281). The new Croatian centre thus, *de facto*, deprived the Serbian elite of its former privileged status.

These Croatian policies confirmed the Serbs' fear of future political deprivation and made the Serbian politicians demand autonomy for the Krajina region. The reaction of the Serbs was also fuelled by the Croatian proposal for a confederation because the Serbian minority feared being left to the mercy of the Croatian majority without the support of the Serbs in Serbia proper (Cohen, 1993: 131).

In conclusion, $H_{2.2}$ is confirmed in the Serbian case because the Serbs, and especially the Serbian elite, lost their former privileged status.

4.2.3 Cultural Colonization

The policies of the Croatian nationalists also involved the adoption of traditional Croatian ethnic symbols, such as a national coat of arms and a national anthem, as the official insignia of Croatia (Cohen, 1993: 131). Furthermore, the Latin script was explicitly identified as the republic's only official alphabet. One consequence of this was that road signs in Cyrillic or in both alphabets in the Serbian majority areas of Croatia were replaced with signs in Latin only (Glenny, 1992: 12). The Croatian national symbols evoked fear among the Serbs because they reminded them of the wartime Croatian Ustasha regime during which the Croats committed a genocide against the Serbs (see Section 3.1.3).

The new Croatian symbolism led Serbian leaders to complain publicly that Serbs were now second-class citizens in Croatia, both politically and culturally (Andrejevich, 1990b: 38). This belief was confirmed when the Croatian authorities refused to give the Serbs cultural autonomy. Such cultural autonomy, including, for example, Serbian schools and media serving areas in Croatia with large Serbian populations, was initially the only demand of the Serbian leaders (Andrejevich, 1990d: 29). But as the Croatian government never made any real concessions on this question, the Serbs went on to demand political and territorial autonomy as well.

Thus, cultural deprivation and frustration played a significant role in the rise of the Serbian national revival, which means that $H_{2.3}$ is also confirmed in the Serbian case.

5 CONCLUSION

In the late 1980s and early 1990s strong national revivals occurred among the Croats and the Serbs in Croatia.

In a primordial perspective, these revivals are explained by reference to the distinct and well-developed ethnic base of both of the nation-groups. The common identity of each group has also been influenced by their historically based antagonistic interrelationship which has made up the basis of a persistent suspicion between the two nation-groups. Moreover, the test of H_1 provides an explanation of why the revivals were initiated in the late 1980s. Although decentralizing reforms had been launched by the federal centre in the late 1960s and early 1970s, the republics could only gradually take advantage of these reforms and obtain a higher degree of self-determination after Tito died in 1980. And when the power of the federal centre weakened still more during the 1980s, the door was opened for the onset of both Serbian and Croatian national revivals. In particular, the revival of the Serbs in Serbia proper influenced the timing of the revivals in Croatia. Furthermore, the Croats could take advantage of the existing republican institutions. However, the constitutional rights through which both the Croats and the Serbian minority sought to legitimize their secessionist policies were of limited value as the opposing sides interpreted them differently and as the legal writ of the federal authorities could no longer be enforced.

In an instrumental perspective, the strong Croatian national revival is explained by reference to the Croats' perception that they were subject to internal colonization by the Serb-dominated federal centre, although the objective deprivation in the economic and cultural spheres in particular was limited. As for the Krajina Serbs, the test of H_2 revealed that they were economically deprived in the Yugoslavian era and as the Croatian revival evolved their frustrations were substantiated further by real deprivation in the economic, political, and cultural spheres.

8 The National Revivals in Czechoslovakia

1 INTRODUCTION

The autumn of 1989 was a time of momentous change for the satellite states in Eastern Europe. After more than 40 years of Soviet hegemony, national movements opting for democracy and market economy were able to gather thousands of people in demonstrations. The communist regimes were overthrown, and soon afterwards the most visible sign of Soviet dominance, the units of the Soviet army, were withdrawn. It was a time of great hope. People expected unification of Europe, a smooth transition to democracy, restoration of basic human rights, and improved living conditions. Yet, the realization of these expectations turned out to be troublesome. At the same time, national identity and the ideology of nationalism began to play a more significant role. As regards Czechoslovakia, for example, the West learned that it was not inhabited by Czechoslovaks but by Czechs and Slovaks. Later, the map of Europe had to be redrawn once again as Czechoslovakia was separated into two separate states.

2 THE NATIONAL REVIVALS

2.1 The Czech National Revival

Following the Soviet-led repression of the 1968 Prague Spring, an orthodox Soviet-sponsored regime was reinstalled and this regime adopted a very hard line towards the remaining opposition (Wolchik, 1991: 152ff; Musil, 1992: 182f). Although a few dissident movements persisted in the ensuing years, they were not joined by new ones until 1988 when they succeeded in involving thousands of people in demonstrations and other unauthorized activities which openly challenged the regime. The movements demanded adherence of human rights and a return to Western-style parliamentary democracy and market economy. The resulting so-called Velvet Revolution in November 1989 led to the fall of the postwar Soviet-influenced communist regime. The Velvet Revolution ended the first phase of the revivals in Czechoslovakia. In the second phase, a distinct

Slovakian national revival evolved which ultimately led to the formation of separate Czech and Slovakian states.

Although opposition movements were also established in Slovakia in 1989, Czech movements and intellectuals were the leading force behind the mass demonstrations which were arranged primarily in Prague. Still, it is questionable whether one can speak of a distinct Czech national revival in a case where both nation-groups initially participated in a movement aiming at establishing a *Czechoslovakian* state fully independent of the USSR and with liberal economic and political institutions, rather than opting for two separate nation-states.[46] Thus, in our view, the first phase of the revivals is most precisely described as a Czech-dominated Czechoslovakian liberal revival.

In the second half of the 1980s the communist regime in Czechoslovakia was still very conservative and adopted only few and moderate reforms. Nevertheless, the reforms of Gorbachev meant that the authorities gradually relaxed censorship and tolerated a more free public debate. This gave the opposition more leeway to mobilize people (Pehe & Obrman, 1989: 18f). But the regime still used anti-riot troops to repress the mass demonstrations which were held in Prague in 1988 and 1989. In November 1989 the confrontation reached a climax when tens of thousands of demonstrators gathered repeatedly in central Prague to demand reforms and the overthrow of the incumbent regime (Pehe, 1990a: 11ff; Bradley, 1992: 66ff). By then, the opposition movements had united in two umbrella organizations – the leading Czech Civic Forum (CF) and the Slovakian sister-organization, Public Against Violence (PAV) – which put the regime under even more pressure by arranging a general strike. Realizing their loss of power, the communist leaders then began negotiations with the CF, and in December the negotiations resulted in the formation of a federal government with a non-communist majority named the Government of National Understanding (Glenny, 1993: 24). In the ensuing weeks, a majority of the communist deputies in the federal parliament were simply replaced with members of the CF and PAV. Thereafter, the parliament amended the constitution by cancelling the article guaranteeing the leading role of the Communist Party of Czechoslovakia (CPC) and elected Vaclav Havel, the most prominent of the Czech opposition leaders, as the new president.

The free general elections held in June 1990 were the first significant event of the second phase of the revivals in Czechoslovakia. The CF confirmed its ascendancy by winning the majority of the seats both in the parliament in the Czech republic and, in coalition with PAV, in the federal parliament (Pehe, 1990b: 11). Only after the Velvet Revolution did some

Czech intellectuals begin to argue against the idea of continued Czechoslovakian statehood, opting instead for an independent Czech state (Martin, 1990b: 15; 1990c: 2f). In the same way, the new Czech republican government formed after the June 1990 elections emphasized the need to create some kind of Czech statehood. However, the majority of both ordinary Czechs and their politicians continued to support a federal state with large powers vested in the central federal government (*ibid.*).[47] But this view was not compatible with that of the Slovaks who wanted most powers delegated to the republican level (see the following section).

After one and a half years with deadlocked Czech–Slovakian negotiations on the future constitutional set-up and the power-sharing between the federation and the constituent Czech and Slovakian republics, general elections were held in June 1992 (Pehe, 1993: 84ff). In the Czech republic, the conservative, pro-market Civic Democratic Party (CDP) became the winning party. In subsequent negotiations with the Slovaks, the Czechs refused to accept the Slovakian demand for a loose confederation. Instead, they preferred the formation of two separate states. This became a reality on 1 January 1993 following the signing of more than 30 treaties governing the post-separation relations between the two republics.

Thus, to the regret of most Czechs, the Czech-dominated Czechoslovakian revival of the late 1980s, which led to the removal of the communist regime and, thereby, of the Soviet influence, also paved the way for an explicit Slovakian national revival. This revival meant that the Czechs, though reluctantly, had to give up the preferred option of continuing the legacy of the interwar independent Czechoslovakian state which was characterized by representative democracy and a well-functioning market economy but also by Czech dominance in all fields of society (see Section 3.1.3).

2.2 The Slovakian National Revival

In the period before the November 1989 Velvet Revolution only a few opposition groups had been formed in Slovakia and the strongest expressions of public activism were demonstrations calling for more religious freedom (Matuska, 1989: 7; Pehe, 1990a: 13).

However, shortly after achieving the common goal of overthrowing the Soviet-influenced communist regime, a split between the Czech and Slovakian movements occurred (Martin, 1990c: 4f; Pehe, 1991a: 11ff).[48] An ever-growing number of Slovakian politicians, though still preferring a continued federation, wanted to change its form by devolving most powers to the republican level. This position was reinforced by the fact that the earlier completely subordinated republican Slovakian parliament began to play a more active role, firstly, as a result of the replacement of communist deputies with opposition members in connection with the Velvet Revolution and, secondly, when nationalist-minded parties won the June 1990 elections in the Slovakian republic.

The still more pronounced Slovakian national awareness and drive for autonomy led to the passing in December 1990 of an amendment to the 1968 constitutional law on the Czechoslovakian federation (Pehe, 1990c: 6ff). After threatening to declare the supremacy of Slovakian laws over those of the federation, the Slovakian politicians persuaded their Czech counterparts to accept the amendment, according to which the country should remain a federal state but the federal institutions should cede many of their powers to the republics. This solution was consistent with the view of the Slovaks, the majority of whom, in June 1990, favoured some kind of common state but with most powers devolved to the republican level (Kusin, 1990: 5f).[49]

However, during the autumn of 1990 and spring of 1991 the Slovakian nationalists who opted for full independence became still more active (Pehe, 1991c: 1ff; 1991d: 2f). For example, in March 1991 demonstrations which attracted several thousand people were held in Bratislava to commemorate the Second World War Nazi-supported semi-independent Slovakian state and to demand a declaration of sovereignty. These activities resulted in a general movement of the Slovakian political scene towards even more emphasis on Slovakian concerns. Thus, in March 1991 the incumbent prime minister of the Slovakian government, Vladimír Mečiar, and his supporters broke out of PAV, which had prevailed until then, and formed a new party with a more clear-cut nationalist programme, the Movement for a Democratic Slovakia (MDS).

Although Mečiar's move paralysed the Slovakian government and although he and the other members of the MDS consequently were forced into opposition, the MDS benefited from the growing national mood. In the June 1992 elections, the party won a plurality (37 per cent) of the Slovakian votes (Obrman, 1992a: 12ff; Pehe, 1993: 84ff). The MDS then formed a majority coalition government with the Slovakian National Party (SNP) which won 8 per cent of the votes. When the Czech government did not accept the Slovakian government's demand for a confederation composed of two sovereign states, the Slovakian parliament adopted a constitution in September that gave Slovakia the attributes of an independent state, and in the remaining months of 1992 an orderly separation was negotiated (see Section 2.1). Thus, the Slovakian national revival resulted in the formation of an independent Slovakian state by 1 January 1993.

3 THE NATIONAL REVIVALS IN A PRIMORDIAL PERSPECTIVE

The Czech-dominated Czechoslovakian revival focused *not* on the establishment of an independent Czech state and an invigoration of Czech culture *per se*, but on political and economic liberalization both in relation to the former dominant Soviet Union and within a common Czechoslovakian state. This absence of a distinct *national* revival among the Czechs could be explained by H_1 if they lacked a strong ethnic base provided by an *ethnie* and the historical interplay with the Slovaks. The Slovakian national revival, on the other hand, could be explained if the Slovaks had a strong ethnic base.

In both cases, however, the temporal location of the revivals could be explained if the formerly repressive Soviet hegemony as well as the political system in Czechoslovakia were liberalized. At the same time, if they existed, administrative units and constitutional rights could have furthered the revivals.

3.1 The Ethnic Base

3.1.1 The Czech Ethnie

The Czechs call themselves so because, according to Czech historians, leading members of the *Cechové* tribe established the golden age Bohemian kingdom in the 10th century (Gawdiak, 1989: 5ff). The Czech myths of common ancestry date back to the Slavic tribes that settled in the present Czech lands (the area of Bohemia, Moravia, and Silesia: see Map 6) around the 5th century.

The association of the Czechs with the Czech lands and many of their historical memories are connected with the Bohemian kingdom which, from the 10th to the 15th century, was a powerful entity in Central Europe (pp. 5ff, 86f). Although the kingdom in the 14th century also controlled principalities in present-day Austria, Germany, and Poland, the Czechs first of all associate with the Czech lands. Thus, the northern, southern, and western borders of the contemporary Czech republic have remained fixed within 50 kilometres of their present location since the 10th century.

The above-mentioned *ethnie* characteristics were reinforced in the first half of the 19th century when Czech intellectuals, under the influence of the enlightenment and the wave of national romanticism, successfully brought about a revival of the Czech culture and self-awareness, thereby transforming the Czech *ethnie* into a nation-group (pp. 21ff). The history and culture of the golden age Bohemian kingdom in particular were intensively cultivated and came to serve as a vital source of Czech national pride. The legends of one of the most famous Czech national heroes, Jan Hus, is also connected with this golden age. Living in the 15th century, he led the so-called Hussite movement, a religious reform movement that triggered a Czech struggle for more autonomy in political and ecclesiastical affairs in relation to the Holy Roman empire. This goal was accomplished but in 1526 the Czech lands were, nevertheless, incorporated into Habsburg Austria. During the 19th century Czech national revival, the Czech leaders also tried to take advantage of the legacy of the Hussite movement and demanded, in vain, an autonomous Bohemia.

In the course of the 19th century revival and afterwards, distinctive elements of Czech culture were also reinforced. Thus, the Czechs pride themselves upon having been a relatively important part of the major intellectual and artistic traditions of Western Europe since the middle ages (pp. 86ff; Cibulka, 1983: 147ff). According to Czech intellectuals, the Czechs influenced movements as diverse as Renaissance music and the Protestant reformation. Nevertheless, the Czech cultural tradition is described as Western-oriented, rationalistic, secular, and anti-clerical in comparison with the Slovakian culture. Another distinctive element is the so-called Svejkian non-violent resistance to whatever regime that holds power, be it represented by Austrian bureaucrats, Soviet-influenced communists, or Warsaw Pact forces.[50]

Although the Czech and Slovakian languages are similar, the Czechs underline the fact that Czech is a much older literary language than Slovakian.[51] Today, several versions of Czech exist but the standard written language, *spisovná cestina*, carries the greatest prestige because it is based on the Czech spoken in 14th-century Prague during the peak of the golden age.

Thus, when the common Czechoslovakian state was established in 1918, a distinct and rather strong ethnic base and national identity existed among the Czechs. And in the late 1980s and early 1990s an explicit Czech national feeling still existed. According to a survey conducted in June 1991, 97 per cent of the Czechs identified themselves as Czechs or Moravians (Rose, 1992: 29). However, like the Moldovan identity, the Czech identity also contained a duality, namely of Czech-ness and Czechoslovakian-ness. After more than 70 years of Czech-led efforts to develop a Czechoslovakian national feeling (see Section 3.1.3), the Czechoslovakian-ness was rather salient to the Czechs. The above-mentioned survey showed that 71 per cent of the Czechs thought of themselves as Czechoslovaks too (p. 30). Of those who had a dual identity, 55 per cent stated that the Czechoslovakian identity was the most important. Thus, approximately one third of the Czechs first of all considered themselves as Czechoslovaks, while two thirds gave priority to the Czech-ness.

On the one hand, the duality of the Czech identity can explain the widespread and strong *Czech* support of the Czechoslovakian revival which led to the Velvet Revolution and to the new status of Czechoslovakia as a fully independent Western-oriented state instead of being a Soviet satellite state. On the other hand, however, the preserved strong and explicit Czech identity cannot explain the reluctant post-1989 support of the few Czech intellectuals and politicians who opted for a separate Czech state.[52] Thus, the coxistence of Czech-ness and Czechoslovakian-ness among the Czechs means that $H_{1.1}$ could not have predicted whether the Czechs would opt for a Czech or a Czechoslovakian state.

3.1.2 The Slovakian Ethnie

Originally, the denomination 'Slovak' meant both Slovak and Slav, but in connection with the 19th century Slovakian national revival the term came to be used as the name of the ethnic group living in Slovakia only (Gawdiak, 1989: 5ff, 16). Like the Czechs, the Slovaks are the descendants of Slavic tribes, in this case those which settled in present-day Slovakia.

If there had been any doubts as to the distinctiveness of the Slovaks in relation to the Czechs and other Slavic groups, Slovakian intellectuals successfully removed them during the 19th-century revival (*ibid.*; Cibulka, 1983: 122ff). Although some Slovakian intellectuals viewed their countrymen as merely a long-separated part of a single Czechoslovakian nation-group, the intellectuals who emphasized the distinctive traits of the Slovaks dominated from the 1840s onwards. They pointed first of all to the fact that the Slovaks had lived separately from the Czechs since the Hungarian invasion of the Moravian kingdom in 907. Although the Slovakian revival started some years later than the Czech, not least because of the much heavier repression of the Slovaks in the Hungarian part of the Habsburg empire, it did not fall short of the Czech revival regarding force and degree of support when it eventually broke out, fuelled as it was by the mounting wave of Hungarian nationalism which had resulted in attempts to assimilate the Slovaks. The Slovakian revival also led to a demand for autonomy, and in 1848 the Slovaks staged a rebellion against the Hungarians. But this was brutally suppressed.

As for historical memories and association with a territory, the Slovaks regard the Great Moravian kingdom (which included both present-day Moravia and Slovakia) of the 9th century as a creation of the Slovaks (Brock, 1976: 3ff). This kingdom, which lasted until the Hungarians conquered the Slovakian part, is celebrated as the Slovakian golden age. Slovakian historians argue that the Slovaks originally entered into a free union with the Hungarians and shared the Slovakian territory with them on equal terms. According to Slovakian intellectuals, the Slovaks even had a civilizing effect on the alleged semi-barbaric Hungarians.

Concerning distinctive elements of culture, the Slovakian language, although rather similar to the Czech, played and still plays a decisive role in the development and preservation of a separate Slovakian nationhood (*ibid.*). In the late 18th century, educator-intellectuals introduced the first version of a Slovakian literary language which replaced Czech as the language used by the Slovakian Christian intelligentsia. However, this version was based on the dialect spoken in western Slovakia. It was not until the 1840s that a unified literary language for the Slovaks of all regions was produced and eventually prevailed.

Finally, a sense of social solidarity among the Slovaks is reflected in the popular legends about the historical figure Jánosík. Living in the 18th century, he acted like a Robin Hood fighting and stealing from the Hungarians to help his poor countrymen (Cibulka, 1983: 148f). Following the 19th-century revival, he has remained a symbol of Slovakian nationalism and rebelliousness against social injustice caused by other dominating groups.

Thus, by the formation of the common Czechoslovakian state in 1918, a fairly strong and explicit national identity also existed among the Slovaks. In contrast to the majority of the Czechs, however, the Slovaks never really accepted the idea of a Czechoslovakian nation-group. According to a survey from June 1991, only 26 per cent of the Slovaks thought of themselves as both Slovaks and Czechoslovaks (Rose, 1992: 30). And of these, only 39 per cent stated that the Czechoslovakian identity was the more important.

In conclusion, the Slovakian national revival could build on a strong common identity provided by the *ethnie*. Thus, $H_{1.1}$ is confirmed in the Slovakian case.

3.1.3 The Historical Interplay between Czechs and Slovaks

The historical record of the pre-1918 interrelations between Czechs and Slovaks does not contain many signs of enmity between the two nation-groups. Only in the 15th century (1438 to 1453) had Czech Hussite armies occupied parts of Slovakia (Gawdiak, 1989: 4ff, 28f). But that occupation was a part of a war between the Bohemian kingdom and the Hungarians, and it was not directed against the Slovaks. On the contrary, during the 19th-century revivals some intellectuals, both Czech and Slovakian, emphasized the friendly interrelations and the common features, especially the common Slavic origin, the closely related languages, and the common adherence to Roman Catholicism. At the end of the 19th century, contacts between Czech and Slovakian intellectuals and political leaders intensified, and still more of these began to advocate the idea of a Czechoslovakian entity (Cibulka, 1983: 123f). During the First World War, Czech and Slovakian leaders in exile managed to gain the support of the Allies for the idea of breaking up the Austro-Hungarian empire and creating a Czechoslovakian state. As the empire turned out to be on the losing side, this idea was realized. Thus, paralleling the Croatian (and Slovenian) leaders, both the Czech and the Slovakian leaders took advantage of the opening window of opportunity to escape Austrian and Hungarian dominance respectively.

While neither the Czech nor the Slovakian *ethnies* or national identities had been marked by any hostile feelings towards one another until then, the picture became somewhat less rosy after 1918. From the outset, the Czechs dominated the so-called First Republic which existed from 1918 to 1938 (Mamatey & Luža, 1973: 39ff). Apart from the numerical dominance of the Czechs,[53] this was based on the fact that the Czech lands under the relatively benign Austrian supremacy had become much more developed, both economically and politically, than the still predominantly rural and impoverished Slovakia. Thus, although the Slovaks had been promised autonomy, the new state, according to the 1920 constitution, nevertheless became a unitary state with Prague as the dominating centre. Politically, Slovakia was merely an administrative unit ruled from Prague, primarily by the Ministry for Slovakia. Economically, the gap in economic development had not been balanced by the end of the interwar period.[54] And culturally, the Czechs pursued a policy of creating a Czechoslovakian identity by way of incorporating the Slovaks into the Czech nation-group, a policy which came to be known as 'Czechoslovakianism'.

Thus, the interwar period was characterized by Czech internal colonization of the Slovaks. Consequently, Slovakian nationalism grew steadily in force, and when Germany occupied the whole of Czechoslovakia in 1939 Slovakian nationalists declared Slovakia an independent state (Kirschbaum, 1993: 73f). In return for Slovakian support of Nazi-Germany, Hitler accepted a formally independent Slovakian state under German protection.

However, in spite of the interwar and war experiences, the historical Czech–Slovakian relations do not contain any violent atrocities committed by any of the sides. This fact clearly differentiates the Czech–Slovakian interrelationship from the Estonian–Russian, Moldovan–Russian, and Croatian–Serbian ones. Therefore, the conclusion to be drawn is that the historical interrelationship was not marked by any significant degree of enmity.

3.2 The Triggering Factors: Recent Developments in the Central European Legal–Political Setting

The appearance of Gorbachev in 1985 and the ensuing liberalizing *perestroyka* reforms were crucial to the success of the Czech-dominated Czechoslovakian revival which led to the fall of the communist regime in 1989. In 1987 Gorbachev turned to the 'young' men in the CPC and made them take away the party leadership from the orthodox Husak in order to advance a Soviet-model reform process in Czechoslovakia (Pehe, 1989: 7f). Subsequently, relatively reform-minded communists took over the power in the CPC. And even if the adopted reforms were only slowly – if at all – implemented, control over public opinion was loosened and this paved the way for the so far repressed opposition to come out into the open. Moreover, in 1989 Gorbachev indicated that the 1968 invasion had been a grave political error, thereby in effect signalling that the Soviet regime would not intervene again to stop political reforms in Eastern Europe by use of violent means (Glenny, 1993: 23).

The regime change in the USSR also exerted a more indirect influence on the events in Czechoslovakia in so far as it triggered regime changes in other East European satellite states as well. Due to the pressure of large-scale mass demonstrations and still more powerful opposition movements, by November 1989 the communist regimes had already fallen in neighbouring Poland and Hungary, and the East German regime was in a process of complete collapse (Bradley, 1992: 48ff). The spill-over effect of these revivals was without doubt an important factor behind the scale of support of the demonstrations held in Prague in the last months of 1989.

When the Velvet Revolution had led to the overthrow of the communist regime, the following Slovakian national revival was eased by the liberal post-1989 political system and by the already existing Slovakian republican unit. Since the adoption of constitutional amendments in 1968, Czechoslovakia had been a federated state consisting of the Czech and Slovakian republics (Wolchik, 1991: 62f). Originally, the federal laws granted considerable powers to the republican governments, but after the Soviet-led Warsaw Pact invasion later in 1968 these powers were reduced by a new series of amendments and the centralized CPC continued to control all policy areas. However, when Slovakian opposition members, following the Velvet Revolution and the June 1990 elections, had replaced most of the former communist deputies in the Slovakian parliament, this institution became an important platform of the Slovakian national revival (Pehe, 1990a: 12; 1991a: 11ff).

Although the preamble and article 1 of the 1968 law on the Czechoslovakian federation stated the right of the two nation-groups to self-determination (Matuska, 1989: 7), the Slovaks never tried to use that law to argue that they had a constitutional right to secede.

In conclusion, the regime change in the USSR was a triggering factor behind the Czech-dominated Czechoslovakian revival, directly by initiating an, albeit hesitant, reform process and more indirectly by accepting the prior national revivals and regime changes in the neighbouring satellite states. Later, the Slovakian revival was eased by the already existing Slovakian republican unit and by the establishment of the democratic Czechoslovakian state that followed the overthrow of the communist regime.

4 THE NATIONAL REVIVALS IN AN INSTRUMENTAL PERSPECTIVE

In contrast to the cases of Estonia, Moldova, and Croatia, Czechoslovakia was subject to *external* colonization in so far as it formally remained an independent state. This, however, does not constitute a hindrance to the basic applicability of the instrumental theories and deduced hypotheses. According to these hypotheses, both the Czech-dominated liberal revival and the Slovakian national revival could be explained if the nation-groups had been subject to economic, political, or cultural colonization.

4.1 External Colonization of the Czechs

To the Czechs (and Slovaks) who initiated and supported the liberal Czechoslovakian revival, the colonizing centre was Moscow, the capital of the USSR.

4.1.1 Economic Colonization

Following the Soviet-supported communist *coup d'état* in 1948, Soviet influence over Czechoslovakia grew markedly in all spheres of society. In the economic sphere, it was exercised not only through the close ties between the CPSU and the subordinated CPC but also through the Czechoslovakian membership of the Council for Mutual Economic Assistance (CMEA) (Wolchik, 1991: 22f, 218ff). Consequently, the industry was nationalized, agriculture was collectivized, and the Soviet planned economy model was implemented.

Thus, the case of the Czechs is rather similar to that of the Estonians. In the interwar period there was a well-functioning market economy in independent Czechoslovakia, and the industry in the Czech lands in particular was competitive in the European markets (Capek & Sazama, 1993: 217f, 231; Wolchik, 1991: 257ff). In that period, the population in Czechoslovakia had a per-capita income at about the same level as the Austrians while by 1988 it had decreased to less than half that of the Spaniards. But still, the living standard of the Czechs continued to be higher than that of the Russians in the Soviet centre.

It is difficult to estimate whether the fact that the Czech standard of living lagged behind the Western can be attributed to an economic deprivation due to the enforced shift from the West to the USSR as the biggest trade partner.[55] On the one hand, Czechoslovakia most probably benefited from the economic relations since it imported raw materials, not least oil and natural gas, at prices below those of the world market and primarily exported finished goods which were no longer competitive on the markets of the West.

On the other hand, the Soviet influence on the economic policies pursued in Czechoslovakia was significant throughout the communist period. When the economy exhibited signs of decline in the 1960s, reform-minded communists launched economic reforms to remedy the situation (Gawdiak, 1989: 93f; Skilling, 1976: 64f).[56] But these reforms conflicted with the Soviet view on how to conduct economic policies, and in the aftermath of the 1968 Warsaw Pact invasion the reforms were brought to a standstill.

Thus, although Czechoslovakia was most probably not economically deprived due to the Czechoslovakian–Soviet trade relations, the Czechs in particular perceived that they were *relatively* economically deprived because of the Soviet influence on the economic policies implemented in the country. When the economic crisis worsened during the 1980s and the regime allowed still more people to visit the West, this feeling became even more pronounced (Pehe & Obrman, 1989: 19f). Therefore, during the Velvet Revolution the Czech opposition movements demanded introduction of market reforms and a reintegration of the Czechoslovakian economy into the economies of the developed West. In this way, it is doubtful whether $H_{2.1}$, when formulated on the basis of deprivations alone, can explain the wide Czech support of the Czechoslovakian liberal revival. However, when economic frustrations are stressed, $H_{2.1}$ is able to explain this revival.

4.1.2 Political Colonization

In the interwar period, Czechoslovakia was the only East European country that maintained a functioning democracy right up until the outbreak of the Second World War – that is, until the German occupation in 1939 (Gawdiak, 1989: 87f, 174f). In 1945, when the Soviet army occupied the country, the period of Soviet external colonization began. The continued presence of the Soviet army facilitated the local communists' efforts to reorganize the militia and the Czechoslovakian army and to place communists in key positions in government institutions. Thereby, the way was paved for the Soviet supported communist *coup d'état* in 1948. Afterwards, Soviet hegemony was strongly reinforced.

Between 1948 and 1953, Czechoslovakia underwent a revolutionary transformation in all spheres of society. Under the leadership of the Czech communist Gottwald who had returned from Moscow in 1945, the new repressive political system in Czechoslovakia became almost a carbon copy of the Stalinist model (Bradley, 1991: 27ff). In deadly fear of the Soviet leader, Gottwald acted almost only on Stalin's instructions. Although the CPC remained formally independent, close connections between it and the superior CPSU were retained. In the second half of the 1950s and in the 1960s when the position of the country as a loyal satellite-state had been secured, the Soviet dominance was somewhat relaxed. But still all power remained concentrated in the CPC which for its part did not deviate from the policies of the Soviet leaders.

Only in the late 1960s did reform-minded communists challenge the Soviet regime. During the Prague Spring in 1968, the Czechs in particular supported the reforms in the so-called Action Programme which would lead to 'socialism with a human face' – that is, a loosening of the power monopoly of the CPC and a reintroduction of basic civil rights (Skilling, 1976: 261ff; Cibulka, 1983: 157ff). However, the leaders in the Soviet centre feared that the reforms would spread to other East European states and that they would endanger the leading role of the CPC and thereby also the Soviet dominance. As a consequence, the Soviet Politbureau had its Czechoslovakian counterpart accept that they must either return to orthodox communism or be forced to do so.[57] Still, the Soviets were far from satisfied, and in August 1968 Warsaw Pact forces invaded the country and made sure that leaders loyal to Moscow took over power again. In the ensuing period of 'normalization', these leaders reestablished Czechoslovakia's status as a committed member of the socialist bloc.

In conclusion, throughout the postwar period the communist elite in Prague remained a mediator-elite in relation to the external centre of the USSR. Although the Czech-dominated periphery elite had a relatively large amount of autonomy in determining, for example, social, educational, and cultural policies (Wolchik, 1991: 60ff), overall policy was not allowed to deviate from the Soviet version of communism. And in the fields of security services, foreign affairs, and military policies the Soviet dominance was almost total.[58] Furthermore, the Soviet centre never allowed the Czech (or Slovakian) communists to challenge the dominance of the Russians in the Soviet centre itself or in the organizations of the Eastern bloc (the Warsaw Pact, CMEA) through which the USSR exercised its influence.

Thus, if we seek to explain the behaviour of the Czech-dominated Czechoslovakian communists, $H_{2.2}$ is of limited use because the non-most-favoured-lords status of this elite did not make them put forward demands for Czechoslovakian decision-making to be independent from Soviet influence. This was the choice of the Estonian, Moldovan, and Croatian communists who eventually agreed with the nationalist opposition that more republican self-determination was required. On the other hand, the political deprivation of Czechoslovakia and the unwillingness of the communist elite to yield to the demand for real self-determination was real enough to frustrate the aspiring, oppositional elite that wanted to substitute liberal democracy for Soviet-guided communist rule. In this sense, $H_{2.2}$ can explain the liberal Czechoslovakian revival by pointing to the deprivation and frustration of the oppositional elite.

4.1.3 Cultural Colonization

While perceptions of economic and political deprivation were significant driving forces in the 1989 revival, the Czechs did not really have any reasons to feel non- or misrecognized as a nation-group by the Soviet centre. In contrast to the nation-groups inside the USSR, the nation-groups in the East European satellite-states were never subject to the Soviet nationalities policy which aimed at creating a sense of belonging to a Soviet people (Djilas, 1986: 375f). Thus, the USSR never tried to change the formal status of Czechoslovakia as an independent state consisting of the Czech and Slovakian nation-groups. And the Czechoslovakian regime had almost no restrictions imposed on their cultural policies.

Only in the field of language was the Soviet influence clear. Russian was a compulsory subject in primary school education, and many Russian words were adopted into the Czech (and Slovakian) language, especially in the areas of economics and politics (Gawdiak, 1989: 100f). In the late 1980s, Czech intellectuals were active in reviving old Czech words or forming new ones from old Czech roots in order to avoid this use of the Russian vocabulary.

Nevertheless, as the Czechs were not culturally deprived, issues concerning Soviet-inflicted cultural deprivation were not salient during the 1989 Czech-dominated revival. Therefore, $H_{2.3}$ cannot be confirmed in this case.

4.2 Internal Colonization of the Slovaks

To the Slovaks the relevant colonizing centre was Prague which after all had some leeway *vis-à-vis* Moscow to run internal affairs and which, after the Velvet Revolution, became the centre of a fully independent Czechoslovakia.

4.2.1 Economic Colonization

In order to create a unified and integrated Czechoslovakian planned economy, the post-1948 communist regime put a high priority on reducing the socio-economic imbalance between the highly industrialized Czech lands and the still predominantly agricultural Slovakian economy. This strategy was implemented by means of higher rates of investment in Slovakia, particularly in industry (Capek & Sazama, 1993: 214ff). Therefore, between 1948 and 1989 republican income in Slovakia increased more than 11 times, whereas in the Czech lands it increased only six times. Industrial output increased 12 times in the Czech lands, while in Slovakia the figure was nearly 33 times. As a result, the levels of economic development and standard of living were gradually equalized. In 1989 the average wage in Slovakia was 99.1 per cent of the level in the Czech lands.

Furthermore, economic evidence did not indicate a cultural division of labour. For example, in 1987 Slovakia had 28 per cent of the country's industrial employment. Thus, Slovaks were only slightly underrepresented as the Slovakian labour force made up 32 per cent of the aggregated labour force (Capek & Sazama, 1993: 226).

Thus, in the communist period the Slovaks were far from being economically deprived by the Prague centre. Nevertheless, even during the reform discussions in the late 1960s, Slovakian communists had wanted to allow for the development of parallel and autonomous Czech and Slovakian economies – in opposition to the Czech demand for more efficiency in an integrated and centralized economy (Gawdiak, 1989: 93). Thus, the leading Czech communists contended that the Slovakian demand for economic autonomy was provincial and anachronistic, and in the period of normalization after the Warsaw Pact invasion such ideas were strongly repudiated.

Yet, Slovakian economic grievances resurfaced in connection with the Czech-dominated revival in the late 1980s. Ignoring the equalized standard of living, some Slovakian opposition members argued that the output deriving from preferential investments did not remain in Slovakia but was distributed at the discretion of the centre (Matuska, 1989: 5). The Slovaks also complained that Prague's policy of industrialization had led to the destruction of vast areas of Slovakian nature (Martin, 1990a: 16).

However, it was not until after the Velvet Revolution that arguments about Czech-caused economic deprivation became effective in mobilizing the Slovaks. The reforms of the Czech-dominated federal government which aimed at transformation to a market economy hit the Slovakian economy harder than the Czech. For example, at the end of 1991 the rate of unemployment was 8.5 per cent in Slovakia, while it was only 4.5 per cent in the Czech lands (Musil, 1992: 186). Therefore, the Slovakian nationalists, not least the PAV/MDS, argued in favour of a much slower process of economic transformation. These views had wide support among the Slovaks who perceived that the reforms were leading to economic deprivation in Slovakia. Thus, according to an opinion poll conducted in September 1991, 70 per cent of the Slovaks wanted the radical economic reforms changed or stopped (Capek & Sazama, 1993: 218). In another poll from October 1991, 64 per cent of the Slovaks disagreed that the resources of the federation were equally distributed between the Czech lands and Slovakia and 67 per cent agreed that the present system favoured Czechs (Deis, 1992: 10f).

In conclusion, the Slovaks were not economically deprived in the communist period. Nevertheless, the radical economic reforms launched by the Czech-dominated federal government in the post-1989 period and the ensuing economic crisis hit the Slovakian economy harder. This meant that the Slovakian perception of being economically colonized by the Prague centre became a significant driving force in the Slovakian national revival. Thus, $H_{2.1}$ is confirmed, also because the Slovaks had reasons to fear a further (short-term) deterioration of their economy as the Czech politicians insisted that the radical reform process should not be slowed down.

4.2.2 Political Colonization

The first signs of Slovakian political frustrations were revealed in the late 1960s when they demanded a federalization of Czechoslovakia and Slovakian autonomy (Gawdiak, 1989: 92f; Bradley, 1991: 75f). The Czech communists gave in to the first Slovakian demand, and in 1968 constitutional amendments were adopted according to which Czechoslovakia became a federation composed of the Czech and Slovakian republics. However, although this reform partly survived the Warsaw Pact invasion, power still remained centralized in the federal institutions.[59] Nevertheless, the Slovaks made moderate gains on the federal level of the political system. In the federal parliament, the principle of parity was introduced in the sense that it became bicameral and the added Nation Chamber consisted of equal numbers of Czech and Slovakian deputies.[60]

However, whatever the structure of the formal political system, real power remained in the CPC which controlled all political institutions including the executive federal ministries. And the CPC was never federalized (Leff, 1988: 243ff). The party was structured according to the so-called asymmetrical model which was also used in the USSR. Just as the Russians never had a republican communist party because they were in full control of the all-Union CPSU, there was never a Czech communist party because they dominated the CPC. And although a Slovakian communist party did exist, it was completely subordinated to the CPC.

The Czech dominance, however, was far from total. Throughout most of the period of communist rule, about one third of the top positions in the CPC – that is, in the Politbureau and the Central Committee – were filled by Slovaks (pp. 253ff). And in the federal period after 1968 the percentage of Slovaks in any government cabinet was around 40 per cent. Thus, the Czech centre elite, without losing its dominant position at any time, had incorporated the peripheral Slovakian elite which in fact enjoyed a status of most-favoured-lords. But, except for the period leading up to the 1968 Prague Spring, only Slovakian communists who fully embraced the basic idea of centralized rule were allowed to rise to top positions in the CPC. These Slovakian communists were co-opted to an extent that the, albeit few, Slovakian dissidents condescendingly branded them Czechoslovaks (p. 199).

After the Velvet Revolution, the Czechs continued to dominate the political institutions of the federation. Thus, Czech deputies constituted a majority in the federal parliament, and ten out of 16 ministers in the post-1990 federal government were Czechs. While the Slovaks were still proportionally represented in these institutions, the Slovakian population was nevertheless unsatisfied with the post-Velvet Revolution system of governing. According to a survey conducted in June 1991, 55 per cent of the Slovaks stated that this system of governing did not treat the Slovaks fairly, while only 20 per cent had the opposite opinion (Rose, 1992: 25).

In conclusion, although the Slovakian elite enjoyed a most-favoured-lords status in the period of communist rule, the lower Slovakian strata were never assimilated to the same extent. Thus, the Slovaks perceived that they were politically deprived, and as the Czechs after the Velvet Revolution consistently demanded a strong and centralized federation, the Slovaks also had reasons to fear future political deprivation.

4.2.3 Cultural Colonization

Although the postwar Czech-dominated communist regime did not continue the efforts to convince the Slovaks that they were in fact part of a common Czechoslovakian nation-group, the formation of a unitary political system, much against the will of the Slovakian communists, did not reflect the existence of a separate and distinct Slovakian nation-group. Furthermore, the regime tried in various ways to suppress remaining expressions of the Slovakian nationalism which had manifested itself during the Second World War. The pro-German, formally independent Slovakian state was condemned and hundreds of Slovaks were sent to prison accused of 'bourgeois nationalism' (Kirschbaum, 1993: 82, 86f). Furthermore, the ruthless oppression of the Catholic Church that continued unabated throughout the communist rule was seen as a misrecognition of the Slovaks since religious belief was much more widespread in Slovakia (Wolchik, 1991: 212f).

In other areas, though, the Slovaks had little or no reason to feel misrecognized. Thus, the constitutional amendment in 1968 formally gave the Slovaks equal status since the unitary state was transformed to a federation consisting of the Czech and Slovakian republics (Matuska, 1989: 4ff). Furthermore, both the Czech and Slovakian languages were recognized as official languages of Czechoslovakia (Gawdiak, 1989: 99f). And although the Czech language dominated, not least because of the Czechs being in the majority, the media used both languages which were understandable to both nation-groups.

Thus, the Slovaks were not culturally deprived to any large extent by the Czech centre, especially not after 1968. This is also reflected in the fact that national symbols became an issue of disagreement only once after the Velvet Revolution though, on that occasion, the question of national symbols revealed its potentially strong moblizing powers. Shortly after the November 1989 events, Czech and Slovakian federal deputies began to discuss a renaming of the country (Martin, 1990a: 14ff). The Czechs preferred to change the name from the Czechoslovakian Socialist Republic to the Czechoslovakian Federal Republic. However, the Slovaks felt that this name reflected the remnants of the policy of Czechoslovakianism implemented in the interwar period (see Section 3.1.3). When the debate resulted in mass demonstrations in Bratislava which soon developed into increasing demands for Slovakian independence, the Czech politicians gave in and the name Czech and Slovakian Federal Republic was adopted to reflect that the country consisted of two equal nation-groups. In the post-1989 Czechoslovakian state, the few reminiscences of cultural deprivation of the Slovaks were completely eliminated. Thus, for example, the issue of religious repression was no longer relevant as the activities of the Slovakian Catholic Church were not restricted any more (Wolchik, 1991: 215f).

The conclusion to be drawn from this analysis is that $H_{2.3}$ must be rejected. Certainly, the Slovaks experienced some degree of cultural deprivation in the communist period, but the cultural liberalization in the new democratic Czechoslovakia gave them no reasons to fear future cultural colonization by the Czechs.

5 CONCLUSION

In the late 1980s a strong revival against Soviet and communist dominance occurred in Czechoslovakia. The initiators and supporters of the revival were predominantly of Czech origin. However, in contrast to the other cases of strong revivals discussed in this book, the Czech-dominated revival was *liberal* rather than *national* in its aim and scope. The liberal revival was successful in that it led to a democratic Czechoslovakia fully independent of the USSR, but as a Slovakian national revival gathered momentum in the following period, the final result was the establishment of two independent states.

The theory of moderate primordialism provides a clear explanation of the Slovakian national revival as the Slovaks had a strong common identity based on their *ethnie* and as they did not embrace the idea of a Czechoslovakian identity. To explain the Czech-dominated Czechoslovakian revival, H_1 must point to the well-developed Czechoslovakian identity among the Czechs. However, H_1 cannot explain why the Czechs, who initiated and supported the Czechoslovakian revival, did not opt for the establishment of an independent Czech state although the ethnically based common Czech identity was at least as important to the majority of the Czechs.

As regards the temporal location of the revivals, the test of $H_{1.2}$ showed that the regime change in the USSR was a triggering factor in relation to the Czech-dominated Czechoslovakian revival and that the post-1989 liberal political system in Czechoslovakia paved the way for the Slovakian revival. Moreover, this revival was eased by the already existing republican institutions.

In an instrumental perspective, the Czech-dominated Czechoslovakian liberal revival was due to the Czechs' perception that they were subject to economic and political deprivation by the Soviet-influenced communist regime – although objective deprivation was primarily evident in the political sphere. With respect to the Slovaks, factors indicating internal colonization by the Czechs were almost absent in the period of communist rule. Nevertheless, as the post-1989 economic reforms had more severe consequences for the Slovakian economy than for the Czech, the Slovaks perceived that they were economically deprived by the Czech-dominated centre. Furthermore, Czech insistence on a strong and centralized federation led to political frustration among the Slovaks who were a numerical minority and who regarded the possibilities for Slovakian self-determination as too restricted. Finally, $H_{2.3}$ is of limited use in the Czech and Slovakian cases as real or perceived cultural deprivation played no significant role in these cases.

9 The National Revivals: Comparison and Conclusions

1 INTRODUCTION

Up to this point Part One has provided an encompassing but separate account of a relatively large number of theories as well as empirical instances of national revivals. Theoretical discussions in Chapters 2 and 3 have reduced the number of relevant theories, and some of these have been tested on each specific case of national revival in Chapters 5 to 8.

Now we can take advantage of the comparative nature of our analysis in order to obtain a more substantiated and generalizable answer to our first question about the causes of national revivals. We do this, firstly, by comparing the dependent variable itself, the national revivals. Secondly, we compare the relative explanatory power of the hypotheses deduced in Chapter 3, thereby providing an overview of the conclusions in Chapters 5 to 8. Thirdly, this comparison gives us an empirical basis for two theoretical discussions. Firstly, we discuss the theoretical relationship between primordial and instrumental explanations on the macrosociological level of analysis, and secondly, we discuss the theoretical relationship between this level of analysis and the microsociological level. Finally, we suggest an integrative model of the causes of national revivals.

2 COMPARISON OF THE NATIONAL REVIVALS

Trying to compare the strength of the revivals using some kind of aggregated absolute measure would clearly be a problematic task. However, the empirical material allows for dividing the national revivals into relatively strong and weak ones (see Figure 1).

It appears that the national revivals of the different East European nation-groups were not as universally strong and comprehensive as they often appear from media reports on the subject. On the contrary, the East Europeans engaged in national movements to very different extents,

● = Yes ○ = No	Many and large demonstrations on issues of nationalism	Strong electoral support of parties and candidates offering autonomy/ independence	Large affirmative turnout in referenda on autonomy/ independence	Achievement of *de jure* or *de facto* national self-determination
Estonian	●	●	●	●
Russian (in Estonia)	○	○	○	○
Moldovan	●	●	None held	●[c]
Russian (in Moldova)	●	●	●	●
Gagauz	●	●	●	●[d]
Croation	●	●	●	●[c]
Serbian	●	None held	●	●[e]
Czech	○[a]	○	None held	●
Slovakian	○	●	None held[b]	●

Figure 1 The national revivals

Notes:

a The large demonstrations in connection with the Velvet Revolution focused not on issues of nationalism but on issues of liberalization, democratization, and economic reforms.

b Although no referenda were held, an opinion poll from 1991 showed that only 23 per cent of the Slovaks favoured a separation of Czechoslovakia.

c The national self-determination did not encompas all of the territory of the former republic.

d Later, in mid-1994, the Moldovans and the Gagauz agreed to make the region an autonomous part of Moldova.

e The Serbs controlled the Krajina area only in the 1991–95 period.

despite the advantages of national movements in the late 20th century. National movements have the general advantages of aiming at control over the vast resources of the modern state and being hard to suppress in a world of well-informed and alleged democratic societies that hail the principle of national self-determination. And, further, in Eastern Europe, *perestroyka* had the effect of allowing alternative groups to be formed, and – not least important – it resulted in an identity crisis that could be solved by taking pride in another but no less ideological group, namely the nation-group.

True, most of our cases exhibit strong national revivals in keeping with these generally benign conditions for national movements in late-20th-century Eastern Europe. Thus, the revivals among the Estonians, Moldovans, Slavs, Gagauz, Croats, and Serbs were characterized by large-scale demonstrations on issues of nationalism, strong electoral support of parties favouring national independence or autonomy, and large affirmative turnouts in referenda on autonomy or independence (only the Moldovans, the Czechs, and the Slovaks did not arrange such a referendum). On the other hand, the revival among the Russians in Estonia was relatively weak. The issue of autonomy only appeared at a relatively late point in time and was then merely supported by a minority. Furthermore, the strength of the Slovakian national revival was somewhat weaker than average. Certainly, almost all Slovakian politicians took on a nationalist image and Slovakian nationalist parties gained fairly strong electoral support, but the prevailing attitude among the Slovakian people seemed to be in favour of a continued Czechoslovakian federation. Finally, the revival among the Czechs is a deviating case since the Czech-dominated Velvet Revolution was actually a Czechoslovakian liberal revival which aimed at establishing an independent state *vis-à-vis* the USSR for both Czechs and Slovaks.

3 COMPARISON OF THE EXPLANATIONS OF NATIONAL REVIVALS

Given this empirical variance in our dependent variable, we need to ask not merely why the national revivals occurred at all but also why they occurred to such different extents.

In order to compare the relatively large number of complex cases analyzed in this book, a certain amount of systematization and categorization is required. When moving from the analysis of specific cases to a comparative analysis, some loss of information is almost unavoidable. In Figure 2, we have made such a systematic but somewhat undifferentiated comparison of the nine cases of national revivals using only three categories: one affirmative, one partly affirmative, and one negative. In the lower part of Figure 2 we have listed the explanatory power of the sub-hypotheses when tried on the slightly reformulated version of our first question about the occurrence of national revivals – that is, when tried on the question of why some national revivals turned out to be strong, while others were moderate or weak. In order not to oversimplify the conclusions, however, we have chosen to include not only the hypotheses and sub-hypotheses presented in Chapter 3 but also the primary elements and variants of the

● = Yes ◗ = To a certain degree, yes ○ = No

	Estonian	Russian (in Estonia)	Moldovan	Russian (in Moldova)	Gagauz	Croatian	Serbian	Czech	Slovakian
Strong national revival	●	○	●	●	●	●	●	◗	◗
Existence of									
an *ethnie*	●	○	◗	◗	●	●	●	◗	●
pluralist policies	●	●	●	●	●	●	●	●	●
republican unit	●	○	●	○	○	●	○	●	●
constitutional rights	◗	○	◗	○	○	◗	◗	◗	◗
Internal colonization by communist centre leading to									
economic deprivation	○	○	●	○	●	○	●	○	○
political deprivation	●	○	●	○	●	◗	○	◗	○
cultural deprivation	●	○	●	○	●	○	○	○	○
Internal colonization by new nationalist centre leading to									
economic deprivation		○		○	●		●		◗
political deprivation		●		◗	◗		●		◗
cultural deprivation		◗		○	○		●		○
Internal colonization leading to									
economic frustration	●	◗	●	●	●	●	●	●	◗
political frustration	●	◗	●	●	●	●	●	●	◗
cultural frustration	●	◗	●	◗	○	◗	●	○	○
Strength/weakness explained by									
$H_{1.1}$	●	●	◗	◗	●	●	●	◗	◗
$H_{1.2}$	●	●	●	◗	◗	●	◗	◗	◗
$H_{2.1}$	●	◗	●	●	●	●	●	◗	●
$H_{2.2}$	●	◗	●	●	●	●	●	◗	●
$H_{2.3}$	●	◗	●	◗	◗	◗	●	●	◗

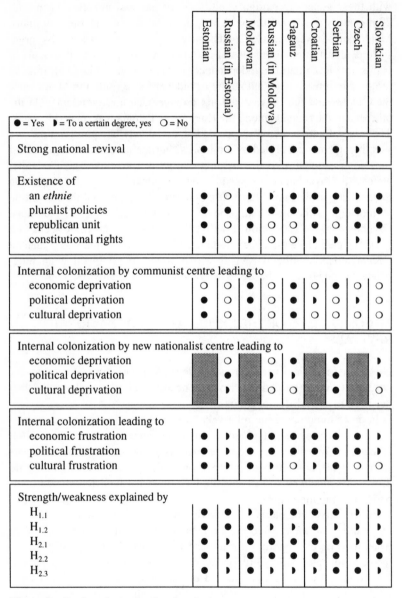

Figure 2 Explanations of national revivals

sub-hypotheses. Read from top to bottom, Figure 2 provides a very short summary of the conclusions in the preceding four chapters. Read from the left to the right, however, it is a practical means to compare the explanatory power of the different hypotheses and sub-hypotheses. Some results of this comparison are especially noteworthy.

First of all, the primordial emphasis on the importance of an *ethnie* as hypothesized in $H_{1.1}$ seems to be a rather good explanation of national revivals, especially if the original question about the occurrence or not of national revivals is considered. In that case, the Russians in Estonia can be regarded as a non-occurrence in contrast to all the other cases, and this could be attributed to their lack of an *ethnie*.

However, when the second question about the strength or weakness of the national revivals is considered, $H_{1.1}$ fares less well. Firstly, $H_{1.1}$ has some difficulties in explaining the strong national revivals in the cases of Moldovans and Slavs in Moldova, where the *ethnies* are present but more equivocal than in the other cases of strong national revivals. The Moldovans have an ongoing discussion about their proper ethnic base: are they Moldovans, Romanians, or both? Although the Moldovans do have a strong and distinct ethnic base as Moldovans, the coexisting element of Romanian-ness makes it impossible for $H_{1.1}$ to predict whether the Moldovan revival would aim at independence or reunification with Romania. At first glance, the Russian national revival in Moldova also seems strange from an 'ethnic' point of view, supported as it was by both Ukrainians and first-generation Russian immigrants, as well as by Russians with a longer history in the Dnestr area. However, in this case $H_{1.1}$ could point to the fact that the Ukrainians were strongly russified and that the Russians who emigrated to the Dnestr region were grafted into an older local Slavic culture. Secondly, $H_{1.1}$ has difficulties explaining why the strong Czech revival had a liberal Czechoslovakian goal rather than a national Czech one, just as it cannot explain why the well-developed Slovakian *ethnie* only resulted in a medium-strong national revival. In all these cases, the primordial hypothesis could explain the occurrence of the revivals post-factually, but it could not have predicted either the strength of the national revivals or which identities would eventually become emphasized in the national revivals.

Nevertheless, $H_{1.1}$ *is* correct in pointing to the necessity of some kind of ethnic base for a national revival to occur. But as we have observed already in the theoretical discussion of primordialism, $H_{1.1}$ obviously needs a supplement of some kind. And the supplement most consistent with the emphasis on the *ethnie* is to point to the influence of external suppression or other political structures as exemplified by $H_{1.2}$. Again, however, the primordial hypothesis fares better in the explanation of the occurrence or not of a national revival than in the explanation of the strength of the national revivals. In the former case, $H_{1.2}$ explains the temporal location of the national revivals, and the consistent finding of liberal policies adopted all over Eastern Europe in the late 1980s could be used to argue that national revivals are the result of existing *ethnies* combined with the adoption of liberal policies in formerly repressive regimes. But the fact that liberal policies were initiated in *all* cases does not help us to explain a dependent variable of *differing* strengths of national revivals.

The explanatory power of $H_{1.2}$ does not increase when we consider whether existing political units or constitutional rights promoted strong national revivals. True, in most cases of strong revivals, such units or rights were present, just as they were absent in the case of the weak Russian revival in Estonia. However, these units and rights were also absent in the cases of the Gagauz and Slavs in Moldova who initiated strong national revivals. Thus, it seems that although existing republican institutions are a helpful basis when a nation-group strives to realize the goal of national self-determination, they are far from being a necessary condition for a strong national revival to occur. As regards formal constitutional rights of national self-determination, they are of very limited value when there is no agreement as to the real content of such rights.

With respect to instrumental theories, it is obvious that deprivations alone – even when the notion is widened to include both political and cultural as well as economic inequalities – cannot explain all the national revivals in Eastern Europe. Objective economic deprivation does explain the strong national revivals of Moldovans, Gagauz, and Serbs as well as the weak revival of the Russians in Estonia. And, if one focuses particularly on political but also on cultural deprivation, it can also explain the Estonian national revival, and to some degree perhaps, the Russian (in Moldova), the Croatian, the Slovakian, and the Czech-dominated Czechoslovakian revivals. But in four of the eight cases of strong and medium-strong national revivals (i.e. Estonian, Russian (in Moldova), Croatian, and Czech) no economic deprivation could be detected, and significant political and cultural deprivation was also absent from half of the eight cases (i.e. Russian (in Moldova), Croatian, Czech, and Slovakian).

This leads us to consider the role of perceptions captured by the notions of economic, political, and cultural frustrations. When formulated in this way, H_2 fares a lot better. In all the cases of strong national revivals (i.e. Estonian, Moldovan, Russian (in Moldova), Gagauz, Croatian, and Serbian), the nation-groups perceived themselves to be unfairly deprived of economic, political, and cultural rights and opportunities by a colonizing centre. Likewise, the medium-strong Slovakian national revival can be explained by the fact that the Slovaks had some, but not strong, economic and political frustrations. H_2 can even explain the strong Czech-dominated liberal revival because, in the instrumental view, any interest group – in this case a Czechoslovakian as opposed to a national Czech one – can be chosen as the vehicle of efforts to correct perceived deprivations.

However, the weak Russian national revival in Estonia cannot be attributed to the absence of such grievances as the Russians experienced a certain level of frustration in all three spheres with the rise and success of the Estonian national movement. To save the instrumental hypothesis in this case, one would have to accord special importance to the more prosperous future of an independent Estonian economy and disregard the Russians' fear for their jobs and their political and cultural rights in this economy.

To summarize the comparative conclusions of each separate hypothesis, H_1 alone can explain the occurrence of the national revivals, but it cannot explain the varying strengths of the revivals, nor why one nation-group initiated a liberal and not a national revival. On the other hand, when frustrations are used as the independent variable instead of deprivations, H_2 has considerable explanatory power as to the strengths of the national revivals. But when this hypothesis is employed alone, we are left with a problem in explaining the weak Russian national revival in Estonia.

4 THE RELATIONSHIP BETWEEN PRIMORDIAL AND INSTRUMENTAL THEORIES

This leads us to the question of whether the primordial and the instrumental views should be combined or whether they are at all combinable. Some students of nationalism, such as Motyl (1990) and Eller and Coughlan (1993), reject this possibility on theoretical grounds, whereas others, such as McKay (1982), Douglass (1988), and Frye (1992) have attempted a theoretical synthesis.

While it is probably true that primordialism in the strong sense is theoretically incompatible with instrumentalism, this does not, in our opinion, apply to the relationship between primordialism in the moderate sense and instrumentalism.

On the theoretical level, the primordial conception of ethnic identities as something 'first created or developed' is compatible with the instrumental conception of reality as a social construct. Moderate primordialism merely draws attention to the fact that culture is not just created by the actions and thoughts of human beings – it also shapes these actions and thoughts. It may be that national identities and institutions can be repeatedly created and recreated, but this does not happen in a vacuum. On the contrary, every recreation or reinvigoration of a national identity – that is, every national revival – takes place on the basis of and inside the existing society and the myths, history, culture, polity, and economy belonging to it. In this respect, primordialism in the moderate sense resembles Giddens's notion of 'duality of structure' which implies that the structural properties of social systems are both the medium and the outcome of the practices that constitute those systems (1984: 25).[61]

But the need for a combination of primordial and instrumental views does not follow solely from theoretical considerations. Our analyses have shown that none of the explanations can be clearly rejected on the basis of the empirical evidence at our disposal. But neither do they independently explain the occurrence and strength of all our cases. Perhaps the most illustrative example of the need for a combination of primordialism and instrumentalism is provided by a comparison of the strong Russian national revival in Moldova and the weak Russian national revival in Estonia – both part of the same mother-nation and both with approximately the same situation as regards frustrations. The most notable difference between these cases is a more developed Slavic *ethnie* in the Dnestr region of Moldova due to their longer history on the left bank of Dnestr and their new and rather short attachment to a Moldovan republic. Thus, a probable outline of the interplay of the two theories could be that the existence of an *ethnie* is a necessary condition on which perceived unfair inequalities or perceived threats can build or even combine to produce a strong national revival, especially when regime changes and a sudden identity crisis open a window of opportunity for nationalist leaders.

5 THE RELATIONSHIP BETWEEN MACROSOCIOLOGICAL AND MICROSOCIOLOGICAL THEORIES

Both primordial and instrumental explanations, however, are macrosociological theories. Their advantage is their ability to detect important historical and structural similarities and differences between groups of individuals. The historical and structural environment and the shared culture and interests of the individuals provide at the same time the limits and the opportunities for individual and collective action. But these macrosociological factors do not, of course, directly determine the behaviour of the individuals. As political scientists, we can only search for some degree of systematic co-variation between, for example, the structural conditions in different societies on the one hand and the probability and intensity of different social events and processes, such as national revivals, on the other.[62]

It is questionable whether we will ever be able to explain the specific considerations, attitudes, and behaviours of each separate individual. Yet, whereas macrosociological theories explain neither why nor how the single individual should act upon these structural conditions, microsociological theories *do* make it possible to get a little closer to a general understanding of the motives of individuals initiating or supporting a national movement. In Chapter 2 we suggested some microsociological theories about the causes of ethnocentrism, ranging from predispositional theories based on biological or psychological drives towards the ingroup to purely rational deliberations about the costs and benefits of such affiliation. Through theoretical discussions of the internal consistency of the theories and their applicability in the analysis of group- and intergroup-level phenomena, we narrowed down the scope of theories to two: rational choice theory representing the cost-benefit view of self-interested individuals maximizing their economic welfare, and social identity theory representing the somewhat broader view of individuals motivated by the need for self-esteem and able to derive some of this self-esteem from a collective that contains something more than the sum of its parts. None of these theories could be dismissed on theoretical grounds and both theories could explain the persistence of national movements in the late 20th century as well as why *national* movements in particular should be initiated in the turmoil of East European *perestroyka*.

To be acceptable, however, the microsociological theories must be consistent with the macrosociological theories – that is, they must not directly contradict the results of the macrosociological analysis. Of course, the reverse holds true as well, but as we have no reliable empirical results on the microsociological level of analysis, this section only examines whether and to what extent rational choice theory and social identity theory are consistent with the comparative macrosociological conclusions made above. As the most powerful macrosociological variables turned out to be the existence of an *ethnie* and real or perceived economic, political, and cultural inequalities, the ability of the microsociological theories to substantiate the macrosociological relationships should be measured against each of these explanations. For convenience, Figure 3 gives a short assessment of these abilities with respect to each macrosociological variable.

Macro Micro	Existence of an *ethnie*	Economic inequalities	Political inequalities	Cultural inequalities
Rational choice theory (RCT)	RCT admits that cultural homogeneity eases group formation but in all other respects RCT rejects the importance of this variable.	RCT accounts for this explanatory variable *par excellence* because individuals are seen as motivated by *economic* deliberations.	RCT can count for the importance of this variable but only if political power is seen exclusively as a means to gain economic benefits through the provision of collective goods and selective incentives.	RCT is hard put to account for the influence of this variable, at least in any direct sense.
Social identity theory (SIT)	SIT is obviously better than RCT to account for the importance of an *ethnie* as individuals derive self-esteem from the social indentity inherent in such groups. SIT, however, does not assert that an *ethnie* will automatically evolve into a national revival, as the individual can choose to enhance his or her pesonal identity as well as several other competing social identities.	SIT cannot displace RCT as a possible microsociological foundation of this variable, but the importance of economic inequalities is not at all inconsistent with SIT. In SIT, relative economic conditions are important to individual status but certainly also to group status which influences individuals' self-esteem independently of their own actual situation.	In contrast to RCT, SIT accounts for this variable by seeing political power not as a means but as a goal in itself. It is important because political self-determination involves recognition of the group's status which in turn has a direct effect on the members' self-esteem.	SIT can easily account for the importance of this variable as culture includes the beliefs, values, myths, symbols, arts, social institutions etc. of a group that lie at the very heart of the group members' social identity.

Figure 3 Ability of microsociological theories to account for the importance of different macrosociological variables

It appears that whereas rational choice theory provides a very plausible microsociological foundation of the importance of economic inequalities as a cause of national revivals, it has obvious problems in accounting for the importance of the other three variables. True, rational choice theory *can* account for the importance of political inequalities by interpreting them as a barrier to satisfactory provision of collective goods to the whole nation-group and selective incentives to activists within the national movement. But the relation between cultural inequalities and the existence of an *ethnie* on the one hand and the economic self-interest of individuals on the other is much more obscure, and this makes rational choice theory at best unsuitable as a microsociological foundation of these explanations.

In contrast, social identity theory can account for the importance of all four variables because status and self-esteem involve economic, political, and cultural elements, and because a positive social identity is likely to be derived from groups (an *ethnie*, for example) that have appropriate identity carriers (symbols, myths etc.) and from which individual exit is associated with difficulties. As a microsociological foundation of the macrosociological explanations of national revivals, social identity theory has two further important advantages. Firstly, it does not necessarily imply that the individual actor's *own* economic, political, and cultural life conditions are considered unfair or threatened. What it does imply is that the individual assesses the conditions of the *group* as undeserved or endangered. This theoretical stance diminishes the risk of ecological fallacies when inferring from group similarities and differences to individual action. Secondly, social identity theory does not *a priori* identify from which groups the individual should derive his or her social identities, just as it allows the individuals to shift allegiances between groups and to give their allegiances to more than one group at a time. Social identity theory even includes the possibility that individuals disregard their social identities and increase their self-esteem by enhancing their personal identity. This theoretical stance diminishes the tendency towards determinism inherent in both primordial and other macrosociological theories as well as pure rational choice theories.

This is not to say that no individual behaviour is governed by rational deliberations about economic self-interest. It would be naïve to reject completely the possibility of such purely utility-maximizing actions in the realm of national revivals. What we do suggest, however, is that such a view of the motivational basis of human behaviour is far too restricted to be able to explain national revivals fully. Thus, instrumentalists and rational choice theorists normally advise us to regard the use of symbols, culture, myths, and history by national leaders as pure rhetoric. While this may be true to some degree, the fact that precisely such arguments occupy a dominant part of national leaders' rhetoric also indicate that history, culture, and political self-determination must have some or perhaps great meaning to the people whom the leaders try to woo.

In conclusion, social identity theory seems to be an apt microsociological foundation of our macrosociological findings with regard to the causes of national revivals. We do not dismiss the influence of rational utility-maximizing considerations about economic self-interest in the decisions of some individuals to support or join a national revival. But in our view, the rational choice assumptions are too restrictive to give a full understanding of the individual and societal processes involved in national revivals.

6 CONCLUSION: AN INTEGRATIVE MODEL OF THE CAUSES OF NATIONAL REVIVALS

We have epitomized our view of the causes of national revivals in the model depicted in Figure 4. In reality, of course, an infinite number of different factors come into play in each specific instance of national revival, and we do not pretend to have found even the main part of them. Our model builds on the assumption that the individual, group, and intergroup levels of analysis must be combined in order to obtain a full picture of the causes of national revivals, and on each level of analysis we have pointed only to those variables that appear to be the most important as a result of our empirical analysis and the accompanying theoretical discussions.

We distinguish between four types of variable: antecedents, orientations, catalysts, and action. Antecedents are characteristics of the individuals, groups, and intergroup relationships that exist prior to the manifest expression of a national revival. Orientations are approaches, attitudes, and perceptions that are applied or held in the early stages of a national revival. Catalysts are neither necessary nor sufficient conditions for a national revival, but circumstances generally conducive to one. And action needs no further description: it involves our dependent variable, a national revival.

Although *catalysts* play a particularly important role in the temporal location of national revivals, they are releasing and conducive factors rather than fundamental causes of national revivals. Thus, it is no coincidence that the turmoil of *perestroyka* sparked off so many instances of national revivals in Eastern Europe. The exposure of the hollowness of the communist regimes which *perestroyka* made possible had the combined effect of diminishing the existing systems' legitimacy and security

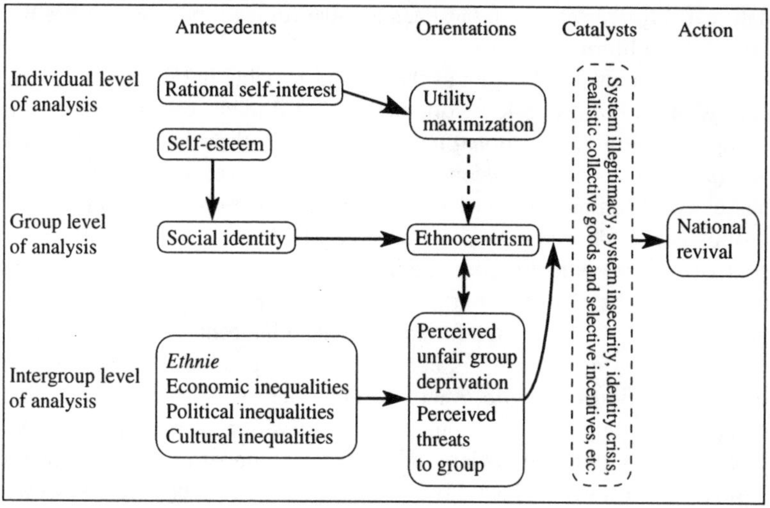

Figure 4 An integrative model of the causes of national revivals

while at the same time producing an identity crisis suitable to be solved by an ideological movement – such as a national one – rather than a simple interest group. Another important catalyst is the ability of national leaders and movements to give reliable promises of provision of attractive collective goods and selective incentives to their members and followers.

The crucial category of variables in our model is *orientations*. It is the degree of ethnocentrism and the intensity of perceptions about the unfairness of the group's relative position and about threats to the group that have the greatest influence on the probability of a national revival.

Ethnocentrism is primarily the result of the human need for a positive self-esteem which can be derived from the ingroup in the shape of a positive social identity. Thus, in our view, the *antecedents* of ethnocentrism are to be found in the insights of social identity theory. The *ethnie* is far from the only possible group in this respect, but it has some advantages over other competing identities. Firstly, it provides a well-developed system of symbols, myths, culture, and history suitable to be a basis for positive identity. Secondly, individual movement out of the *ethnie* might prove more difficult in practice than it appears theoretically, partly as a result of the limitations posed by the modern bureaucratic state and the condemnation from co-nationals, and partly as a result of the individual's own emotional investment in his or her *ethnie*. And thirdly, the idea of national self-determination has been a powerful legitimizer ever since the French Revolution.

Ethnocentrism can be seen as the pivotal variable in our model, firstly, because it is the group-level orientation that directly corresponds to the group-level action of national revivals. As such, the ethnocentrism of an *ethnie* can be seen as a precondition for a national revival. Secondly, if it has evolved, ethnocentrism has a major influence on the tendency of a group to feel deprived or threatened. Part of the syndrome of ethnocentrism is the contention that the ingroup is worth more and therefore is more deserving than the outgroup. Thus, even total equality between groups would not be enough for an obstinate ethnocentrist.

Ethnocentrism, however, is not enough to explain why some national movements flourish while others do not. The decisive variable in this respect is perceptions of unfair group deprivation or perhaps of direct threats. Such perceptions are inherently a comparative phenomenon involving the status and actions of other coexisting groups. This is why a macrosociological analysis is inevitable in the explanation of national revivals.

Unfortunately, the factors and processes that influence perceptions are far from well known, and the *antecedents* of perceptions cannot therefore be described fully or precisely. Yet, there is no doubt that objective economic, political, and cultural inequalities are most often the foundation of such perceptions. The problem is that perceptions can form without any solid objective foundation. One explanation of negative perceptions where no objective inequalities are present has to do with the comparative nature of social identity. Thus, the choice of the relevant reference group is obviously important to the perceived fairness of one's own group's situation. A clear-cut example of this is the Estonians who compared their present status with either the present-day Scandinavian countries or the relative status of the interwar independent Estonia, but certainly not with the other periphery Soviet republics or even with the Russian republic in the centre of the USSR. Another explanation is that perceptions are often formed by analogy and that historical experiences play a major role in determining which analogies are plausible. Thus, perceptions of unfair deprivation or threats with no obvious objective reason are more likely to evolve between groups with a historical relationship characterized by suppression or enmity. The best examples of such influence of the historical interplay between *ethnies* are the Croats and the Slavs who were frustrated and feared for their future despite their advantageous position.

As mentioned above, a high level of ethnocentrism has a direct effect on perceptions. The opposite causal direction holds true as well. Discriminations or threats to an individual on the grounds that he or she belongs to a certain group are bound to make his or her group membership salient. Thus, perceived unfair deprivation and threats often lead to higher levels of ingroup favouritism and idealization and outgroup derogation and hatred.

However, the most important role of perceptions in our model is the powerful conditional effect they have on the relationship between ethnocentrism and national revivals. To evolve into a powerful national revival, ethnocentrism must be combined with perceptions of unfair deprivation or threats.

Part Two: The Consequences of National Conflicts

10 Processes of Intergroup Conflict

1 INTRODUCTION

If we accept Pruitt and Rubin's definition of conflict as 'perceived divergence of interest' (1986: 4), it follows from Part One that a national revival must almost necessarily entail a national conflict of some kind. This is because, as we concluded in Chapter 9, the decisive cause of national revivals is a wish to correct or counter perceived inequalities or threats caused by another nation-group. This does not, however, mean that national revivals must necessarily lead to intense and violent conflict, although such conflicts are often the most salient ones to the ordinary observer, not least because of the news criteria of the modern mass media.

In this part of our book, we shall examine the reasons why some national conflicts escalate into violence whereas others remain on a controlled level or perhaps even get solved. As in Part One, we begin on the microsociological level of analysis. In contrast to the microsociological chapter of Part One, however, we have chosen to discuss *processes* of intergroup conflict rather than the individual motivational basis of intergroup conflict.

There are two main reasons for this focus, apart from the fact that Chapter 2 indirectly covers the microsociological motivational basis of national conflicts as well as revivals. Firstly, the escalation of a conflict obviously presupposes an interaction between two parties, and national conflicts thus, even more clearly than national revivals, belong to the *intergroup* level of analysis. Therefore, it is difficult to approach the microsociological level of analysis in terms of individual motives alone as we did in Part One. Secondly, whereas the causes of conflicts as such might be found primarily in antecedents such as diverging interests, the causes of diverging intensity of conflicts are obviously connected to the specific *processes* that accompany each conflict as it evolves.

Our acknowledgement of the primacy of *intergroup* variables and *processes* of escalation over the influence of individual- and group-level antecedents does not, however, prevent us from analysing the influence and self-reinforcing consequences of intergroup conflict on individuals and groups. Neither does it prevent us from analysing the influence of some central individuals and groups on the intergroup conflict. In this chapter these two relationships are discussed in turn. First, however, we shall give a short and general description of the characteristics of escalation which normally precede our dependent variable when it takes the form of violent national conflict.

2 CHARACTERISTICS OF ESCALATION

Whereas a broad definition of conflict is defendable in order not to prematurely restrict conceptual analysis of conflict in general (Fink, 1968: 453ff), the phenomenon of *escalation* is obviously related to manifest conflicts involving certain types and especially certain developments of interaction.

Pruitt and Rubin summarize the characteristics of escalation as at least five types of incremental transformation that occur on both sides of an escalating conflict (1986: 64f). Firstly, and most characteristically, *light* attempts to influence or control the adversary, such as persuading or promising, gradually give way to *heavier* tactics, such as threats, irrevocable commitments, or even violence. Secondly, *small* issues and resources invested in the conflict increase and become *larger* as the conflict evolves. Thirdly, *specific* issues are often supplanted by more *general* issues. Fourthly, the parties' objectives tend to change from a simple interest in doing well for themselves via *winning over* the adversary, to *hurting the other* at least as much as oneself has been hurt. Finally, escalating conflicts seem to start with *few* participants and end up with *many*.

In accordance with this conception of escalation, we regard violent conflict and full-scale war not as a category by itself but as an extreme instance or result of an escalatory process. This permits us, in this and the following chapter, to draw on general theoretical insights about conflict and escalation in order to explain the occurrence or not of violent national conflicts.

3 PROCESSES OF ESCALATION

The chain of events in escalating conflicts can be generalized in three ways (Pruitt and Rubin, 1986: 89). In the *aggressor–defender model*, escalation is seen as a result of an aggressor trying to serve his or her interests which are at odds with the interests of the defender. Escalation results if the defender refuses to give in and the aggressor continues to pursue his or her goals using more and more contentious tactics.

While the conflicting parties often picture the escalating process in terms of the aggressor–defender model, the understanding of escalation has been widened with the introduction of the *conflict spiral model* (pp. 90f). This model sees escalation as the result of a vicious circle in which both parties see their negative perceptions of the other party confirmed in the hostile actions, of that party. The negative perceptions then legitimize the party's own hostile actions, thereby fuelling the circle's next iteration.

Finally, Pruitt and Rubin introduce a third model, *the structural change model* (1986: 92ff). In this model, each escalatory step is seen as changing the functioning of the individuals and groups involved in the conflict as well as the members of the surrounding community. Thus, Pruitt and Rubin mention psychological changes such as the development of negative attitudes and perceptions, group changes such as the development of certain norms, and changes in the broader community such as a tendency towards polarization. Each structural change leaves a residue that encourages further escalation and the changes seem to have a lasting influence on psychological and group structures, thereby making de-escalation more difficult.

Structural changes contribute to escalation in three ways. Firstly, they are intervening variables in a conflict spiral model as described above. Thus, hostile actions by one party tend to produce structural changes in the adversary. The structural changes then motivate similar actions by the adversary which, in turn, tend to produce structural changes in the party itself. Secondly, hostile actions by one party produce structural changes not only in the other but also directly in the first party. Thus, the very fact of defending one's nation-group against another is likely to create more negative attitudes towards the adversary. Finally, structural changes tend to erode the norms and institutions that normally limit escalatory conflicts.

The structural change model is useful in this chapter because it explicitly focuses on the relationship between intergroup conflict and individual and group actors. In comparison with the aggressor–defender model and the conflict spiral model, it also has the advantage of allowing a more precise identification of the mechanisms through which conflicts escalate. In the following subsections we shall describe the most important structural changes in individuals and groups and the subsequent self-reinforcing consequences of intergroup conflict.

3.1 Individual Changes: Perceptual and Cognitive Biases

Perceptual and cognitive filters are a 'must' to all human beings who have to deal with the confusing and immense complexity of the world. An important tool in this filtering process is *stereotyping* – that is, the formation of an expectation that a set of traits is associated with membership in a particular social group (Ashmore & Del Boca, 1981: 21).[63] However, stereotypes have been shown to influence both our attention to and our perception and memory of events or information in ways that confirm our preconceived opinions (Grant, 1990: 41f). This tendency is compounded in times of conflict when negative attitudes and perceptions often have severe behavioural implications.

In the context of national conflicts, several authors prefer the concept of *images* which refers to 'the organized representation of an object in an individual's cognitive system ... the individual's conception of what the object is like' (Kelman, 1965: 24). Thus, national images are the basic attitudes that different nation-groups hold towards themselves and others.[64] Often, groups involved in prolonged international conflicts seem to develop images of each other that are very alike; the images are, so to speak, mirror images (Bronfenbrenner, 1961: 46). The influence on international conflict of such images and other pre-existing beliefs – especially those held by decision-makers – has been shown by many studies (e.g. Jervis, 1976, and White, 1984).

The influence of pre-existing beliefs and feelings, such as stereotypes and national images, on perceptions and behaviour can be explained through cognitive dissonance theory (Festinger, 1957; Jervis, 1976: 382–406). According to this theory, individuals strive to reduce inconsistencies which may arise in their knowledge about their attitudes, behaviour, and environment. If a person, for example, receives some 'dissonant' information about the environment, the resulting inconsistency can be reduced by assimilating the new information into one's preconceived opinions or by completely disregarding the information. This cognitive distortion leads to a confirmation of the pre-existing beliefs or policy preferences which is irrational and, in the case of escalating conflict, often fatal.

3.1.1 The Effects of Conflict on Beliefs

Conflict is undoubtably a social phenomenon that is sure to bring about negative feelings and beliefs.[65] Conflict that involves interaction creates negative feelings and beliefs in two ways.

The most obvious way is by aversive behaviour, which is blamed on the adversary, producing an angry reaction. This anger may result in some kind of aggression (see Section 3.2.3 of Chapter 2 on the frustration–aggression theory), but most often it simply causes negative feelings and beliefs about the adversary (Pruitt and Rubin, 1986: 102f).

The less obvious way is by one's *own* hostile actions contributing to the formation of negative feelings and beliefs (pp. 103f). According to the theory of cognitive dissonance presented above, dissonant information not only about the environment but also about one's own behaviour can lead to cognitive inconsistency. Again, this inconsistency can be reduced by assimilating one's feelings and beliefs through a process of rationalization. Thus, if an adversary is unjustifiably hurt by a person, it is not unlikely that this person will react by adjusting his or her feelings and beliefs about the adversary, so that the hostile action can be perceived as warranted.

Of course, negative beliefs are most influential when they have gained cultural acceptance and have become widely held stereotypes or national images. Thus, we should expect groups that have been engaged in manifest conflict for a long time or repeatedly through history to display particularly negative beliefs about each other and therefore to be especially susceptible to escalating conflicts.

3.1.2 The Effects of Negative Beliefs on Conflict

Escalation-promoting cognitive errors on the basis of negative beliefs function in many ways. Most generally, pre-existing beliefs affect present perception and behaviour through the psychological mechanism of selective perception. Under conditions of conflict and widespread negative beliefs, selective perception can take three interrelated forms (see Cooper & Fazio, 1979: 153ff, who cite evidence for each form).

Firstly, *distorted evaluation of behaviour* means that the behaviour of both ingroups and outgroups is evaluated positively or negatively in accordance with one's expectations. As an example, members of one nation-group much more often 'see' the violent actions of the opposing nation-group than those of their own.

Secondly, a conflicting party has a tendency to ask the questions that will confirm his or her preconceptions. In this way, the party is reaffirmed in his or her negative beliefs through a false *'discovery' of confirming evidence.*

Thirdly, there is an overwhelming tendency among conflicting parties to engage in *attributional bias* – that is, to attribute different causes to the same kind of behaviour depending on who performs it. Even with no conflict, the behaviour of people who are perceived to be members of groups tends to be explained in terms of group rather than individual characteristics (Wilder, 1986: 299f). When conflict is present, undesirable actions by outgroup members (and desirable actions by ingroup members) tend to be attributed to the inherent bad character of members of the outgroup (and respectively the good character of the ingroup members) – that is, to dispositional causes. Conversely, desirable actions by outgroup members (and undesirable actions by ingroup members) tend to be attributed to external constraints or forces – that is, to situational causes (Hewstone, 1988: 49ff). As Pruitt and Rubin comment, the net effect of this process is that there is virtually nothing that the opposing group can do to dispel one's negative expectations if this mechanism is allowed unhindered functioning (1986: 116).

These three mechanisms preserve and reinforce negative feelings and beliefs about the adversary. Negative feelings and beliefs and the mechanisms of selective perception generate expectations that the adversary's behaviour has bad intentions and harmful effects. And, especially in situations where information is ambiguous (as information most often is), human beings tend to perceive the situation in accordance with their expectations. In turn, the perception of bad intentions and harmful effects will serve to legitimize defensive or even pre-emptive actions that feed the escalation spiral by initiating the same type of processes in the adversary. As the adversary responds in what he or she sees as a defensive or pre-emptive manner, one's own negative beliefs are reaffirmed and probably strengthened, thus making them a self-fulfilling prophecy.

3.2 Group Changes: Cohesiveness and Constituent Pressure

At the group level, the perceptual and cognitive biases described above are often socially reinforced or even magnified. This is due to the fact that groups tend to develop norms for socially acceptable opinions and behaviour. If negative and hostile attitudes towards the outgroup become group norms, the majority of the group will stop questioning their justification at all, and those who do become subject to pressures of conformity in both subtle and more obvious ways.

Group discussions can even make individual feelings and beliefs more extreme (Pruitt and Rubin, 1986: 105). This polarization effect can be seen as related to the conformity effect, so that individuals will strive not only to conform to the content of group norms but also to hold an opinion that is at least as extreme in the direction favoured by the group as that advocated by the average group member.

Apart from conformity to and the frequent polarization of group norms, increased group cohesion stands out as one of the most generally observed consequences of intergroup conflict.

3.2.1 The Effects of Conflict on Group Cohesiveness

Although there is no generally accepted definition of group cohesiveness, the concept usually refers to the degree of attraction that members have towards the other group members and the degree to which they are motivated to remain in the group (Shaw, 1981: 213).

The idea that external conflict tends to increase group cohesion is normally attributed to Coser (1956: 87ff). Coser, however, recognized that conflict does not necessarily increase cohesion. In fact, under some conditions it can lead to anomie (p. 92). On the basis of a comprehensive review of studies in sociology, anthropology, psychology, and political science, Stein (1976) summarizes the conditions under which external conflict seems to increase group cohesion. According to Stein, the external conflict needs to involve some threat, to affect the entire group, and to seem solvable by group efforts. Furthermore, the group must have had some preexisting cohesion or consensus as well as a centralized political system and a leadership that can intervene to create or increase cohesion (p. 165).

When these conditions are met – as they are very likely to be in national conflicts – the external conflict itself seems to increase group cohesion. In terms of ingroup survival and functioning, high group cohesion has, of course, many positive effects. This is probably also true with regard to some aspects of intergroup relations, such as when the groups have to cooperate. However, in cases of conflictual intergroup relations, the negative effects of high ingroup cohesion are the most salient.

3.2.2 The Effects of Group Cohesiveness on Conflict

High group cohesion can contribute to the escalation of a conflict in at least three ways. Firstly, group cohesion encourages conformity to and polarization of group norms (Shaw, 1981: 218ff). These effects, in turn, serve to magnify the influence of perceptual and cognitive biases described above.

Secondly, group cohesion increases the group's ability to execute coordinated actions. Thus, goals – including contentious ones in an intergroup conflict – can be pursued more effectively by highly cohesive groups (pp. 222ff).

Finally, in part through the processes of conformity and polarization, group cohesion increases constituent pressure on leaders (Fisher, 1990: 83). That is to say that although leaders have some leeway in relation to their group, they cannot afford to depart seriously from the prevailing wishes of the group (Sherif, 1966: 16). This holds true both in democracies and in, for example, authoritarian polities as all political systems need a certain level of legitimacy. And when external conflict causes group opinions to homogenize and perhaps even polarize, the latitude of the leaders diminishes. Knowing that they can be held accountable to their constituencies may even make the official statements and actions by leaders more rigorous than necessary because representatives typically view their constituency as non-conciliatory (Pruitt and Rubin, 1986: 30). This makes the concessions that are necessary to stop escalation and initiate de-escalation difficult to make because leaders fear that it will expose them as weak or soft in the eyes of their constituents.

3.3 Community Changes: Polarization

Even if some individuals or groups in the community feel that they have no part of the conflict, they may often find it very difficult to remain neutral as the conflict escalates. This is due to two processes (Pruitt and Rubin, 1986: 108). Firstly, they will often be forced or at least pressed by parties of the conflict to take sides through statements like 'either you are with us or against us'.

Secondly, as the means used in an escalating conflict become more and more aversive, the moral question of who is right and who is wrong becomes more salient. And if the aversive means even begin to affect formerly neutral individuals or groups more directly, they are likely to join the side of the party to which they were initially closer or which seems to have contributed less to the escalation and hence to be more properly considered the defender.

3.4 Escalation-Limiting Processes

Of course, the conflicting parties are not completely enslaved to the malignant processes of escalation described above. Some notable processes, norms, and institutions can reduce or at least limit the processes of escalation.

In particular, realistic empathy with the adversary – that is, an understanding of the adversary's thoughts and feelings – usually serves as a corrective to the perceptual biases towards escalation (White, 1984: 160ff).[66] The probability of realistic empathy is increased if an individual has personal relations with members of the opposing group, but it can also exist without such. The problem is, however, that as a conflict escalates a 'good guys/bad guys' picture often develops in the minds of the participants. And as realistic empathy is a dangerous challenge to this cherished image of the conflict, people tend to avoid engaging too seriously in realistic empathy (pp. 165f).

Secondly, fear of escalation can limit the tendency towards escalation. The greater the capacity and will of the adversary to retaliate and the greater one's own cognition of this, the greater inducements not to engage in escalatory actions.

Finally, on the group level, social norms, institutions, and bonds can limit escalation. Cultures can be more or less conflict-accepting. Institutions can exist either to mediate in conflicts or to prevent them by force from escalating. And finally, individuals and groups can have a feeling of interconnectedness and interdependence that prevent them from escalating conflicts even if they perceive that they have diverging interests on some issues.

More generally, the point is that although socially reinforced negative attitudes and beliefs can stack the deck against peace, the cards still have to be played. In other words, escalation presupposes inter*action* and interaction involves not only the preceding attitudes and perceptions but also the actual decisions of actors. It is to the influence of such actors on the escalation of a national conflict that we now turn.

4 ACTORS OF ESCALATION

On closer examination, the concept of actors is very complex. In fact, all individuals and groups, passive as well as active, that are conscious of a potential or manifest conflict qualify as actors of escalation. In an effort to impose order on this complexity and to reduce the number of relevant actors to a manageable level, we narrow down the perspective of this section in two ways. Firstly, we focus exclusively on actors in *national* conflicts, and secondly, we provide a typology including only the most *important* actors in national conflicts.

Following the typology of actors of escalation, we proceed to discuss how each type of actor can influence the escalation of national conflicts primarily through their impact on the above-mentioned processes of escalation.

One obvious role of actors in conflicts is that it is actors who perceive divergence of interests, have perceptual and cognitive biases, exert constituent pressure, make decisions, and carry out actions and reactions. However, an analysis of the role of actors from this perspective of *actors as carriers of conflict* would amount to little more than a generalized description of conflicts. Instead, we shall focus attention on how the actions of central actors influence the *general opinion climate* in which attitudes are formed and decisions are taken and carried out.

The general opinion climate in our conception denotes the overall balance of attitudes, norms, and perceptions in a community as they appear to the individual who must form his or her own ideas in this climate. It does not imply only those attitudes, norms, and perceptions about which there is explicit or implicit agreement in the community. Rather, it should capture the spectrum of approaches and especially the prevalence of certain approaches to different issues. The issue of interest to us is, of course, the latent or manifest national conflict. Thus, in this section we propose to focus on how important actors of escalation affect the context in which the processes of escalation take place.

4.1 A Typology of Important Actors

We have chosen to discuss the influence of four types of actor on national conflicts: strategists, mobilizers, activists, and intermediaries. The definition of these types builds on a typology involving two dimensions (see Figure 5).

First, we distinguish between leaders and independents. Leaders, in our context, are defined as individuals or groups that take decisions on behalf of larger societal groups of individuals or collectives. Thus, for example, chief state officials, leaders of national movements, elected representatives, and dominant political parties qualify as leaders in this respect. In contrast, independents are defined as individuals or groups that – at least formally – act independently of such larger societal groups and their leaders.

These two categories of actor are then divided with respect to their immediate target group: the ingroup or the outgroup. In relation to the ingroup, leaders must make sure they get and maintain the support of the group in order to serve both their private interests in the conveniences of leadership and the goals they pursue on behalf of the group. In this role as *mobilizers* they can contribute to the intensity of a conflict by influencing the perceptions of the group and by mobilizing groups around goals that are either compatible or incompatible with the goals of the outgroup. In relations with the outgroup, leaders act as *strategists*. Their choice of strategy, of course, directly influences the chain of events that leads to escalation or solution. What is important in an assessment of the overall opinion

	Actions directed primarily towards:	
	ingroup	outgroup
Leaders	*Mobilizers*	*Strategists*
Independents	*Intermediaries*	*Activists*

Figure 5 Typology of important actors of escalation

climate, however, is the signal effects in the ingroup as well as the perceptions in the outgroup of the actions of strategists.

Likewise, independents appear as two types of actor. By *intermediaries* we refer to independent actors who significantly influence the formation of perceptions in the ingroup, thereby indirectly influencing the extent of escalation. Such intermediaries could be teachers, writers, and other intellectuals, but first and foremost we believe that the modern mass media play an important role as an intermediary between social events and group perceptions of them. Finally, *activists* are independent actors who increase or reduce tensions between the conflicting groups by initiating contentious or conciliatory actions towards the outgroup. Such activists include grass roots movements, from peace groups to violent extremists. As with strategists, the importance of activists with regard to the general opinion climate is the signals they send to the ingroup and the perceptions in the outgroup of their actions.

There is a considerable overlapping and interlinking between the four types of actor. Firstly, the same individual or group may appear as more than one type of actor. The most obvious example is that leaders almost by definition act both as strategists in the intergroup conflict and as mobilizers of their own groups. Secondly, the actions of one type of actor most often influence the other types considerably. For example, leaders may exert a considerable influence – in both overt and covert ways – on formally independent actors. At the same time, leaders are constrained by the reactions and perceptions that independents generate in both conflicting groups. And thirdly, our reference to the *immediate* target group does not deny that actions apparently directed towards one group are often intended to generate effects in the other.

However, although the different types of actor are neither exhaustive nor mutually exclusive, the typology provides a useful ordering of what we believe to be the most influential actors in national conflicts. Thus, as *roles* the four types of actor are sufficiently distinctive to warrant the separate discussion of their influence on the general opinion climate that we now provide.

4.2 Mobilizers

The importance of mobilizers in group formation in order to pursue common interests has long been recognized. Thus, for example, Dahrendorf mentions the need for leaders and founders as an empirical condition in order for conflict groups to emerge from so-called quasi-groups – that is, groups with common interests (1959: 185). In several rational choice theories about group formation, political entrepreneurs have even assumed a central theoretical role. Thus, Frohlich, Oppenheimer and Young suggest that part of the solution to the problem of collective action could be that some individuals might be interested in working for the provision of a collective good for their own career reasons (1971: 18ff; the problem of collective action was presented in Section 3.3 of Chapter 2). Such political entrepreneurs can promote group formation, among other ways by articulating the presumed common interests of the group and a corresponding policy, by organizing and distributing selective incentives, and by facilitating cooperation through organizing meetings etc.

In relation to the influence of mobilizers on the general opinion climate, our focus of attention is both narrower and broader than this list of the tools of a mobilizer. It is narrower because we deal only with mobilizers' articulation of interests, ideas, and policies. And it is broader because we focus on the overall supply of such mobilizers in the nation-group as a whole. Thus, we assume that mobilizers have to compete with other mobilizers over the same constituencies, and more importantly, that the decisions of constituents to support or desert one mobilizer are dependent not only on the constituents' ideal preferences but also on the availability and strength of alternative mobilizers who are either more in agreement with their preferences or more able to fulfil at least some of their preferences.

More precisely, we suggest that the overall political spectrum and distribution of strength between political leaders in the different nation-groups are central to the general opinion climate because they determine the degree of qualified debate about the potential or manifest national conflict. In other words, if most or all leaders have a non-conciliatory stance towards the opposing nation-group, the general opinion climate is malign with respect to processes of escalation, whereas it becomes more benign if critical and more conciliatory leaders are present or even dominant.

4.3 Strategists

Pruitt and Rubin distinguish between five possible strategies that conflicting parties can choose (1986: 25f). Firstly, *contending* means trying to impose one's preferred solution on the other party without regard to that party's interests. Secondly, *yielding* means lowering one's aspirations and settling for less than one would have liked. Thirdly, *problem solving* means pursuing an alternative that satisfies the aspirations on both sides. Fourthly, *withdrawing* means leaving the scene of the conflict permanently. And finally, *inaction* means doing nothing at least for the time being.

In national conflicts, the strategists to be considered are the leaders who take decisions and actions on behalf of the *entire* nation-groups in question. This means that our broad definition of leaders must be somewhat restricted in practice. What matters in relations with the outgroup is the actual actions taken by the ingroup as a whole because the outgroup typically regard the ingroup as a unitary actor, and, in any event, the outgroup is likely to be more interested in the output of the ingroup decision process than in the process and discussions leading to that output.

In relation to an assessment of the general opinion climate, one aspect with regard to strategists is, of course, their choice of strategy and the signals this choice sends to the ingroup. An even more important aspect, however, is how different actions are perceived by the *outgroup*. Thus, for example, if neutral or even conciliatory actions of the strategists of one nation-group are perceived by other nation-groups as expressions or cover-ups of an underlying contentious strategy, this would be an indication that the general opinion climate is malign with respect to processes of escalation.

4.4 Intermediaries

Intermediaries play an important role in the provision and interpretation of the information upon which the members of one nation-group build their attitudes towards and perceptions of other nation-groups. As the mass media are among the most important institutionalized communication channels in modern societies, they are obviously also among the most important intermediaries with respect to national conflicts. However, we should be careful not to overestimate the importance of the mass media in the formation of opinions and beliefs. Firstly, the mass media do not seem to have a very great effect on well-established attitudes (Davison, 1974: 10). And more basically, the mass media are themselves part of the broader community, and they can to some extent be said to mirror the surrounding attitudes and beliefs as well as creating them in their own right (Schlesinger, 1991: 108).

Whether the media mirror or create reality, they are central to the general opinion climate. From the perspective of media as 'mirroring society', they are a direct indicator of the general opinion climate. And, from the perspective of media as 'creating reality', they are central in the formation of the general opinion climate. With respect to this last perspective, we can point to at least two mechanisms by which the mass media have a large *potential* influence on the general opinion climate through their influence on attitudes and perceptions.

Firstly, as soon as the first signs of a conflict appear, the media are likely to cover it because conflict is one of the most important types of news. In this way, the attention of people is focused on the evolving conflict, and under certain conditions this is often enough to promote escalation. Thus, Price (1989: 203f) contends that a news report emphasizing intergroup conflict over an issue cues members of the groups in question to think about the issue through their particular group perspective. This in turn leads to polarized or exaggerated perceptions of group opinions, and finally it leads to expressions of personal opinion consistent with these exaggerated perceptions of group norms. Furthermore, we would suggest that audio-visual coverage by television of open confrontations are especially likely to cue the recipients to think about the conflict and to form biased opinions about it (see Olien, Donohue & Tichenor, 1984: 2, for an American study).

Secondly, to the extent that the mass media are themselves more than normally biased,[67] they are a powerful means to disseminate stereotyped perceptions of other nation-groups, thereby enhancing the prevalence and salience of such perceptions. Furthermore, they can stress economic, political, and cultural deprivations as well as ethnic symbols, a glorious ethnic past, and antagonistic historical relations with other nation-groups that, we know from Part One, can cause national revivals. And finally, by presenting the evolving conflict selectively and in a biased manner, they can create and reinforce negative attitudes and beliefs about the opposing nation-group as well as about the events of the conflict and their reasons.

Thus, in sum, biased mass media are among the prime sources (or expressions) of a general opinion climate that is malign with respect to processes of escalation.

4.5 Activists

Whereas the study of leaders has a long history in social sciences, the role of activists has been less thoroughly examined. Nevertheless, it is far from unrealistic to assume that they play a role with regard to the character of the general opinion climate.

One type of activist that could be expected to influence the general opinion climate is peace groups that strive to enhance international understanding or other grass roots movements with an explicit aim of serving human interests regardless of nationality.

Although we would not dismiss the possible influence of peace groups or, for example, environmental groups, the sad fact is that their ability to reduce escalation is far less than the ability of violent extremists to promote escalation. True, as shown in Part One, general deprivation or frustration of a nation-group can lead to a national revival in order to redress the perceived inequalities. But violent assaults on innocent members of a nation-group with their group membership as the sole justification can contribute directly to the escalation of a national conflict by arousing anger and a call for revenge, especially if the legal system is unable or unwilling to punish the evil-doers (Kim & Smith, 1993: 38f).

As in the case of strategists, the importance of activists with respect to the general opinion climate is not only how their actions themselves are expressions or carriers of the conflict, but also how the actions are perceived by the groups. Of course, the mere presence of extremists does influence the general opinion climate. But if the actions of extremists are taken by the outgroup to be representative of the nation-group in question, the general opinion climate is especially malign.

5 CONCLUSION

This chapter has discussed the processes of escalation that generally accompany intergroup conflicts and the ways in which certain important actors can influence these processes in national conflicts. As in the microsociological chapter (ch. 2) of Part One, we have not deduced hypotheses from the theories presented in this chapter. This time, however, there is both an epistemological and an ontological reason.

The epistemological reason is the same that prevented us from deducing hypotheses in Chapter 2: we simply lack the kind of evidence that is needed to test microsociological hypotheses about the national conflicts in Eastern Europe. To do this, we would need comparative data about, for example, negative beliefs, group cohesion, and community polarization, as well as detailed content analyses of statements by mobilizers and the news coverage of the mass media.

More important, however, is the ontological question about the causal status of any hypotheses that we might deduce on the basis of the processual theories of this chapter. The problem is that even if we could test the hypotheses deduced from the structural change model, not much would be gained in terms of explanatory power because the core of the structural change model is the self-reinforcing consequences of conflict. Thus, even if we could detect a correlation between any of the variables presented above and the degree of escalation, we would not be able to determine which came first – the attitudes, beliefs, norms, polarization, or the escalation itself. In that way we would end up explaining escalation with conflict, and that would be both deterministic and obviously wrong.

Instead, we shall use the concepts presented in this chapter in an exploratory attempt to identify the general opinion climate in Eastern Europe in the late 1980s and early 1990s. More specifically, in Chapter 12 we shall search for escalation-promoting and escalation-reducing traits and actions of the important actors in Eastern Europe in order to assess whether the general opinion climate was benign or malign with respect to processes of escalation. In a way, the concept of a general opinion climate reflects very well the above-mentioned dialectical status of the processes of escalation. Our assertion is that the general opinion climate influences our dependent variable, national conflicts, but at the same time it is, of course, shaped by the actors and events involved in the conflicts.

For the present moment, however, we must search for causal variables that can more unambiguously be identified as antecedents of the escalation of national conflicts in order to gain both more generalizable and more reliable knowledge about the intensity of national conflicts. This is not to say that processes and actors do not matter. On the contrary, they are the very essence of national conflicts (as well as national revivals). The task that we turn to now, however, is to search for general macrosociological patterns that might reasonably be said to constrain the involved actors and provide them with opportunities of action.

11 Explanations of National Conflict Intensity

1 INTRODUCTION

In the preceding chapter we discussed some self-reinforcing processes of escalation that often occur in individuals and groups involved in conflict, and we directed attention to how certain actors of escalation can influence these processes of escalation as well as the context in which they occur. In this chapter, we turn to macrosociological theories that seek to explain the underlying reasons why some national conflicts escalate into violent conflicts while others remain non-violent.

The study of conflict by social scientists has a long and varied history. Conflict has been an immanent element in several classical works, such as those of Machiavelli, Hobbes, Marx, and Weber. As an object of study *per se*, social conflict gained prominence in the 1950s as several authors directed attention to the need for a general theory of social conflict (e.g. Mack & Snyder, 1957; Fink, 1968). Some writers even sought to build a general theory of sociology around the concept of conflict (e.g. Dahrendorf, 1959). Other writers have argued that a general theory of social conflict is not recommendable because true knowledge about a specific instance of conflict lies in the peculiarities of each case. Of special relevance for our study is the variant of the latter argument that war cannot be understood as a result of the same dynamics that pertain to other manifestations of conflict (e.g. Aron, 1957: 180; Singer, 1981: 3).

The present work adopts a middle stance as to the claim of theoretical generality. Because of our focus and theoretical preferences, we narrow down the scope of our investigation by focusing on certain *units*, *modes*, and *sources* of conflict.

Firstly, what we have set out to explain is the intensity of *national* conflicts. This means that our interest is confined to the class of conflicts involving nation-groups as units. It does not mean, however, that general statements about this class are avoided. On the contrary, we believe that a search for generalizable variables that can explain national conflict intensity is needed if we are not to leave this question completely to descriptive and ideographic analyses by historians and journalists. Nor does it mean that insights about social conflict in general are disregarded if they are applicable to national conflicts. Our use of such general insights has already been exemplified by the description of processes of escalation in Chapter 10.

Secondly, even if we assume that generalized knowledge about national conflict intensity is obtainable, the acquisition of such knowledge is compounded by the methodological problem that a proper operationalization of the concept of 'intensity' is very difficult to reach. Ideally, the intensity of specific conflicts should be identifiable on a continuous scale ranging from low to high intensity. However, because the perceptions entering our definition of conflict as 'perceived diverging interests' are difficult to measure, some behavioural measurement of intensity might be more practicable. Having said that, even a confinement to behavioural criteria does not solve the problem of rank ordering of, for example, strikes, demonstrations, and civil disobedience. Because of this problem, we distinguish between only two modes of conflict, namely violent and non-violent, which seems to be the most unambiguous way to distinguish between high- and low-conflict intensity. This does not, however, mean that we agree with the above views of Aron and Singer that war merits explanations that do not pertain to other levels of conflict. On the contrary, we treat the question of violent or non-violent conflict as a matter of degree to be explained by the same underlying variables. This viewpoint has been expressed excellently by Carl von Clausewitz in his famous statement that war is nothing but the continuation of state politics with other means (1966 [1832]: 77).

Finally, we believe that the sources of intergroup conflict, and thus of conflict intensity, should be found at the intergroup level of analysis. In consequence, we accord special importance to the theories presented in this macrosociological chapter. Furthermore, the nature of the sources that in our opinion are most likely to yield generalizable explanations of national conflict intensity are *realistic* as opposed to *non-realistic* (a distinction made by Coser, 1956: 48ff). Realistic sources of conflicts are characterized and caused by opposed means and ends and by incompatibility of values and interests. In contrast, non-realistic sources of conflicts are certain personality traits, displacement of frustrations, and other mainly psychodynamic sources (see Chapters 2 and 10). We do not deny the influence of non-realistic sources on national conflict intensity altogether. But we do assert that *when* non-realistic sources play a part in the escalation, they do so primarily through the processes of escalation described in Chapter 10. And the conflictual interaction involved in these processes of escalation is itself based on the competing interests which are the subject of this chapter.

Thus, in short, we shall in this chapter seek generalizable macrosociological explanations of violent (and non-violent) national conflicts based on the competing interests of the groups involved. We do so firstly by distinguishing between two categories of interest, tangible and intangible, and then by deducing hypotheses about national conflict intensity from theories based on each category of interest. Unfortunately, the focus of most relevant theories is often somewhat different from our interest in national conflict intensity. For example, international relations theory offers explanations of war between *states*, and those theories that deal with national conflicts are often implicit about the *intensity* of them. Therefore, we have adapted both the theories and the hypotheses to the present context.

2 THE CONCEPT OF INTERESTS

Conflict within and between groups has been attributed to real conflicting group interests at least since the writings of Marx, and it has been the predominant approach to social conflict in sociology and political science. Even social psychology, which was for a period preoccupied with nonrealistic sources of conflicts, has, since the work of Muzafer Sherif, acknowledged that realistic sources are vital to an understanding of intergroup conflict. In one of his later volumes, Sherif captures the view that to sociologists and political scientists is often too obvious to merit special treatment:

> What determines the positive or negative nature of interaction between groups? In large part, it is the reciprocal interests of the groups involved and their relative significance to the group in question. The issues at stake between groups must be of considerable concern to the groups, if they are to play a part in intergroup relations. They may relate to values or goals shared by group members, a real or imagined threat to the safety of the group, an economic interest, a political advantage, a military consideration, prestige, or a number of others. (1966: 15)

The relatively long and far from exhaustive list of interests provided by Sherif in this quotation reveals that the concept of interests is so inclusive as to cover a large array of human aspirations. To generate substantial explanations, interest theories must distinguish between different types of interest and then specify which types are most important to the intensity of various conflicts. However, as several reviews make clear (e.g. Mack &

Snyder, 1957; Fink, 1968), there is no general agreement between analysts with respect to either a typology of conflict sources or the role of different sources in the escalation of a conflict. Even without reviews, it is not difficult to imagine that conflicting interests can be categorized as, for example, religious, political, military, ecological, cultural, ideological, and economic, just to mention some.

As a preliminary effort to categorize the various types of interest, we suggest distinguishing between material and profane interests on the one hand, and expressive and sacred interests on the other. Material and profane interests are found in areas such as the economy, politics, and the military. In contrast, expressive and sacred interests are found in areas such as culture, ideology, norms, and values. We shall refer to the former category of interest as tangible interests and to the latter as intangible interests, knowing well that tangibility is often more a question of degree than of categories. Furthermore, although interests of one category that have no connection to interests of the other can probably be found, there are often enough linkages between the categories to make our distinction purely analytical. However, analytical distinctions are exactly what is needed to impose order on a complex reality.

3 TANGIBLE INTERESTS

Theories on national conflict intensity based on tangible interests see violent conflict as an extreme result of groups' competition for scarce resources or physical possessions. Though a lot of variants of this position could be imagined, we shall deduce only two central hypotheses based on tangible interests. The first hypothesis is based on the security interest prominent in international relations theory. The second hypothesis draws on the potential for conflict explanation inherent in the instrumental theories of national revivals presented in Chapter 3. Because the latter set of theories has been extensively discussed in Part One, we shall dwell considerably longer on the former theories.

3.1 Security Interests

The explanation of conflict and war among states has been a preoccupation in international relations theory. This is especially true with regard to the so-called realist school which, in terms of interests, focuses on the basic need for states to secure the physical survival and territorial sovereignty of the state.

3.1.1 Realist International Relations Theory

In order to generate hypotheses about national conflicts from the realist school, we must apply its assumptions about states to nation-groups. Realists assume firstly that states are unitary in the sense that internal disagreements are ultimately resolved so that the state eventually speaks with one voice. Secondly, it is assumed that states are rational in the sense that they choose the best among feasible alternatives to achieve whatever might be their goals. And thirdly, states are seen as preoccupied with questions of national security (Viotti & Kauppi, 1987: 32f).

Traditional realists explained war almost exclusively by reference to attributes of states themselves. Thus, for example, Morgenthau viewed international politics as a struggle for power, and he saw the quest for power as rooted ultimately in the nature of man (1960: 34). In any case, according to Morgenthau, states pursue and use power whenever they can in order to serve their interests or achieve their objectives (p. 27).

This view has been thoroughly revised by the so-called neorealists. Instead of pointing to the intrinsic nature of states, neorealists point to the characteristics of the international system as the central cause of conflict among states. The essential structural quality of the international system is anarchy – that is, the absence of any hierarchy of authority (Waltz, 1979: 102ff). In a state of anarchy, nobody can rely on others to help them serve their interests, however justified these interests might be. Because the anarchic order is a system of self-help, it is not strange that states come to rely on their own power if they want to survive.

Thus, too little power can be fatal to states because it makes them vulnerable to external attacks. But so can too much power. The enhancement of one state's security through an increase of its powers is bound to make other states insecure because the anarchic order offers no guarantee that these powers will not be used aggressively. Consequently, other states will also seek to increase their (military) powers or even launch a pre-emptive attack in order to enhance *their* security, and this again has the similar reciprocal relationship with respect to the security of the former state. In this way, the anarchic international system gives rise to a security dilemma (Herz, 1950: 157ff).

3.1.2 Realist Theory Applied to National Conflicts

The security dilemma stemming from anarchy has recently been applied to national conflicts in Eastern Europe by Posen (1993). Posen argues that the commitment of soldiers is a major determinant of a nation-group's ability to defend itself when it suddenly finds itself responsible for its own security due, for example, to collapse of a previous imperial order (pp. 29f).

Therefore, a national revival on the basis of a strong national identity enhances the power of a nation-group because national identity is one of the main motivating factors for soldiers. And as opposing nation-groups cannot determine whether this power is purely defensive or whether it will be used for offensive purposes, national revivals give rise to security dilemmas. In addition, the identity mobilization of opposing nation-groups is often purposely interpreted as offensive in nature by leaders who strive to mobilize their own nation-groups (p. 31). This fact makes the potential for escalation of national conflicts even greater than for interstate conflicts caused by 'normal' security dilemmas.

The problem for both Posen and other neorealists is that whereas anarchy can account for the general recurrence of war through history, specific wars cannot be explained by anarchy alone.[68] In fact, anarchy and the security dilemma account so well for conflict among states and independent nation-groups that the phenomenon to be explained is rather the periods of stability than those of conflict in the international system. Various explanations of stability have been forwarded by neorealists, but generally they all centre on power and power relations among states as the central variable, just as traditional realist explanations did. More specifically, neorealists propose that the safest way to maintain international peace and stability is for states to join alliances and, by pooling their powers, obtain a balance of power between states or groups of states. Although there is some disagreement among neorealists as to whether the optimal balance of power is obtained in a bipolar or a multipolar world (see Waltz, 1964, versus Deutch & Singer, 1964, for opposing views on this matter), the fact remains that gross imbalances of power can be seen as one of the main factors contributing to war because of the temptations under such conditions for the more powerful to make use of their power if they feel threatened.

The solution offered by Posen to the differing intensity of national conflicts in Eastern Europe is essentially of the same kind. What matters is power. Thus, after the collapse of empires, the emerging nation-groups must calculate their power relative to each other both in the short and the long run (1993: 34f). If the power of a nation-group outweighs the powers of opposing groups in the short run, but if there is risk that the powers will be balanced later, the powerful group will have a great incentive to solve outstanding issues while it is stronger.[69]

3.1.3 Discussion and Deduction of a Hypothesis

Thus, whether we adopt a traditional or a structural realist view, relations between states are ultimately seen as characterized by *Realpolitik* on the basis of distribution and use of power. Imbalances of power are seen as the major cause of wars because more powerful states have incentives to dominate less powerful states if they perceive a threat to their security in the short or the long run stemming from the opposing but less powerful states.

In order to formulate testable hypotheses on the basis of realist international relations theory in general and Posen's application of it in particular, we must make some comments and reservations.

Firstly, we note that the nation-groups involved in national conflicts in Eastern Europe were either far from being the nation-*states* that realists regard as the principal actors in international relations, or they were in an uncertain initial phase of such statehood. Nevertheless, we shall apply the above-mentioned assumptions about states to nation-groups because the lack or inadequacy of state institutions does not necessarily imply that nation-groups are not subject to the same constraints and endeavours that characterize states and their environment. This is ultimately an empirical question to be solved through a test of the hypothesis deduced from the theory.

Secondly, when applied to national conflicts as opposed to conflicts between states, Posen's theory claims to be valid only when central authority has recently collapsed. Of our cases of conflict in Eastern Europe, the conflicts in Estonia, Moldova, and Croatia obviously meet this demand in the period following the collapse of the USSR and the Socialist Federal Republic of Yugoslavia respectively. But the conflict in Czechoslovakia could also be said to have gained renewed possibilities of expression when Gorbachev abandoned the Brezhnev doctrine. Following Buzan's theory of security complexes, the European security complex was, from the Second World War until 1989, characterized by a state of overlay from the global security complex formed by the superpower rivalry (1991: 219f). During this period of overlay, local security concerns were subordinated to the security orientation of the dominating power, and this orientation was reinforced by the stationing of that power's military forces directly within the local complex. When the overlay was lifted, all nation-groups – including the Czechs and the Slovaks – in the East European satellite-states found themselves without the dominant central authority provided by the USSR.

Thirdly, we accept Posen's assertion that a national revival in one group poses a security problem to the opposing nation-group and that this security problem must be solved, if necessary and possible, through the use of force. Thus, an evolving national revival in the opposing nation-group is seen as the prime motivation of the *wish* to use force in a national conflict.[70] Whether this wish is reflected in actual use of force is dependent on whether such use is *feasible*, and this, in turn, is determined by the relative power of the nation-groups in question.

The above simplification that national revivals in opposing nation-groups are the only security concerns covered by the theory raises the question of whether it applies to cases where a national revival occurs only in one of the parties. There are two possible variants of such cases. If a national revival occurs only in the stronger nation-group, the theory would predict non-violent conflict because the weaker group would lack the power to engage in violent conflict. But there is no guarantee, of course, that the stronger nation-group would not use force against the weaker, which it can do at relatively low cost. Precisely because the motivations to use power are purposely simplified in the theory, it would be wrong to reject it on the basis of such instances. The other variant, in which a national revival occurs only in the weaker nation-group so that the stronger has both the wish and the power to engage in violent conflict, could still, however, be used as a test case. For, if the violent conflict predicted in this case fails to manifest itself, the theory should be rejected.

Fourthly, we must specify more clearly what is meant by the central variable that converts a security interest in the light of opposing national revivals into violent conflict. That is, the content of 'power' must be specified. Despite its centrality to realist theory, however, there is no generally accepted definition of the concept. In our view, the optimal definition of power would include objective capabilities within an almost infinite number of realms, such as military, economic, technological, diplomatic, human, societal, and natural resources, *and* the willingness to use these capabilities *as well as* other actors' perceptions and actual acceptance of these capabilities and the willingness to use them. Again, however, we shall simplify matters somewhat. Firstly, we focus only on objective capabilities assuming, as described above, that the willingness to use them is present if a national revival occurs in an opposing nation-group following the collapse of central authority. And secondly, we focus exclusively on military capabilities as violent national conflict naturally must presuppose use of military power above all.

Finally, we must decide which entities are to be examined with respect to military capabilities. Until now we have discussed only nation-groups as if they act independently in each case of national conflict. However, as mentioned earlier, it is central to the realistic balance of power concept that states can pool their powers in order to obtain this balance. Because help sometimes does come from the outside despite the state of anarchy, it would be wrong to consider only the military capabilities of those nation-groups that found themselves within the borders of Estonia, Moldova,

Croatia, and Czechoslovakia. If there is high probability that help would be provided from the outside in the case of violent conflicts, the relevant military capability of each nation-group is comprised of that group's own military capability as well as the amount of help it can rely on from external sources. To narrow down the number of possible alliance partners to be examined, we assume that external help is most likely to come from members of the same mother-nation – that is, from republics, states, and (federal) armies dominated by members of the mother-nation.

On the basis of this discussion we formulate the following hypothesis:

> **H_3** Violent national conflicts result from a security interest to counter threats from opposing nation-groups initiating a national revival in connection with the collapse of a central authority. If a potentially threatening national revival occurs in at least the weaker nation-group under such conditions, a violent national conflict commences if the difference between the military capabilities of the nation-groups is sufficiently great to make use of force feasible.

3.2 Instrumental Interests

The second type of tangible interest that we propose as an explanation of national conflict intensity is rather a group of interests. The hypothesis to be deduced in this section builds on the primary interests identified by instrumentalists as the explanation of national revivals.

3.2.1 Instrumental Theories of National Revivals Applied to National Conflicts

The potential for explaining conflict is inherent in instrumental explanations of national revivals. It will be recalled that, according to instrumentalists, national identity is merely a convenient base on which groups can be mobilized in the competition for scarce resources (see Section 3 of Chapter 3). In other words, national revivals arise simply *because* a prior conflict of interests exists.

At the same time, a national revival serves to intensify the national conflict. If nationalist mobilizers succeed in launching a strong national revival on the basis of an alleged incompatibility of interests between the nation-group in question and other groups, the resulting political movement will intensify the pre-existing conflict in the same way as usual interests groups intensify conflicts by making explicit claims and employing more or less severe sanctions if the claims are disappointed. Thus, a national revival is what makes latent national conflicts manifest. Apart from the effects of a national mobilization, however, instrumentalists are tacit as to what accounts for the degree of national conflict intensity.

3.2.2 Discussion and Deduction of a Hypothesis

There are two central questions in relation to instrumental theories of national revivals that must be answered before we can formulate a hypothesis about national conflict intensity.

The first question has been touched upon above. If a national revival is the mechanism that makes a latent conflict manifest, what then explains why some manifestations of conflict are violent while others remain non-violent? In the answer to this question, we follow the tradition of von Clausewitz (see Section 1). Thus, as noted earlier, we see the level of conflict intensity as a matter of degree depending on the underlying interests of the nation-groups.

We suggest that three properties of the underlying interests are especially important to the level of national conflict intensity. Firstly, a nation-group involved in a national revival must perceive its interests to be incompatible, or *conflicting*, with those of an opposing nation-group. Such perception is inevitable at least towards one other nation-group in so far as it is the condition for a national revival in the first place. However, it does not mean that the nation-group involved in a national revival must necessarily perceive its interests as conflicting with *all* other groups. Whether it does so or not and whether this perception is correlated with a high level of conflict intensity is an empirical question.

Secondly, a national conflict is likely to reach a high level of intensity if *both* nation-groups involved perceive that they have conflicting interests. In this case, both nation-groups should be reluctant to make concessions to their opponents.

Finally, to be willing to endanger lives through the use of force, both parties must perceive to have *strong* conflicting interests. This is the clearest heritage from von Clausewitz: we suggest that the level of conflict corresponds to the strength of interests involved.

The second question to be answered is what exactly counts as instrumental interests? In Chapter 3 we presented three main groups of instrumental explanations relating national revivals to economic, political, and cultural deprivation and frustration. We then noted that proponents of cultural explanations might find themselves uncomfortable in the company of hard-core instrumentalists. The reason why we categorized cultural deprivation and frustration as an instrumental explanation in connection with national revivals is that the instrumental view sees national revivals as an attempt to correct the perceived deliberate deprivation of one nation-group by another also in the cultural sphere. The instrumental focus on the perception of a *present* intolerable situation was contrasted in that chapter with the *historical* emphasis of the primordialists.

In this chapter, however, our main distinction is between tangible and intangible interests, and the need for recognition involved in the cultural instrumental explanation of national *revivals* can hardly be termed a tangible interest when explaining national *conflicts*. Thus, as instrumental interests we consider those identified in Part One in the tests of $H_{2.1}$ and $H_{2.2}$, but not those that appear from the tests of $H_{2.3}$. That is, instrumental interests originate in economic and political deprivation or frustration, and not in cultural deprivation or frustration. More specifically, interests in correcting perceived unfair economic and political deprivations caused by the opposing nation-group (felt colonization) and also interests in preventing future economic and political deprivations caused by the opposing nation-group (feared colonization) count as instrumental interests.

On this basis we formulate the following hypothesis:

H_4 The probability of violent national conflict is high if both nation-groups perceive that they have strong conflicting instrumental interests, that is if they feel or fear economic and political deprivation caused by the opposing nation-group.

4 INTANGIBLE INTERESTS

The concept of intangible interests could be seen as stretching the concept of interests rather far. And, indeed, some writers prefer to reserve the concept of interests to situations of resource scarcity as opposed to value disagreements (e.g. Aubert, 1963: 27ff). Nevertheless, we believe that the concept of intangible interests is not self-contradictory for, as McKay points out, 'besides political and economic interests, humans struggle over *ideal* interests', such as values, moral questions, and other elements of culture (1982: 400; emphasis in the original).

We propose to deduce hypotheses from two types of intangible interests. Firstly, we consider theories that view violent national conflicts as the result of certain types of nationalism, and on the basis of one such theory we deduce a hypothesis linking an ideological interest in implementing a certain type of nationalism to violent national conflicts. Following this, we deduce a hypothesis based on the primordial explanations of national revivals presented in Chapter 3. In the same way as instrumental interests, we propose to conceive of primordial interests and to link these interests to national conflict intensity.

4.1 Ideological Interests

Much theoretical effort has been made to distinguish between different types of nationalism, and some of the resulting typologies have related different types of nationalism to the degree of violence in their wake. Typologies can be based on an almost infinite number of criteria. But if the criteria pertain to the *content* of different types of nationalism, it follows from our definition of nationalism as an ideology (see Chapter 1) that distinguishing between different types of nationalism is synonymous to identifying different ideologies (or different versions of the ideology) of national revivals.

The aim of this section is to formulate a hypothesis about the relationship between certain variants of the ideology of nationalism and national conflict intensity. As a point of departure, we discuss some attempts to relate typologies of nationalism to national conflict intensity.

4.1.1 Typologies of Nationalism Applied to National Conflicts

One of the most extensively employed distinctions between different types of nationalism is that made by Kohn (1955) and Plamenatz (1976) between a Western, rational, liberal version of nationalism and an Eastern, mythical version.[71] These two types of nationalism are seen as having different origins and consequences. The Western type is seen as more benign because it is based on the idea of a social nation that could encompass more than one ethnic group, whereas the Eastern type is inherently less benign because it is based on the idea that only members of one ethnic group should be allowed to live in the nation-group's territory.

Thus, the type of nationalism is linked to the intensity of ensuing national conflicts in a general way. Exactly which aspects of the two types account for the differing consequences is a matter of dispute, though. The disagreements on this point are closely connected to what is seen as the origins of the two types of nationalism. In the following paragraphs we shall discuss two opposing views of these origins: those of Gellner (1983) and Smith (1991).

Gellner maintains the distinction between Western and Eastern nationalism though renaming them 'classical liberal Western nationalism' and '"Habsburg" (and points east and south) nationalism' (1983: 94). Gellner explains nationalism in general as the struggle between two or more cultures to become accepted as a nation-group with the right to form a state and thereby to promote its culture through the education system. Promoting culture through the education system is important because the resulting high-culture then forms the basis of standardized communication within the territory of the state, which is a functional imperative of the industrial society.

The difference between Western and 'Habsburg' nationalism, according to Gellner, is due to differences in access to education among the unprivileged cultures who initiated national revivals in the 19th century. In the West (e.g. Germany and Italy), the national movements could draw on an already codified high-culture, and what was needed was merely a fight to shift the balance of power from the dynasties to the new-born nation-groups. In contrast, Eastern cultures had to fight not only against the power-holders, but also against other low-cultures in order to become *the* cultural basis of a new high-culture.

Thus, according to Gellner, the violent national conflicts in areas where 'Habsburg' nationalism prevailed followed from the struggle of aspirant high-cultures 'to preside, in ferocious rivalry with similar competitors, over a chaotic ethnographic map of many dialects' (1983: 100). In other words, it is the environment of 'Habsburg' nationalists rather than some characteristic qualities or attributes of them that accounts for the tendency towards violent national conflict.[72]

Smith's explanation of this tendency of Eastern nationalism differs from Gellner's both in being more explicit about the content of the two types of nationalism and in pointing to other factors as their origin.

Smith prefers the more neutral and analytical terminology of territorial nationalism (the Western kind) and ethnic nationalism (the Eastern kind) (1991: 79f). Territorial nationalism is inspired by the idea of a civic nation that followed from lateral *ethnies'* bureaucratic incorporation of lower social strata (see Section 2.2 of Chapter 3 for the distinction between lateral and vertical *ethnies*). This view entails a nation with, among other things, legal–political equality of members who have the opportunity to adopt the national culture – and thereby become members – regardless of their ethnicity. In contrast, ethnic nationalism is inspired by the vernacular mobilization of vertical *ethnies*, and in the resulting conception of an ethno-nation members are defined by their descent. It follows that ethnic nationalism tends to be more exclusive than territorial nationalism, and therefore more disagreeable to minorities.

So, the explanation of national conflict intensity following from this view is that intensity will be higher when the state-bearing nation-group exhibits ethnic nationalism because the discrimination towards minorities inherent in ethnic nationalism presumably will lead to greater resistance from minorities caught on the territory of the titular nation-group.

4.1.2 Discussion and Deduction of a Hypothesis

Thus, Gellner and Smith explain the different consequences of the two types of nationalism in two very different ways. Smith talks about the different *conceptions* of a nation following different political processes in late medieval and early modern Europe, and Gellner points to time-specific *functional imperatives* of the industrial society, namely the struggle to become *the* high-culture. To Smith, the consequences are results of ideas, whereas Gellner explains the violent conflicts in Eastern Europe in the 19th century as stemming 'from the inescapable logic of the situation' (1983: 101).

Gellner's focus on the environment rather than the content of different types of nationalism makes his theory unsuitable for our present purposes in two ways. Firstly, it is a major drawback because it limits the explanatory power to the historical period lasting from the introduction of industrial production until the establishment of a high-culture. And as a high-culture in Gellner's definition is established with the introduction of a state-run mass education system, Gellner's theory is of little relevance in explaining the intensity of the national conflicts which have taken place in modern and developed states.

Secondly, by pointing to the functional imperatives of the industrial society as the explanation of the different consequences, Gellner actually dissolves the distinction between Western and Eastern nationalism as a distinction between two different sets of ideas. What matters to Gellner is not the ideology of nation-groups but their material conditions of existence. In other words, Gellner's typology of nationalism is rather a typology of conditions than of content, and his distinction between Western and 'Habsburg' nationalism is therefore ill suited as the basis of a hypothesis about the relationship between national ideology and national conflict intensity.

In contrast, Smith's typology has the advantage of generating general statements about the *content* of different nationalisms, while still linking them to their historical roots. And as statements about the content of nationalism is tantamount to conceiving of national revivals and conflicts as fuelled by a wish to implement certain ideologies, Smith's distinction between territorial and ethnic nationalism is well suited for an ideological hypothesis about national conflict intensity. The ideological interest connected to ethnic and territorial nationalism can, with Smith's terminology, be described as exclusive and inclusive nationalism respectively.

Having chosen Smith's typology as the foundation of a hypothesis about the relationship between the ideologies of nation-groups and national conflict intensity, we must make a few comments before formulating the hypothesis.

Firstly, as mentioned in Chapter 3, Smith focuses on the historical origins of nationalism, and we should therefore not be prejudiced by observations that the first wave of nationalism in Eastern Europe was a result of a vernacular mobilization of vertical *ethnies*. Whether today's nationalism in Eastern Europe is territorial or ethnic must be subject to an empirical analysis.

Secondly, the mechanism through which the type of nationalism influences national conflict intensity essentially depicts an aggressor–defender conflict model (see Section 3 of Chapter 10). It is the ideology of the majority nation-group in each case of conflict that determines whether the minority nation-group is compelled to resistance. More specifically, the exclusive quality of ethnic nationalism in majority nation-groups is seen as increasing national conflict intensity because the minority is assumed to feel threatened by it. Conversely, the inclusive quality of territorial nationalism in majority nation-groups serves to avoid national conflicts or to keep them non-violent because the minority will have few incentives to resist it. Consequently, what needs to be examined is only the dominant ideology of the majority nation-group, as the minority nation-group is expected simply to react to the stimuli presented to it.

Finally, we must decide how to identify the dominant ideology of the majority nation-group. We propose to use the actual actions taken by members of the majority nation-group towards the minority nation-group(s) as an indicator of the underlying ideology. This is perhaps not a direct measure but, in any case, it is reasonable to assume that the actions indicated the majority group's ideology towards members of the minorities.

In other words, we propose to use *policies of nationalism* as a measure of the dominant type of nationalism in the majority nation-group. In a Western context, 'policies' normally refer to the plans of action of a government, thereby making 'policies' an official notion almost by definition. However, in the late-20th-century East European context of collapse of old states (and governments) and building of new states, we believe that unofficial actions should be included if not in the concept itself, then at least as indicators of the dominant ideology of the new state-bearing nation-groups towards their minorities. As indicated by our broad definition of the concept in Chapter 1, we have decided to include these unofficial actions in 'policies of nationalism'.[73]

With these remarks, we can now formulate the following hypothesis:

> **H_5** Violent national conflicts are the result of an ideological interest of the majority nation-group in implementing an ethnic version of nationalism through the adoption of exclusive policies of nationalism towards minority nation-groups. Conversely, the probability of

violent national conflict is low if the ideology of the majority nation-group is territorial nationalism leading to inclusive or neutral policies of nationalism adopted towards minority nation-groups.

4.2 Primordial Interests

In contrast to the above hypothesis which assumes the existence of *different* types of nationalist interest, the theories in this section assume that all national conflicts following from national revivals are expressions of essentially the *same* kinds of interest. The content of these interests is derived primarily from the primordial explanations of national revivals presented in Chapter 3.

4.2.1 Primordial Theories of National Revivals Applied to National Conflicts

Recalling our distinction between strong and moderate primordial explanations of national revivals, there are two corresponding ways to explain national conflicts.

Primordialism in the strong sense explains the seemingly irrational use of violence involved in national conflicts either metaphysically by reference to a wounded *Volksgeist* or age-old, but temporarily suppressed, group hatreds, or biologically by reference to the primordial sentiments of kinship based on the imperatives of natural selection. As we commented in Chapters 2 and 3, however, this version of primordialism is heavily compromised by its inherent determinism. In its logical conclusion, it asserts that the existence of a nation-group must necessarily lead to violent national conflict.

In contrast, primordialism in the moderate sense does not envisage an inevitable clash between opposing nation-groups. On the other hand, moderate primordialism is seldom explicit about what accounts for the differing levels of national conflict intensity. Smith's theory of the origins and consequences of ethnic and territorial nationalism presented above is one attempt to link the ethnic foundation of a national revival – the *ethnie* – to the level of conflict intensity. Smith's solution is to distinguish between different types of *ethnie* whose cultural and historical background made them adopt different versions of the ideology of nationalism.

4.2.2 Discussion and Deduction of a Hypothesis

In our opinion, however, it is not necessary to distinguish between different *kinds* of nationalism to formulate a plausible explanation of the varying intensity of national conflicts. As with regard to instrumental interests, it suffices to distinguish between different *degrees* of the same kinds of national interest.

As a basis for this proposition, we propose to recall the assumptions of social identity theory (presented in Section 3.4.1 of Chapter 2) as well as the quotation by Charles Taylor (in Section 3.3 of Chapter 3). Both of these theories have at their core an assumption that man needs an identity and that this identity can be attached to a group. If this need is interpreted as an interest, we can formulate a hypothesis on the basis of the aforementioned view that violent conflict intensity is a function of interest strength. Thus, the basic proposition of the hypothesis is that if the primordial interests as well as the barriers blocking their realization are felt to be strong enough, then national conflicts can escalate into violence. Furthermore, as in H_4 about instrumental interests, we regard *strong* and *conflicting* primordial interests in *both* groups as contributing to the probability of violent national conflict.

The foundation of our conception of primordial interests is the assumption that individuals need identity and often attach this identity to a group. Before presenting the final formulation of the hypothesis, however, we must specify which properties of this group should be seen as providing for strong primordial interests. We suggest three such properties and, for simplicity, we assume that each of these properties adds in its own right to the strength of perceived primordial interests.

First and foremost, membership of an *ethnie* provides a ready focus of group identity for the individual. Thus, one way for a member of an *ethnie* to enhance his or her self-esteem is to seek recognition of one's *ethnie*. And as an association with a given territory is an integrated part of an *ethnie*, one obvious way to seek this recognition is to strive for a place in the system of nation-states. Just as obvious in this connection, however, is the fact that two *ethnies* cannot use the same territory for this purpose. Thus, the first instance of conflicting primordial interests is present if two strong *ethnies* compete over the same territory.

Secondly, we suggest that present conceptions of group identity are very much informed by the past, both in the form of historical myths and symbols, and in the form of interpretations of present events through analogies with the past. Furthermore, we believe that the historical interplay between two nation-groups serves as an obvious inventory of available analogies from which the present and the prospects for the future can be interpreted. Thus, the second instance of conflicting primordial interests is present if the opposing groups have an antagonistic history of interaction.

Finally, we include as primordial interests those that originate in cultural deprivation or frustration, that is those that can be derived from the tests of $H_{2.3}$. Paralleling the instrumental interests, this means that interests in correcting perceived unfair cultural deprivation caused by the opposing nation-group (felt colonization), and also interests in countering future cultural deprivation caused by the opposing nation-group (feared colonization) count as primordial interests.

The final hypothesis about the relationship between primordial interests and national conflict intensity can be expressed as follows:

H_6 The probability of violent national conflict is high if both nation-groups perceive that they have strong conflicting primordial interests – that is, if both groups 1) are characterized by strong *ethnies* competing for sovereignty in the same territory, 2) have an antagonistic history of interaction, and 3) feel or fear cultural deprivation caused by the opposing nation-group.

5 CONCLUSION

Although national conflict is an almost inescapable concomitant of national revivals, and although as a consequence we should expect a close relationship between national revivals and national conflicts, we are still far from an unequivocal determination of the factors that account for national conflict *intensity*.

The first problem in this respect was encountered in the previous, microsociological chapter. No conflict gains intensity without a preceding process of escalation. And in the process of escalation, a lot of structural changes in individuals, groups, and societies combine to impede solution or de-escalation of the conflict. There are, however, three problems connected with an application of this structural change model in our study. Firstly, due to lack of empirical evidence, we cannot identify the structural changes in the East European populations in any detail. Secondly, the structural changes are as much results as causes of conflict escalation, and therefore even if we could identify them, we would not be able to determine their causal status. And thirdly, even if we assumed that structural changes are causes of escalation, we would still be left with the question why some conflicts escalate while others do not, or, in other words, why structural changes occur in some cases and not in others.

Yet, in the previous chapter we made the first foundation for an examination of the conditions under which structural changes take place during national conflicts. Through the introduction of the concept of a general opinion climate and the presentation of the most influential actors of escalation in national conflicts, we believe that it is possible to attain some impression of the extent to which structural changes have taken place in the society as a whole, as well as of the probability that social events and intergroup contact will be interpreted so as to further or lessen escalation of the national conflict. The analysis of the general opinion climate in our five cases is carried through in the following chapter. Due to the ambiguous causal status of the general opinion climate, however, this analysis can only be an exploratory one.

The foundations for a proper *explanatory* analysis of the causes of national conflict intensity has been developed in this chapter. In our search for antecedents, we have focused on realistic sources of intergroup conflict and this has led us to examine national conflict intensity from an interest perspective. Although it disregards non-realistic sources of conflict, the concept of interests, however, must be limited further in order to generate testable hypotheses. We have done this, firstly, by employing a distinction between tangible and intangible interests. Tangible interests are the material and profane interests found primarily in the realms of economy, politics, and military power, whereas intangible interests are the expressive and sacred interests found in the realms of ideology, culture, and history.

From each category of interests we have then formulated two hypotheses. The first hypothesis in each category has been deduced from existing macrosociological theories of conflict. H_3, which sees national conflict intensity as the result of the security interests of the nation-groups involved, is inspired by realist international relations theory and in its concrete formulation it has been deduced from Posen's theory of ethnic conflicts (1993). Likewise, H_5, which sees national conflict as the result of the ideological interest of the majority nation-group, is inspired by a common typology of nationalism and in its concrete formulation it has been deduced from Smith's theory of nationalism (1991).

The two following hypotheses in each category are, in fact, based on macrosociological theories of national revivals. The notions of instrumental interests in H_4 and primordial interests in H_6 relate to the theories presented in Part One about the causes of national revivals rather than to national conflicts. To convert the existing theories of national revivals into theories of national conflict intensity, we must adapt them, firstly, by specifying which properties of nation-groups should count as instrumental or primordial interests and, secondly, by specifying which properties of instrumental or primordial interests account for violent national conflict. As for the first specification, we have pointed to felt or feared economic and political colonization as tangible, instrumental interests, whereas felt or feared cultural colonization, as well as strong *ethnies* competing for sovereignty in the same territory and an antagonistic history of interaction between the *ethnies*, count as primordial interests. The second specification of the properties of the interests relevant to national conflict intensity has been solved in three steps. Firstly, the instrumental or primordial interests must be perceived as conflicting with the interests of the opposing nation-group in question. Secondly, this must be so for both nation-groups involved in a particular national conflict. And thirdly, we draw on von Clausewitz when we suggest that the intensity of the conflict corresponds to the strength of the involved interests.

As in Part One, the theoretical chapters in this part have not given the answers to all questions pertaining to national conflict intensity. What we have done so far is to provide the necessary theoretical elements for an analysis of the consequences of nationalism in Eastern Europe. How the different elements – particularly the microsociological and macrosociological ones – relate to each other is discussed in the conclusion of Part Two. At that point, we have the advantage of the empirical results of the analysis which can be used to develop an integrative model of the causes of national conflict intensity.

Until then, however, the empirical evidence in each case must be analyzed in depth. We do this in Chapter 12 through an exploratory analysis of the general opinion climate in the countries of Eastern Europe. Then, in Chapters 13 to 16 we turn to a detailed search for the explanations of the differing intensity of the national conflicts in each of our cases. This search is based on the hypotheses deduced in this chapter. Finally, in Chapter 17 we compare the results of the analyses and use this as a point of departure for a further discussion of the above-mentioned theoretical questions.

12 The Conflict Climate in Eastern Europe

1 INTRODUCTION

Before we turn to a detailed examination of the explanations of national conflict intensity, we shall in this chapter explore the context in which the national conflicts in Eastern Europe developed. Our purpose is to determine whether some generalizable statements about the general opinion climate in Eastern Europe can be made. More precisely, we will assess whether the presence, support, and influence of important actors of escalation affected the general opinion climate in directions benign or malign with respect to the processes of escalation presented in Chapter 10. Or, in other words, we examine whether a conflict climate was prevalent in the late 1980s and early 1990s in Eastern Europe.

This chapter bears certain resemblances to the exploratory analysis in Chapter 4 in that it applies microsociological concepts and assumptions in an attempt to assess the context of the dependent variable. Yet, it differs in some important respects. Firstly, Chapter 4 used microsociological theories to generalize about factors conducive to national revivals on the basis of *general* observations about national movements and Eastern Europe in the late 20th century. In contrast, this chapter seeks generalization on the basis of *specific* empirical examples drawn from the nation-groups and countries under investigation. Secondly, Chapter 4 described externally inherited or initiated constraints and opportunities such as concrete social changes (e.g. *perestroyka*) and social organization (e.g. the power and legitimacy of the nation-state and the principle of national self-determination). In contrast, this chapter analyses the more diffuse concept of a general opinion climate which can be described as internally generated constraints and opportunities in the form of social moods and popular attitudes. Thus, apart from serving their individual purposes in each part of this book, Chapter 4 and the present chapter also have a complementary relationship with regard to the necessary description of the social context in which the national revivals and national conflicts in Eastern Europe took place. They are complementary both in the sense that Chapter 4 analyses the influence of real social changes and social organization whereas this chapter analyses the influence of more evasive social moods and dispositions, and in the sense that Chapter 4 adopts a top-down approach in the analysis whereas this chapter adopts a bottom-up approach in focusing explicitly on the important actors in specific nation-groups.

As the main frame for the analysis we examine the four types of important actors of escalation presented in Chapter 10. For each type of actor, we look first at the occurrence and support of actors who can be assumed to have influenced the general opinion climate in ways that were malign with respect to processes of escalation. Then we go on to examine whether such actors were balanced or perhaps even outweighed by actors who took a more conciliatory stance in the national conflicts. Finally, we assess the net effect of each type of actor on the general opinion climate in Eastern Europe.

2 THE MOBILIZERS IN EASTERN EUROPE

In this section we shall assess the political spectrum and the distribution of strength between the various leaders in the nation-groups in Eastern Europe. Firstly, we examine the occurrence, support, and influence of leaders who mobilized by espousing an exclusive conception of nationalism and, thus, had a non-conciliatory stance towards the opposing nation-group. Then we go on to examine to what extent such leaders were balanced or outweighed by leaders with an inclusive conception of nationalism (if they espoused nationalism at all) and a conciliatory attitude towards the opposing nation-group.

2.1 Non-Conciliatory Leaders

At first glance, it seems as if non-conciliatory leaders were clearly dominating the East European political scenes.

In the case of Estonia, Estonian leaders seeking to mobilize on the basis of exclusive Estonian political programmes gradually came to dominate the political life as the Estonian national revival progressed. In the pre-independence period, nationalist parties such as the Estonian National Independence Party played an oppositional role *vis-à-vis* the more moderate PFE which took over governmental power in the spring of 1990 (Nørgaard, 1994: 79ff). Nevertheless, these parties clearly influenced the opinion climate in a direction malign to processes of escalation. For instance, they arranged elections to an alternative parliament, the so-called Estonian Congress, in which only pre-1940 citizens and their descendants could participate (Taagepera, 1993: 174f). Following the achievement of independence, new nationalist parties such as those in the coalitions Pro Patria and Secure Homeland were added, and the influence of the leaders of these parties grew even larger as they won the 1992 elections and then formed a majority coalition government (Lieven, 1993: 285).

As for the leaders of the Russian minority in Estonia, those with a non-conciliatory attitude towards the Estonians were preponderant in the pre-independence period. Thus, the leaders of the Intermovement and the closely related UCWC and UWC organizations, who sought to mobilize the Russians to support the goal of preserving status quo, were the dominant Russian political force in Estonia in that period (Ilves, 1991: 72f).

In Moldova, too, practically all of the political leaders of the titular nation-group took up a non-conciliatory position towards the Russian and Gagauz minorities in the pre-independence period. Besides the dominating PFM, several small movements were founded (Socor, 1992i: 5). However, they all belonged to the so-called national bloc led by the PFM, and all sought to mobilize the Moldovans by espousing specifically Moldovan goals.

In the two break-away regions, the majority of the leaders also adopted non-conciliatory positions towards the Moldovans. Thus, paralleling the demands forwarded by the Russian leaders in Estonia in the pre-independence period, they demanded that Moldova remained a part of the USSR and that most of the reform laws were nullified (Socor, 1992a: 43).

Turning to Croatia, the CDC became the dominating Croatian political force following the elections in the spring of 1990 as the CDC, in coalition with five small parties, won a majority of the seats in the parliament and subsequently formed a majority government (Andrejevich, 1990b: 41). The leaders of the CDC consistently stressed the primacy of Croatian interests in relation to the Serbian minority (Cohen, 1993: 96ff). Thus, a favourite theme of the CDC leader, Tudjman, was the affirmation of Croatian identity and sovereignty and complaints about Serbian over-representation in, for example, the Croatian media.

Regarding the Serbian minority, the SDP emerged as the principal voice of the Serbs. The attitude of the leaders of the SDP towards the Croats was strongly non-conciliatory. Thus, SDP leader, Rašković, stated that the Serbian minority would never accept a separation of Croatia from Yugoslavia as they did not want to be left at the mercy of the Croatian majority (pp. 130f).

Finally, in Czechoslovakia the majority of the Slovakian parties that competed in the 1992 elections had nationalist agendas and demanded either a further weakening of the federal institutions or an independent Slovakia (Pehe, 1992b: 25). Furthermore, following the election victory of the MDS and SNP, leaders with a non-conciliatory stance towards the Czechs also took over governmental power in Slovakia.

2.2 Conciliatory Leaders

Although non-conciliatory leaders were the most conspicuous in Eastern Europe, some conciliatory leaders did influence the general opinion climate.

In Estonia, the PFE actually took up a relatively conciliatory position towards the Russians in the pre-independence period. Thus, Savisaar, the leader of the PFE-dominated government, was a consistent advocate of compromise with the Russian minority (Lieven, 1993: 277).[74] However, in the first post-independence elections held in 1992, the PFE won only 15 per cent of the seats and consequently became a less influential opposition party (Nørgaard, 1994: 82). Thus, Estonian leaders with a conciliatory attitude were present throughout the Estonian–Russian conflict. But their numbers and influence gradually decreased.

Only after Estonian independence had become a reality did a moderate Russian political force appear in Estonia. It was the Russian Democratic Movement whose leaders stressed their loyalty to the new Estonia (Lieven, 1993: 281). By way of negotiations the leaders of this movement tried to make the best of the situation for the Russians. Thus, in contrast to the development among the Estonian leaders, the number and influence of Russian leaders with a conciliatory attitude was initially very low but then gradually rose.

Also in contrast to the situation in Estonia, leaders of the titular nation-group in Moldova with a conciliatory stance primarily appeared after the achievement of independence – and in particular after the failed attempt to prevent the Dnestr republic from seceding by means of force. Thus, an increasing portion of those Moldovan parliamentary deputies who were elected in the spring of 1990 switched to a more moderate position during the post-independence period – that is, after August 1991 (Socor, 1992i: 5ff). In November 1992 this process resulted in the formation of a so-called government of national consensus which was more willing than the former to offer the break-away regions substantial autonomy. However, it is important to note that the Moldovan leaders with a conciliatory attitude prevailed only after the escalation of the conflict when the non-conciliatory strategy had proven futile to the Moldovan aims.

As among the Russians in Estonia, moderate Slavic leaders appeared only after the establishment of Moldovan independence. However, these moderates, who had formed the movements Democratic Moldova and

Accord, were only present in Moldova proper where they sought to further the interest of those Russians who did not live in the Dnestr republic (Socor, 1992a: 43). Thus, a moderate Russian opposition eventually appeared in Moldova as well. But its influence on Moldovan–Slavic relations was relatively weak as it was not paralleled by an opposition in the Dnestr republic where the hard-line leaders continued to dominate unabated.

As for the leaders of the Gagauz minority, the situation was different because a moderate opposition, the CM, existed from the outset of the Gagauz national revival (Cavanaugh, 1992: 12). And although the CM remained in opposition, this was an important difference compared with the situation in the Dnestr republic.

In Croatia several parties involved in the spring 1990 elections – in particular the CLC, which at that time had added 'Party of Democratic Change' to its name – did not espouse explicit nationalist viewpoints (Andrejevich, 1990a: 34ff). However, due to electoral defeat, these parties were reluctant to continue arguing for the preservation of a federated Yugoslavia and the protection of civil rights irrespective of nationality. Thus, in the period leading up to the outbreak of full-scale war in the late summer of 1991, a moderate Croatian opposition did exist but its political influence was relatively small.

In the Serbian minority in Croatia, a few politicians did not firmly oppose the new nationalist Croatian leadership. In contrast to the deputies of the SDP who boycotted the work of the Croatian parliament, some of the Serbian deputies of the CLC continued to attend the sessions and tried to build a bridge of confidence between the two nation-groups (Andrejevich, 1990c: 40f). However, the SDP launched a campaign against these deputies, labelling them traitors of the Serbian cause, and due to this they gradually lost their support from the Serbian minority.

Finally, as regards Czechoslovakia, the Czech leaders differed from the leaders of the other nation-groups as virtually all of the Czech politicians had a conciliatory attitude towards the Slovaks. While opting for the preservation of Czechoslovakia, they were ready to go a long way to fulfil the Slovakian demands for more autonomy. For example, almost all Czech politicians voted for the constitutional amendment in December 1990 according to which the federal government was to cede many of its powers to the republican governments (Pehe, 1990c: 6).

Among the Slovakian politicians, relatively many had a conciliatory attitude towards the Czechs in the first months after the Velvet Revolution. Thus, during the election campaign preceding the June 1990 elections, not a single Slovakian politician argued that Slovakia should take steps in the direction of secession (Pehe, 1991f: 12). However, in the ensuing period, the number of Slovakian politicians who adopted a non-conciliatory attitude towards the Czechs grew so much that they became a majority.

2.3 Preliminary Conclusion

The general picture emerging from the above analyses is that leaders with a conciliatory attitude towards the outgroup did exist in all of the nation-groups. However, with the exception of the Czech leaders and the Moldovan leaders after the failed war with the Slavs, leaders with a conciliatory attitude were in a minority. Furthermore, it seems likely that if the leaders of merely one of two opposing nation-groups mobilize on the basis of non-conciliatory viewpoints, an opinion climate malign to processes of escalation is created. Consequently, we conclude that a decisive part of the mobilizers in our cases of national conflict influenced the opinion climate in a direction malign to processes of escalation.

3 THE STRATEGISTS IN EASTERN EUROPE

We now turn to an assessment of the general opinion climate from another angle. The focus will be on whether those leaders who were in a position to act on behalf of the ingroup towards the outgroup chose a contending or a non-contending strategy. The influence of strategists on the general opinion climate is, of course, mediated by the outgroup's perception of their actions. Therefore, we include an examination of how the nation-groups reacted to actions directed towards them by leaders of the opposing nation-group. In this connection it is not so interesting to examine reactions to contentious strategies as a nation-group subject to such strategies presumably reacts negatively. Instead, we concentrate on how non-contentious actions were perceived by the outgroups. If such actions were perceived as cover-ups of an underlying contending strategy, it is a clear indicator of an opinion climate conducive to processes of escalation.

3.1 Contending Strategies

The choice of a contending strategy seemed to be the norm rather than the exception among leaders of nation-groups in Eastern Europe in the late 1980s and early 1990s. Yet, it is possible to distinguish between those leaders who persistently chose the contending strategy and those who chose it only at particular times.

Among the majority national leaders, the Estonian leaders belonged to the first category. In the period preceding the August 1991 unilateral declaration of independence, they sought to impose the option of independence, paying only little attention to the interests of the Russian minority. Thus, the demands of the Intermovement were largely neglected (Hosking, 1992: 190f). And having achieved independence they continued to neglect the demands of the Russians by adopting a range of discriminatory laws (see Section 5 of Chapter 13).

The Croatian leaders also consistently pursued a strategy of contending towards the Serbian minority. Neither during nor after the pre-independence period were they willing to compromise with the Serbs' demand for autonomy (see Section 2 of Chapter 15).

Among the national leaders of the minority nation-groups, the Slavic leaders in Moldova and the Serbian leaders in Croatia also stuck to a contending strategy throughout the conflicts. Both sets of leaders wanted to preserve the status quo without regard to the interests of the titular nation-groups. As they were not able to prevent the secessions of the titular nation-groups, they took unilateral steps in order to establish independent state-like formations.

Except for the Czech leaders, the rest of the national leaders chose a contending strategy at some point during the national conflicts. Thus, the Moldovan leaders pursued a strategy of contending towards the Russian minority until the failed attempt of preventing the Dnestr republic from seceding by violent means, and towards the Gagauz minority until some months after the Gagauz leaders had declared a separate Soviet republic in their area. Likewise, the Russian leaders in Estonia chose a contending strategy in the pre-independence period, the Gagauz leaders chose the same strategy until they decided to participate in negotiations with the Moldovan government on the future status of their region, and the Slovakian leaders did so as they repeatedly threatened to take unilateral steps towards secession if the Czech leaders did not comply with their demands for more autonomy.

3.2 Non-Contending Strategies

Some, albeit few, leaders in Eastern Europe did adopt non-contending strategies. This was most evident in the case of Czechoslovakia.

In the period between the November 1989 Velvet Revolution and the partition of Czechoslovakia by January 1993, the Czech leaders chose a strategy of yielding almost all the time. Although their professed goal was a strong and centralized federation, they lowered their aspirations and gave in to the Slovakian demands for more autonomy. However, following the June 1992 elections, the majority of both the Czech and Slovakian leaders shifted to a problem-solving strategy as they pursued an alternative – Czech and Slovakian independent states – which by then satisfied the aspirations of both sides.

The Moldovan leaders also chose a strategy of yielding towards the Gagauz as they eventually accepted the Gagauz demand for autonomy, thereby giving up the original goal of establishing a unitary state. For their part, the Gagauz leaders also shifted to the yielding strategy as they accepted the autonomy option instead of the option of being a separate unit belonging to the CIS or Russia.

Finally, the leaders of the Russian minority in Estonia – except for those in Narva who tried in vain to gain support of a declaration of independence of the north-eastern part of the country – also chose a yielding strategy as they accepted Estonian independence and simply strived to secure the interests of the Russians as well as possible by way of negotiation.

3.3 Reactions to Non-Contending Actions

Although they were not particularly widespread, conciliatory actions or proposals were sometimes agreed upon by the leaders of the opposing nation-groups.

For example, in January 1991 the Moldovan parliament considered a law on local self-government according to which a special Gagauz county was to be created in the southern part of the republic (Cavanaugh, 1992: 14f). However, the dominant GP rejected that proposal. In May 1991 the oppositional CM then launched a proposal which implied a somewhat larger degree of autonomy (*ibid.*). Yet, the Moldovan parliament's Commission on Human Rights and Nationality Affairs and on Local Self-Government considered the proposal for a year before finally rejecting it.

The case of Croatia provides another example. In July 1990 the leader of the CDC, Tudjman, met with the leader of the SDP, Rašković. During this meeting, Tudjman indicated that Croatia's Serbs could achieve cultural autonomy (Andrejevich, 1990b: 41f). However, the proposition was made too late and the Serbian side was not convinced of its credibility. Instead, the Serbs arranged a referendum on Serbian territorial autonomy in the following month.

In both instances, otherwise non-contending actions were perceived as ill intended. This was probably due to a profound mistrust between the nation-groups, and this is yet another evidence of an opinion climate malign with respect to processes of escalation.

3.4 Preliminary Conclusion

The above analyses show that the choice of a contending strategy was indeed more frequent than the choice of non-contending strategies among the leaders of the nation-groups in Eastern Europe. This indicates that the general opinion climate was not particularly benign with respect to processes of escalation. Furthermore, the refusal of the leaders of the opposing nation-groups to accept conciliatory proposals also substantiates the malign character of the prevailing opinion climate.

4 THE INTERMEDIARIES IN EASTERN EUROPE

During the period of communist rule in Eastern Europe, the mass media were controlled by the party and state apparatus. Consequently, the media primarily functioned as a mouthpiece of the communist regimes. And as issues pertaining to nationalism were tabooed, it was very difficult for journalists – if they so wished – to influence perceptions of, for example, national identity.[75] Therefore, it was only with the gradual lifting of censorship in the second half of the 1980s (see the sections on the triggering factors in Chapters 5 to 8) that the media potentially could play a role in the national revivals and conflicts.

Our survey of the media landscape in Eastern Europe in that period firstly assesses the prevalence of nationalist-biased media. Then we examine the extent to which such media were balanced by others which strived to act as neutrals *vis-à-vis* the opposing nation-groups.

4.1 Nationalist Mass Media

Concerning the mass media in Croatia, the findings of a content analysis of selected Croatian and Serbian newspapers covering the period from August 1991 to January 1992 is telling. The analysis examined whether the media used value-laden (e.g. 'aggressor', 'Chetnik', or 'Ustasha') or neutral (e.g. 'armed citizens' or 'territorial defence forces') characterizations when referring to the other side of the conflict (Malesic, 1993: 73ff). The main conclusion drawn from the analysis was that over time the frequency of neutral characterizations decreased while the frequency of value-laden characterizations increased, resulting in an overall dominance of the latter. The study also concluded that the causal explanations of the conflict offered by the media were clearly biased (p. 32).[76]

In the other cases of conflict no content analyses are available. Therefore, we must rely on evaluations made by outside observers. Thus, analysing the media in Moldova, one observer stated that, following the election victory of the PFM in the spring of 1990, adherents of the PFM made up a relatively large proportion of the staffs of the Moldovan-speaking media (Socor, 1992g: 77ff). This meant that pro-PFM leanings were often evident in the treatment of the news, in the tone of the commentaries, and in the selection of opinion articles by outside contributors. Also, a profusion of materials on the national history and culture of Moldova was published in the media (Socor, 1991a: 25). On the other hand, the contents of the Russian- and Gagauz-speaking media were biased by a blend of Soviet ideology and Russian or Gagauz nationalism (p. 80).

In Estonia, most of the printed media formally declared their independence in relation to political interests following the abolishment of the censorship system in 1989 (Lauristin & Vihalemm, 1991: 99f). This was clearly a reaction to the, until then, so pervasive interference in the workings of the media by the CPE and the CPSU. Nevertheless, practically all of both the Estonian- and Russian-language media became involved in the ongoing national conflict (*ibid.*). Another observer analysing the media in Estonia concluded that in the majority of the Estonian language media, the analyses were often simplistic, demagogic, and anti-Russian (Kionka, 1992c: 63f). And with respect to the Russian language media, pro-Soviet and pro-Russian attitudes prevailed (*ibid.*).

As for Czechoslovakia, one observer noted that very few journalists were able to stand above politics and not let a particular ideology influence their reporting which was often incomplete and biased (Pehe, 1992c: 34ff). In Slovakia, a large number of journalists were reported to support Mečiar, the leader of PAV and later of the MDS. In the spring of 1992 some of these journalists founded an association called For the True Picture of Slovakia. As for the electronic media, republican radio and television companies were established in early 1991 due to demands from Slovakian politicians. Thus, Mečiar and other nationalist politicians claimed that the federal television and radio were hostile to Slovakia's efforts to achieve autonomy (p. 37). And the establishment of republican electronic media without doubt enhanced the probability of biased media coverage.

4.2 Neutral Mass Media

It is, nevertheless, possible to detect a few countervailing tendencies in the East European media landscape. Starting with Croatia, a Croatian language press in opposition to the CDC government did exist. In particular, the newspapers *Globus* and *Danas* tried to take a neutral stand regarding the evolving national conflict, for example by pointing out violations of human rights committed by both sides in the conflict (Malesic, 1993: 43). However, as the conflict escalated into full-scale war during the autumn of 1991, both newspapers officially distanced themselves from their previous neutral approach.

In Estonia and Moldova, the governments tried to counter the prevailing tendency for the Russian minorities primarily to receive information from pro-Russian mass media, including those based in Russia. Thus, one of the channels of each of the Estonian and Moldovan republican radio continued to broadcast only in Russian (Socor, 1992g: 81; Nørgaard, 1994: 198f). However, although Russian journalists produced the programmes, there were limits as to how critical they could be because their programmes were submitted to control before being released (*ibid.*).

In Czechoslovakia, despite the biased attitude of most journalists regarding the evolving Czech–Slovakian conflict, some journalists strived to remain neutral. Thus, editors of several leading Slovakian newspapers complained about government efforts to limit their independence, especially following the formation of the MDS–SNP coalition government in June 1992 (Pehe, 1993: 87f). The background was that prime minister Mečiar had called for a so-called ethical self-regulation of journalists in accordance with the interests of Slovakia and had threatened to punish those newspapers that did not tell the truth. Also, the leadership of Slovakian television protested against government efforts to intimidate them to report pro-government and pro-Slovakian viewpoints. However, Mečiar pursued his media policy unaffected, and in October 1992 Slovakian television officials on the media supervisory board opposed to Mečiar lost their jobs, and followers of the prime minister were elected instead.

4.3 Preliminary Conclusion

Summing up the above analyses, the majority of the mass media in Eastern Europe in the late 1980s and early 1990s became entangled in the politics of nationalism as biased editorials and news coverage were widespread. Thus, the media probably both reflected and influenced the nationalist attitudes and interests of the opposing nation-groups, thereby contributing to the formation of an opinion climate which was conducive to processes of escalation.

5 THE ACTIVISTS IN EASTERN EUROPE

Activists operating independently in relation to the leaders of nation-groups make up another group of actors which could influence the general opinion climate in Eastern Europe. In this section, we examine the occurrence of violent extremist groups and peace groups in our cases of national conflict. Furthermore, we try to assess how the actions of these groups were perceived by the opposite nation-group.

5.1 Violent Extremist Groups

Although violent extremist groups existed all over Eastern Europe, there were large differences with regard to their prevalence as well as the number and character of their actions.

In Estonia a few Estonian extremist anti-Russian groups appeared in the course of the conflict with the Russian minority. The most conspicuous was the so-called Defence Union, a civil militia formed in May 1990 (Kionka, 1992b: 34ff). Yet, throughout the conflict, members of the Defence Union only engaged in violent actions a few times during the summer of 1992.[77] As a result of the Defence Union members' efforts to restrict the movements of the Soviet forces still stationed in Estonia, incidents involving exchange of fire occurred. However, no casualties were reported. As for other extremist groups, none of them used violent means. For example, an organization named the Estonian Decolonization Fund was formed in February 1993 (Girnius, 1994a: 7f). The publicly stated goal of the organization was to make as many Russians as possible leave for Russia. To achieve this end, the organization raised funds in order to assist Russians who were willing to leave the country.

From the Russian side, only very few incidents of violence against Estonians committed by extremists occurred. Among these, the most serious happened immediately after the failed Moscow coup when a bomb attack on the headquarters of the Estonian Home Guard seriously wounded one Estonian (Lieven, 1993: 198).

In Moldova the situation was different. Moldovan, Slavic, and Gagauz extremist volunteers and paramilitary units all played a significant role during the conflicts. But for their part, the Moldovan extremists reacted strongly against the Slavic and Gagauz declarations of independence. For example, when in October 1990 the Gagauz leaders arranged elections to a Gagauz national parliament, several thousand Moldovans headed for the Gagauz region to try to prevent the elections from taking place (Cavanaugh, 1992: 13f). Due to the interference of Moldovan police forces and troops from the USSR Ministry of Internal Affairs, violent clashes were prevented. However, the intentions of the Moldovan volunteers were not easily misunderstood as they shouted slogans such as 'Moldovans, to arms' and 'Never yield an inch of Moldovan land' (*ibid.*).

Among the Slavs and Gagauz, numerous paramilitary groups appeared in connection with the secessions. Yet, it is rather difficult to determine to what extent the local Slavic and Gagauz authorities controlled these units. However, they were most probably not fully controlled in the initial phase when the local authorities were still consolidating their power in the regions. Thus, the Dnestr authorities were reported to have arrested volunteers on several occasions for having disobeyed military orders (Kolstø et al., 1993: 987). Anyway, while the Gagauz paramilitary units only engaged in relatively few violent actions towards Moldovans, the Slavic units were very active.[78] In the period preceding the outbreak of full-scale war in the spring of 1992, the paramilitary units gradually seized police stations, administrative bodies, and local newspapers in the Dnestr region and forced the Moldovan police officers and officials to leave (Socor, 1992b: 9f).

In Croatia, the prevalence and activities of violent extremists were even more conspicuous. Among the Croatian extremist groups, the Croatian Defence Forces (CDF), which were the paramilitary branch of the Croatian Party of Historical Rights (CPHR), were dominant (Moore, 1994: 80ff). The CDF attracted young militants who were eager to fight for Croatia. Besides members of CPHR, these also included members of strongly anti-Serbian, neofascist organizations such as the Ustasha Youth and the Black Legion. Neither before nor during the large-scale fightings in the autumn of 1991 did the Croatian government fully control the actions of the CDF. During the war, the volunteers of the CDF fought more fiercely and aggressively than the conscripts of the Croatian army. Furthermore, they openly claimed to take up the legacy of the Croatian Ustasha units which operated during the Second World War.

On the Serbian side, violent extremist groups also played a very active role. Even before the outbreak of the war, Serbian irregulars were involved in several incidents. For example, in May 1991 Serbian irregulars from the village Borovo Selo opened fire on Croatian policemen as the latter broke an agreement not to enter the village (Glenny, 1992: 75ff). The clash led to the death of 12 Croatian policemen and three Serbs. Furthermore, the Serbian Krajina extremists were joined by members of a host of paramilitary organizations from Serbia proper (Markotich, 1994: 95f). With names such as the White Eagles, the Knights and the Chetniks, the Serbian extremist groups also evoked memories of atrocities committed during the

Second World War. And during the war in the autumn of 1991, history repeated itself as both Croatian and Serbian extremists committed atrocities against civilians in particular and conducted campaigns of ethnic cleansing. As for the question of independence *vis-à-vis* the national leaders, the local Serbian extremists were brought under the command of the Serbian Krajina authorities as full-scale war broke out in July 1991, while the extremist units from Serbia proper were put under YPA control in December that year (Gow, 1992: 21ff).

Turning to Czechoslovakia, the situation was more similar to that in Estonia than those in the two other cases. Although a few Czech radical nationalist groups, such as neo-Nazis and skinheads, emerged in the post-1989 period, their political influence remained limited (Pehe, 1994: 50ff). Furthermore, the activities of these groups, primarily demonstrations but also some cases of violent attacks, were directed against Romanies, Jews, and foreigners from developing countries – not against Slovaks.

In Slovakia, a number of extremist groups similar to those in the Czech lands appeared after the Velvet Revolution (Fisher, 1994: 68ff). The aggressions of these groups were directed against the same targets – not against the Czechs. However, in addition to these, Slovakian nationalist groups espousing explicit anti-Czech attitudes were also formed, for example the Stefanik Legion, the Slovakian National Unity Party, and the Association of Jozef Tiso.[79] Yet, only on very few occasions did the supporters of these groups act directly aggressively towards Czechs. For example, president Havel was intimidated and jostled when he appeared at a rally organized in March 1991 to commemorate the anniversary of the founding of the Slovakian semi-independent state at the beginning of the Second World War (Pehe, 1991e: 5).

5.2 Peace Groups

Peace groups and similar grass roots movements seeking to establish trust and conciliation were not completely absent in Eastern Europe. In Slovakia, for example, the Young Democratic Left and the Slovakian Union for Peace and Human Rights called for an end to racism, intolerance, and nationalism (Fisher, 1994: 71). However, some of the groups which allegedly pursued pacifist goals in fact also harboured other goals. In Moldova, for example, the Christian-Democratic Women's League and the Organization of the Democratic Youth repeatedly arranged anti-military demonstrations where demands such as the immediate abolition of conscription and the transformation of Moldova into a demilitarized zone were forwarded (Socor, 1990b: 20f). Yet, the demonstrations were in fact protests against the presence of Soviet 'occupation forces' in Moldova and against the continued obligation of young Moldovans to serve in the USSR armed forces.

Besides the relatively few and small peace groups, other groups appeared with the apparent aim of serving general human interests. Among these, ecological movements were the most widespread. However, they rarely functioned as bridge-builders between the opposing nation-groups. In Estonia, for example, the Green Movement protested against the still worsening state of the environment in the republic (Taagepera, 1993: 120ff). Yet, the issue of the environment was closely connected to that of nationalism as only the ministries of the Soviet centre were blamed for the environmental problems. Phosphorite mining, for example, was perceived as a typical case of colonial exploitation and as just another pretext for bringing more Russian 'colonists' into Estonia.

5.3 Preliminary Conclusion

The prevalence and activities of the extremist groups were, thus, far from matched by peace groups in our cases of national conflict – in particular in Croatia and Moldova. Furthermore, there is little doubt that the mere presence of extremist groups contributed to an opinion climate malign to processes of escalation. And when the actions of the extremists were intensively covered by the mass media, this effect was most probably multiplied.[80] With respect to the question of how the actions of the extremists were perceived by members of the opposite nation-group, we have no empirical evidence. However, we assume that the opposing nation-groups in Moldova and Croatia were most likely to perceive the actions of the extremists as representative of the intentions of the nation-groups as such because the extremists were numerous and played a relatively big role during those conflicts.

6 CONCLUSION

The individuals' interpretation of reality, opinion formation, decision-making, and actions are all to some – often large – extent dependent on the social context in which they take place. The problem is which aspects of the social context are the most important. The present chapter has tried to infer some general statements about the general opinion climate in late-20th-century Eastern Europe from specific analyses of selected East European societies. The general opinion climate is only one aspect of the social context, and, admittedly, it is not an aspect that lends itself to any quantitative or exact measurement. Nevertheless, we believe that an assessment of the general opinion climate is important in order to understand the potential for escalating conflicts.

On the background of examples from some East European societies, our impression is that the general opinion climate in late-20th-century Eastern Europe – except perhaps in the Czech republic – was malign with respect to processes of escalation. That is, virtually all important actors of escalation in Eastern Europe were individuals and groups who favoured non-conciliatory, exclusive actions towards outgroups and who tried to make their own populations perceive outgroup relations as characterized by incompatible interests and goals. In very few instances were there any influential critical opposition, mass media, or grass roots movements which could counterbalance the preponderance of non-conciliatory mobilizers, contending strategists, nationalist-biased media, and extremist activists. Thus, although there were important differences among the East European societies, we believe that, on balance, it is warranted to describe the social mood in which opinions and interpretations of social events were formed as a conflict climate.

The conflict climate in Eastern Europe helps us to understand the difficulties of keeping the potential for conflict inherent in national revivals under control. But, unfortunately, it does not bring us decisively closer to an answer to the main question of Part Two, namely why some national conflicts in Eastern Europe escalated into intense, violent conflicts, while others were solved or at least remained non-violent. This is what we set out to do now.

In the following chapters we search for macrosociological explanations of the intensity of the national conflicts in Estonia, Moldova, Croatia, and Czechoslovakia. Each chapter begins with a short description of the national conflicts. The descriptions focus on issues of disagreement and the actions taken by the opposing nation-groups. In particular, we examine the extent to which the parties employed violent means to solve issues of disagreement. The time period covered reaches from the rise of the national revivals and the concomitant national conflicts in the second half of the 1980s until the conflicts were solved or until a *modus vivendi* was reached through third-party mediation. Then we turn to a test of the hypotheses H_3 to H_6 through an examination of the nation-groups' security, instrumental, ideological, and primordial interests.

13 The National Conflict in Estonia

1 INTRODUCTION

Notwithstanding the Estonian national revival and subsequent secession, the presence of a relatively large Russian minority in Estonia, and the overwhelming power of the Russian-dominated USSR and later of the Russian Federation, the national conflict in Estonia remained non-violent. Thus, the relationship between Estonians and Russians in Estonia illustrates that national conflicts do not necessarily escalate.

2 THE NATIONAL CONFLICT

The Russian minority in Estonia did react to the appearance of still more overtly nationalist Estonian politicians and especially to the nationalist laws adopted by these politicians as they came to dominate the revived Estonian parliament (see Section 2 of Chapter 5). In particular, those laws that pertained to the status and rights of the Russians led to disagreements between the two nation-groups. Thus, laws on issues such as national symbols, language, immigration, citizenship, and suffrage resulted in Russian protests. Yet, the response of the Russian minority was remarkably restrained. Although organizations such as Intermovement were formed, the leaders of these organizations never succeeded in mobilizing the Russians on any larger scale. Thus, neither the Estonians nor the Russians employed violent means to solve the issues of disagreement. Only in the summer of 1992 did the Estonian Defence Union get involved in a few skirmishes (see Section 5 of Chapter 12). However, these actions were directed against the Soviet troops, not against the local Russians. Instead, negotiations between Estonian government commissions and representatives from Russian organizations were held frequently (Nørgaard, 1994: 199f). Although these negotiations often ended in a deadlock, it is notable that disputed issues remained negotiable.

At the beginning of 1993 the possibilities of conflict management increased as the OSCE (Organization of Security and Cooperation in Europe – until 1994 called the Conference on Security and Cooperation in

Europe) established a mission in Estonia. Although Western diplomacy had been rather slow to get to grips with the potential dangers of the ethnic situation in Estonia, the issue was internationalized during the summer of 1992 as the Russian government still more loudly protested against the Estonian government's treatment of the Russian minority (Lieven, 1993: 378ff). Thus, Russia directed complaints through the channels of the OSCE, the UN, and the Council of Europe. Following these complaints, the OSCE decided to establish a conflict-mitigating mission. This had the important effect of giving local Russians a voice in the West and without doubt restrained the behaviour of the majority nation-group (wanting, as it did, to retain the image of Estonia as a liberal and democratic state deserving membership of Western organizations such as the Council of Europe). The influence of international organizations became clear in the summer of 1993 when the law on aliens resulted in international criticism from both Russia and the West and led to the holding of a referendum by the city councils of Narva and Sillamäe on the question of autonomy (Raun, 1994: 173). Subsequently, president Meri declined to sign the bill already passed by the parliament and sent it to the OSCE and the Council of Europe for expert assessment. These organizations suggested some minor changes which were nearly all accepted by the Estonian parliament.

Thus, the Estonian–Russian national conflict did not escalate into large-scale and violent conflict. On the contrary, peaceful crisis resolution characterized the conflict. And following the events of the summer of 1993 and the local elections in the autumn of 1993 which resulted in considerable Russian representation in the city councils in Tallinn and in the Narva region (Nørgaard, 1994: 177), the two nation-groups seemed to have reached a *modus vivendi*.

3 THE SECURITY INTERESTS OF THE NATION-GROUPS IN ESTONIA

As the powers of the federal Soviet authorities gradually weakened, the nation-groups in Estonia found themselves responsible for their own security to a still larger degree. As only the Estonian national revival was strong, H_3 would predict that the Russians should perceive the Estonian revival as a security problem and not vice versa. Yet, the Estonian–Russian conflict remained non-violent. In accordance with H_3, this development could be explained if the difference between the military capabilities of the Estonians and Russians was relatively small so that use of force by the Russians was not feasible.

3.1 The Military Capability of the Estonians

When the Estonians achieved full independence in August 1991, the Estonian authorities had to start almost from scratch as they began to form national armed forces. The only basis to build on was the Defence Union, a civilian militia group formed in May 1990 (Kionka, 1992b: 34ff). Following the establishment of independence, this unit became subordinated to the newly formed Estonian Ministry of Defence and came to function as a national guard component of the nascent armed forces.

Yet, the formation of the armed forces progressed only slowly. This was, first of all, due to a pronounced lack of armaments and equipment. Thus, the Estonians inherited only very few of the Soviet arms which were still located in the republic. When negotiating with the USSR, and later with the Russian, government on the future of the Soviet units stationed in the republic, the Estonian representatives did not try to achieve a transfer of jurisdiction over some of these units but simply opted for a withdrawal of the troops as fast as possible (Bungs, 1993: 55f). In addition, the Estonian politicians were willing to allocate only modest financial means to the armed forces (Huldt, 1992: 67, 75).

Furthermore, the Estonians could not, of course, rely on the support of an outside mother-nation. And although the attitude of the Western states towards the newly independent Estonia was indeed positive, they nevertheless kept a low profile concerning military assistance and in particular security guarantees – at least in the immediate post-independence period (Knudsen, 1993: 11f). One consequence of this reluctant attitude was that the Western countries were not willing to sell arms to Estonia in that period (Nørgaard, 1994: 214).

Therefore, the military capability of the Estonians was not overwhelmingly large. By June 1992, almost one year after the achievement of independence, the Estonian armed forces consisted of approximately 2000 servicemen who were equipped with light arms only (Huldt, 1992: 75).[81]

3.2 The Military Capability of the Russians

When the Estonian national revival in August 1991 resulted in the declaration of an independent state, approximately 36 000 Soviet troops, the majority of whom were Russians, were stationed in Estonia (Clarke, 1992: 43). The Soviet forces included both an army division, and air and naval forces.

However, the local Russian minority did not undertake any concerted efforts to establish cooperation with the Soviet units in order to make them interfere on their behalf. Although some cases of illegal sales of arms to the local Russians were reported, these sales were never organized in a systematic way and occurred only on a small scale (Lieven, 1993: 206). On the contrary, the Russian commanders in Estonia seemed to prefer not to get involved in the Estonian–Russian conflict. Thus, when conservative Russians, who strongly resisted the Estonian efforts to achieve independence, attempted to carry out the coup in Moscow in August 1991, the Russian officers in Estonia did comply with the order to declare a state of emergency but did nothing whatsoever to implement it (p. 202). And in November 1991 a group of officers of the Tallinn garrison took matters into their own hands and issued a document in which they stated that the Soviet armed forces in Estonia recognized the government of the republic of Estonia and that they had no interest in heightening tensions (Kionka, 1991: 27f).

Furthermore, the central Soviet – and later the Russian – authorities only indirectly made use of the Soviet forces stationed in Estonia.[82] In October 1992, after several months of negotiation with the Estonians on the future of the former Soviet forces, Russian president Yeltsin signed a directive suspending the withdrawal of these troops (Bungs, 1993: 50ff). Yeltsin argued that the Estonian authorities were discriminating against the local Russians. Nevertheless, the Estonian authorities did not yield to the Russian pressure, and the pull-out of the troops, which had started already shortly after the Estonian declaration of independence, continued. Thus, while approximately 23 000 soldiers were still stationed in Estonia in June 1992, the number had decreased to only 7000 in June 1993 (*ibid.*; Huldt, 1992: 75).[83]

3.3 The Explanatory Power of H_3

The above analysis shows that the Russians in Estonia potentially had a very large military superiority compared to the Estonians. However, notwithstanding the strong Estonian national revival and the potentially huge military capability of the Russian minority, the Russians never tried to make any direct use of the military superiority. And as H_3 is not able to provide an explanation of the passive behaviour of the Russians, we conclude that H_3 is not confirmed in this case.

4 THE INSTRUMENTAL INTERESTS OF THE NATION-GROUPS IN ESTONIA

According to H_4, the non-escalation of the Estonian–Russian conflict could be explained if both or at least one of the nation-groups did not feel or fear significant economic and political deprivation caused by the opposing nation-group and, thus, had either non-conflicting or weak conflicting instrumental interests.

4.1 The Instrumental Interests of the Estonians

The Estonians were not economically deprived by the Russian-dominated Soviet centre in so far as the economy of the Estonian SSR was one of the most developed in the USSR and the standard of living of the Estonians was above that of the USSR average (see Section 4.1.1 of Chapter 5). Nevertheless, the Estonians perceived that they were economically deprived by the Russians. The Estonians compared their standard of living with that of West European nation-groups and blamed the forced incorporation of the Estonian economy into the Soviet planned economy for the ensuing and still larger gap with regard to economic welfare. And although the Estonian economy was advanced by Soviet standards, the Estonians also complained that they had very limited control over their raw materials, the production processes, and the distribution of the output. Thus, the Estonians perceived themselves to have a clear interest in correcting their alleged undeserved economic backwardness by establishing an independent state in which Estonian control over the economy could be achieved and market economy reforms introduced.

Moreover, the Estonians were politically deprived by the Soviet centre (see Section 4.1.2 of Chapter 5). The Estonian elite was not granted a most-favoured-lords status as it was underrepresented in the ruling organs of the communist party not only at the all-Union but also at the republican level. And the Estonians were underrepresented regarding ordinary membership of the party, too. Therefore, the Estonians also had a strong interest in regaining political power and self-determination in an independent state.

And precisely because they blamed the Russians of economic and political colonization, the Estonians perceived their instrumental interest in correcting the deprivations as conflicting with the interests of the Russians. The Russians in Estonia were seen as representatives of the colonizing Soviet centre (Raun, 1994: 169f). As for the question of economic deprivation, the Estonians perceived the bulk of the local Russians as economic immigrants or colonists who came to Estonia mainly because of the relatively high standard of living. And concerning the issue of political deprivation, local Russian party officials and members of the military and the KGB in particular were perceived as occupiers.

4.2 The Instrumental Interests of the Russians

Due to the dominance of the Soviet centre, the Russians in Estonia were not economically deprived (see Section 4.2.1 of Chapter 5). On the contrary, they were well-off in relation to the Estonians. Naturally, the Russians had an interest in prolonging this position. And as the Estonian national revival progressed, it could very well be seen as a threat to the economic position of the Russians. Thus, especially the predominantly Russian managers of the all-Union controlled factories feared for their future. Accordingly, they played a dominant role in the Intermovement, the UWC, and the UCWC (Hosking, 1992: 189). These organizations strongly opposed the Estonian demand for economic autonomy which they branded as 'economic separatism'. In general, however, the Russian minority did not offer significant support to these organizations. While the ordinary Russians did notice that their economic position was becoming more insecure, they nevertheless perceived that their economic interests were better served in Estonia than in Russia. Thus, if the Russians can be said to have perceived conflicting economic interests with the Estonians, these interests were weak as the Russians believed that coexistence with the Estonians was better than secession or emigration.

The Estonian national revival also meant that the Russians became politically deprived as the Estonian centre gained still more political leverage (see Section 4.2.2 of Chapter 5). While the Estonians in the pre-independence period only threatened to exclude the Russians from citizenship and suffrage rights, this became reality soon after independence was achieved. So, as regards political rights and influence, the Russians had conflicting interests in relation to the Estonians. Still, the Russians did not seem to give the question of citizenship and voting rights high priority. Thus, the June 1992 referendum on the new Estonian constitution and the September 1992 parliamentary elections which excluded non-citizens from participation proceeded calmly without any significant interruptions or demonstrations by the Russians (Pettai, 1993: 124f). And according to a survey from September 1993, 64 per cent of the Russians gave the Estonian system of government a positive or neutral rating (Rose & Maley, 1994: 35ff).

4.3 The Explanatory Power of H_4

H_4 is able to provide an explanation of the non-violent character of the Estonian–Russian conflict as only one of the parties in the conflict, the Estonians, perceived that they had strong conflicting instrumental interests in relation to the opposing nation-group. As for the other party, the instrumental interests of the Russians were relatively weak and only partly conflicting with those of the Estonians on the issue of political influence and rights.

5 THE IDEOLOGICAL INTERESTS OF THE ESTONIANS

According to H_5, the non-violent character of the Estonian–Russian conflict could be explained if the majority nation-group, the Estonians, had an ideological interest in adopting a territorial version of nationalism which resulted in inclusive or neutral policies of nationalism towards the minority nation-group, the Russians.

5.1 Official Estonian Policies

Starting with the language law in January 1989, which made knowledge of Estonian a prerequisite for many jobs, the Estonian parliament adopted a series of laws that, while not explicitly discriminating on ethnic grounds, in effect put most of the Russian-speaking population at a disadvantage. The bulk of this legislation was enacted after the achievement of independence in August 1991 which seems to have constituted a turning point as earlier statements from Estonian politicians revealed a somewhat more liberal stance towards the Russian minority (Lieven, 1993: 276, 302f).

In February 1992 the citizenship law of 1938 was reinstated. In consequence, only citizens of pre-war Estonia and their direct descendants were automatically recognized as citizens. Anyone else was required to satisfy a two-year residence qualification counting from 30 March 1990, take an oath of loyalty, and pass a language examination which most Russians perceived as a nearly insurmountable hurdle (Sheehy, 1993: 8). With a one-year waiting period, this meant that no one could receive citizenship before 30 March 1993. The citizenship law, together with the law on national elections from April 1992 and the law on local elections from May 1993, effectively disfranchised the majority of the Russians in the referendum on the new constitution and the first post-independence parliamentary elections in June 1992. And in the local elections in October 1993, non-citizens were only allowed to vote, not to run as candidates (*ibid.*). Finally, according to the law on aliens from June 1993, all non-citizens were declared aliens and granted a two-year respite to apply for residence and labour permit (p. 9).

The exclusion of the Russians from the above-mentioned legal–political rights made them vulnerable to possible future discrimination between citizens and non-citizens not only in the political field, but also in the fields of property ownership, choice of occupation, government employment, social welfare, unemployment benefits, pensions, and health care; especially as the Estonian constitution does not explicitly rule out such discrimination (CE, 1992: arts. 28-32; Lieven, 1993: 314).

5.2 Unofficial Estonian Policies

On the unofficial level, too, the Estonian policies of nationalism seemed to be at variance with the interests of the Russian minority. Lieven (1993) mentions that the Baltic universities increasingly operated only in the Baltic languages and quietly discriminated against Russian applicants (p. 315). Further, Russian officials were dismissed in the name of 'desovietization' (p. 289). This could be an offshoot of the above-mentioned language law which provided that command of Estonian was obligatory in some specified jobs (DAT, 1992: 4). Moreover, very few resources were allocated to teaching Estonian to interested Russians. Thus, there were numerous complaints by Russians that instruction in Estonian was simply not available (Raun, 1994: 167).

5.3 The Explanatory Power of H_5

The above analysis reveals that the Estonian nationalism was far from territorial as the Estonians adopted and implemented policies of nationalism which were clearly of an exclusive nature. Moreover, the fact that the Estonians primarily launched exclusive policies after the achievement and international recognitions of full independence indicates that the relatively neutral policies of the pre-independence period were tactically motivated. However, despite the ethnic nationalism of the Estonians, the reaction of the Russian minority was remarkably restrained. Many Russians even stated that they did not see any problems in the minority policies of Estonia. Thus, according to a survey from September 1993, 58 per cent of the Russians disagreed with the claim that 'non-citizens and minority nationalities are being badly treated here' (Rose & Maley, 1994: 39f). Therefore, we must reject H_5.

6 THE PRIMORDIAL INTERESTS OF THE NATION-GROUPS IN ESTONIA

According to H_6, the limited Estonian–Russian conflict could be explained if both or at least one of the nation-groups perceived that their primordial interests were either weak and conflicting or non-conflicting in relation to those of the opposing nation-group. In order to find out whether this was actually the case we examine the elements on which the nation-groups' primordial interests were formed (the *ethnie*), the history of interaction, and the issue of cultural deprivation.

6.1 The Primordial Interests of the Estonians

First of all, the Estonians had a strong ethnic base as they scored high on all the characteristics of an *ethnie* (see Section 3.1.1 of Chapter 5). Actually, the transformation of the Estonian *ethnie* into a national identity had occurred already in connection with the first national revival in the second half of the last century, and the subsequent ambition of the Estonians to establish a state on the territory with which they associated was crowned with success shortly after the First World War when the independent republic of Estonia came into being. However, the Estonian state-building project ceased with the Soviet occupation during the Second World War. Therefore, the Estonians, whose ethnic and national identity by the 1980s was still intact, had a strong primordial interest in regaining full control over the territory which had earlier formed the basis of an Estonian nation-state.

Furthermore, the Estonians' primordial interest in establishing a nation-state was reinforced and perceived to be conflicting with the interests of the Russians because of two factors. Firstly, the Estonian national identity was characterized by an anti-Russian attitude due to the experience of Russian dominance since the early 18th century, except for the interwar period (see Section 3.1.3 of Chapter 5). This experience included large-scale atrocities committed by the Russians in the shape of deportations of thousands of Estonians, especially during the Second World War and the subsequent years of Stalinism.

Secondly, the Estonians perceived that they had been subject to Russian-led cultural deprivation throughout the Soviet period (see Section 4.1.3 of Chapter 5). The russification policies of the Soviet centre and the presence of large numbers of Russian immigrants made the Estonians perceive that their culture and language were threatened, and they felt mis-recognized as a nation-group. Therefore, they had a clear interest in avoiding this cultural deprivation.

6.2 The Primordial Interests of the Russians

In contrast to the Estonians, the Russians in Estonia lacked a distinct and historically deep-rooted ethnic base and national identity (see Section 2.2 of Chapter 5). This was first of all due to the fact that the majority of the

Russians had immigrated to Estonia in the postwar Soviet period. Instead, the identity of the Russians was centred on the Soviet culture. And although this identity, to a still larger extent, became a phenomenon of the past, only relatively few efforts were made by Russian leaders and intellectuals to invigorate a Russian identity. A survey from September 1993 substantiated this. When asked which term best described how they usually thought of themselves, only 28 per cent of the Russians answered 'Russian' while 52 per cent answered in terms of 'city/locality' (Rose & Maley, 1994: 51). Thus, the vague ethnic base of the Russians, not least the lack of a historical association with a territory in Estonia, meant that their primordial interest in establishing a separate state unit or seeking unification with Russia was weak.

Furthermore, the historical interrelationship with the Estonians, which had never entailed organized Estonian persecution of Russians (see Section 3.1.3 of Chapter 5), did not contribute to a strengthening of the primordial interests of the Russians.

Yet, as a consequence of the Estonian national revival, the Russians increasingly experienced some cultural deprivation and misrecognition (see Section 4.2.3 of Chapter 5). Of special importance in this respect were the Estonian efforts to diminish the status of the Soviet culture and the Russian language *vis-à-vis* the Estonian. In this last respect, therefore, the Russians did have an interest in avoiding the rising cultural deprivation.

6.3 The Explanatory Power of H_6

H_6 provides an explanation of the non-violent character of the Estonian–Russian conflict as only the Estonians perceived that they had strong conflicting primordial interests. The primordial interests of the Russians were relatively weak as they were only driven by a desire to avoid the rising cultural deprivation. Thus, H_6 can explain why the reaction of the Russians towards the Estonian national revival was so weak that the conflict did not escalate.

7 CONCLUSION

Due to the strong Estonian national revival and the potentially overwhelming military superiority of the Russians in Estonia, H_3 would have predicted outbreak of violent conflict as a consequence of a Russian attempt to solve the security problem. Yet, the conflict remained non-violent, and this indicates that the Russians did not perceive that their security interest was threatened by the Estonian revival.

Nevertheless, the passive behaviour of the Russian minority was surprising given the Estonian ideological interest in implementing an ethnic version of nationalism. Thus, the Estonians conducted clearly exclusive policies of nationalism towards the Russians, especially after independence was achieved. Consequently, both H_3 and H_5 must be rejected in this case.

The tests of H_4 and H_6 did, however, point out reasons why the Russians reacted relatively calmly to the Estonian revival. Thus, although the Russians did have some conflicting interests with the Estonians, these interests were weak. The instrumental interests of the Russians were weak as they believed that their economic interests were best served within an independent Estonia. The political prospectives of the Russians were less attractive, but the Russians regarded political rights as not really important, and their instrumental interests were also rather weak in this respect. The same holds true with respect to the primordial interests of the Russians. They did experience an increasing cultural deprivation, but on the other hand they lacked a distinct ethnic base and they had never been victims of atrocities organized by Estonians. So, the character of the instrumental and primordial interests of the Russians explains why they did not undertake any comprehensive efforts to avoid the consequences of the Estonian national revival.

14 The National Conflicts in Moldova

1 INTRODUCTION

The case of Moldova provides an example of three simultaneous, strong national revivals. Yet, the resulting national conflict between the Moldovans and the Slavs escalated into extensive warfare while the Moldovan–Gagauz conflict remained much less intensive. This chapter examines the reasons why these two conflicts developed so differently.

2 THE NATIONAL CONFLICTS

2.1 The Moldovan–Slavic Conflict

Apparently, the issues of disagreement between the Moldovans and the Slavs were rather similar to those between the Estonians and the Russians. Thus, the Slavs also protested against laws on issues such as state language, national symbols, and immigration which were adopted by the Moldovan parliament following the victory of Moldovan nationalists in the March 1990 elections (see Section 2.2 of Chapter 6). However, the reaction of the Slavs was much stronger, especially among those living in the Dnestr region. The protest strikes and demonstrations arranged by the Slavic leaders attracted large numbers of dissatisfied Slavs, and when the leaders in the Dnestr region had won the local elections in the spring of 1990, they responded to the Moldovan declaration of sovereignty by declaring the Dnestr area a separate SSR.

So far, the conflict had been non-violent, but as the Moldovan authorities reacted by declaring the secession illegal, dissolving the local Soviets, introducing direct presidential rule, and, finally, in early November 1990 sending in police troops in order to enforce these decisions, violence broke out (Fane, 1993: 139f). Although the violence resulted in bloodshed[84] and both Moldovan and Slavic paramilitary volunteer units were formed, the conflict did not escalate at this point in time, primarily due to the reluctance of the Moldovan authorities to employ military means.

Thus, the Moldovan attempts to regain full control over the area did not succeed. On the contrary, during the first months of 1992 the Dnestr authorities gradually seized all police stations and removed remaining Moldovan officers (Socor, 1993: 13ff). By then, the Dnestr authorities had established fully fledged conventional military units, armed and trained by the (former Soviet, then Russian) 14th Army which was based in the region.

However, in March 1992 the conflict escalated anew as the Moldovan side tried to stop what it called 'the Creeping Putsch in Eastern Moldova' (Socor, 1992b: 8). Thus, from March to July 1992 warfare of growing intensity took place as newly formed Moldovan army units tried in vain to defend Bendery, a largely Slav-populated city on the west side of the river Dnestr, and two remaining bridge-heads in the Dnestr area (Socor, 1993: 13ff). The Moldovan units lacked heavy arms and suffered several hundred casualties during the clashes. Consequently, the Moldovan authorities saw themselves compelled to ask Moscow to help mediate a peaceful solution. In September 1992 a Yeltsin-sponsored cease-fire agreement was signed and Russian peacekeeping forces moved into the area.

Since then, the cease-fire has been observed, but although some negotiations between the Moldovan government and the Dnestr Slavs about the future status of the Dnestr region have been held, no compromises have so far ended the Dnestr impasse (Duplain, 1995: 10; Ionescu, 1995: 14f). Thus, the status quo has been preserved while the Dnestr republic has continued to consolidate its territory and state structures.

2.2 The Moldovan–Gagauz Conflict

As early as November 1989, following the adoption of the Moldovan language law, the Gagauz reacted to the Moldovan national revival by proclaiming the Gagauz region an ASSR (Fane, 1993: 143f). This move probably also reflected the frustrations of the Gagauz that they had never been granted any distinct administrative unit by the Soviet regime. However, the Moldovan authorities promptly rejected the idea of an autonomous Gagauz entity.

Nevertheless, the Gagauz national revival proceeded, and less than a year later, in August 1990, the Gagauz announced the secession of the Gagauz region and the formation of a separate Gagauz SSR (*ibid.*). The Moldovan authorities did not accept this move either. They declared the secession illegal, banned the GP, and assumed direct control of police units in Gagauz-inhabited rayons (Socor, 1990a: 11). At first, the Moldovan authorities responded to the Gagauz declaration of independence in much the same way as to the Slavic declaration. However, they soon took a more conciliatory stand towards the Gagauz. In October 1990 Moldovan police forces, assisted by troops from the USSR Ministry of Internal Affairs, stopped Moldovan volunteers from intervening in the elections to the newly created Gagauz national parliament (Cavanaugh, 1992: 13). The Moldovan authorities also supported the idea of cultural autonomy for the Gagauz and promised to allocate funds for the economic development of the Gagauz region, but stopped short of agreeing to grant territorial autonomy or independence.

Although negotiations were held repeatedly, no compromise solution was reached. As the GP dominated over the CM, the Gagauz demands focused on a dissolution of Moldova into Moldovan, Dnestr, and Gagauz republics while preserving overall Soviet rule in the region (pp. 14ff). In May 1991 the CM presented a compromise proposal entailing autonomy within a Moldovan state in an attempt to bridge the opposing positions of the Moldovan authorities and the GP. But this was not accepted by the Moldovan side, and in August 1991 the split between GP and the Moldovan authorities deepened as the ruling Gagauz hard-liners hailed the attempted *coup d'état* in Moscow.

While full-scale war was raging along the Dnestr river in the spring of 1992, only a few skirmishes took place in the Gagauz area which developed into a 'grey zone' where neither side was in complete control (pp. 16f). The Gagauz did establish some paramilitary units but Moldovan police and border troop units still remained in the area. The latter did not seek to disarm the Gagauz units which for their part did not confront the Moldovan units. And in the ensuing period no skirmishes were reported (Socor, 1994b: 19f). Thus, the Moldovan–Gagauz conflict never assumed the violent character of the Moldovan–Slavic conflict, although the issue of the status of the Gagauz region long remained unresolved due to the intransigence of both sides.

Only in late July 1994, following protracted negotiations between Moldovan and Gagauz representatives, did the Moldovan parliament approve an article in the country's new constitution promising a special status to certain localities in southern Moldova (Socor, 1994c: 20ff). Later, in December 1994, the parliament approved a law according to which the Gagauz were to have an autonomous region named Gagauz Eri (the Gagauz Land) with an elected legislature and executive authorities. Although this law was promulgated by the Moldovan president in January 1995, the actual jurisdiction and extent of decentralization of the Gagauz Eri remains ambiguous and subject to the exact implementation of the law (King, 1995: 21ff).

3 THE SECURITY INTERESTS OF THE NATION-GROUPS IN MOLDOVA

As the collapse of the USSR appeared imminent, the Moldovans, Slavs, and Gagauz in Moldova could not, to the same extent, count on the security forces of the USSR to manage local security problems. Consequently, according to H_3, each of the three nation-groups should perceive the national revivals of the others as a security problem. Thus, H_3 would expect the outbreak of violent national conflict between the Moldovans and the Slavs to be a consequence of a large difference between their military capabilities, while attributing the largely non-violent Moldovan–Gagauz conflict to a military balance between these two nation-groups.

3.1 The Military Capability of the Moldovans

By June 1992, almost a year after the Moldovan national revival had led to the declaration of an independent state, the Moldovan armed forces consisted of approximately 12 000 soldiers plus another 4000 from the national guard of the Ministry of Internal Affairs, the so-called *Carabinieri* (Huldt, 1992: 80). Yet, the historical record of these units was at that time very short.

Two years earlier, in August and September 1990 when the Gagauz and Dnestr regions declared themselves independent SSRs, the newly appointed Moldovan government had at its disposal only a small police force of the republican Ministry of Internal Affairs (Socor, 1990b: 21f). Moreover, this police force was badly equipped after years of neglect under Soviet rule. In September 1990, therefore, the Moldovan parliament directed the government to submit a programme for the formation of republican regular armed forces (*ibid.*). The government also announced plans to create the abovementioned corps of *Carabinieri* under the republican Ministry of Internal Affairs, to be modelled after Italy's force carrying the same name. However, the government began to take concrete steps towards implementation of these plans only after full independence was achieved a year later. One such step was the introduction of national conscription in November 1991 (Socor, 1992a: 44). Yet, the Moldovan authorities faced no problem regarding recruitment as they received a great number of applications from Moldovan volunteers willing to do military service for the newly independent state. But paralleling the situation in the Estonian armed forces, the overriding problem was lack of experienced personnel, equipment, and armaments.

The Moldovan authorities did succeed in gaining control over a small part of the military hardware of the Soviet forces which were stationed in the republic. Like the Estonians, the Moldovan government initially demanded the complete withdrawal of all Soviet forces, but after independence was achieved it changed strategy and tried to negotiate a transfer of jurisdiction over these forces (Socor, 1992f: 38ff). However, the Soviet authorities completely rejected this idea. Therefore, the units remained under the jurisdiction of the USSR Ministry of Defence until the formal dissolution of the USSR in December 1991. When the units subsequently fell under the jurisdiction of the joint CIS forces, the Russian position apparently softened, and in March 1992 an agreement was signed according to which Moldova was to take over the control of a few units placed on the west bank of the Dnestr river. However, this agreement did not last long, for in April 1992 the forces in Moldova were incorporated into Russia's armed forces, and in May the Russian government suspended the ongoing transfer of weapons and equipment from the above-mentioned units to the nascent Moldovan forces. As the reason for the suspension, the Russian authorities referred to the Dnestr conflict for which they held the Moldovan government responsible.

Not least because of these problems, the Moldovan government turned to Romania for support in the formation of its armed forces shortly after the achievement of independence. The Moldovan approach was not neglected. Thus, in May 1992 Romanian president Iliescu publicly stated that Romania had offered both technical and material assistance (Socor, 1992e: 43f). However, the assistance had not been provided on a large scale. In June 1992 the Russian commander of the CIS border troops, which at that time still controlled the Romanian–Moldovan border, stated that by the end of May that year Romania had only delivered 20 armoured personnel carriers, some pontoon equipment, and some consignments of hand weapons and ammunition (*ibid.*).

Nevertheless, on the basis of the – albeit limited – armaments inherited from the Soviet forces and those received from Romania, the Moldovan authorities were gradually able to build up armed forces of their own. In the beginning of 1992 the first units of the *Carabinieri* force became operational, and in May 1992 the first army battalions came into being (Socor, 1992g: 41f). However, the former units were only armed with hand weapons while the latter were equipped with armoured personnel carriers and light artillery.

3.2 The Military Capability of the Slavs

In contrast to the Russians in Estonia, the Slavs in the Dnestr region took active measures to enhance their military capability. Alongside the declaration of an independent SSR in September 1990, the local leaders set up paramilitary so-called Worker Detachments (Socor, 1992b: 9f). Building on that force, the Dnestr authorities then gradually built up a regular army unit named the Republican Guard whose first battalion became operational in September 1991, shortly after the Moldovan declaration of independence.

The reason why the Dnestr Slavs were able to establish these forces was the close cooperation with the Soviet troops stationed in Moldova – that is, the 14th Army whose units were primarily located in the Dnestr region (Huldt, 1992: 80). The majority of the Soviet officers were Russians and, in contrast to their colleagues in Estonia, they openly sided with the Slavic minority. Thus, in the aftermath of the failed coup in August 1991, the Soviet units responded to appeals from the Dnestr authorities and held assemblies of the officers that passed resolutions supporting the Dnestr republic and declaring their opposition to any withdrawal from the area (Socor, 1992b: 10). Another indicator of the attitude of the Russian officers was the decision of the commander of the 14th Army in December 1991 to agree to serve as Minister of Defence in the Dnestr republic (p. 11).

The active involvement of the Soviet forces in the Moldovan–Slavic conflict also had more tangible consequences. Especially after the Moldovan declaration of independence, the Soviet forces openly engaged in training and arming the Republican Guard (Socor, 1992g: 41ff). Initially, only hand weapons and ammunition were transferred to the local Slavs. But during the spring of 1992, when the Moldovan side tried to stop the Slavic forces from gaining control over the whole of the Dnestr region, the Republican Guard also received armoured personnel carriers, battle tanks, and heavy artillery. Moreover, numerous commissioned and non-commissioned officers joined the Republican Guard and served as commanders in these units (Socor, 1992f: 42). And finally, especially during the most heavy clashes in June and July 1992, entire units of the 14th Army actually participated in the confrontations (Socor, 1992g: 44ff).

Furthermore, the Soviet – and later the Russian – authorities did not undertake any actions to prevent the open involvement of the 14th Army. While some Russian officials, such as Marshal Shaposhnikov, the commander of the CIS Joint Forces, persistently claimed that the army remained neutral, others, such as President Yeltsin, admitted that the forces had been involved in the clashes but he justified their actions by referring to them as self-defence (*ibid.*).

Thus, the military capability of the Slavs in Moldova was considerably larger than that of the Moldovans. By June 1992 the Republican Guard consisted of approximately 15 000 men while the 14th Army numbered approximately 10 000 (Huldt, 1992: 80; Socor, 1992f: 40). Although they had built up armed forces of their own, the Moldovans were still considerably inferior in terms of number of soldiers and, more importantly, they were even more inferior in terms of armaments.

3.3 The Military Capability of the Gagauz

Following the declaration of an independent Gagauz SSR in August 1990, the Gagauz authorities also strived to establish military forces. However, their opportunities for doing so were limited by the fact that no mother-nation could provide support to this end. Furthermore, no Soviet military units were located in the Gagauz area (Huldt, 1992: 80).

Nevertheless, the close cooperation that developed between the Gagauz and Dnestr authorities meant that the latter covertly arranged transfers of weapons from the Dnestr region to the Gagauz (Cavanaugh, 1992: 16). However, not all of these weapons reached their destination as the Moldovan authorities on several occasions succeeded in discovering the weapon transfers.[85] Yet, a Soviet division located only three kilometres south of the Gagauz region in Ukraine was apparently another source of weapons and logistical support for the Gagauz units (Socor, 1992f: 40). Consequently, the Gagauz authorities also managed to establish a so-called Republican Guard.

Still, due to the size of the Gagauz population (153 000) and the problems connected with obtaining weapons, the military capability of the Gagauz was most probably small.[86]

3.4 The Explanatory Power of H_3

The strong Moldovan national revival presented the Slavic minority with a security problem. To solve this, they opted for and succeeded in making use of the Soviet forces located in their region. Thereby, the local Slavs obtained a superior military capability and were, thus, able to establish a separate state unit by use of violent means. Thus, H_3 is able to explain the Moldovan–Slavic conflict by reference to the Slavic reaction to the Moldovan national revival.

The Gagauz minority also reacted to the strong Moldovan national revival by building up military forces in order to ensure the sovereignty of their self-proclaimed state unit. Although we lack exact information on the size of the Gagauz forces, we estimate that the military capability of the Gagauz was somewhat smaller than that of the Moldovans – especially as the post-independence Moldovan build-up of independent armed forces progressed. In so far as the Gagauz military capability was in fact considerably smaller, H_3 cannot be confirmed as the Moldovans did not launch any violent action to deal with the Gagauz revival. Yet, in this case the empirical evidence is not sufficient to either reject or confirm H_3.

4 THE INSTRUMENTAL INTERESTS OF THE NATION-GROUPS IN MOLDOVA

According to H_4, the violent Moldovan–Slavic conflict could be explained if both nation-groups perceived that they had strong conflicting instrumental interests. On the other hand, the non-violent Moldovan–Gagauz conflict could be explained if at least one of these nation-groups perceived that their instrumental interests were either non-conflicting or weak and conflicting.

4.1 The Instrumental Interests of the Moldovans

Unlike the Estonians, the Moldovans were clearly economically deprived by the Soviet centre (see Section 4.1.1 of Chapter 6). The Russian-dominated centre institutionalized a cultural division of labour which meant that the Moldovan economy largely remained a producer of agricultural raw materials, the majority of which were processed and consumed in the all-Union economy. The limited resources allocated to industrialization resulted in a per-capita income level that continued to be well below the all-Union average. Thus, it was not surprising that the Moldovans perceived themselves to be economically deprived and had an instrumental interest in correcting this relation by achieving Moldovan control over the economy. Furthermore, paralleling the Estonian case, this interest was not perceived to be compatible with that of the Slavs in Moldova as they were seen as representatives and part of the colonizing Soviet centre.

The Moldovans' instrumental interest in establishing an independent state was also driven by the perception that they were politically deprived (see Section 4.1.2 of Chapter 6). Though making up an increasing proportion of the republican communist party as well as its ruling organs, the Moldovans remained heavily underrepresented. And in the organs of the Soviet centre, where most power was located, the underrepresentation was even heavier. Also in this respect, the Moldovans perceived their instrumental interest in correcting the political deprivation to be in conflict with the Slavic minority, precisely because the Moldovans wanted to diminish the so far dominant political influence of both the Soviet centre and the local Slavs.

In contrast, the Moldovans did not perceive their instrumental interests in avoiding the economic and political deprivation to be in conflict with the interests of the Gagauz. The Gagauz were not perceived to be a cause of the deprivation so far, and neither were they perceived to be a potential future threat in this respect. On the contrary, there was widespread acknowledgement among the Moldovans that the Gagauz had been even more economically underprivileged than themselves under Soviet rule and that the two nation-groups had a common interest in opposing the Russian-led Soviet dominance (Socor, 1990a: 12f).

With respect to political issues, the Moldovans did not consider the Gagauz a threat to the functioning of a (Moldovan-dominated) democracy because of the sheer size of the Gagauz minority. In the same vein, the Moldovans perceived that Gagauz cultural autonomy was compatible with their political interests.

4.2 The Instrumental Interests of the Slavs

The economic situation of the Slavs in Moldova was better than that of the titular nation-group because the former were overrepresented as regards employment in the relatively small industrial sector with the best paid jobs (see Section 4.2.1 of Chapter 6). As Moldovan nationalist politicians began to propose either the creation of an independent Moldovan economy or a fusion with the Romanian, the Slavic minority, in contrast to the Russians in Estonia, did not perceive its economic interests to be compatible with those of the titular nation-group. Living in a relatively underdeveloped Moldovan economy separated from the Soviet one but with no ties to Western economies as a counterbalance, not to mention the possibility of a fusion with the even more backward Romanian economy, was not perceived as an economically lucrative option. Thus, the Slavic minority had a strong instrumental interest in avoiding the perceived future economic deprivation or even discrimination.

Furthermore, the instrumental interests of the Slavs were reinforced as they also feared future political deprivation. This fear was caused by the political development in the wake of the Moldovan national revival (see Section 4.2.2 of Chapter 6). While the local Slavs throughout the Soviet period had a disproportionate political influence due to their overrepresentation in the CPM, this power base eroded as the first democratic elections shifted the locus of power to the parliament. The new government which was almost completely dominated by Moldovans soon adopted measures which removed the so far absolute power of the CPM. In addition, the fear of political deprivation was strengthened by some Moldovan politicians' call for reunification with Romania which had a malign record of minority treatment.

4.3 The Instrumental Interests of the Gagauz

The Gagauz region was even more underdeveloped than Moldova and the standard of living of the Gagauz was lower than the Moldovan average (see Section 4.3.1 of Chapter 6). The Gagauz thus had a strong instrumental interest in correcting the economic deprivation. However, they were divided on the question of whether this interest was compatible with the economic interests of the Moldovans. The Gagauz opposition perceived that the economic interests of the Gagauz were compatible with those of the Moldovans as it also supported the introduction of market economy reforms and trusted that the Moldovan offers on economic assistance to the Gagauz region were credible. However, the strong support for the dominant Gagauz leaders in the GP indicates that many Gagauz shared the perception that their economic interests were conflicting with those of the Moldovans. According to this perception, the Moldovans were blamed for the economic backwardness of the Gagauz region, market economy reforms were not seen as a solution to the economic grievances of the Gagauz, and it was not taken for granted that the Moldovans would have the will or the means to correct the economic deprivation of the Gagauz.

The same pattern was relevant concerning the issue of political deprivation. The Gagauz were clearly politically deprived as they were never assigned a separate administrative unit and were underrepresented in the organs of the CPM (see Section 4.3.2 of Chapter 6). Consequently, the Gagauz also had a strong instrumental interest in enhancing their political status and influence. But again the perceptions of the Gagauz were not unequivocal. The opposition and its followers perceived that their interests were compatible with Moldovan independence and the introduction of democracy if the Gagauz were granted autonomy. However, the dominant wing and its followers strongly opposed the idea of an independent Moldova and opted instead for a separate Gagauz unit as a constituent part of the USSR or the CIS.

4.4 The Explanatory Power of H_4

As it appears from the above analyses, H_4 provides an explanation of the violent character of the Moldovan–Slavic conflict as both nation-groups perceived that they had strong and conflicting instrumental interests. The Moldovans' interests were driven by the desire to correct the economic and political deprivation. And as the Slavs were perceived to be the cause of this deprivation, the Moldovans perceived their interests to be conflicting with those of the Slavs. For their part, the Slavs feared that the evolving Moldovan national revival would lead to future economic and political deprivation.

Regarding the Moldovan–Gagauz conflict, H_4 also points out convincing reasons why this conflict did not escalate into large-scale use of violent means. Firstly, although the Gagauz had a strong interest in correcting the economic and political deprivation, some of the Gagauz did not perceive this interest to be conflicting with those of the Moldovans. Secondly, there was a widespread perception among the Moldovans that their economic and political interests were, if not identical, then compatible with those of the Gagauz.

5 THE IDEOLOGICAL INTERESTS OF THE MOLDOVANS

According to H_5, the violent Moldovan–Slavic conflict could be explained if the majority nation-group, the Moldovans, had ideological interests in implementing an ethnic version of nationalism through the adoption of exclusive policies towards the Slavs. On the other side, the non-violent Moldovan–Gagauz conflict could be explained if the Moldovans adopted inclusive or neutral policies towards the Gagauz.

5.1 Official Moldovan Policies

The Moldovan citizenship law adopted in June 1991 represented a 'zero option'. Thus, all persons who, by the date of the Moldovan declaration of sovereignty (23 June 1990), had a permanent place of residence automatically became citizens of Moldova (Nedelciuc, 1992: 48f). However, this solitary example of inclusive policies was adopted by the Moldovans approximately one year *after* the secessions of the Slavs and the Gagauz. Similarly, the law on Gagauz Eri granting some autonomy to the Gagauz was not adopted until several years after the outbreak of the national conflicts, and it contained no similar rights to the Dnestr Slavs (see Section 2).

The language law adopted in August 1989 was fairly similar to the Estonian version. Thus, the preamble stated that the aim of the law was to protect the Moldovan language and assure its functioning in all spheres of public life (pp. 45ff). Although the status of Russian and Gagauz was protected in so far as they were to be used as, respectively, a language of inter-ethnic communication and in areas densely populated by Gagauz, other paragraphs of the law were, nevertheless, exclusive towards non-Moldovans. Public employees who occupied positions involving contact with citizens were expected to speak both Moldovan and Russian in order to make citizens' choice of language possible. In the field of education, the curriculum of all schools, irrespective of the language of instruction, was nationalized (Kolstø et al., 1993: 982). In history, for example, this meant that the history of the USSR was replaced with the history of the Romanians and Moldovans. The case of Moldova also provides an example of a classic exclusive policy, namely strict immigration laws. In January 1991 the Moldovan parliament passed a law which was explicitly designed to stop the influx of people, primarily Russians, from the USSR (Socor, 1992a: 44). According to this law, immigration was to be limited to an annual quota equivalent to 0.05 per cent of the permanent population of Moldova. Natives of Moldova seeking repatriation were exempted from the quota.

The above-mentioned policies hit all non-Moldovans alike. But on some points, the policies of the new Moldovan government, which came to power in the spring of 1990, were differential. Thus, towards the Gagauz the government conducted a less exclusive policy than towards the Slavs, but mainly concerning cultural issues. The government thus recognized the cultural rights of the Gagauz and promised to foster the development of their cultural life (Nahaylo, 1992: 42f see also Section 4.3.3 of Chapter 6). For example, in July 1991 the government decided to hold a week-long celebration of Gagauz culture in the republic.

5.2 Unofficial Moldovan Policies

The language law contained a number of loopholes which cleared the way for unofficial exclusive policies. Soon after the adoption of the law, for example, the Slavs complained that Moldovans were given high priority in admission to higher education and in employment because they, naturally, spoke the new state language fluently (Kolstø et al., 1993: 981).

5.3 The Explanatory Power of H_5

Apart from the law on citizenship, the Moldovans adopted a range of exclusive official and unofficial policies of nationalism towards the Slavic and Gagauz minorities. As a consequence, H_5 would predict intense national conflicts between the majority nation-group and the minority nation-groups. Because the Moldovan–Slavic conflict was indeed violent, H_5 is able to explain the intensity of this national conflict.

However, the fact that the policies towards the Gagauz were only slightly less exclusive does not seem to be a satisfactory explanation of the strongly differing characters of the two national conflicts. Therefore, H_5 must be rejected in the Moldovan–Gagauz case.

6 THE PRIMORDIAL INTERESTS OF THE NATION-GROUPS IN MOLDOVA

According to H_6, the violent Moldovan–Slavic conflict could be explained if both nation-groups perceived that they had strong conflicting primordial interests, while the non-violent Moldovan–Gagauz conflict could be explained if at least one of these nation-groups perceived that its primordial interests were either non-conflicting or weak and conflicting.

6.1 The Primordial Interests of the Moldovans

The ethnic base and national identity of the Moldovans consisted of a blend of Romanian-ness and Moldovan-ness (see Section 3.1.1 of Chapter 6). Thus, the Moldovans had a primordial interest either in the re-establishment of the interwar Great Romania which also included Bessarabian Moldova or in taking up the legacy of the golden age medieval Moldovan principality and establishing an explicit Moldovan state. Thus, regardless of whether the Romanian-ness or the Moldovan-ness dominated, the Moldovans had a primordial interest in assuming control over what they perceived as ancestral Moldovan lands. According to the Moldovans, these lands also included the regions largely populated by the Gagauz and Slavs (Furtado & Chandler, 1992: 293).

Furthermore, the primordial interest of the Moldovans in establishing an independent state or reuniting with Romania was strengthened by their anti-Russian attitude (see Section 3.1.4 of Chapter 6). This attitude was rooted in the antagonistic historical relations with the Russians which had implied suppression by the tsarist regime in the 19th century and large-scale atrocities in the shape of deportations and enforced collectivization during and after the Second World War. However, the Moldovans did not have an antagonistic history of interaction with the Gagauz (see Section 3.1.5 of Chapter 6). Thus, the Moldovans had never before experienced the Gagauz acting collectively against their interests.

Finally, the primordial interests of the Moldovans were enforced by the misrecognition and cultural deprivation they perceived themselves to have been subject to during the Soviet period (see Section 4.1.3 of Chapter 6). The Moldovans complained about russification policies in fields such as language, education, and writing of history. Moreover, the Moldovans' interest in correcting this deprivation was not perceived to be compatible with the interests of the local Slavs. Thus, the mere presence of the Russian-dominated Slavic minority, the size of which had grown considerably in the course of the postwar period, was seen as a threat to the Moldovan language and culture. On the other hand, the Moldovans perceived themselves to have compatible interests on the issue of cultural deprivation with the far smaller Gagauz minority which had also been subject to russification policies.

6.2 The Primordial Interests of the Slavs

While the Slavs in Moldova, like the Russians in Estonia, associated with the Soviet culture, the Slavs substituted a revived Russian identity for the outlived Soviet one much more easily and quickly (see Section 3.1.2 of Chapter 6). This was due not merely to the more comprehensive efforts of dedicated local mobilizers to revive the Russian identity but also to the circumstance that they could take advantage of a more well-developed local ethnic base. In particular, the historically large number of Slavic settlers in the Dnestr region meant that the Slavs living there had a strong association with that territory which they called 'a little piece of Russia'. Consequently, the Dnestr Slavs had a primordial interest in preserving Russian control over the region. Moreover, they could refer to a historical precedent of a state-like unit in the Dnestr area, the interwar Moldavian ASSR.

In addition, the historical interplay between the Moldovans and the Slavs merely enforced the primordial interests of the latter in avoiding the expected malign consequences of the Moldovan national revival (see Section 3.1.4 of Chapter 6). Thus, the romanophobia of the present-day Slavs was due to the historical memory of the suppression of the Russian minority in the interwar Great Romania and of the deportations of large numbers of Russians during the Second World War when the Romanians and Moldovans sided with Nazi-Germany.

Finally, the national revival of the Moldovans made the Slavs fear that they would become a culturally deprived minority in an independent Moldova or perhaps in a reunited Romanian state (see Section 4.2.3 of Chapter 6). This fear was caused by the efforts of the Moldovans to upgrade the status of their language and culture in relation to the so far dominant combination of the Russian language and the Soviet culture.

6.3 The Primordial Interests of the Gagauz

The Gagauz had a strong ethnic base as they shared all the characteristics of an *ethnie* (see Section 3.1.3 of Chapter 6). Although they had distant roots in the Turkish nation-group, they had over the centuries come to regard themselves as a distinct group, especially following the first national revival at the end of the 19th century. Of special importance was their strong association with the southern region of Moldova where Gagauz had lived since the beginning of the 19th century when the area was allotted to them by the tsar. Yet, the Gagauz had always been regarded merely as an ethnic minority which, therefore, was not entitled to a territory of its own. But as approximately 90 per cent of *all* Gagauz, as of 1989, lived in the southern part of Moldova and in the contiguous Odessa Oblast in Ukraine (Fane, 1993: 141f), this was the only place which would make sense as a Gagauz nation-state. Therefore, the so far misrecognized Gagauz had a strong primordial interest in striving, if not for an independent state, then at least for some kind of autonomous status, be it within the boundaries of the USSR or within an independent Moldova.

On the other hand, in contrast to the Slavs, the primordial interests of the Gagauz were not strengthened by past experiences of atrocities committed by Moldovans (or Romanians) (see Section 3.1.5 of Chapter 6). Although the Gagauz had not been accorded any minority rights in the interwar period, they were not subject to any violent persecution, either before or during the Second World War.

Moreover, the cultural deprivation of the Gagauz was the result of russification policies and not of moldovanization policies (see Section 4.3.3 of Chapter 6). This was indicated, for example, by the 1989 Soviet census, according to which only 4 per cent of the Gagauz claimed to speak Moldovan (Socor, 1990a: 9). So, while the Gagauz had a strong interest in correcting the cultural deprivation, they could hardly perceive this interest as conflicting with those of the Moldovans as the latter had offered cultural autonomy to the Gagauz from the outset of the Moldovan national revival.

6.4 The Explanatory Power of H_6

The test of H_6 showed that this hypothesis provides significant clues to the understanding of the character of the two national conflicts in Moldova. Thus, the violent Moldovan–Slavic conflict could be explained by reference to the perception of both of these nation-groups that they had strong conflicting primordial interests. The ethnic bases of the two groups implied overlapping associations with territory. The level of mutual mistrust and fear was high due to the fact that both groups had experienced past atrocities committed by members of the other group. And finally, the Moldovans wanted to correct cultural misrecognition and deprivation while the Slavs wanted to avoid any future developments in that direction.

As regards the Moldovan–Gagauz conflict, these two *ethnies* also competed for sovereignty in the same territory. However, their primordial interests were not conflicting to the same extent because their historical interrelationship did not contain use of violence, and because the two groups neither did nor intended to misrecognize or culturally deprive each other.

7 CONCLUSION

As regards the Moldovan–Slavic conflict, it seems that it can be explained by all the hypotheses. In contrast to the Russians in Estonia, the Slavs in Moldova apparently felt that the Moldovan national revival posed a threat to their security. And while the Moldovans were still striving to build up military forces of their own, the Slavs took advantage of their military superiority and gained control over the Dnestr region by way of a series of pre-emptive strikes. So, H_3 was confirmed in the case of the Moldovan–Slavic conflict.

This was also the case with respect to H_5 which pointed to the fact that the Moldovan national revival led to the adoption of a range of exclusive policies towards the Slavs. In accordance with H_5, these policies made the Slavs take up arms – with a violent national conflict as the result.

Finally, H_4 and H_6 provided an explanation of the intensity of the Moldovan–Slavic conflict as both the Moldovans and the Slavs perceived that they had strong conflicting instrumental and primordial interests.

Regarding the Moldovan–Gagauz conflict, the Gagauz had a security interest in countering the Moldovan national revival. Their formation of armed units could be seen as an indication that H_3 in this case was right in its prediction that a national revival poses a security problem to opposing nation-groups. Yet, neither the Gagauz nor the Moldovans tried to gain full control over the Gagauz region through use of violent means. This could be explained by reference to a balance between the two nation-groups' military capabilities. But as we lack exact information on the size and armaments of the Gagauz units, H_3 can neither be rejected nor confirmed.

In contrast, H_5 can be clearly rejected in this case. The overwhelming part of the Moldovan policies towards the Gagauz were exclusive. And although the Gagauz did react by trying to establish a separate state-like unit, they did not try to secure full control over this unit through use of violent means.

However, the tests of H_4 and H_6 pointed to reasons why the national conflict did not escalate. True, the Gagauz had conflicting interests with the Moldovans in several respects. While some of the Gagauz did not perceive their instrumental interests to be conflicting with those of the Moldovans, the dominant political organization of the Gagauz did. As for the primordial interests of the Gagauz, they were strong and conflicting on the territorial question while weakened by the absence of antagonistic historical relations and cultural colonization by the Moldovans.

But, apart from the question of supremacy over the Gagauz region, the Moldovans perceived their instrumental and primordial interests to be compatible with those of the Gagauz. And as only one of the two nation-groups involved in the conflict perceived itself to have strong conflicting interests, H_4 and H_6 are confirmed.

15 The National Conflict in Croatia

1 INTRODUCTION

The Yugoslavian tragedy has, at the time of writing, lasted half a decade. Following the short and limited war in Slovenia in the end of June 1991, a full-scale civil war was fought in Croatia in the second half of 1991. In March 1992 violent national conflict also broke out in Bosnia-Hercegovina. And in May and August 1995 the still unresolved conflict between the Croats and the Krajina Serbs escalated into war once again as the Croats took advantage of the breathing space provided by the overlay of the UN peacekeeping force. Thus, employing their now relatively strong army, the Croats succeeded in regaining control over the territory of the self-proclaimed RSK (Republic of Serbian Krajina). And once again the civil population came to bear the brunt of the sufferings – some 160 000 Krajina Serbs fled towards the Serbian-controlled regions in Bosnia and towards Serbia proper. In this chapter we examine the underlying reasons why the national conflict between the Croats and the Serbian minority in Croatia was so intensive.

2 THE NATIONAL CONFLICT

The Croatian national revival, which started in 1989, accelerated and intensified the national revival among the Serbs in Croatia (see Section 2 of Chapter 7). Survey research conducted during the spring 1990 election campaign revealed that a large majority of the Serbian citizens in Croatia were strongly opposed to plans by Croatian nationalists such as Tudjman to restructure the Yugoslavian federation on a confederal basis or perhaps even to declare Croatia independent (Cohen, 1993: 99).

When the Croatian nationalist parties eventually won the elections, took over governmental power, and began to adopt a range of policies of nationalism, the anxiety among the Serbs increased even more and the Serbian leaders called upon the Croatian government to grant autonomy to regions with a Serbian majority. When this was refused, the leaders of the SDP organized a referendum in August 1990 on independence of the Krajina region.

However, like the Slavs in Moldova, the Serbs not only made far-reaching demands but had also taken measures to arm themselves. This resulted in small-scale clashes when the Croatian authorities tried to prevent the holding of the referendum in August 1990 (Andrejevich, 1990b: 42). These first clashes primarily took place in and around the town of Knin, the later capital of the RSK. During the autumn of 1990 and spring of 1991, the Serbs formed paramilitary units throughout the entire Krajina area (Malesic, 1993: 15ff). Arms were provided at the local depots of the YPA and the Territorial Defence.[87] Although the YPA officially remained neutral during the conflict, it became in fact ever more openly involved in military actions in support of the Krajina Serbs. This became apparent in the spring of 1991 when the Croatian authorities initiated a republican-wide blockade of YPA barracks and convoys in response to the federal government's authorization of the YPA to disarm the Croatian police force which by then was evolving into army-like units.

However, it was only after the unilateral Croatian declaration of independence in June 1991 that the character of the conflict changed into a full-scale war (*ibid.*). During the remaining months of 1991 the Serbian paramilitary forces, supported by regular YPA units, repeatedly forced the relatively poorly armed Croatian forces to withdraw. By the end of 1991 approximately one third of Croatia's territory was under Serbian control. Massacres of civilians were committed by both sides, and large numbers of Croats and Serbs were either forced out or fled from the territory controlled by the opposing party.

In April 1992 the first UN peacekeeping forces arrived in the Krajina area and, until the summer of 1995, only minor hostilities occurred. The presence of the UN forces meant that the status quo continued, but a political compromise solution could not be agreed upon. And in May and August 1995 the Croatian government lost patience and launched a large-scale attack on the RSK (Fedarko, 1995: 22ff). In a few days of intense fighting, the Croats regained control over the majority of the territory of the former Yugoslavian republic of Croatia.

3 THE SECURITY INTERESTS OF THE NATION-GROUPS IN CROATIA

Concurrently with the gradual weakening of the power of the federal Yugoslavian authorities, the constituent nation-groups found themselves responsible for their own security to a still larger degree. In accordance with H_3, we would expect that the violent conflict between Croats and Serbs in Croatia could be explained by a large difference between the military capabilities of the two nation-groups so that the one with a superior capability would take violent action to deal with the security problem posed by the national revival in the opposing nation-group.

3.1 The Military Capability of the Croats

As nationalist Croatian politicians took over governmental power in Croatia in May 1990, they had very few military means at their disposal. Moreover, the republican police force consisted of a majority of Serbian police officers (Markotich, 1993: 29). Therefore, the Croatian government began to dismiss Serbian police officers and to establish special police units under the Ministry of Internal Affairs (Cohen, 1993: 133, 189).[88] These units were composed of Croats only and were equipped with light arms and armoured personnel carriers. The government also set out to form regular republican armed forces, termed the Croatian National Guard.

However, the Croatian authorities faced serious problems regarding armaments, especially heavy ones. Thus, in the early spring of 1990, as the electoral victory of the Croatian nationalist parties appeared imminent, the YPA high command subordinated the Territorial Defence units located in Croatia to itself and simply transferred the arms of these units to YPA units (Bebler, 1992: 135). Furthermore, the Croatian government was not able to gain control over the arms of the YPA units located in the republic as the YPA became still more openly involved in the conflict on the Serbian side (see the next section).

In addition, the Croats could not, in contrast to the Serbian minority, rely on the support of a mother-nation. And although some of the Western states, in particular Germany and Austria, adopted a positive attitude towards the Croatian efforts to achieve autonomy and later independence (see e.g. Moore, 1991: 34f), it is unclear whether this support included military assistance.[89]

Nevertheless, the efforts of the Croatian government to build armed forces did progress. Thus, by June 1991, at the time of the declaration of independence, the Croatian special police forces and the National Guard consisted of approximately 22 000 soldiers (Heisbourg, 1991: 97). In addition, the independent paramilitary units, primarily the Croatian Defence Forces (see Section 5.1 of Chapter 12), numbered an estimated 10 000–15 000 men (Gow, 1992: 19).

3.2 The Military Capability of the Serbs

Following the referendum on secession of the Krajina region in August 1990, the leaders of the Serbian minority gradually built up paramilitary forces and established the Krajina area as an exclusion zone into which the Croatian authorities could not gain entry without risking bloodshed (Gow, 1992: 20f). The largest of these forces, the Martićevci force, was founded and led by Martić, one of the Serbian police chiefs who had been dismissed by the Croatian authorities.[90] And as full-scale war broke out in the late summer of 1991 the Krajina authorities succeeded in bringing the various local paramilitary forces under their command. By that time, the Serbian Krajina forces numbered approximately 50 000 men (*ibid.*).

Paralleling the Slavs in Moldova, the Serbian minority's formation of military units was supported by the armed forces of the federation, the YPA. Thus, in the year leading up to the Croatian declaration of independence the YPA, in particular the Knin corps which was located in the Krajina region, gave the Krajina Serbs access to weapons and ammunition (Cohen, 1993: 225). This assistance was a consequence of the still more active involvement of the YPA in politics as the Croatian (and Slovenian) national revivals evolved. Thus as early as November 1990 one of the generals of the YPA high command publicly stated that the YPA would not accept any political development that threatened the unity of the federation (p. 187). The attitude of the YPA, in which 60 per cent of the officers were Serbs (Gow, 1992: 19), was also revealed in January 1991 when the YPA launched a proposal that the nascent Croatian and Slovenian armed forces should be dissolved and disarmed (Cohen, 1993: 189f).[91]

The YPA became directly involved in the Croatian–Serbian conflict when the Croatian government declared Croatia an independent state in June 1991. With the active support of YPA units, the military capability of the Krajina Serbs greatly exceeded that of the Croats, not only in terms of manpower but primarily in terms of heavy armaments (Gow, 1992: 19f). Therefore, paralleling the development in the Dnestr region, the Krajina Serbs were able to repel the attempts of the Croatian forces to regain control over the Krajina region and instead launch an offensive which eventually led to Serbian control of approximately one third of the territory of the republic of Croatia.

3.3 The Explanatory Power of H_3

The analysis of the military capabilities of the Croats and of the Serbian minority in Croatia shows that the military capability of the latter was considerably superior due to the active support of the YPA. And as the Serbs took advantage of their military superiority and used violent means to solve the security problem that the Croatian national revival posed, we can conclude that H_3 is confirmed in this case.

4 THE INSTRUMENTAL INTERESTS OF THE NATION-GROUPS IN CROATIA

In accordance with H_4, the violent conflict between Croats and Serbs could be explained if both nation-groups perceived that they had strong and conflicting instrumental interests.

4.1 The Instrumental Interests of the Croats

Like the Estonians, the Croats were not economically deprived by the federal centre in so far as the GDP per capita was considerably above the Yugoslavian average (see Section 4.1.1 of Chapter 7). Nevertheless, the Croats perceived that the federal centre was to blame for the fact that the Croatian economy lagged behind Western ones. The Croats argued that the principles of a socialist economy and the financial transfers to the poorer republics had a restrictive influence on the development of the Croatian economy. And when the federal authorities sought to impose a recentralization of economic policies and planning in the 1980s, the Croats' perception of themselves as victims of economic deprivation was only reinforced. Consequently, the Croats had a strong economic interest in correcting this situation.

As for political deprivation, the Croats were not deprived in so far as some political power had been decentralized to the republican level in the 1970s and as the federal state presidency was characterized by consociational features (see Section 4.1.2 of Chapter 7). On the other hand, the Serbs dominated both the federal state presidency and federal repressive organs, and they were overrepresented in the CLC and the republican police force. Thus, the instrumental interests of the Croats were strengthened by the desire to escape the perceived political deprivation also.

And as the Croats regarded the disproportionate Serbian influence in both Croatia and the rest of Yugoslavia to be the cause of their perceived disadvantageous economic and political situation, they did not perceive their instrumental interest in diminishing this influence as compatible with the interests of the Serbs.

4.2 The Instrumental Interests of the Serbs

Paralleling the Gagauz, the standard of living of the predominantly rural Krajina Serbs was below that of the titular nation-group (see Section 4.2.1 of Chapter 7). However, the local Serbs' perception that the titular nation-group was to blame for the relative underdevelopment of the Krajina area was more well founded than the similar perception of the dominant

Gagauz leaders and their followers because the Croats had more leeway regarding allocation decisions at the republican level. So, the Krajina Serbs had a strong instrumental interest in avoiding continued economic deprivation. And as they had been economically deprived even during the Yugoslavian era when the federal authorities, and thereby the Serbs of Serbia proper, had some influence over the Croatian economy, they had little reason to expect improvements of their economic situation in an independent Croatia. Thus, the Krajina Serbs' interest in avoiding continued economic deprivation was perceived as conflicting with the Croats' desire to separate the Croatian economy from the Yugoslavian.

On the other hand, the Serbs were not politically deprived in the Yugoslavian republic of Croatia (see Section 4.2.2 of Chapter 7). Like the Russian minority in Estonia and the Slavs in Moldova, they were overrepresented in the republican communist party and its ruling organs. However, the Serbs were frustrated by the actions of the new Croatian nationalist elite. As the latter had taken over governmental power, it initiated a series of dismissals of high-ranking republican and local Serbian officials. Thus, the instrumental interests of the Serbs were reinforced by the desire to escape future political deprivation.

4.3 The Explanatory Power of H_3

By pointing to the circumstance that both Croats and Serbs in Croatia had strong and conflicting instrumental interests, H_3 is able to explain why members of the two opposing nation-groups were willing to employ violent means when pursuing their interests. The Croats wanted to escape the perceived Serbian-caused economic and political deprivation and eventually saw Croatian secession and independence as the only solution to their grievances. On the other hand, the Serbs strongly resisted this option as they feared that the Croat-caused economic deprivation would worsen and that their so far privileged political status would become a phenomenon of the past.

5 THE IDEOLOGICAL INTERESTS OF THE CROATS

According to H_5, the violent conflict in Croatia could be explained by the character of the ideological interests of the majority nation-group, the Croats. Thus, H_5 would expect that the Croats implemented an ethnic version of nationalism by adopting exclusive policies towards the minority nation-group, the Serbs.

5.1 Official Croatian Policies

By 1992, Croatia had an extensive legal framework guaranteeing equal rights for all Croatian citizens. It included provisions of fundamental freedoms and rights in the constitution (CC, 1990: arts. 14, 15), the 'Constitutional Law on Human Rights and Freedoms and the Rights of National and Ethnic Communities or Minorities in the Republic of Croatia' (1991), and a law on abolition for war crimes ('Zakon o oprostu…', 1992). In spite of this, the UN Special Rapporteur on Human Rights reported a considerable number of human rights violations including arbitrary arrest and dismissal from employment (Mazowiecki, 1992: 22; see also Corell et al., 1992: 11–23).

Yet, both the adoption of the legal framework (which was a condition of the West European states for recognizing Croatia) and the reported violations occurred when the conflict had already escalated to a point of no (easy) return. Of more interest for our purposes are the policies adopted until the outbreak of the civil war.

Officially, during and immediately after the April 1990 election campaign, president Franjo Tudjman reluctantly supported the initial Serbian demand for cultural autonomy (Andrejevich, 1990b: 41), but no concrete progress in that direction was made. Instead, the government formed special police units composed only of Croats and ordered that the arms of police reserve units in towns with large Serbian populations be reduced by 60 per cent. This led to clashes between the special police and Serbs in such towns (Andrejevich, 1990d: 29ff).

Furthermore, after the 1990 election victory of the CDC, the new government displayed an extraordinary preoccupation with national symbols (see Section 4.2.3 of Chapter 7). Unfortunately, some of these, such as the coat of arms, were intimately linked with Croatia's fascist past. And Tudjman did not distance himself and his government from this Second World War past. Instead he tried to belittle the scope of the Croatian persecution of the Serbs, claiming, for instance, that no more than 70 000 people died at Jasenovac which was the largest KZ-camp set up by the Ustasha regime (Markotich, 1993: 29f).

5.2 Unofficial Croatian Policies

In the case of Croatia, unofficial policies contributed significantly to the Serbs' feeling of being threatened. For instance, road signs in Cyrillic or in both alphabets in the Serb majority areas were replaced with signs in Latin only (Glenny, 1992: 12). More importantly, perhaps, was the commencement of a series of dismissals of Serbian public employees in order to redress the alleged disproportionate number of these (*ibid.*). This move was seen by the Serbs as a sign of apartheid-like policies of the government, and the most serious reactions came from the Serbian police for whom it entailed not only dismissal but also disarmament.[92]

5.3 The Explanatory Power of H_4

Although the Croats did adopt inclusive laws, this did not happen until after the outbreak of large-scale violent conflict and only when the EC, the United States, and other Western powers had made the adoption of such laws a precondition for recognition of Croatia as an independent state. Until then, the Croats in fact implemented a series of exclusive policies towards the Serbian minority, not least on the unofficial level. Thus, H_4 is able to explain why the Serbs reacted so intensely to the Croatian national revival, and it is, therefore, confirmed in this case.

6 THE PRIMORDIAL INTERESTS OF THE NATION-GROUPS IN CROATIA

According to H_6, the character of the primordial interests of the opposed nation-groups is the factor which is decisive as to whether a conflict escalates or not. Thus, in accordance with H_6, we would expect that the violent Croatian–Serbian conflict was due to the perceptions of both nation-groups that they had strong and conflicting primordial interests.

6.1 The Primordial Interests of the Croats

The Croats had a strong common identity (see Section 3.1.1 of Chapter 7). During the first national revival in the second half of the 19th century, intellectuals had reinforced the Croatian ethnic base and transformed it into a popular national identity. And since then, the sense of Croatian-ness had been kept well alive by Croatian politicians and intellectuals. As late as 1971 the so-called Croatian Spring bore witness to the continued strength of the Croatian national identity (Čuvalo, 1990). Thus, the Croats had a strong primordial interest in establishing an independent nation-state. Furthermore, the Krajina region was a part of the territory that the Croats perceived to be ancient Croatian land.

Moreover, the Croats' ambition to create a Croatian nation-state was reinforced by the antagonistic nature of the Croatian–Serbian historical interplay (see Section 3.1.3 of Chapter 7). Thus, the Croats had resented the settlement of Serbs on Croatian lands which took place during the rule of the Habsburg empire and the semi-autonomous status that was granted to the Serbs in that period. The presence of the Serbian minority was perceived as an encroachment of the Croats' right to that territory and, in addition, the Croats feared that the Krajina Serbs might unite with the other Serbs in a Great Serbia. When the Serbian minority, shortly after the elections in the spring of 1990, arranged a referendum on autonomy of the Serb-populated areas, the Croats perceived this action as a confirmation of their fear.

Finally, the primordial interests of the Croats were also founded on the perception that their language, culture, and history had been misrecognized by the alleged Serb-dominated Yugoslavian authorities (see Section 4.1.3 of Chapter 7). Consequently, the Croats had an interest in avoiding this cultural deprivation by establishing an independent state in which the status and influence of the Croatian culture *vis-à-vis* the Serbian could be enhanced.

6.2 The Primordial Interests of the Serbs

Unlike the Russians in Estonia but paralleling the Dnestr Slavs and the Gagauz in Moldova, the Krajina Serbs in Croatia emphasized that they had a unique identity (see Section 3.1.2 of Chapter 7). The claim of the Krajina Serbs was not unfounded as their historical roots in the area stretched back to the early 16th century. Of special importance in relation to the Serbs' primordial interests was the fact that the strong ethnic base of the Serbs implied a close association with the Krajina area which their ancestors defended against the Turks during several centuries. Consequently, the Serbs had a strong interest in securing the largest possible degree of control over the area. So, when the Croats claimed in the late 1980s that the Krajina area was rightfully a part of Croatia while at the same time threatening to secede from Yugoslavia, the primordial interests of the Serbs were clearly at odds with those of the Croats.

The character of the historical interplay between the Croats and Serbs only added to the Serbs' perception that their primordial interests were conflicting with those of the Croats. Thus, the Serbian minority had not forgotten that the Croats had tried virtually to exterminate them when the opportunity and the powers to do so were present in the wake of Nazi-Germany's invasion of Yugoslavia (see Section 3.1.3 of Chapter 7).

Furthermore, the Croatian national revival resulted in actions which made the Serbs fear that they would end up as a culturally deprived and misrecognized minority. First of all, traditional Croatian national symbols which had also been used by the Ustasha regime, such as the Croatian coat of arms, replaced the Yugoslavian symbols. In addition, the status of the Cyrillic alphabet was diminished in relation to that of the Latin. Consequently, the Serbs also had a primordial interest in avoiding future cultural deprivation.

6.3 The Explanatory Power of H_6

The test of H_6 provides an explanation of the violent Croatian–Serbian conflict which is similar to the one provided in the case of the Moldovan–Slavic conflict. Thus, both the Croats and the Serbs had strong and conflicting primordial interests. Firstly, both the titular nation-group and the minority nation-group had a strong ethnic base, and the two groups also competed for sovereign control over a territory with which both associated. Secondly, the Croats and Serbs had an antagonistic history of interaction which raised the level of mistrust and made the Serbs fear a repetition of past atrocities. And finally, the Croats wanted to avoid continuation of the perceived Serb-caused cultural deprivation, while the Serbs feared future Croat-caused cultural deprivation.

7 CONCLUSION

As the situation in Yugoslavia became still more anarchic in the sense that the power and authority of the federal authorities eroded concurrently with the increasing scope of the national revivals of the constituent nation-groups, both the Croats and the Krajina Serbs had reasons to perceive the national revival of the other as conflicting with their security interests. In consequence, both nation-groups made great efforts to enhance their military capabilities. Due to the open support of the YPA, however, the Krajina Serbs' military capability was clearly superior, and therefore they succeeded in gaining control over practically all areas in Croatia populated by Serbs, except for the capital Zagreb. In this way, H_3 was confirmed in the case of the Croatian–Serbian conflict.

The test of H_4 also resulted in an explanation of the violent behaviour of the nation-groups: they both perceived that they had strong and conflicting instrumental interests. That is, while the Croats were strongly motivated to achieve the establishment of an independent state which they saw as the only way out of the perceived Serb-caused economic and political deprivation, the Serbian minority vehemently resisted this prospect as they feared it would lead to political deprivation and increased economic deprivation.

Moreover, H_5 was also able to explain the escalation of the national conflict in Croatia as the Serbian minority reacted to the range of exclusive policies which the Croats adopted and implemented towards them.

Finally, H_6 was confirmed as it revealed that the two groups also had strong and conflicting primordial interests: they had overlapping associations with the Krajina territory, their historical interrelationship was marked by mutual animosity, and the Croats wanted to escape what they regarded as Serb-caused cultural misrecognition by establishing an independent state, while the Serbs feared that they would then become subject to cultural colonization.

16 The National Conflict in Czechoslovakia

1 INTRODUCTION

In the wake of the regime change in 1989, the Czech–Slovakian conflict became an example of a national conflict that was solved peacefully. In contrast to the marriage between the south Slavic Croats and Serbs which ended in a violent row, the conflict between the west Slavic Czechs and Slovaks thus ended with a subdued divorce.

2 THE NATIONAL CONFLICT

Having overthrown the Soviet-influenced communist regime in 1989 together, the number of issues of disagreement between the Czechs and the Slovaks grew still larger (see also Section 2 of Chapter 8). However, the ensuing conflict was neither violent nor characterized by unilateral actions by the opposing sides. True, on several occasions the Slovaks in particular threatened to take unilateral steps, as, for example, in the autumn of 1990 when they warned the Czechs that they would declare the supremacy of Slovakian laws over those of the federation if their demand for decentralization of the powers of the federal authorities was not met (Pehe, 1990c: 6ff). But still, issues of disagreement were handled at the negotiation table before any action was taken. Thus, in the above-mentioned instance, a compromise was reached in the December 1990 law on power-sharing in which the federal government agreed to cede many of its responsibilities to the republican governments until new federal and republican constitutions could be drafted (p. 9).

The still more pronounced Slovakian national awareness and the demand of a growing number of Slovakian politicians that Czechoslovakia should be a confederation was not compatible with the Czechs' demand for a centralized federation. Thus, although protracted negotiations were held, the fundamental questions regarding the constitutional set-up and the power-sharing could not be solved. Furthermore, this stalemate meant that it was difficult to adopt and implement other reforms, such as the much-needed economic reforms (Martin, 1991: 6ff). Also, foreign investors hesitated due to the confused situation.

As the Czechs and Slovaks, in June 1992, elected politicians whose views on the above-mentioned questions were still very far from being compatible, the second best solution was eventually accepted by the majority of both Czech and Slovakian politicians. Thus, the two nation-groups did not need a third party to solve the national conflict. On 1 January 1993 Czechoslovakia was split into two independent states following the signing of more than 30 treaties governing the post-separation relations between the two republics. And since then, no serious issues of disagreement have appeared.

3 THE SECURITY INTERESTS OF THE NATION-GROUPS IN CZECHOSLOVAKIA

When the USSR abandoned the Brezhnev doctrine, the overlay on the East European security complex was significantly reduced. According to Buzan's theory of security complexes, this development should allow local security dynamics renewed expression. Thus, the probability that local security problems came to play a decisive role increased.

In the case of Czechoslovakia, only the Slovakian national revival could pose a security problem to the Czechs in the sense of H_3. H_3 would not predict the Slovaks to be threatened by the Czechs as the Czech-dominated Czechoslovakian revival was not a distinct Czech national revival. According to H_3, the non-violent character of this conflict could be explained as follows: although they perceived the Slovakian national revival as a security problem, the Czechs refrained from use of violent means because of the small difference in the military capability of the two nation-groups.

3.1 The Military Capability of the Czechs

In contrast to the situation in Estonia and Moldova, the Soviet forces stationed in Czechoslovakia played no role in relation to the military capabilities of the Czechs and Slovaks. As early as the spring of 1990 an agreement was signed between the Czechoslovakian and USSR governments that the Soviet forces should be withdrawn, and in June 1991 the last unit left the country (Pehe, 1992a: 86).

However, like the other East European satellite states and Yugoslavia, Czechoslovakia had its own armed forces. For strategic reasons, the greatest part of these forces were located in the Czech lands during the cold war. Following the Velvet Revolution in November 1989 this was still the case. Thus, in June 1991 eight out of ten divisions were stationed in the Western Military District of Czechoslovakia – that is, in the Czech republic (Heisbourg, 1991: 86f). Yet, notwithstanding the evolving Slovakian national revival, the Czech politicians took no steps towards establishing separate Czech armed forces. This attitude was in line with that of the ordinary Czechs. When asked in the autumn of 1991 whether they agreed with the statement that 'our security should be based on separate Czech and Slovak home defence forces', only 19 per cent agreed strongly or somewhat (Deis, 1992: 11). And as for the armed forces themselves, they remained neutral and under joint federal command throughout the Czech–Slovakian conflict in contrast to the YPA in Croatia and the Soviet forces in Moldova (Huldt, 1992: 65).

3.2 The Military Capability of the Slovaks

By 1991 only two out ten divisions of the Czechoslovakian federal army were located in Slovakia (Heisbourg, 1991: 86f). However, separate military powers were not an important issue on the Slovakian (and Czech) agenda until after the June 1992 elections when the Czech and Slovakian politicians decided, in principle, to establish two separate states.[93] During the subsequent negotiations on the future of the Czechoslovakian armed forces, the Czechs initially demanded that the military assets should be divided according to the so-called territorial principle – that is, the assets should remain in the possession of the republic on whose territory they were located (Pehe, 1992d: 10). The Slovaks strongly protested against this demand as 80 per cent of the military assets were located in the Czech lands, and eventually the two parties agreed to divide the armed forces on the basis of a 2:1 ratio (Pehe, 1992e: 2). Consequently, during the last months of 1992 large numbers of troops and military hardware were transferred to Slovakia.

3.3 The Explanatory Power of H_3

Although it would have been easy for the Czechs to establish a superior military capability in relation to the Slovaks by unilaterally taking control of those units of the federal armed forces which were located in the Czech republic, this did not happen. Furthermore, the fact that the Czechs agreed to narrow the gap between the military capabilities of the two nation-groups by transferring large amounts of military equipment to the Slovaks indicates that the Czechs did not perceive the Slovaks as constituting a security risk. Therefore, H_3 is not confirmed in the Czech–Slovakian case of national conflict. On the contrary, paralleling the Estonian–Russian conflict, the above analysis shows that a national revival of one nation-group is not necessarily perceived as a security problem by opposing nation-groups.

4 THE INSTRUMENTAL INTERESTS OF THE NATION-GROUPS IN CZECHOSLOVAKIA

According to H_4, we should focus on the instrumental interests when trying to explain the non-violent character of the Czech–Slovakian national conflict. So, according to H_4 we should expect that neither or only one of the nation-group felt or feared economic and political deprivation caused by the opposing nation-group – that is, perceived itself to have weak and non-conflicting instrumental interests.

4.1 The Instrumental Interests of the Czechs

Like the Estonians and the Croats, the Czechs felt that they were relatively economically deprived because of the Soviet influence on the economic policies implemented in the country in the postwar period (see Section 4.1.1 of Chapter 8). Accordingly, the Czechs had an instrumental interest in abandoning the Soviet-model planned economy and instead starting a transition towards a market economy and reorienting their trade relations towards the West. Unlike the Russians in Estonia, the Slavs in Moldova, and the Serbs in Croatia, however, the Slovaks did not belong to the nation-group which was blamed for the perceived economic deprivation of the majority nation-group. On the contrary, until the fall of the Soviet-influenced communist regime, the Czechs had a shared instrumental interest with the Slovaks in correcting the perceived undeserved economic backwardness.

Nor did the Czechs have any reason to feel economically colonized by the Slovaks in the post-Velvet Revolution period. Certainly, some Czech politicians did complain that the contribution of the Slovakian republic to the federal budget was far too little in relation to that of the Czech republic, and they questioned the redistribution of financial resources at the federal level towards the Slovakian republic (Pehe, 1991f: 13). In the same vein, an opinion poll conducted in the autumn of 1991 revealed that only 34 per cent of the Czechs agreed strongly or somewhat that the resources of the federation were equally distributed between the Czech lands and Slovakia (Deis, 1992: 10). However, the widespread perception that the

Slovaks were becoming an economic burden – and the Slovakian politicians' reluctant attitude towards rapid economic reforms – meant that the Czechs eventually did not regard the Slovaks' ambitions of autonomy as conflicting with their economic interests.

As for political deprivation, the situation was rather similar. The Soviet hegemony meant that the opportunities for the Czechs (and Slovaks) to pursue independent policies were strongly circumscribed (see Section 4.1.2 of Chapter 8). The Soviet-influenced communist regime also deprived the Czechs (and the Slovaks) of basic civil rights and of the opportunity to exercise political influence by participating in democratic elections. Consequently, the Czechs had an instrumental interest in correcting the political deprivation. Yet, this interest was also perceived to be identical rather than conflicting with the interests of the Slovaks.

The Velvet Revolution crowned the aspiration of the Czechs to establish a fully independent and democratic Czechoslovakia with success. And as the numerical majority of the Czechs secured them a continued dominance of the federal organs, they had no reason to fear political deprivation caused by the Slovaks either.

True, as the growing Slovakian demand for autonomy threatened to erode the Czech ambition to build a strong and relatively centralized federation, the Czechs no longer perceived their instrumental interests to be identical with those of the Slovaks. However, the Czechs did not fear direct political deprivation. Rather, they disagreed with the Slovaks' demand for decentralization of most powers to the republican level as they feared that it would make the federation weak and dysfunctional. Therefore, the Czechs eventually did not regard the separation of the federation as incompatible with their political interests although they had preferred a strong and centralized federation. President Havel probably represented the stand of most Czech politicians when he stated that a separation of the republics would be preferable to a federation that would be nothing but an empty shell (Pehe, 1991f: 14).

4.2 The Instrumental Interests of the Slovaks

During the communist era, the Slovaks were not economically deprived in so far as their standard of living rose almost to the same level as that of the Czechs due to relatively high rates of investment in industry in particular (see Section 4.2.1 of Chapter 8). Still, the economy in Slovakia was managed by the centre in Prague. And when the post-1989 Czech-dominated federal government decided to follow a radical economic transition strategy and the economic reforms hit the economy in Slovakia especially hard, the perception among the Slovaks that they were subject to economic deprivation caused by continued Czech domination of the federation became widespread. Therefore, they had an instrumental interest in avoiding this deprivation. And when the Czechs proposed a partition of the common state, the Slovaks could hardly claim that their economic interests were conflicting with those of the Czechs.

Regarding political deprivation, the Slovakian elite enjoyed a most-favoured-lords status throughout the period of communist rule (see Section 4.2.2 of Chapter 8). Nevertheless, the Slovaks as such never fully embraced the idea of Czechoslovakian-ness (see also Section 3.1.2 of Chapter 8). Instead, following the Velvet Revolution the Slovaks supported those nationalist Slovakian politicians who argued that the Czech demand for a strong and centralized federation would mean continued Czech dominance. So, the Slovaks also feared political deprivation which led them to opt for maximum political autonomy inside a weak federation. However, as with regard to economic interests, the Slovaks could not claim to have conflicting political interests with the Czechs when they eventually offered complete self-determination to the Slovaks.

4.3 The Explanatory Power of H_4

H_4 is able to explain the non-violent character of the Czech–Slovakian conflict as neither side had conflicting instrumental interests.

The instrumental interests of the Czechs in building a strong and centralized Czechoslovakian federation were initially conflicting with the ambitions of the Slovaks. However, following more than two years of discussions on the set-up of the post-communist federation and with a strongly diminished chance of finding a compromise solution after the June 1992 elections, the arguments in favour of 'letting the Slovaks go' were the most weighty. The less competitive Slovakian economy and the unwillingness of the Slovaks to support radical economic reforms were perceived as a barrier to the expected fast transition to a prosperous market economy. Furthermore, the Czechs feared that devolving most powers to the republican level would result in a dysfunctional federation. As a result, the Czechs came to see a partition of the federation as compatible with their instrumental interests.

As for the Slovaks, they feared future economic and political Czech domination. Therefore, they opted for autonomy within a weak federation. And when the Czechs proposed a partition of the common state, this was sufficiently close to the Slovakian preferences as to make their interests compatible with the Czech proposal.

5 THE IDEOLOGICAL INTERESTS OF THE CZECHS

In accordance with H_5, the non-violent character of the Czech–Slovakian national conflict could be explained by an ideological interest of the majority nation-group, the Czechs, in adopting a territorial type of nationalism which implied inclusive or neutral policies of nationalism towards the minority nation-group, the Slovaks.

5.1 Official Czech Policies

In contrast to the Estonians, Moldovans, and Croats, the Czechs, who constituted a majority in the federal parliament and government of Czechoslovakia in the 1989–93 period (see Section 4.2.2 of Chapter 8), did not use this position to force through exclusive policies directed at the Slovaks. Thus, the Czechs opted for a Czechoslovakian state, supported a continued 'zero option' regarding citizenship,[94] and were willing to reduce, though not completely lose, their former dominance in order to preserve the common state. This willingness was expressed, for example, in the December 1990 agreement which delegated significant powers to the republican level (see Section 2).

Only when the negotiations on the future constitutional structure of the federation had come to a complete deadlock after the June 1992 elections and a preliminary decision on the split of the common state had been reached did the Czech politicians begin to favour some exclusive policies. Thus, in negotiations in the autumn of 1992 on the future regulations regarding citizenship, the Czech side did not accept dual citizenship and demanded that a citizen of one republic should be treated as a foreigner in the other republic (Pehe, 1992d: 7ff). On the other hand, the Slovakian side proposed dual citizenship and recommended that a citizen of one republic should have the legal rights of a citizen in the other republic. However, although the Czechs were not willing to negotiate a compromise explicitly on the citizenship issue, they nevertheless signed non-discriminatory agreements with the Slovaks on related issues. Thus, one agreement secured the free movement of citizens of both republics across the common border, and another stipulated that no working permit would be needed if a citizen of one republic wished to work in the other. In any case, the decisive argument is still that in the period *prior* to the Czech–Slovakian agreement to form two separate states, the Czech politicians did not demand the adoption of exclusive policies towards the Slovaks.

5.2 Unofficial Czech Policies

Although a few Czech radical nationalist groups, such as neo-Nazis and a Czech version of the German Republican Party, emerged in the post-1989 period, their political influence remained limited (Pehe, 1994: 50ff).[95] Furthermore, the discriminatory activities of these groups, primarily peaceful demonstrations but also some cases of violent attacks, were directed against Romanies and foreigners from developing countries – not against Slovaks. On the contrary, the Republican Party, for example, blamed the federal government for the worsening relations between Czechs and Slovaks as it feared the possibility of a separation of the country.

The absence of any significant unofficial Czech policies of nationalism against the Slovaks is also underpinned by the fact that only among the relatively few Slovaks living in the Czech lands[96] were some accusations made that they had been subject to discrimination by Czechs (Kirschbaum, 1993: 78). However, these accusations were not substantiated by arguments about how the alleged discrimination had been pursued.

5.3 The Explanatory Power of H_5

The above analysis shows that the Czech-dominated liberal revival leading to the Velvet Revolution had a territorial character. The following absence of Czech exclusive policies towards the Slovaks can explain that the scope and content of the Slovakian revival was moderate and that the Czechs and Slovaks throughout the national conflict were able to negotiate peacefully the disagreements regarding the interrelations of the two nation-groups. Therefore, H_5 is confirmed.

6 THE PRIMORDIAL INTERESTS OF THE NATION-GROUPS IN CZECHOSLOVAKIA

H_6 offers a different explanation of the national conflict in Czechoslovakia. According to H_6, the non-violent conflict could be explained if both or at least one of the nation-groups perceived that their primordial interests were either non-conflicting or weak and conflicting in relation to those of the opposing nation-group.

6.1 The Primordial Interests of the Czechs

By the late 1980s, a strong and explicit Czech ethnic base and national identity still existed (see Section 3.1.1 of Chapter 8). Yet, the existence of a Czech-dominated Czechoslovakian state since 1918 meant that a majority of the Czechs also perceived themselves as Czechoslovaks, although only approximately one third of the Czechs considered the Czechoslovakian identity as the more important. Consequently, the Czechs only had a weak primordial interest in preserving the Czechoslovakian state. And in fact it is questionable whether this interest can be termed primordial at all since its historical foundation was so young and lacked a distinct ethnic base. Moreover, as the explicit Czech identity was still the most salient to the majority of the Czechs and as the Czechs were historically associated with the Czech lands,[97] the Czechs did not have a primordial interest conflicting with the Slovaks' wish for control over the Slovakian territory.

Furthermore, the primordial interests of the Czechs were not marked by an antagonistic historical interrelationship with the Slovaks (see Section 3.1.3 of Chapter 8). In the period prior to the founding of the Czechoslovakian state, the Czechs had never been subject to violent attacks by Slovaks. And although later Slovakian attempts to gain autonomy, primarily the establishment of the Slovakian quasi-state at the beginning of the Second World War, were perceived as a betrayal of the Czechoslovakian state-building project, these attempts were not accompanied by antagonistic Slovakian actions towards the Czechs. Thus, the historical interrelationship did not contain events which could make the Czechs associate the present Slovakian striving towards autonomy with an inherent danger for the Czechs.

Finally, the primordial interests of the Czechs were not driven by a desire to correct cultural deprivation or frustration since they had never experienced Slovakian misrecognition or cultural colonization (see Section 4.1.3 of Chapter 8).

6.2 The Primordial Interests of the Slovaks

By the early 1990s only approximately one quarter of the Slovaks associated with Czechoslovakia in the sense that they identified themselves as being not only Slovaks but also Czechoslovaks (see Section 3.1.2 of Chapter 8). In contrast, the Slovaks had preserved a strong ethnic base which included a historical association with the territory of the Slovakian republic. Thus, the Slovaks had a primordial interest in achieving autonomy or independence. Initially, the Slovaks perceived their primordial interests to be conflicting with those of the Czechs in so far as the latter were not prepared to fulfil the Slovakian demand for extensive autonomy. But as the Czechs – in contrast to the Estonians, Moldovans, and Croats – did not insist on maintaining a common territory with the Slovaks, the primordial interests of the two nation-groups turned out to be compatible in this respect.

Furthermore, the primordial interests of the Slovaks were not strengthened by an historically ingrained anti-Czech attitude (see Section 3.1.3 of Chapter 8). Before 1918, Czech–Slovakian relations were characterized by amity rather than enmity. And although the Slovaks were subject to internal colonization in the interwar period, they never experienced any instances of violent persecution.

Finally, the Slovaks had no primordial interest in correcting cultural misrecognition or deprivation since the communist regime abandoned the idea of a Czechoslovakian nation and, from 1968 onwards, recognized the equal status of the Slovaks by transforming the unitary state into a federation (see Section 4.2.3 of Chapter 8). Also, the fact that both the Czech and the Slovakian languages enjoyed the status of official languages points to the absence of Czech cultural deprivation of the Slovaks. Nor did the development in the wake of the Velvet Revolution contain any events that could make the Slovaks fear future cultural deprivation. For example, the Czechs yielded to the Slovakian demand that the name of the federation should be changed to the Czech and Slovakian Federal Republic instead of the Czech proposal, the Czechoslovakian Federal Republic.

6.3 The Explanatory Power of H_6

H_6 provides a convincing explanation of why the national conflict between the Czechs and the Slovaks after the Velvet Revolution never escalated into violent conflict but ended with a peaceful and negotiated separation into two independent states. First of all, although the Czechs associated with the Czechoslovakian identity to a larger extent than the Slovaks, both *ethnies* remained the most salient basis of national identity, and as the historical territories of the two nation-groups were non-overlapping, there was no competition for sovereignty over the same territory. Secondly, the two groups did not have a history of interaction that exhibited instances of mutual violent persecution. And thirdly, neither of the two nation-groups felt or feared cultural deprivation caused by the opposing group. In short, both nation-groups perceived that their primordial interests were relatively weak and non-conflicting.

7 CONCLUSION

The test of H_3 led to a rejection of the hypothesis. Thus, although the potential military capability of the Czechs was superior and although the Czech politicians did not agree with the increasing Slovakian demand for extensive autonomy, they did not take any steps towards trying to solve the disagreements by way of violent means. On the contrary, the Czech side gave in to the Slovakian demands on several occasions, such as when the constitution was amended in December 1990 to allow for devolving more powers to the republican level.

In contrast, H_5 could explain why the intensity and scope of the Slovakian national revival was limited. The character of the Czech-dominated Czechoslovakian revival was territorial rather than ethnic and therefore the majority nation-group did not demand the adoption of exclusive policies towards the minority nation-group.

H_4 could also explain the non-violent character of the national conflict. Certainly, the instrumental interests of the two nation-groups were initially at odds as the Czechs wanted to implement comprehensive market economy reforms and preserve a strong federation while the Slovaks preferred a slower reform process and autonomy within a weak federation. However, the less competitive Slovakian economy and the Slovakian refusal to implement comprehensive and fast economic reforms and build a centralized and strong federation made the Czechs perceive their instrumental interests to be better served by a partition of the common state. As this proposal was close to the Slovakian demands, the instrumental interests of the two nation-groups turned out to be non-conflicting.

Finally, the test of H_6 revealed that the primordial interests of both nation-groups were non-conflicting. Although both had a strong *ethnie*, neither *ethnie* had any claims as to the territory with which the other associated. Furthermore, the historical relationship between Czechs and Slovaks did not involve any instances of violent persecution. And finally, neither group perceived or feared cultural colonization by the other.

17 The National Conflicts: Comparison and Conclusions

1 INTRODUCTION

In order to obtain generalizable knowledge about the causes of national conflict intensity, the preceding separate accounts of theories and cases have to be compared and evaluated. This is the task of the present chapter.

As in Chapter 9, we begin with a comparison of the dependent variable, national conflict intensity. Then we proceed to compare the relative explanatory power of the hypotheses deduced in Chapter 11. These comparisons are then used as the foundation for a discussion of the relationship between the different theories of interests and of the relationship between macrosociological and microsociological theories. Finally, we epitomize our conclusions in an integrative model of the causes of national conflict intensity.

2 COMPARISON OF THE NATIONAL CONFLICTS

Of course, each case of national conflict has its own specific combination of issues of disagreement, events, escalation, and attempts to solve the conflict.

In the course of the Estonian national revival from 1987 onwards, the potential for escalatory conflict between Estonians and Russians in Estonia increased considerably as the number of Estonian policies of nationalism on issues such as national symbols, language, immigration, citizenship, and suffrage multiplied. Nevertheless, no violent means were used to solve the issues of disagreement. And after the establishment of an OSCE mission in Estonia in 1993, the two nation-groups seem to have found, if not a solution to their conflictual relationship, then at least a *modus vivendi.*

In the Moldovan–Slavic conflict, the issues of disagreement were initially practically the same as in Estonia. But when, in the spring of 1990, both Moldovans and Dnestr Slavs declared the sovereignty of Moldova and the Dnestr region respectively and took measures to secure control over the claimed areas, the seeds of a more serious conflict than that in Estonia were sown. The potential for escalation was realized with the outbreak of full-scale war in the spring of 1992 after a period of consolidation and rearmament on both sides since the first limited skirmishes between Moldovan police troops and Slavic paramilitary units took place in the autumn of 1990. After the Moldovan defeat in this war, Russian peace-keeping forces were sent to the Dnestr area. These Russian units have maintained the status quo and, thus, secured the *de facto* independence of the Dnestr republic.

The potential for escalatory conflict seemed the same in the Moldovan–Gagauz relationship as almost the same issues of disagreement were prevalent from 1990 onwards and as both sides claimed supremacy over the same Gagauz-inhabited area. The potential for escalation was maintained for a long time as no real solution to the issue of Gagauz autonomy was found and as both Moldovan troops and Gagauz paramilitary units remained in the area. However, neither side had full control over the area and, most importantly, neither side sought to attain this through violent confrontation with the other side. Thus, the Moldovan–Gagauz conflict remained non-violent, and in the summer of 1994 the decisive step towards a solution was made as the Moldovan parliament in the new constitution guaranteed autonomy and decentralization to the Gagauz-inhabited area.

Just as with the relationship between Moldovans and Slavs, the national conflict between Croats and Serbs in Croatia escalated into a violent conflict. The main differences were that it happened quicker, that the violent means employed were more brutal and hit the civilian population to a far greater extent, and that the violence could not be stopped even with a large international intervention through UNPROFOR (United Nations Protection Force) which was deployed in Croatia in early 1992. As in Moldova, violent skirmishes began following disagreement about the issue of autonomy for the minority population. The Serbs found no understanding of their demands within the Croatian nationalist government elected in the spring of 1990. On the contrary, the Croatian authorities insisted on establishing full control of the area by dismissing Serbian police officers and other public employees and by sending police forces staffed by Croats to the Serb-inhabited areas. Meanwhile, the Serbs took measures to arm themselves with the help of the YPA and the Territorial Defence. As a result, the relationship between the two nation-groups deteriorated until, finally, full-scale war broke out following the Croatian declaration of independence in the summer of 1991. The war lasted several months and continued even some time after the deployment of UNPROFOR. And although a relatively stable cease-fire was observed for a long period, the international involvement was not able to prevent the conflict from re-escalating as the heavily rearmed Croatian army attacked and conquered the Krajina area in the summer of 1995.

Finally, the Czech–Slovakian conflict approaches a text-book example of peaceful conflict solution. Following the Velvet Revolution in 1989, the two nation-groups disagreed considerably about the central issue of power-sharing between the federal and republican levels – an issue that was decisive for continued coexistence. The Czech position, which favoured a strong and centralized federation, was so far from the Slovakian preference for a decentralized confederation that a potential for escalation was certainly present. However, following a long period of negotiations, the conflict was solved as both nation-groups settled for their second-best option, realizing that they could not attain their preferred solution. The second-best option was a peaceful partition of the Czechoslovakian federation which took effect from 1 January 1993.

The five national conflicts have in common the basic disputed issue: who or which institutions have the right to govern which nation-groups and territories, and what does this right imply? Furthermore, in almost all cases (except perhaps for the Czech republic), the dispute over this issue took place in a social context that was conducive with respect to processes of escalation. Critical oppositions, neutral mass media, and conciliatory grass roots movements were seldom present, and when they existed they were not so influential as to counterbalance the preponderance of non-conciliatory mobilizers, contending strategists, nationalist-biased media, and extremist activists.

Nevertheless, as the above summary shows, the national conflicts in Eastern Europe escalated to very different levels of intensity before they were settled (in the Czech–Slovakian case), reached a peaceful *modus vivendi* (in the Estonian–Russian case with help from international organizations, and in the Moldovan–Gagauz case without such help), or resulted – at least temporarily – in an internationally supervised cease-fire following large-scale military confrontation (in the Moldovan–Slavic and the Croatian–Serbian cases). Despite the variety of national conflict intensities in Eastern Europe, we have decided to distinguish only between violent and non-violent conflict because any other scaling of the concept of conflict intensity, as discussed in Section 1 of Chapter 11, is connected with serious difficulties. With this criterion, we can distinguish between, on the one hand, the Moldovan–Slavic and the Croatian–Serbian national conflicts that escalated into violent conflict and, on the other hand, the Estonian–Russian, the Moldovan–Gagauz, and the Czech–Slovakian national conflicts that remained non-violent.

3 COMPARISON OF THE EXPLANATIONS OF NATIONAL CONFLICT INTENSITY

As we noted in the concluding chapter of Part One, the shift from analyses of specific national revivals to a general and comparative analysis almost necessarily implies some level of simplification and some loss of information. This is true also when we compare the explanations of national conflict intensity. In Figure 6, we have summarized the results from the previous four chapters using only three categories: one affirmative, one partly affirmative, and one negative.

In the upper part of Figure 6, the relationships towards the opposing nation-groups as seen from each nation-group involved in a national conflict are compared. This amounts to ten instances of perceived relationships as the Moldovan nation-group must be analysed both with respect to the Slavs and to the Gagauz. As parameters, we include the essential elements of each hypothesis deduced in Chapter 11 – that is, the questions of security interests (national revival in the opposing group), military superiority, instrumental interests (economic and political), ideological interests (exclusive policies of nationalism by the state-bearing nation-group), and primordial interests (*ethnies* competing for a certain territory, antagonistic historical relationship, and cultural interests). In the lower part, then, these elements are used to determine the explanatory power of the hypotheses in our two cases of violent national conflict and three cases of non-violent national conflict.

Like Figure 2 in Chapter 9, Figure 6 can be used both as a summary of the preceding chapters and as a comparison of the cases. As a summary – that is, read from above – the figure indicates, for example, that all hypotheses were confirmed in the two cases of violent conflict. Thus, it seems that all kinds of interests – security interests as well as instrumental, ideological, and primordial interests – combined to make the Moldovan–Slavic and the Croatian–Serbian conflicts violent. However, if we want to determine the ability of the hypotheses to explain national conflict intensity in general, we have to compare the explanatory power of the hypotheses with respect to both violent and non-violent conflicts. That is, we must conduct a comparative analysis. Read horizontally instead of vertically, the figure thus reveals two especially obvious comparative points.

Firstly, although the hypothesis based on Posen's (1993) theory about the relationship between the security dilemma created by national revivals in the territory of collapsing empires on the one hand and the use of military power in national conflicts on the other seems confirmed in the cases of violent national conflicts, it has difficulties explaining why

● = Yes ◗ = To a certain degree, yes
○ = No

	Estonians (vs. Russians)	Russian (vs. Estonians)	Moldovans (vs. Slavs)	Slavs (vs. Moldovans)	Moldovans (vs. Gagauz)	Gagauz (vs. Moldovans)	Croats (vs. Serbs)	Serbs (vs. Croats)	Czechs (vs. Slovaks)	Slovaks (vs. Czechs)
Strong national revival in the opposing nation-group	○	●	●	●	●	●	●	●	◗	◗
Military superiority over the opposing nation-group	○	●	○	●	◗	○	○	●	●	○
Strong economic interest conflicting with the opposing nation-group	●	○	●	●	○	◗	●	●	○	○
Strong political interests conflicting with the opposing nation-group	●	●	●	●	○	◗	●	●	○	○
Exclusive policies of nationalism adopted by the majority nation-group		●		●		●		●		○
Strong *ethnie* associated with territory claimed by the opposing nation-group	●	○	●	●	●	●	●	●	○	○
Past atrocities committed by the opposing nation-group	●	○	●	●	○	○	●	●	○	○
Strong cultural interests conflicting with the opposing nation-group	●	●	●	●	○	○	●	●	○	○

		Estonian–Russian	Moldovan–Slavic	Moldovan–Gagauz	Croatian–Serbian	Czech–Slovakian
Violent national conflict		○	●	○	●	○
Coflict intensity explained by:	H_3	○	●	◗	●	○
	H_4	◗	●	●	●	●
	H_5	○	●	○	●	●
	H_6	◗	●	◗	●	●

Figure 6 Explanations of national conflict intensity

the nation-groups in some cases did not turn to violent means when a national revival occurred in the opposing nation-group. Most notably, it must be surprising to Posen and other realists that the Russians in Estonia did *not* rebel against the strong Estonian national revival although they could most probably have counted on an overwhelming military superiority due to their powerful mother-nation. In the same vein, the peaceful settlement of the Czech–Slovakian conflict fits badly into Posen's theory as the Czechs were willing to balance the military power of the two republics by transferring large numbers of units and equipment to Slovakia despite the security threat which the national revival in Slovakia, according to the theory, posed to the Czech nation-group. Finally, although we lack exact information about the military strength of the Gagauz, a probable estimation is that it was exceeded by the military power of the Moldovans simply due to the small size of the Gagauz nation-group. If this was so, H_3 cannot explain why the Moldovans did not counter the strong national revival among the Gagauz by use of force.

Secondly, the ideological content of the nationalism of the majority nation-group does not seem to be a stable explanation of national conflict intensity either. H_5 fares somewhat better than H_3 in that it can explain the two cases of violent national conflict as well as the Czech–Slovakian non-violent conflict. In both cases of violent national conflict, the minority nation-groups faced a large number of exclusive policies of nationalism, and in the non-violent Czech–Slovakian conflict such policies were absent. However, as exclusive policies of nationalism were also adopted towards the Russians in Estonia and towards the Gagauz in Moldova, H_5 cannot explain why the Estonian–Russian and the Moldovan–Gagauz conflicts remained non-violent, and it is therefore unable to account for national conflict intensity in general.

In contrast, neither H_4 nor H_6 could be clearly rejected in any of the cases. In the Moldovan–Slavic and Croatian–Serbian violent conflicts, both nation-groups perceived themselves to have strong and conflicting instrumental and primordial interests. Both nation-groups were competing for economic and political power in a territory to which both claimed historical ethnic rights, and both nation-groups wanted to counter cultural misrecognition and repetition of past atrocities. At the other end of the spectrum, the non-violent Czech–Slovakian conflict also fits well with the predictions of the hypotheses as neither nation-group perceived their instrumental or primordial interests to be conflicting. The non-violent Estonian–Russian and Moldovan–Gagauz conflicts are less clear, but nevertheless explainable by both hypotheses. In the Estonian–Russian case, there is no doubt that the Estonians perceived both their instrumental interests and their primordial interests to be strong and conflicting with those of the Russians. But this is not enough to reject the hypotheses as *both* nation-groups are required to think in this way in order for the conflict to escalate. The fact that the Russians, to some extent, perceived their political and cultural interests to be conflicting with those of the Estonians weakens both hypotheses a little, though still not enough for a complete rejection as the Russians neither perceived conflicting economic interests, associated ethnically with the Estonian territory, nor had been subject to any past atrocities committed by Estonians. In the same way, the Moldovans and the Gagauz did compete for the same territory and some Gagauz did perceive their economic and political interests to be conflicting with the Moldovans. But the instrumental interests were not strong and were counterbalanced by other Gagauz who rejected the view that Moldovans and Gagauz had strong, conflicting interests, and the primordial interests were weakened by the absence of historical antagonism and cultural misrecognition. In any case, the Moldovans did not perceive their primordial and instrumental interests to be conflicting with the Gagauz. The hypotheses can therefore not be rejected in the case of the Moldovan–Gagauz conflict either.

With these empirical results as a foundation, we are able to give a more substantiated discussion of the theoretical relationship between different kinds of interests and the causal role of the different kinds of interests in the escalation of national conflicts.

4 THE RELATIONSHIP BETWEEN DIFFERENT THEORIES OF INTERESTS

The single-factor hypotheses about national conflict intensity – that is, Posen's emphasis on a narrow concept of security interest based on relative military power and Smith's focus on the ideological content of different types of nationalism – could not resist a closer examination of the empirical evidence. In contrast, the hypotheses based on instrumental and primordial interests proved resistant in the empirical tests. This difference is, of course, primarily due to the greater explanatory power of H_4 and H_6. However, in our view, H_4 and H_6 also have at least three general theoretical advantages over the hypotheses based on Posen's and Smith's theories.

Firstly, they recognize that the occurrence or non-occurrence of escalating national conflicts is not attributable to any single cause. Thus, both H_4 and H_6 are compounded of several elements, and they do not, as H_3 and H_5, hinge upon the existence of a single, crucial interest.

Secondly, they explicitly recognize that interests are *variable*. Thus, both H_4 and H_6 focus on the *strength* of instrumental or primordial interests and formulate probabilistic predictions of the outcome, whereas H_3 and H_5 express a more mechanistic view of nation-groups as billiard balls which always react when stimulated in a certain way.

Finally, H_4 and H_6 are explicit about the importance of *mutual perceptions*. H_3 and H_5 are less insistent on the importance of perceptions, and they focus almost exclusively on the situation of *one* of the nation-groups. True, a comparison of the relative military power of the opposing nation-groups *is* involved in H_3, but it is sufficient that this comparison is conducted in one of the nation-groups only. Even more obvious is H_5's statement that the minority group's experience of exclusive policies of nationalism is enough to provoke escalation. In contrast to these hypotheses, H_4 and H_6 build on the basic fact that a social conflict is comprised of at least two parties, and they argue that *all* (or both) parties in a conflict must have conflicting interests to defend in order for the conflict to escalate. Furthermore, these hypotheses emphasize that the important characteristic of such mutual, conflicting interests is the *perception* in the two nation-groups of their strength.

These theoretical disadvantages of H_3 and H_5 and their disability to account for the intensity of all our cases of national conflict do not, however, render military capabilities and exclusive policies of nationalism inconsequential to national conflicts altogether. It is our view that these factors do influence the course and intensity of national conflicts although their causal status, of course, is not that proposed by H_3 and H_5. Whereas relative military capabilities cannot explain in all cases why a national conflict does or does not escalate into violent conflict, it would be naïve completely to exclude the conducive effect of large military superiority on the decision of force employment in some cases as well as the corresponding dampening effect of military inferiority in other cases. In any case, it is obvious that military capabilities are central to the course, duration, and outcome of a violent conflict once it has started. In the same vein, there is no doubt that exclusive policies of nationalism are conducive to conflict escalation. To assert otherwise would be to deny the possibility of countering escalation through wise and restrained policy-making. The point is, however, that the presence or absence of such policies cannot by itself explain the intensity of a national conflict. In our view, the conducive effect of exclusive policies of nationalism is not least due to the influence of such policies on the perceptions of instrumental and primordial interests. Through policies of nationalism, the majority nation-group not only attains concrete political goals which by themselves affect the instrumental and primordial interests of the minority groups, but also – deliberately or unwillingly – sends signals to the minority groups that make them think twice about their future life conditions in an independent state dominated by the majority nation-group.

The fact remains, however, that H_4 and H_6 proved most resistant to the empirical tests conducted in the previous chapters. Thus, both instrumentalists and primordialists can claim to be able to explain national conflict intensity. However, in line with the conclusion of Part One, we believe that instrumental and primordial explanations should be combined. We shall not recapitulate the theoretical argument for such combination but, in the remaining part of this section, show that it can only strengthen the explanatory power of each hypothesis separately.

What we propose is that a proper macrosociological explanation of national conflict intensity should be found in the constellations of primordial and instrumental interests between the opposing nation-groups. The consistent finding of our empirical investigations is that *both* opposing nation-groups involved in a violent conflict perceived strong, conflicting instrumental *and* primordial interests, whereas in non-violent conflicts none or only one nation-group did so. To give a graphical illustration of this, in Figure 7 we have plotted the strength of the perceived conflicting instrumental and primordial interests of each nation-group with regard to the relevant opposing nation-group. Of course, the determination of the strength of an interest is to a certain degree dependent on the interpretation by the analyst. To minimize this problem, we have measured the strength of the nation-groups' instrumental and primordial interests by the number of elements in each kind of interest which were answered in the affirmative in Figure 6. By simply adding the effect of each element in this way, we avoid the extra layer of interpretation involved in an assessment of the combined strength of the elements. Thus, for instance, the Russians in Estonia had strong, conflicting cultural interests but no *ethnie* that associated with Estonian territory and no past experiences of Estonian persecutions, and they are therefore placed in the '1' area of the abscissa. Likewise, they perceived strong, conflicting political interests but non-conflicting economic interests. Their position on the ordinate should therefore also be in the '1' area. Each pair of opposing nation-groups are then connected with a bold line to distinguish the conflicts from each other.

Figure 7 clearly shows that the top right corner is the most dangerous with respect to conflict escalation. Both Croats and Serbs, and Moldovans and Slavs perceived strong instrumental and primordial interests conflicting with those of the opposing nation-group. The presence of the Estonians in this corner underlines the fact that conflicts tend to escalate only when *both* nation-groups have strong and conflicting interests. The Estonian–Russian conflict also provides an example of how the explanatory power of the two types of interest can be mutually reinforcing. Whereas it can be discussed which predictions should follow from H_4 if the constellations of the two nation-groups' instrumental interests – as in this case – were strong (the Estonians) vs. medium-strong (the Russians), H_6 can support a non-violent prediction as the primordial interests of the Russians were clearly weak. As for the Czech–Slovakian and Moldovan–Gagauz conflicts, they are both safely placed in the bottom left corner of Figure 7.

Unfortunately, our selection of national conflicts lacks proper cases for a test of the relative explanatory power of instrumental and primordial interests. To test the relative strength of H_4 and H_6 against each other, we need conflicts in which the constellations of interests centred either in the top left corner or the bottom right corner of the figure so that the results of, for example, strong and mutually conflicting instrumental interests com-

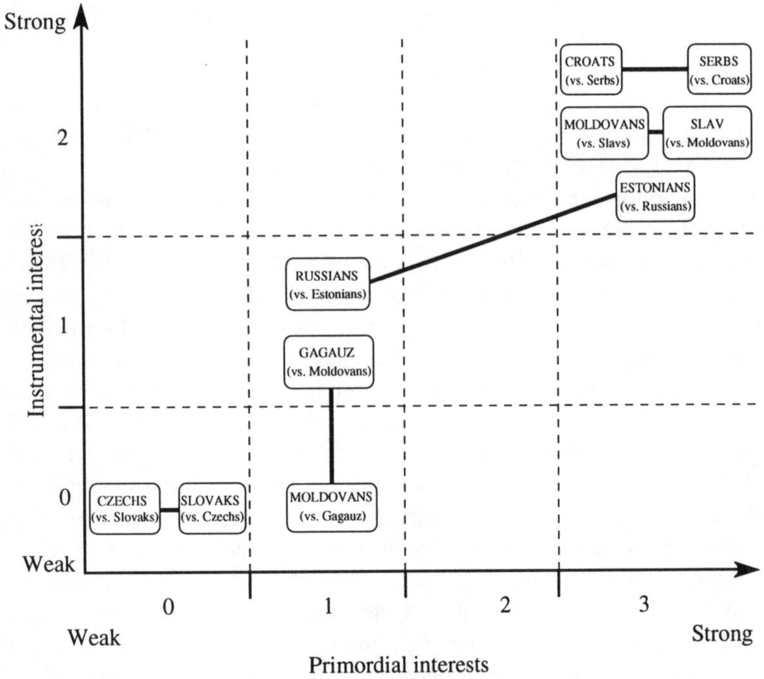

Figure 7 Constellations of perceived primordial and instrumental interests

bined with weak or non-conflicting primordial interests could be observed. Until such test cases are revealed, we must content ourselves with the empirical confirmation of both hypotheses and our theoretical assertion that they should be integrated.

In sum, our theory is that the potential for intense (and ultimately violent) national conflict is highest when the opposing nation-groups perceive strong primordial and instrumental interests which both or all groups perceive as conflicting with the interests of the opposing nation-group(s).

5 THE RELATIONSHIP BETWEEN MACROSOCIOLOGICAL AND MICROSOCIOLOGICAL THEORIES

Having identified constellations of primordial and instrumental interests between nation-groups as the most important macrosociological explanation of national conflict intensity, we must hasten to recognize that several layers of perceptions, moods, processes and decisions enter the causal relationship between these interests and the ensuing character of the conflict. Thus, it would be wrong to accord the theories of interests any inexorable logic. The probabilistic formulation of H_4 and H_6 captures exactly this point: even the most ominous constellation of interests depends on the actions of individuals and groups of individuals in order to result in violent conflict. We have comprised the contingencies that influence the thoughts and behaviour of the individual members of a nation-group under the designation of microsociological theories although, perhaps, categories such as structure-agency or structure-process might have been at least as adequate with conflict escalation as the object of inquiry.

In the case of national conflicts, the individuals are influenced not only by the constellation of interests but also by the social context of the conflict and the structural changes in individuals, groups, and communities that the process of escalation by itself brings about.

The first point to be made in this respect is that the importance of individual thoughts and considerations is present already in the formulation of the macrosociological hypotheses about instrumental and primordial interests. Both hypotheses are founded on the premise that *perceptions* are central to the effect of interests on conflict intensity,[98] and with this premise they recognize the importance of microsociological elements even in a macrosociological theoretical context.

Apart from this recognition by the macrosociological theories themselves, we have pointed to several other microsociological factors that influence the perceptions and actions of individual members of nation-groups and thus the course of national conflicts. Most prominent among these are the effects that conflictual interaction itself has on individuals, groups, and communities through the structural changes it occasions in these entities.

First of all, intergroup conflict tends to make the perceptions and attitudes of individuals negatively biased against members of the outgroup. This is due not only to the aversive actions of some members of the outgroup but also to a wish to avoid the cognitive dissonance that arises from one's own aversive actions against members of the outgroup. Negative beliefs then tend to escalate conflict by further reinforcing the bias against the outgroup through selective perception of its actions and motives.

Secondly, intergroup conflict most frequently increases intragroup cohesion. Group cohesion, in turn, reinforces the intensity of the conflict by increasing the pressures of conformity to group norms which, in times of conflict, often encompass negative beliefs about the adversary. Group cohesion also furthers the ability of executing coordinated actions, and finally, it increases the constituent pressure on leaders who, to some extent, have to abide by the prevailing norms and wishes of the group.

Finally, intergroup conflict has a polarizing effect on the wider community partly because of pressures from the actively involved group members and partly because escalating conflicts tend to affect still more people who are cued to take sides as the conflict and its aversive consequences become salient to them. Perhaps this polarizing effect is even more pronounced in national conflicts than in other kinds of intergroup conflict precisely because the combatants of national conflicts insist that they fight on behalf of nation-groups to which the individual either belongs or does not belong. In this way, even non-combating civilians of the opposing nation-group are seen as potential enemies against whom employment of, for example, 'ethnic cleansing' is warranted.

The course of a national conflict, and thus the above-mentioned structural changes involved in processes of escalation, is also heavily dependent on the actions of the central actors. We have identified four important groups of actors of escalation which significantly influence the course of events as well as the social context in which perceptions are formed and decisions are made. Of course, strategists are the most important immediate carriers of a national conflict because they represent whole nation-groups and have the authority to initiate coordinated action on behalf of their groups. Thus, for example, the immediate cause of the difference between the Croatian decision to send police troops to take control of the Krajina area in 1990 and the simultaneous but opposite Moldovan decision to send police troops to prevent interference with the Gagauz elections must be ascribed to the decisions of strategists. However, an analysis of the effects of actions on the course of a national conflict based exclusively on an identification of the immediate decision-makers amounts to little more than an ideographic description of the conflict.

Instead, we have focused on the indirect influence that important actors of escalation have on the intensity of national conflicts through their aggregated effect on the social context of the conflict. For this purpose not only strategists but also mobilizers, intermediaries, and activists are important because they all influence and express what we have called the general opinion climate – that is, the social mood in which perceptions are formed and decisions to support, execute, or counter conflictual actions are made. The general opinion climate is influenced and expressed by the political spectrum and strength of mobilizers, by the actions and signals of strategists, by the degree of nationalist bias in the mass media, and by the existence and actions of various grass roots movements.

As a result, the individual members of different nation-groups cannot be expected to assess their primordial and instrumental interests in a neutral way. In the perception of their interests, the individuals will be influenced not only by actual events and structural conditions but also by their own perceptual and cognitive biases as well as the pressures to conform to group norms and to take sides in the conflict. If, in addition, the general opinion climate is biased towards a conflictual interpretation of the relationship between one's own and other nation-groups, the individual group member will find it increasingly difficult to ameliorate the menacing prospects of escalation by attempts to find at least some common ground between the interests of the nation-groups in question.

6 CONCLUSION: AN INTEGRATIVE MODEL OF THE CAUSES OF NATIONAL CONFLICT INTENSITY

As in Part One, we conclude our examination of the consequences of national conflicts with an integrative model which epitomizes the variables that appear to be the most important in the light of our empirical and theoretical investigations (see Figure 8). As in Figure 4, we employ the categories of antecedents, orientations, catalysts, and action, but this time we group antecedents and orientations together in order to give special prominence to processes as a fifth category of variables. In each category of variables, we distinguish between individual-, group-, and intergroup-level variables.

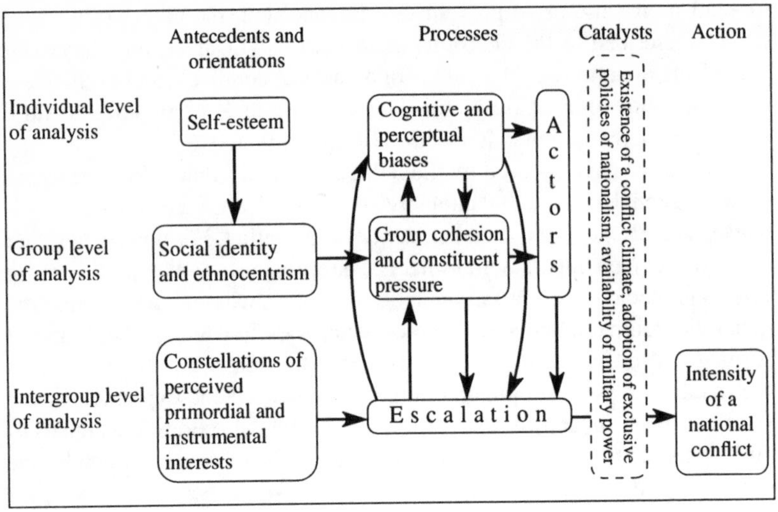

Figure 8 An integrative model of the causes of national conflict intensity

The dependent variable of the model is intensity of a national conflict. This variable, of course, presupposes that some kind of national conflict exists at all – that is, that two nation-groups perceive themselves to have diverging interests at least to some degree. Our empirical operationalization of this variable was limited to only two values: violent and non-violent national conflict. Nevertheless, as we think of violent and non-violent conflicts as extremes on a continuum rather than two different categories, we believe that the theoretical model applies also to a more exhaustive division of the variable if this had been possible.

The intensity of a national conflict is, of course, first of all dependent on the chain of events and interaction that actors carry out in the course of the conflict. In other words, intense national conflict presupposes a *process* of escalation. This process involves not only concrete interaction but also processual changes of the functioning of individuals and groups. Because these processes are extremely complex and vary extensively from case to case, it is very difficult to extract any generalized theory about the intensity of national conflicts from the processual category of variables. At the most, we are able to point to some generally observed structural changes that conflictual interaction between groups frequently occasions in individuals, groups, and communities. The perceptual and cognitive functioning of the individual as well as the cohesion, polarization, and constituent pressure of the group are changed in ways that promote further escalation by making group members still more biased against the outgroup. The functioning of central actors of escalation are, of course, no exception to these processes. First of all, the structural changes occur in the actors themselves, but apart from this their roles as mobilizers, strategists, intermediaries, and activists make them dependent on the structural changes that occur in the people around them. This effect is relevant to all important actors, but it is most clear in the process of constituent pressure on leaders of nation-groups.

From these observations we can extract the common-sense truth that conflict tends to breed conflict, and that it is essential to avoid escalation in the first place if one's goal is peaceful settlement of the conflict. But this does not bring us significantly closer to a general explanation of why only some national conflicts escalate although the potential for such escalation seems to be present in most national conflicts. The complexity of processes of escalation and the ambiguity of their causal status make it necessary to search for such general explanations in the antecedents, orientations, and catalysts of the social context of the conflict. The obvious centrality of processes of escalation, however, also cautions us not to make too definitive statements about national conflict intensity on the basis of antecedents, orientations, and catalysts.

In our view, the most important *catalysts* of national conflict escalation are existence of a conflict climate, adoption of exclusive policies of nationalism, and availability of military power. As catalysts, these variables are neither sufficient nor necessary causes of escalation, but they can act conducively to an escalation of a national conflict.

The effect of a conflict climate in which the general opinion climate is heavily biased towards a conflictual interpretation of the intergroup relationship is to further the structural changes in individuals, groups, and communities that follow escalation. Our assertion of this effect builds on the basic assumption that individuals are never totally free to form their own beliefs about their situation. On the contrary, they are always to some degree influenced by the society around them. And if no important and opinion-shaping actors in that society advocate conciliation and compromises, there is great probability that they will come to think of such a strategy as unwarranted or at least unrealistic.

The effect of exclusive policies of nationalism is to give very direct signals to the minority nation-group about the attitude of the majority nation-group. Exclusive policies of nationalism influence the perceived interests of the minority nation-group both through their direct consequences for the present situation of the group and through their influence on the minority's assessment of its future prospects. They do not, however, by themselves *determine* these interests, and this is why we have limited their location in the model to the role of catalysts.

Finally, military power does, of course, play a role in the intensity of national conflicts. Most obviously, its centrality is due to the fact that most violent national conflicts are fought with military equipment and tactics. However, the causal role of military power is ambiguous as the military superiority of one group does not necessarily bring it to employ its power, and it does not necessarily prevent the inferior nation-group from engaging in a violent conflict anyway. Thus, military power is not a general cause of national conflict escalation although, in some cases, it might act as a catalyst (or a dampener) of escalation.

As with respect to national revivals, the most important generalizable explanations of national conflict intensity are to be found among *antecedents* and *orientations*. Some explanation can be derived already from the individual- and group-level causes of national revivals. The proclivity towards ethnocentrism caused by the possibility of increasing one's positive self-esteem through adoption of a social identity (see Part One) has as central effects that the cohesion of the ingroup is increased and that intergroup differences are highlighted at the expense of intergroup commonalities.

The decisive causes of national conflict escalation, however, must be found at the intergroup level of analysis. We have found that the probability for a violent conflict between two nation-groups is high when the constellation of their primordial and instrumental interests is characterized by strong and conflicting perceptions in both groups. Thus, although primordial and instrumental theorists *can* explain the varying intensity of the East European national conflicts without referring to the theories of their theoretical opponents, we have asserted that the two kinds of explanation should be combined to explain not only national revivals but the intensity of the ensuing national conflicts as well.

In our view this assertion is not at all implausible. There is no doubt that instrumental interests stemming from real, perceived, or feared deprivation of rights and livelihood exclusively due to one's nationality can act as a powerful incentive for individuals and groups to engage in national conflicts. But for large numbers of individuals to be willing to kill and mutilate in protracted and violent national conflicts, something more is needed. This 'more', in our opinion, is captured in the notion of primordial interests. An already existing group solidarity, for example in the form of a strong *ethnie*, is important to a sense of common cause not only in correcting the tangible injustice felt by the group members but also in attaining more intangible goals such as cultural recognition of the group.

Furthermore, historical analogies are an important means for interpretation of present events and interests, and an antagonistic historical relationship is therefore very likely to enhance both the strength and the incompatibility of the perceived interests. It is probably also the sense of a common cause and a group solidarity which reaches beyond the particularities of the moment that secure continued group solidarity even under conditions of war and severe hardships.

18 Conclusion

1 INTRODUCTION

In the late 1980s and early 1990s the inhabitants of Eastern Europe participated in or witnessed not only the overthrow of the repressive regimes but also intense and violent clashes between nation-groups with horrifying consequences for the civilian population. To the outside observer as well, these epoch-making years were instructive. What seemed earlier to be a monolithic glacier changed almost overnight into a roaring débâcle, creating numerous new states in its train and drawing attention to the existence of an even larger number of previously ignored nation-groups.

Whether the consequences are viewed as positive or negative, participants and observers alike are bound to wonder what it is that fuels the coordinated actions of large numbers of individuals in the name of some entity called a nation-group. This is the basic question that we have set out to answer. In this concluding chapter, we shall sum up our conclusions both as regards our empirical object of inquiry, the nationalism in late-20th-century Eastern Europe, and as regards the implications for theories of nationalism in general. As we have already given an extensive treatment of this in the concluding chapter of each part, this summary will be very brief. Furthermore, we discuss the future prospects for nationalism in Eastern Europe and give some suggestions for future research. Finally, we touch upon what seems to be the most serious challenge of the future as well as the present: how can the persistent ideology of nationalism be reconciled with a political system of liberal democracy and the basic respect for other human beings that lies at its core?

2 NATIONALISM IN LATE-20TH-CENTURY EASTERN EUROPE

The prevalence and the fatality of nationalism in Eastern Europe were the immediate reasons for our interest in the subject of nationalism. On the basis of empirical examinations of nine cases of national revivals and five cases of national conflicts, we have tried to identify which variables are able to account for the simultaneous rise of nationalism all over Eastern Europe (the prevalence of nationalism) and for the very differing intensities of the ensuing national conflicts (the potential fatality of nationalism). Moreover, through comparisons of these empirical investigations, we have centred on the causal variables that seem to have more than just ideographic importance to the national revivals and conflicts.

2.1 The Prevalence of Nationalism

The most important explanatory variables that are generally valid in Eastern Europe are to be found in the functions that nationalism fulfils for the individual members and in the structural commonalities between the members of certain nation-groups as well as the relationships between different nation-groups.

2.1.1 Individuals and National Revivals

We believe that the inhabitants of Eastern Europe – as, indeed, all human beings – are and were motivated by a basic desire for a positive self-esteem. Membership of a nation-group and support of a national revival of this group were means to enhance this positive self-esteem because humans derive identities not only from their individual achievements but also from their group membership. This is the main reason for the universal tendency towards ethnocentrism which is the precondition for national revivals. Certainly, some participants in national movements also profited from the national revivals in economic ways, but in our view the identity-providing functions of nationalism were the most important to the majority of the East European populations.

Moreover, the importance of the national revivals to the individuals as revealed by social identity theory and rational choice theory can help us to understand why the East European populations chose to form groups on the basis of nationality rather than some other common attribute.

Firstly, some of the characteristics of late-20th-century *national* movements in general made it more likely that the thought of joining or supporting a national movement would appeal to the East European citizen. Thus, in modern societies national movements are privileged in relation to other groups due to the practical advantages that cultural homogeneity and common language have to group formation as well as to the potential of modern states with respect to production of collective goods and selective incentives. Moreover, national movements profit from the illegitimacy of discriminating multinational states which have to observe human rights to some degree in order to obtain internal legitimacy and a good reputation in the international community. This is due to the fact that, today, people know sufficiently well that things could be different and to the fact that basic liberal and democratic rights have gained prominence to the extent that open suppression of such rights has become much more suspect. Furthermore, individuals are often prevented from changing nationality due to political norms and rules as well as to their emotional investment in the group membership. This makes individual action to counter any discrimination less likely than collective action.

Secondly, some of the characteristics of the late-20th-century *East European* societies also favoured the formation of national movements as opposed to other kinds of groups. Thus, national movements could take advantage of the renewed opportunity to form groups outside communist control as well as a lower group solidarity within the communist organizations due to the consequences of Gorbachev's *perestroyka* reform programme. Finally, the national movements had the very important advantage of offering an alternative unifying and identity-providing ideology at a time when the legitimacy, the security, and the alleged positive qualities of the communist regimes vanished.

Yet, these characteristics were merely benign conditions for the individuals' decision to initiate, support, or join a national movement. Whether the national revivals served psychological or economic purposes for the individual members, this does not bring us closer to the reasons why the national revivals occurred in Eastern Europe in the late 1980s and the early 1990s. In other words, a functional analysis of the East European national revivals in terms of their consequences for identity or economic welfare cannot count as a causal explanation of their occurrence in the first place. In our search for a valid causal explanation, we have centred on the structural conditions influencing the perceptions of the nation-groups in question.

2.1.2 Structural Conditions and National Revivals

The decisive causes of the East European national revivals are to be found in the structural conditions of the nation-groups. Two main groups of conditions are important in this respect: primordial and instrumental.

Thus, we found that all cases of strong national revivals exhibited strong ethnic foundations in the form of *ethnies*. This primordial insistence on the importance of myths, ancestry, symbols, history, and association with a certain territory was, however, not sufficient, for a strong *ethnie* by itself did not in all cases lead to a strong national revival. Yet, when combined with the instrumental conditions of *perceived* unfair economic, political, and cultural deprivations due to colonization by either a communist centre or a new nationalist centre, the nation-groups in Eastern Europe with strong ethnic bases were easy to mobilize under the banners of national movements.

In any case, it is obvious that the mobilization of nation-groups with the combined characteristics of strong *ethnies* and economic, political, or cultural frustrations was eased by the liberal policies adopted by the formerly repressive regimes in the second half of the 1980s. These policies made it possible to formulate the ideas of nationalism in public and made it less likely that the communist regimes would interfere and try to revert the unfolding revivals.

2.1.3 Probable Scenarios

Given the prevalence of nationalism in Eastern Europe in the late 1980s and early 1990s, one could pose the question whether it is likely that more national revivals will take place in Eastern Europe in the coming years. In other words, will the ideal of the nation-state and the ideology of nationalism continue to prevail in Eastern Europe?

On the one hand, many nation-groups' aspirations to establish states of their own have now been satisfied. This is the case with respect to the titular nation-groups in the former Soviet West and in Yugoslavia, and the titular nation-groups in the former East European satellite states have also gained self-determination after the removal of the Soviet overlay.

On the other hand, the potential for future national revivals is far from exhausted. Most present-day East European states have large or small minorities who have lived in these states for centuries and who will therefore most often have a well-developed *ethnie*. And if the titular nation-groups carry out any kind of economic, political, or cultural discrimination, such *ethnies* can quickly become politically aware and form national movements with the aim of achieving autonomy or, perhaps, (re-)unification with other members of the mother-nation.

Therefore, we believe that the ideal of the nation-state and the ideology of nationalism will continue to prevail for many years to come. Today, almost all East European states are undergoing a painful process of transition which most probably will last quite a few more years. And in a time of economic suffering and social insecurity, the legitimizing and mobilizing resources of the ideology of nationalism are a ready-made political tool to any reformist leadership.

Both because of the likelihood of nationalist rhetoric and actions by reformist leaders and because perceptions or fear of deprivations are probable among both majorities and minorities in times of scarcity, the potential for further national revivals in Eastern Europe is likely to be high. Furthermore, the idea of national self-determination continues to enjoy world-wide legitimacy. Thus, in sum, nothing indicates that the popularity of the ideology of nationalism is waning.

2.2 The Potential Fatality of Nationalism

The explanations of the differing intensity of the national conflicts in Eastern Europe must be found in a combination of the processes that influence the individuals, the social context in which individuals and nation-groups form their perceptions, and, most importantly, the character and strength of their perceived interests.

2.2.1 Individuals and National Conflicts

Whether they were active participants or not, many individual members of nation-groups involved in escalating conflicts probably experienced the self-reinforcing consequences of the conflict. At the individual level, negative feelings and cognitive biases with respect to the adversary were created and reinforced. And at the group level, these feelings and biases were socially reinforced and polarized – often to the extent that it became almost impossible to remain neutral.

Some individuals and groups of individuals played especially important roles as actors of escalation. Apart from influencing the specific chain of events involved in any escalation, they influenced and expressed the general opinion climate. Our analysis of the general opinion climate in Eastern Europe revealed that the majority of potential actors of escalation favoured non-conciliatory, exclusive actions towards the opposing nation-groups and tried to make their own nation-groups perceive relations with these nation-groups as characterized by incompatible interests and goals. In other words, only in very few instances were there any influential critical opposition, mass media, or grass roots movements that could counterbalance the preponderance of non-conciliatory mobilizers, contending strategists, nationalist-biased media, and extremist activists. Thus, the general opinion climate in Eastern Europe was indeed malign with respect to processes of escalation.

However, the general observation of a conflict climate in Eastern Europe does not explain why some national conflicts escalated into intense, violent conflicts while others remained non-violent or were solved.

2.2.2 Constellations of Interests and National Conflicts

The intensity of the East European national conflicts must basically be explained by reference to the interests of the opposing nation-groups. However, although some conducive effect of military opportunities and adoption of exclusive policies of nationalism could be detected, neither security interests nor ideological interests were generally applicable as explanations of the varying intensity of the national conflicts.

Instead, we found that the intensity of the national conflicts in Eastern Europe was closely related to the constellations of the perceived strength and character of the primordial and instrumental interests of the opposing nation-groups. More precisely, the violent conflicts between the Moldovans and Slavs and between the Croats and Serbs were caused by the fact that *both* of the opposing nation-groups perceived that they had strong conflicting primordial *and* instrumental interests. As for the other national conflicts, at least one of the opposing nation-groups perceived that it had either weak and conflicting or non-conflicting primordial and instrumental interests.

2.2.3 Probable Scenarios

It is a central question of more than theoretical importance whether national conflicts will continue to mark interrelations between the nation-groups of Eastern Europe and whether possible future conflicts will escalate into large-scale war.

On the one hand, the problems in connection with the transition process from a one-party system and a centralized planned economy towards liberal democracy and a market economy increase the likelihood of national conflicts. Thus, when the fight for scarce resources – that is, not only for economic ones but also for political power – becomes more intensive, the likelihood increases that opposing nation-groups perceive their instrumental interests as conflicting. Furthermore, in times of economic crisis and social insecurity, the probability of perceptual and cognitive biases (e.g. negative stereotypes of an opposing nation-group) also increases. In addition, it is not difficult to imagine that the leaders of a majority nation-group could try to divert dissatisfaction by promoting negative perceptions and feelings towards other (minority) nation-groups.

On the other hand, a new kind of overlay has been introduced in Eastern Europe. Western organizations (in particular the EU and NATO) have begun discussions and negotiations about enlargement eastward, and various international regimes (in particular those within the OSCE process) have increasingly supported the principle that human rights do not represent an internal issue to be left to the discretion of sovereign states. All of these organizations seek to avoid violent means being used to solve conflicts. Furthermore, as the vast majority of the East European states have expressed an explicit wish to 'return to Europe' – that is, to carry through a catch-up modernization and establish well-functioning economic markets and political democracies – and as an important means as well as an important symbol of this aspiration is admission to the international organizations, it is likely that this alone will have a moderating effect on any wishes to employ violent means in the external and internal national conflicts of the states.

Thus, although national conflicts can hardly be completely avoided, we contend that the probability that they will escalate into large-scale war is considerably smaller than in the wake of the First World War, the last time European empires broke down and made the establishment of a range of new East European states possible.

3 THEORIES OF NATIONALISM

A huge number of theories related to the subject of nationalism has been produced by historians, philosophers, and sociologists as well as by political scientists. We have not intended to cover all these theories in this book. Instead, we have tried to present an overview of the available theories and then choose those which are theoretically coherent and seem to be most relevant to the questions we have set out to answer. Furthermore, we have not employed any of the selected theories in their original version, so to speak. Instead, using an eclectic approach, we have adapted and integrated these theories into 'middle-range' theories of our own in order to be able to deduce hypotheses relevant to our questions of investigation.

3.1 Theories about National Revivals

As a combination of the primordial and the instrumental hypotheses about national revivals was needed in order to explain the national revivals of Eastern Europe fully, we were led to the conclusion that the theoretical trench warfare between primordialists and instrumentalists is futile. Furthermore, it is also theoretically unfounded as the differing points of the two groups of theories of nationalism are not incompatible – at least not as regards moderate versions of the theories. Thus, in our view, national revivals occur when the present economic, political, and cultural situations of nation-groups are interpreted on the basis of a pre-existing social solidarity expressed through a strong *ethnie*. In other words, instrumentalists are right when asserting that reality is a social construct, but wrong when ignoring that it is always construed on the basis of already existing social constructs such as *ethnies*.

Most primordialists and instrumentalists, however, fail to examine the microsociological foundations of their macrosociological explanations. In other words, they take for granted that their explanations of group movements actually correspond with the motives and drives of the individual group members. It is our opinion that the macrosociological effects of economic, political, and cultural frustrations and strong *ethnies* can best be founded on the basic assumption that individuals strive to maintain or increase a positive self-esteem and that this can be accomplished both through individual action and by enhancing one's social identity. Of course, it cannot be ruled out that individual self-interest plays a role when groups are formed to produce and consume collective goods. But there is no doubt that membership of a nation-group forms part of the individual's identity, and it is because of the urge for a positive social identity that ethnocentrism in the form of ingroup preference and outgroup derogation is so prevalent among nation-groups. If the individual member of a nation-group perceives that the group is unfairly deprived by another nation-group with respect to its economic, political, or cultural status, his or her self-esteem will be affected negatively because part of his or her identity is derived from the overall status of the nation-group. In that case, he or she will frequently find it more feasible to engage in collective action in the form of a national revival to correct the undue inequalities than to attempt individual amelioration of the situation, for example by moving out of the nation-group.

3.2 Theories about National Conflicts

As with respect to national revivals, it is essential that any macrosociological explanation of national conflict intensity incorporates the thoughts and psychological functioning of the individuals and groups involved in the conflict. These microsociological variables play a central role in the process of escalation that leads to intense or even violent national conflicts. Thus, escalation of national conflicts most often involves increasing perceptual and cognitive biases among individuals and still more polarized groups and communities.

On the other hand, national conflict intensity is not alone rooted in psychological processes or even instigations to aggression as some social-psychological theories suggest. In contrast, to explain the intensity of conflicts between large societal groups such as nation-groups, we must concentrate on the intergroup level of analysis and search for macrosociological explanations. In our view, nationalist conflict intensity is best explained by reference to the constellations of primordial and instrumental interests of the opposing nation-groups. True, exclusive policies of nationalism and military imbalances between the nation-groups can often contribute to escalation of national conflicts, but the most generally valid explanation of national conflict intensity is that nation-groups can perceive their economic and political as well as their ethnic, historical, and cultural interests to be more or less strong and more or less conflicting with the interests of other groups. And it is when two groups *both* perceive their primordial and instrumental interests to be strong and conflicting that the risk of escalation into violent conflicts is highest.

3.3 The Relationship between National Revivals and National Conflicts

As national revivals are political movements formed on the basis of *ethnies* to correct perceived unfair deprivations by a colonizing centre, national conflicts in the form of perceived divergence of interests between nation-groups follow as a matter of definition. However, this argument says nothing about the likely number of national conflicts or the intensity of them.

First of all, because of its origins, a national movement is almost always directed against a specific alleged colonizing nation-group. Thus, the immediate consequence of a national revival will be a conflict with the nation-group representing the colonizing centre. However, as a national revival of one nation-group involves heavy use of national symbols and – if it is successful – most often adoption of exclusive policies, *all* minorities living in the territory of that nation-group will be more or less affected, and many members of these minorities will begin to perceive the status of their groups as threatened. In this way, a national revival is likely to spark off several more national conflicts than its primary aspiration would predict.

However, the national conflicts resulting from a national revival do not necessarily escalate into violent conflicts. Whether they do this or not depends on the perceived interests of the nation-groups involved. And as the strength and character of these interests are shaped also during the process of mobilization in national revivals, the intensity of national conflicts will, to some extent, depend on the specific development of the preceding national revivals.

3.4 Suggestions for Further Research

We have made the above-mentioned theoretical conclusions about national revivals and conflicts on the basis of available theories and empirical evidence. Of course, with the complex object of inquiry of nationalism, a more thorough theoretical knowledge as well as more adequate empirical evidence would have been preferable in many instances.

As regards empirical evidence, we have especially lacked comparable, individual-level statistical data in order to test the microsociological theories. More of such data could also have further substantiated our macrosociological conclusions about the perceptions of nation-groups. However, even if we had undertaken such a data collection after the occurrence of the national revivals and conflicts, we could not have been sure to get any valid data because human perceptions most often change over time and the course of events. Thus, if the aim is to infer generalized knowledge about national revivals, we would also recommend a study of some of the minorities in Eastern Europe that have not yet initiated national revivals in the hope that examinations of possible future revivals will be able to make use of the data.

With regard to theoretical development, we suggest two lines of research. Firstly, there is the question of theoretical generality. Our conclusions have been made on the basis of a careful selection of national revivals and conflicts. Moreover, this selection is not chosen from the whole populations of national revivals and conflicts – neither in time nor in space. Therefore, it would obviously be interesting to examine whether our conclusions hold true with regard to cases of national revivals and conflicts outside Eastern Europe and under other temporary conditions.

Secondly, we believe that the microsociological foundations of group movements and conflicts have been neglected in political science. As a consequence, we have lacked proper theoretical tools to investigate the motives and thoughts of individuals. For example, we would have liked to go deeper into the mechanism and conditions of group mobilization. But with the available microsociological tools, we have not, unfortunately, been able to examine this important intervening variable sufficiently.

4 NATIONALISM AND DEMOCRACY IN THE MODERN WORLD

4.1 The Positive Consequences of Nationalism

In large parts of this book, we have been preoccupied with the serious and sometimes disastrous consequences of nationalism. On this basis, one might get the impression that nationalism is primarily a negative phenomenon. This is also the conclusion drawn by most intellectuals, especially in the West but also within the East European intelligentsia. And it is consistent with the tendency of most people to associate the term 'national*ism*' as opposed to 'national *identity*' with something negative. Yet, this does not capture the whole truth about the phenomenon.

In our opinion, nationalism is also a positive force. In the East European context, the idea of a nation-group provided the alienated East Europeans with an identity and a source of self-esteem when the hollowness of the identity as citizens in a so-called socialist or communist society was revealed. Moreover, nationalism is the expression of the idea that one nation-group should not be ruled by members of another nation-group. On the contrary, according to the ideology of nationalism, a nation-group has a right to self-determination. As such, nationalism is an inherently legitimate ideology as it builds on the basic liberal assertion that people should govern themselves. The mobilizing powers associated with the identity-providing functions of nationalism and the legitimacy of national self-determination could not only make members of East European nation-groups engage in contending or outright violent actions towards other nation-groups; the feelings of national identity and the ideology of nationalism have also helped them to endure a painful transition process towards a market economy and democracy and contributed to the legitimacy and coherence of the new-born states.

Those who associate the term 'nationalism' with something negative tend to forget that a difficult transitional period – often referred to as modernization – also preceded the hailed present economic and political system of the West in which most conflicts are arbitrated through well-established institutions and, ultimately, through the democratic process. And one of the driving powers of modernization and, thus, of the democratization involved in modernization was, in fact, nationalism and its assertion that people should be ruled by neither foreign powers nor autocrats. Therefore it is not at all unlikely that the forces of nationalism might also prove to offer a road towards catch-up modernization in Eastern Europe.

4.2 The Competing Logics of the Nation-State and Democracy

The problem is, however, that although nationalism played an important role in the democratization of today's West, the ideas of nationalism and democracy are not always compatible. Empirically, there are few polities in the world that are simultaneously a state, a nation, and a democracy. Indeed, if one employs systematically these three concepts it is impossible that most polities could be all three simultaneously. This is because throughout most of the globe there is such an overlapping and intermixing of different nation-groups that the possibility of clear territorial boundaries that are congruent with even a very small nation-state cannot be obtained, short of ethnic cleansing and mass migrations. In other words, the effort to combine the three ideas risks leading to the erosion of the conditions needed for consensual democracy or even territorial integrity of the state. Therefore, since democracy implies rights of minorities, some reconciliation between the three concepts is necessary. A political–legal structure that gives some guarantees to a state's different nation-groups is essential to achieve such a reconciliation. The necessary guarantees include rights of citizenship, cultural rights of minority nation-groups, and the creation of institutional arrangements which allow for cultural expression, political representation, and influence of all the constituent nation-groups.

As mentioned earlier, there are small or large minorities in all of the present-day East European states. What are the prospects, then, that these states will succeed in mitigating the competing logics of democracy and nation-state?

On the one hand, our analyses have showed that ethnic nationalism and exclusive policies of nationalism were widespread phenomena in Eastern Europe in the late 1980s and early 1990s. This fact does not seem promising for the future coexistence of several nation-groups in the same democratic state.

On the other hand, there are some developments that point in a positive direction. Thus, the case of Moldova provides an example of how a conflict between a majority and a minority nation-group can be solved without disintegrating the territory of the state. According to the 1994 constitution, the Gagauz are guaranteed autonomy and a range of other rights. Moreover, not all of the new East European laws on, for example, citizenship and franchise are in fact so restrictive that they exclude future integration of minority nation-groups. For instance, the Estonian law on citizenship requires that applicants have been residents for two years, take an oath of loyalty, and pass a language examination. Furthermore, in several instances international pressure has made majority nation-groups adjust their originally exclusive policies and choose a more conciliatory strategy towards minorities.

In conclusion, we believe that the ideal of the nation-state and the ideology of nationalism will continue to prevail in Eastern Europe for many years to come. Yet, we also contend that although national conflicts can hardly be avoided, the likelihood that they do not escalate into large-scale war and the likelihood that the competing logics of democracy and nation-state can be reconciled is greater than ever before in the history of Eastern Europe.

Notes

1 In the rest of this book, we shall for convenience frequently refer to Czechoslovakia although we are, of course, very well aware that this state ceased to exist in January 1993.

2 In this respect, the theory of the authoritarian personality resembles the frustration–aggression theory treated below.

3 It should be noted, however, that Geertz in the rest of his essay (despite the allegation made by Eller & Coughlan, 1993) uses the concept in a more historical way – more in accordance with what we have called primordialism in the moderate sense. For example, he states that the 'givens' more accurately should be called 'the assumed "givens"' as culture is inevitably involved in such matters.

4 Smith also points to other significant factors, such as the success of the first nation-states, the importance attributed to the nation-state by the international system, and the crystallizing effect on national sentiments exercised by expanding capitalism through its wars and rivalries and its provision of classes that can act as bearers of the national interest *vis-à-vis* other nation-states (1991: 163ff). However, the important part of his argument is based on cultural and historical factors, not economic and structural factors.

5 The notion that ethnicity is a comparative concept has been advocated by Horowitz, among others (1985; see Newman, 1991: 464) and it is present also in the importance allotted to social comparison by social identity theory (see Section 3.4.1 of Chapter 2).

6 Smith himself has also emphasized contemporary forces in an article focusing on the cultural heritage of Marxist and Leninist USSR (1992). However, we prefer Kellas's more general argument because it is easier to conceptualize and test.

7 In the remaining part of the book, we shall frequently use the term 'confirm' although, strictly speaking, a confirmation of a hypothesis only means that it cannot be dismissed.

8 A theory which resembles the theory of Laitin in this respect has been suggested by Anderson (1991). However, Anderson makes the same point regarding the Creoles in the Americas, thus explaining the rise of nationalism on the background of deprived elites in *external* colonies.

9 We should note that other instrumentalists acknowledge the fact that not only disadvantages, but also advantages can lead to a national revival (e.g. Gellner, 1983: 109).

10 See, for example, Smith (1991), Gellner (1983), Anderson (1991), Kellas (1991), and Connor (1994).

11 A more elaborate discussion of the influence of modern mass media on national conflicts is given in Chapters 10 and 12.

12 In the former Yugoslavia, citizens also had the option of calling themselves 'Yugoslavians'. This possibility, however, was used only by a minority. In the 1981 census, for example, only 5.4 per cent of the population identified themselves as Yugoslavians (Cohen, 1993: 175).

13 The high probability that multinational states are perceived as illegitimate is one side of the coin. The other side of the coin is the efforts of most such states to homogenize their populations in order to achieve the legitimate status of a nation-state. This is often done by way of harsh migration and assimilation policies.

14 Before the mid-1980s, only few students of Eastern Europe and the USSR stressed the continued importance of ethnic and national allegiance and identity and warned about the potential disruptive powers of nationalism. One example was Hélène Carrère d'Encausse (1979).

15 Those of Estonian heritage who, previous to 1940, were either born or spent their formative years in Russia were called Russian–Estonians.

16 The importance of the annual song festivals to the Estonian national revival made it known as 'the singing revolution'.

17 Two other similar organizations, the Union of Work Collectives (UWC) and the United Council of Work Collectives (UCWC), were also formed. However, the Intermovement dominated (Ilves, 1991: 72).

18 According to a survey conducted in 1993, one third of the Estonians had a family member imprisoned, deported, or killed by the Soviet regime (Rose & Maley, 1994: 59).

19 Actually, Moscow agreed to formal Estonian economic autonomy in the autumn of 1989, but as the central ministries took counter-measures to prevent the implementation of the enabling laws, economic autonomy was never realized (Taagepera, 1993: 162ff).

20 In interwar independent Estonia, 88 per cent of the population was Estonian (Misiunas & Taagepera, 1983: 272), while this figure decreased to 62 per cent in 1989 (Kaplan, 1993: 208).

21 On 5 June 1990 the republican parliament amended the constitution to change the republic's name from the Moldavian Soviet Socialist Republic to the Soviet Socialist Republic of Moldova, thereby modifying the pronunciation to reflect its name in Moldovan (Fane, 1993: 149f). A further amendment on 23 May 1991 changed the republic's name to the Republic of Moldova. As 'Moldova' is the official name of the new state, we have chosen to use this form instead of the Russian 'Moldavia' except when referring explicitly to Soviet inspired names such as the Moldavian SSR, the Communist Party of Moldavia, and the self-proclaimed Dnestrian Moldavian Republic.

22 At one demonstration on 27 August an estimated 100 000 took part (Crowther, 1991: 195).

23 In mid-1991, the PFM adopted a new stance on this issue as it decided to aim at reunification with Romania. However, due to this change, its support among the Moldovans sharply declined just as the main part of its parliamentary deputies switched to other parties (Socor, 1992c: 30).

24 In Romanian and Moldovan, the area is called Trans-Dnestr as it is situated on the left bank of the river Dnestr – that is, beyond the river as seen from Romania. The Russian name, Pridnestrov'e, simply means 'by the river Dnestr'.

25 During the Moldovan national revival of the late 1980s and early 1990s the head of an aurochs became part of the new Moldovan coat of arms (Socor, 1991a: 26).

26 The Moldovan principality did not become an Ottoman vassalage until 1541 (Dima, 1975: 32).

27 While spoken Moldovan is considered a Romanian dialect which is understood by Romanians without problems, the literary languages resemble each other even more closely (Dima, 1975: 38).

28 The Romanian state was originally formed in 1859 by the unification of the principality of Wallachia and the western part of the Moldovan principality, but it was not internationally recognized until 1878 (Dima, 1991: 14f).

29 Bessarabia was situated in the area between the rivers Prut and Dnestr. The area roughly equals the territory of the present Moldova (see Map 3).

30 In Moldova 12 per cent (352 000) of the population were Russians in 1930 (Fane, 1993: 137). In Estonia, 8 per cent (91 000) of the population were Russians in 1934 (Kirch, 1992: 206).

31 In 1924, a so-called Moldavian ASSR was established in the left-bank Dnestr region, which the USSR retained following the First World War. However, the Moldavian ASSR was most probably only created as a springboard for a reconquest of Bessarabian Moldova.

32 The main cause of this situation is probably that Moldova, and thereby the Gagauz, was not incorporated into the USSR until 1940, while almost all Soviet autonomous units were established in the interwar period. By giving autonomy to the Gagauz relatively late, the Soviet authorities would have risked other parallel demands in the region, for example from the Crimean Tatars.

33 These Slavs were recruited from the leadership of the Moldavian ASSR established in 1924 in the left-bank Dnestr region. When Bessarabian Moldova was reconquered during the Second World War, the communist cadres of the Moldavian ASSR were placed in top positions in the new Moldavian SSR comprised of both Bessarabian Moldova and the left-bank Dnestr region (Bruchis, 1984: 72ff).

34 22 out of the 23 members of the cabinet were Moldovans (Nedelciuc, 1992: 53).

35 For a treatment of the conditions of minorities in Romania see Verdery (1993).

36 Due to the subtropical climate of southern Moldova, the fertility of the soil depends particularly on irrigation (Socor, 1990a: 9).

37 The Moldovan government hesitated concerning this issue by arguing that there was simply not enough land to satisfy the demands of the farmers in the densely populated rural areas of Moldova (Socor, 1990a: 12f).

38 Later, in January 1991, about half a year after the Gagauz SSR had been proclaimed, the new Moldovan government tried to negotiate a compromise with the Gagauz leaders by proposing to create a special Gagauz county (Cavanaugh, 1992: 14). For all practical purposes, however, that proposal did not even meet the demand for autonomy by the Gagauz opposition since the proposed organ of local self-government was not allowed to make decisions on political or state legislation questions. Consequently, the proposal was rejected by the Gagauz.

39 At the end of 1989 the CDC already had about 50 000 members (Irvine, 1993: 278).

40 According to the official election results, 99 per cent of the voters supported independence.

41 At the same time, the state was renamed 'Yugoslavia'.
42 The exact number is disputed. The official Yugoslavian estimate was some 700 000, but scholars have later revised the number to 350 000–400 000 (Ramet, 1992: 69).
43 Approximately 2 per cent of the republic's social product.
44 It was widely recognized that, in addition to the vote of the Serbian republic, the Serbs controlled the vote of the republic of Montenegro and of the two autonomous provinces of Vojvodina and Kosovo.
45 Unfortunately, we have not been able to obtain the exact results of the survey which Cohen refers to.
46 Leading Czech intellectuals during the Velvet Revolution used the slogan 'Strength in Unity' (Musil, 1992: 182).
47 This stand was reflected repeatedly in opinion polls: for example, in June 1990 42 per cent of the Czechs preferred a strong centralized federation (Kusin, 1990: 5f). In the autumn of 1991, only 13 per cent of the Czechs agreed with the statement that Czechoslovakia should be split into two independent states (Deis, 1992: 9).
48 By 1988, the Czechs made up 63 per cent (9 808 000) of the population in Czechoslovakia, while the Slovaks constituted 32 per cent (4 984 000). In the Czech republic, the Czechs made up 94 per cent of the population, while the Slovaks made up 87 per cent of the population in the Slovakian republic (Kirschbaum, 1993: 78).
49 This majority was composed of 41 per cent who favoured a common state with large powers vested in Czech and Slovakian national governments and 30 per cent who favoured a confederation (Kusin, 1990: 5f). This attitude was confirmed in a survey in the autumn of 1991 when only 23 per cent of the Slovaks agreed with the statement that Czechoslovakia should be split into two independent republics (Deis, 1992: 9).
50 Svejk was the Czech protagonist in Jaroslav Hasek's famous and still popular novel, *The Good Soldier Svejk.*
51 While Slovakian did not become a literary language until the late-18th-century national revival, the oldest written records of the Czech language are found in 11th-century texts (Gawdiak, 1989: 101).
52 A survey from the autumn of 1991 revealed that only 13 per cent of the Czechs agreed with the statement that Czechoslovakia should be split into two independent states (Deis, 1992: 9)
53 According to the 1921 census, the Czechs constituted 51 per cent of the population. The Slovaks made up only 15 per cent while the Germans were the second largest group representing 23 per cent of the population (Gawdiak, 1989: 268).
54 Throughout the period, Slovakia's share in total national income remained approximately 12 per cent (Capek & Sazama, 1993: 212).
55 The trade with the USSR increased steadily during the postwar period, and by 1987 it accounted for 44 per cent of the country's total foreign trade turnover (Wolchik, 1991: 257f).
56 The reform programme called the New Economic Model implied substantial autonomy for individual enterprises and a normalization of the trade relations with capitalist countries (Skilling, 1976: 64f).
57 This policy came to be known as the 'Brezhnev doctrine'.

58 For example, the military in Czechoslovakia was in reality accountable only to the Soviet regime and the Soviet military via the Warsaw Pact, with the CPC merely playing a supervisory role for the Soviets. The Ministry of Defence in Prague simply put into practice the policies outlined by the Soviets (Szayna & Steinberg, 1992: 19, 33).

59 In 1970 an amendment was passed that gave the federal government the right to overrule laws passed by the republican parliaments (Kusin, 1990: 12). Thus, the Leninist principle of democratic centralism was reconfirmed.

60 Thus, the Slovaks were actually overrepresented in the Nation Chamber since they only made up 29 per cent of the population in 1970. By 1984 this figure had increased to 31 per cent (Gawdiak, 1989: 268).

61 While Giddens's structuration theory is one of the most coherent and comprehensive attempts at a structure–agency integration, the insight presented above is far from new in the history of sociological thought, as shown by the following citation: 'Men make history, but they do not make it just as they please; they do not make it under circumstances chosen by themselves, but under circumstances directly encountered, given, and transmitted from the past' (Marx, 1963 [1869]: 15).

62 It is worth considering whether the detection of such co-variation between structure and action deserves to be called an 'explanation' at all given the kaleidoscopic nature and seemingly infinite number of factors and considerations that come into play in each individual's thoughts and actions. Nevertheless, this is the common stance in political science and it is reflected also in our terminology as we refer to our macrosociological hypotheses as 'explanations of national revivals'.

63 Tajfel contends that stereotypes also have other and even more important functions. They help individuals to defend or preserve their value systems; they contribute to the creation and maintenance of group ideologies explaining or justifying a variety of social actions; and they help to preserve or create positively valued differentiations between social groups (1981: 146; see also Chapter 2 on Tajfel's social identity theory). For our present purposes, however, the cognitive function of bringing order into a chaotic world is the most important.

64 And, due to ethnocentrism, national images will most often be biased in favour of the ingroup (see Chapter 2).

65 The formation of negative beliefs about the adversary and positive beliefs about oneself or one's own group can also be seen as subconsciously motivated by a need to think well of oneself or one's own group. Such motives could be seen as the foundation of common mirror images in conflicts, such as a diabolical enemy-image and a moral self-image (White, 1984: 138). However, as we have covered the motivational basis of ingroup preference and outgroup derogation in Chapter 2, we concentrate for the present moment on the 'isolated' effects of conflictual interaction on the formation of negative beliefs.

66 White distinguishes empathy from sympathy which comprises not only understanding but also feeling for the adversary (1984: 160).

67 Of course, due to the necessary editorial and journalistic selection of news, the mass media can never be completely neutral. What we mean to say is that sometimes certain media or even all important media of a

nation-group can be systematically biased towards one particular image of the conflict.

68 This is recognized explicitly by the well-known neorealist, Waltz (1988: 44).

69 One factor that, according to Posen, makes nationalism less relevant as a way to serve security interests is the presence on both sides of nuclear weapons which increases the cost of force employment to the unbearable (1993: 32). Because of the extraordinary effect accorded to nuclear weapons, Posen's empirical analysis is actually biased towards a confirmation of his theory. He sees the violent conflict between Serbs and Croats in the former Yugoslavia as following directly from security concerns about the national revivals in the opposing group. But in his test case of non-violent conflict between Russians and Ukrainians, the presence of nuclear weapons on both sides makes the cases virtually incomparable.

70 This is, of course, a simplification as other reasons for using force could easily be found. For example, the Estonians who did not face a strong Russian national revival (see Chapter 5) could still use force for other purposes, such as simply to rid their country of Russians or to defend themselves from any aggression from internal or external actors. These motivations, however, are not included in our resulting hypothesis.

71 Examples of more recent theorists who employ this distinction are Gellner (1983: 99ff), Kellas (1991: 73f), and Smith (1991: 79f). Gellner and Kellas employ the distinction as one among several others, whereas Smith makes it his main distinction. The distinctions of Gellner and Smith are discussed below.

72 By pointing to structural properties of the nation-groups' environment, Gellner comes very close to a realist international relations interpretation of violent national conflict. The 'ferocious rivalry' in which aspirant 'Habsburg' high-cultures find themselves is very close to the realist view of the anarchic international system. Gellner differs only in specifying the 'national interest' as a functional imperative of industrialization and by restricting his analysis to the period in history when high-cultures were established and to the geographic areas where different aspirant high-cultures had to fight each other in order to prevail.

73 The distinction between official and unofficial policies bears a superficial resemblance to our earlier distinction between the actions of strategists and activists (see Chapter 10). Certainly, the actions of activists must be regarded as unofficial policies of nationalism. But strategists initiate both official policies through their authority as leaders and semi-official policies through informal signals about their ideology to their administrative apparatus and the majority population in general.

74 Although it is difficult to determine whether the conciliatory attitude of Savisaar and other PFE leaders was rooted in strategic considerations *vis-à-vis* the USSR centre or in a sincere inclusive nationalist attitude, the decisive point is that the PFE mobilized on the basis of a relatively conciliatory attitude.

75 Journalists who wanted to express, for example, anti-Soviet or anti-Russian attitudes had to resort to caricatures and parodies which could not so easily be subjected to censorship (Lauristin & Vihalemm, 1991: 100f).

76 Thus, the Croatian media accused Serbian nationalism for causing the conflict and vice versa (Malesic, 1993: 32). In the same vein, the Croatian media spoke of an insurrection by the Serbs while the Serbian media stressed the legitimate right of the Serbian nation-group to self-determination. Thus, the media of the conflicting parties presented mirror images of each other in accordance with the assertions, '*we* are innocent, only defend ourselves, and tell the truth; while *they* are guilty, are the aggressors, and lie' – a clear instance of ethnocentrism (see Section 2.1 of Chapter 2).

77 Actually, the Defence Union became subordinated to the newly established Estonian Ministry of Defence shortly after independence was achieved (Kionka, 1992b: 34ff). However, the ministry only managed to obtain full control over the Defence Union members when a limited purge of its leadership was conducted following the incidents in the summer of 1992.

78 The local Russian extremists were also joined by nationalist Cossacks from Russia (Socor, 1994a: 21).

79 Jozef Tiso was the leader of the Slovakian state which, during the Second World War, achieved a status of semi-independence under the supremacy of Nazi Germany (Mamatey & Luža, 1973: 276).

80 For instance, the incident in the Serbian village Borovo Selo was front page news in both the Croatian and Serbian media (Glenny, 1992: 76). In the Croatian press, the story was illustrated with photographs apparently showing the mutilated bodies of Croats returned by the Serbs.

81 Information on the size of the Defence Union is not available.

82 In January 1992 Russia assumed jurisdiction over the Soviet forces in the Baltic region (Bungs, 1993: 51).

83 On 26 July 1994 a final agreement on the withdrawal of the remaining former Soviet units was signed and in late August the last soldier left Estonia (Girnius, 1994b: 32).

84 The first clashes left six people dead and 30 wounded (Socor, 1990c: 11).

85 The Dnestr and Gagauz regions were separated by land controlled by the Moldovans (see Map 2).

86 No source is available as to the size of the Gagauz units.

87 The Territorial Defence units were established in the 1960s as a home guard force and were organized on a republican basis (Cohen, 1993: 184).

88 The Croatian name of the Ministry of Internal Affairs is *Ministarstvo Unutarnjih Poslova* (MUP). Therefore, these special police forces were called *Mupovci*.

89 In the period preceding the declaration of independence, the Croatian government clandestinely imported arms from Hungary and Czechoslovakia (Cohen, 1993: 189). Yet, no sources are available as to the scope of these imports.

90 When the Serbian leaders in December 1990 proclaimed the Serbian Autonomous Region Krajina, Martić became minister of defence (Gow, 1992: 20f).

91 Although the federal state presidency subsequently voted to adopt this proposal, the Croatian (and Slovenian) government formally agreed to comply with the demand but in fact did nothing to implement it. And the federal authorities did not instruct the YPA to take any concrete action (Cohen, 1993: 189f).

92 By 1992 Croatia's police force consisted almost exclusively of Croats (Markotich, 1993: 29).

93 Until then, only two Slovakian soldier organizations, the Association of Slovakian Soldiers and the Stefanik Legion, advocated the formation of a separate Slovakian army or home guard (Szayna & Steinberg, 1992: 22f). However, only some of the politicians in the SNP shared their viewpoints. And in a survey from the autumn of 1991 only 36 per cent of the Slovaks agreed with the viewpoint that 'our security should be based on separate Czech and Slovakian home defence forces' (Deis, 1992: 11).

94 The 'zero option' also included other nationalities living in Czechoslovakia, such as the rather large Hungarian minority (585 000) in Slovakia (Pehe, 1991b: 1ff).

95 The extremist groups remained small and disunited. Only the Republicans established a political party which failed to win any seats in the 1990 elections but gained 6 per cent of the vote and 7 per cent (14) of the seats in the Czech parliament in the 1992 elections (Pehe, 1994: 50ff).

96 In 1988 Slovaks made up 4 per cent (419 000) of the population in the Czech republic (Kirschbaum, 1993: 78).

97 During the existence of the Czechoslovakian state, rather few Czechs moved to Slovakia. By 1988 only 63 000 Czechs lived in Slovakia, constituting no more than 1.2 per cent of the population (Kirschbaum, 1993: 78).

98 In fact, it is an old discussion whether interests are at all conceivable without recognition by the people who hold them – that is, whether it is possible to speak of objective interests (see e.g. Stone, 1988: 166ff). With our emphasis on perceptions, we have avoided this discussion.

References

Adorno, Theodor W., Else Frenkel-Brunswik, Daniel J. Levinson & R. Nevitt Sanford (1950), *The Authoritarian Personality*, New York: W.W. Norton & Co.

Andersen, Erik A. (1991), 'Demokrati og menneskerettigheder i de baltiske lande' in *Vindue mod øst*, no. 17, pp. 22–5.

Anderson, Benedict (1991), *Imagined Communities*, 2nd revised and extended ed, New York: Verso.

Andrejevich, Milan (1990a), 'Croatia Goes to the Polls' in *Report on Eastern Europe*, 4 May, pp. 33–7.

Andrejevich, Milan (1990b), 'Croatia between Stability and Civil War (Part I)' in *Report on Eastern Europe*, 14 September, pp. 38–44.

Andrejevich, Milan (1990c), 'Croatia between Stability and Civil War (Part II)' in *Report on Eastern Europe*, 28 September, pp. 38–44.

Andrejevich, Milan (1990d), 'Crisis in Croatia and Slovenia: Proposal for a Confederal Yugoslavia' in *Report on Eastern Europe*, 2 November, pp. 28–33.

Andrejevich, Milan (1991), 'Relations between Croatia and Slovenia' in *Report on Eastern Europe*, 22 March, pp. 33–41.

Andrejevich, Milan, Patrick Moore & Duncan M. Perry (1991), 'Croatia and Slovenia Declare Their Independence' in *Report on Eastern Europe*, 12 July, pp. 24–8.

Aron, Raymond (1957), 'Conflict and War from the Viewpoint of Historical Sociology' in Jessie Bernard, T.H. Pear, Raymond Aron & Robert C. Angell from the International Sociological Association (eds), *The Nature of Conflict: Studies on the Sociological Aspects of International Tensions*, Paris: UNESCO, pp. 177–203.

Ashmore, Richard D. & Frances K. Del Boca (1981), 'Conceptual Approaches to Stereotypes and Stereotyping' in David L. Hamilton (ed.), *Cognitive Processes in Stereotyping and Intergroup Behavior*, Hillsdale, N.J.: Lawrence Erlbaum.

Aubert, Vilhelm (1963), 'Competition and Dissensus: Two Types of Conflict and of Conflict Resolution' in *Journal of Conflict Resolution*, vol. 7, no. 1, pp. 26–42.

Banac, Ivo (1984), *The National Question in Yugoslavia: Origins, History, Politics*, London: Cornell University Press.

Bebler, Anton (1992), 'Political Pluralism and the Yugoslav Professional Military' in Jim Seroka & Vukasin Pavlovic (eds), *The Tragedy of Yugoslavia: The Failure of Democratic Transition*, New York: M.E. Sharpe.

Berkowitz, Leonard (1962), *Aggression: A Social Psychological Analysis*, New York: McGraw-Hill.

Berkowitz, Leonard (1969), 'The Frustration–Aggression Hypothesis Revisited' in Leonard Berkowitz (ed.), *Roots of Aggression: A Re-examination of the Frustration–Aggression Hypothesis*, New York: Atherton Press, pp. 1–28.

Berlin, Isaiah (1972), 'The Bent Twig: On the Rise of Nationalism' in *Foreign Affairs*, vol. 51, reprinted in Henry Hardy (ed.), *Isaiah Berlin: The Crooked*

Timber of Humanity. Chapters in the History of Ideas, London: John Murray, pp. 238–61.

Bradley, John F.N. (1991), *Politics in Czechoslovakia 1945–1990*, New York: Colombia University Press.

Bradley, John F.N. (1992), *Czechoslovakia's Velvet Revolution: A Political Analysis*, New York: Colombia University Press.

Brass, Paul R. (1985), 'Ethnic Groups and the State' in Paul R. Brass (ed.), *Ethnic Groups and the State*, London: Croom Helm, pp. 1–56.

Brewer, Marilynn B. (1979), 'The Role of Ethnocentrism in Intergroup Conflict' in William G. Austin & Stephen Worchel (eds), *The Social Psychology of Intergroup Relations*, Monterey, Calif.: Brooks/Cole, pp. 71–84.

Brewer, Marilynn B. (1981), 'Ethnocentrism and Its Role in Interpersonal Trust' in Marilynn B. Brewer & B.E. Collins (eds), *Scientific Inquiry and the Social Sciences*, San Francisco: Jossey-Bass, pp. 345–60.

Brock, Peter (1976), *The Slovak National Awakening*, Toronto: University of Toronto Press.

Bronfenbrenner, Urie (1961), 'The Mirror Image in Soviet–American Relations: A Social Psychologist's Report' in *Journal of Social Issues*, vol. 17, no. 3, pp. 45–56.

Brown, Roger W. (1986), *Social Psychology*, 2nd edn, New York: The Free Press.

Bruchis, Michael (1984), *Nations – Nationalities – People: A Study of the Nationalities Policy of the Communist Party in Soviet Moldavia*, Boulder, Col.: East European Monographs.

Bungs, Dzintra (1993), 'Progress on Withdrawal from the Baltic States' in *RFE/RL Research Report*, 18 June, pp. 50–9.

Buzan, Barry (1991), *People, States and Fear: An Agenda for International Security Studies in the Post-Cold War Era*, New York: Harvester Wheatsheaf.

Capek, Ales & Gerald W. Sazama (1993), 'Czech and Slovak Economic Relations' in *Europe–Asia Studies*, vol. 45, no. 2, pp. 211–35.

Cavanaugh, Cassandra (1992), 'Conflict in Moldova: The Gagauz Factor' in *RFE/RL Research Report*, 14 August, pp. 11–17.

CC (abbreviation of the Constitution of the Republic of Croatia) (1990), promulgated on 22 December 1990.

CE (abbreviation of the Constitution of the Republic of Estonia) (1992), adopted following a referendum on 28 June 1992.

Cibulka, Frank (1983), *Nationalism, Communism and Collaborationism: A Study of the Soviet-Led Invasion of Czechoslovakia and its Aftermath*, Michigan: University Microfilms International.

CIS: The Commonwealth of Independent States 1992 (1992), London: Europa Publications.

Clarke, Douglas L. (1992), 'Former Soviet Armed Forces in the Baltic States' in *RFE/RL Research Report*, 17 April, pp. 43–9.

Clausewitz, Carl von (1966 [1832]), *Vom Kriege: Hinterlassenes Werk des Generals Carl von Clausewitz*, Bonn: Ferd. Dümmlers Verlag.

Coakley, John (1990), 'National Minorities and the Government of Divided Societies: A Comparative Analysis of Some European Evidence' in *European Journal of Political Research*, vol. 18, no. 1, pp. 437–56.

Cohen, Lenard J. (1993), *Broken Bonds: The Disintegration of Yugoslavia*, Oxford: Westview Press.

Connor, Walker (1973), 'The Politics of Ethnonationalism' in *Journal of International Affairs*, vol. 27, no. 1, pp. 1–21.
Connor, Walker (1977), 'Ethnonationalism in the First World' in Milton J. Esman (ed.), *Ethnic Conflict in the Western World*, Ithaca: Cornell University Press, pp. 19–45.
Connor, Walker (1994), *Ethnonationalism: The Quest for Understanding*, Princeton: Princeton University Press.
'Constitutional Law on Human Rights and Freedoms and the Rights of National and Ethnic Communities or Minorities in the Republic of Croatia' (1991), adopted on 4 December 1991. Printed in Gisbert H. Flanz, 'Republic of Croatia' in Albert P. Blaustein & Gisbert H. Flanz (eds) (1992), *Constitutions of the Countries of the World*, Dobbs Ferry, New York: Oceana Publications.
Cooper, Joel & Russell H. Fazio (1979), 'The Formation and Persistence of Attitudes that Support Intergroup Conflict' in William G. Austin & Stephen Worchel (eds), *The Social Psychology of Intergroup Relations*, Monterey, Calif.: Brooks/Cole, pp. 149–59.
Corell, Hans, Helmut Türk & Gro H. Thune (1992), *Report: Rapporteurs (Corell – Türk – Thune) under the Moscow Human Dimension Mechanism to Croatia, 30 September–5 October 1992*, Vienna: CSCE (now OSCE).
Coser, Lewis A. (1956), *The Functions of Social Conflict*, Glencoe, Ill.: Free Press.
Crow, Suzanne (1992), 'Russian Moderates Walk a Tightrope on Moldova' in *RFE/RL Research Report*, 15 May, pp. 9–12.
Crowther, William (1991), 'The Politics of Ethnonational Mobilization: Nationalism and Reform in Soviet Moldavia' in *The Russian Review*, vol. 50, April 1991, pp. 183–202.
CUSSR (abbreviation of the Constitution of the USSR) (1987), adopted on 7 October 1977 and amended on 24 June 1981. Printed in *Konstitutsiya (Osnovnoy Zakon) Soyuza Sovetskikh Sotsialisticheskikh Respublik*, Moscow: Yuridicheskaya Literatura.
Čuvalo, Ante (1990), *The Croatian National Movement 1966–1972*, New York: Columbia University Press.
Dahrendorf, Ralf (1959), *Class and Class Conflict in Industrial Society*, Stanford, Calif.: Stanford University Press.
DAT (abbreviation of the Danish Embassy in Tallinn) (1992), *Redegørelse om forholdet mellem nationaliteterne i Estland*, Tallinn: The Danish Embassy.
Davies, James C. (1962), 'Toward a Theory of Revolution' in *American Sociological Review*, vol. 27. Partly reprinted in Leonard Berkowitz (ed.), *Roots of Aggression: A Re-examination of the Frustration–Aggression Hypothesis*, New York: Atherton Press, pp. 119–30.
Davison, W. Phillips (1974), *Mass Communication and Conflict Resolution: The Role of the Information Media in the Advancement of International Understanding*, New York: Praeger.
Deis, Michael J. (1992), 'A Study of Nationalism in Czechoslovakia' in *RFE/RL Research Report*, 31 January, pp. 8–13.
d'Encausse, Hélène C. (1979), *Decline of an Empire: The Soviet Socialist Republics in Revolt*, New York: Newsweek Books.
Deutch, Karl W. & J. David Singer (1964), 'Multipolar Power Systems and International Stability' in *World Politics*, vol. 16, no. 3, pp. 390–406.

Dima, Nicholas (1975), 'Moldavians or Romanians?' in Ralph C. Clem (ed.), *The Soviet West: Interplay between Nationaliy and Social Organisation,* New York: Praeger.

Dima, Nicholas (1991), *From Moldavia to Moldova: The Soviet–Romanian Territorial Dispute*, Boulder, Col.: East European Monographs.

Djilas, Milovan (1986), 'Eastern Europe within the Soviet Empire' in Robert Conquest (ed.), *The Last Empire: Nationality and the Soviet Future*, Stanford: Hoover Institution Press,

Dollard, John, Leonard W. Doob, Neal E. Miller, O. Hobart Mowrer & Robert R. Sears (1939), *Frustration and Aggression*, New Haven: Yale University Press.

Dougherty, James E. & Robert L. Pfaltzgraff, Jr. (1981), *Contending Theories of International Relations: A Comprehensive Survey*, 2nd edn, New York: Harper & Row.

Douglass, William A. (1988), 'A Critique of Recent Trends in the Analysis of Ethnonationalism' in *Ethnic and Racial Studies,* vol. 11, no. 2, pp. 192–206.

Duplain, Julian (1995), 'Chisinau's and Tiraspol's Faltering Quest for Accord' in *Transition*, 20 October, pp. 10–13.

Eckhardt, Wilhelm (1991), 'Authoritarianism' in *Political Psychology*, vol. 12, no. 1, pp. 97–124.

Eller, Jack D. & Reed M. Coughlan (1993), 'The Poverty of Primordialism: The Demystification of Ethnic Attachments' in *Ethnic and Racial Studies*, vol. 16, no. 2, pp. 183–202.

Englefield, Greg (1992), *Yugoslavia, Croatia, Slovenia: Re-emerging Boundaries*, Durham: International Boundaries Research Unit Press.

Fane, Daria (1993), 'Moldova: Breaking Loose from Moscow' in Ian Bremmer & Ray Taras (eds), *Nation and Politics in the Soviet Sucessor States*, Cambridge: Cambridge University Press, pp. 121–53.

Fedarko, Kevin (1995), 'New Victims, New Victors' in *Time Magazine*, 21 August, pp. 22–5.

Festinger, Leon (1957), *A Theory of Cognitive Dissonance*, New York: Row Peterson.

Fink, Clinton F. (1968), 'Some Conceptual Difficulties in the Theory of Social Conflict' in *Journal of Conflict Resolution*, vol. 12, no. 4, pp. 412–60.

Fisher, Ronald J. (1990), *The Social Psychology of Intergroup and International Conflict Resolution*, New York: Springer-Verlag.

Fisher, Sharon (1994), 'Slovakia' in *RFE/RL Research Report*, 22 April, pp. 68–71.

Flakierski, Henryk (1989), *The Economic System and Income Distribution in Yugoslavia*, New York: M.E. Sharpe.

Frohlich, Norman, Joe A. Oppenheimer & Oran R. Young (1971), *Political Leadership and Collective Goods*, Princeton, N.J.: Princeton University Press.

Frye, Timothy M. (1992), 'Ethnicity, Sovereignty and Transitions from Non-Democratic Rule' in *Journal of International Affairs*, vol. 45, no. 2, pp. 599–623.

Furtado, Charles F. & Michael Hechter (1992), 'The Emergence of Nationalist Politics in the USSR: A Comparison of Estonia and the Ukraine' in Alexander J. Motyl (ed.), *Thinking Theoretically about Soviet Nationalities: History and Comparison in the Study of the USSR*, New York: Columbia University Press, pp. 169–204.

Furtado, Charles F. & Andrea Chandler (eds) (1992), *Perestroika in the Soviet Republics: Documents on the National Question*, Boulder, Col.: Westview Press.

Gabanyi, Annett U. (1993), 'Die Moldaurepublik zwischen Wende und Rückwendung' in *Südosteuropa*, vol. 42, nos 3–4, pp. 163–207.

Gapinski, James H., Borislav Skegro & Thomas W. Zuehlke (1989), *Modeling the Economic Performance of Yugoslavia*, New York: Praeger.

Gardels, Nathan (1991), 'Two Concepts of Nationalism: An Interview with Isaiah Berlin' in *The New York Review of Books*, 21 November, pp. 19–23.

Gawdiak, Ihor (edn) (1989), *Czechoslovakia: A Country Study*, 3rd edn, Washington DC: Federal Research Division, Library of Congress.

Geertz, Clifford (1973), 'The Integrative Revolution: Primordial Sentiments and Civil Politics in the New States' in *The Interpretation of Culture: Selected Essays by Clifford Geertz*, New York: Basic Books, pp. 255–310.

Gellner, Ernest (1983), *Nations and Nationalism*, Oxford: Basil Blackwell.

Geron, Leonard (1991), 'Roads to Baltic Independence' in *The World Today*, August/September 1991, pp. 135–8.

Giddens, Anthony (1984), *The Constitution of Society: Outline of the Theory of Structuration*, Berkeley, Calif.: University of California Press.

Girnius, Saulius (1994a), 'The Baltic States' in *RFE/RL Research Report*, special issue on 'The Politics of Intolerance', 22 April, pp. 5–8.

Girnius, Saulius (1994b), 'Relations between the Baltic States and Russia' in *RFE/RL Research Report*, 26 August, pp. 29–33.

Glazer, Nathan & Daniel P. Moynihan (1975), 'Introduction' in Nathan Glazer & Daniel P. Moynihan (eds) *Ethnicity: Theory and Experience*, Cambridge, Mass.: Harvard University Press, pp. 1–26.

Glenny, Misha (1992), *The Fall of Yugoslavia: The Third Balkan War*, London: Penguin Books.

Glenny, Misha (1993), *The Rebirth of History: Eastern Europe in the Age of Democracy*, 2nd edn, London: Penguin Books.

Götz, Roland & Uwe Halbach (1991), *Daten zur Geographie, Bevölkerung, Politik und Wirtschaft der nichtrussischen Republiken der ehemaligen UdSSR*, Bundesinstitut für ostwissenschaftliche und internationale Studien.

Gow, James (1992), 'Military–Political Affiliations in the Yugoslav Conflict' in *RFE/RL Research Report*, 15 May, pp. 16–25.

Grant, Peter R. (1990), 'Cognitive Theories Applied to Intergroup Conflict' in Ronald J. Fisher, *The Social Psychology of Intergroup and International Conflict Resolution*, New York: Springer-Verlag, pp. 39–57.

Griffiths, Stephen I. (1993), *Nationalism and Ethnic Conflict: Threats to European Security*, Stockholm: Stockholm International Peace Research Institute.

Gross, Mirjana (1981), 'On the Integration of the Croatian Nation: A Case Study in Nation Building' in *East European Quarterly*, vol. 15, no. 2, pp. 209–25.

Hardin, Russell (1982), *Collective Action*, Baltimore: Johns Hopkins University Press.

Hechter, Michael (1975), *Internal Colonialism: The Celtic Fringe in British National Development, 1536–1966*, ch. 2, London: Routledge & Kegan Paul.

Hechter, Michael (1985), 'Internal Colonialism Revisited' in Edward A. Tiryakian & Ronald Rogowski (eds), *New Nationalisms of the Developed West*, Boston: Allen & Unwin, pp. 17–26.

Hechter, Michael (1987a), *Principles of Group Solidarity*, Berkeley, Calif.: University of California Press.

Hechter, Michael (1987b), 'Nationalism as Group Solidarity' in *Ethnic and Racial Studies*, vol. 10, no. 4, pp. 414–26.

Heisbourg, François (ed.) (1991), *The Military Balance 1991–1992*, London: Brassey's.

Heitmann, Klaus (1989), 'Probleme der moldauischen Sprache in der Ära Gorbachev' in *Südosteuropa*, vol. 38, no. 1, pp. 28–53.

Herz, John H. (1950), 'Idealist Internationalism and the Security Dilemma' in *World Politics*, vol. 5, no. 2, pp. 157–80.

Hewstone, Miles (1988), 'Attributional Bases of Intergroup Conflict' in Wolfgang Stroebe, Arie W. Kruglanski, Daniel Bar-Tal & Miles Hewstone (eds), *The Social Psychology of Intergroup Conflict: Theory, Research and Applications*, Berlin: Springer-Verlag.

Hirschman, A.O., (1972), *Exit, Voice, and Loyalty: Responses to Decline in Firms, Organizations, and States*, 2nd edn, Cambridge, Mass.: Harvard University Press.

Horowitz, Donald L. (1985), *Ethnic Groups in Conflict*, Berkeley, Calif.: University of California Press.

Horowitz, Donald L. (1992), 'How to Begin Thinking Comparatively about Soviet Ethnic Problems' in Alexander J. Motyl (ed.), *Thinking Theoretically about Soviet Nationalities: History and Comparison in the Study of the USSR*, New York: Columbia University Press, pp. 9–22.

Hosking, Geoffrey A. (1992), 'Popular Movements in Estonia' in Geoffrey A. Hosking, Jonathan Aves & Peter J.S. Duncan, *The Road to Post-Communism: Independent Political Movements in the Soviet Union 1985–1991*, London: Pinter, pp. 180–201.

Huldt, Bo (ed.) (1992), *The Military Balance 1992–1993*, London: Brassey's.

Ilves, Toomas H. (1991), 'Reaction: The Intermovement in Estonia' in Jan A. Trapans (ed.), *Toward Independence: The Baltic Popular Movements*, Oxford: Westview Press.

Ionescu, Dan (1995), 'Russia's Long Arm and the Dniester Impasse' in *Transition*, 20 October, pp. 14–15.

Irvine, Jill A. (1993), *The Croat Question*, Oxford: Westview Press.

Jackman, Mary R. & Michael J. Muha (1984), 'Education and Intergroup Attitudes: Moral Enlightenment, Superficial Democratic Commitment, or Ideological Refinement?' in *American Sociological Review*, vol. 49, December, pp. 751–69.

Jelavich, Charles (1967), 'The Croatian Problem' in *Austrian History Yearbook*, vol. 3, pp. 83–115.

Jervis, Robert (1976), *Perception and Misperception in International Politics*, Princeton, N.J.: Princeton University Press.

Kand, Villu (1994), 'Estonia: A Year of Challenges' in *RFE/RL Research Report*, 7 January, pp. 92–5.

Kaplan, Cynthia (1993), 'Estonia: A Plural Society on the Road to Independence' in Ian Bremmer & Ray Taras (eds), *Nation and Politics in the Soviet Sucessor States*, Cambridge: Cambridge University Press, pp. 206–21.

Karger, Adolf (1992), 'Die serbischen Siedlungsräume in Kroatien' in *Osteuropa*, vol. 42, no. 2, pp. 141–46.

Karlsson, Klas-Göran (1992), 'Nationalism och miljöproblem i de baltiske republikerne' in *Aktuelt om historia*, vol. 3, no. 4, pp. 65–77.

Kellas, James G. (1991), *The Politics of Nationalism and Ethnicity*, London: Macmillan.

Kelman, Herbert C. (1965), 'Introduction' in Herbert C. Kelman (ed.), *International Behavior: A Social-Psychological Analysis*, New York: Holt, Rinehart & Winston.

Kim, Sung H. & Richard H. Smith (1993), 'Revenge and Conflict Escalation' in *Negotiation Journal*, vol. 9, no. 1, pp. 37–43.

King, Charles (1993), 'Moldova and the New Bessarabian Questions' in *The World Today*, vol. 49, no. 7, pp. 135–9.

King, Charles (1995), 'Gagauz Yeri and the Dilemmas of Self-Determination' in *Transition*, October 1995, pp. 21–5.

Kionka, Riina (1990), 'Estonians' in Graham Smith (ed.), *The Nationalities Question in the Soviet Union*, London: Longman, pp. 40–53.

Kionka, Riina (1991), 'Officers in the Baltic Take the Initiative' in *Report on the USSR*, 15 November 1991, pp. 27–9.

Kionka, Riina (1992a), 'Estonia: A Break with the Past' in *Report on Eastern Europe*, 3 January, pp. 65–7.

Kionka, Riina (1992b), 'Armed Incidents Aggravate Russian–Estonian Relations' in *RFE/RL Research Report*, 28 August, pp. 34–7.

Kionka, Riina (1992c), 'Estonia' in *RFE/RL Research Report*, 2 October, pp. 62–5.

Kionka, Riina (1993), 'Estonia: A Difficult Transition' in *RFE/RL Research Report*, 1 January, pp. 89–91

Kirch, Aksel (1992), 'Russians as a Minority in Contemporary Baltic States' in *Bulletin of Peace Proposals*, vol. 23, no. 2, pp. 205–12.

Kirschbaum, Stanislav J. (1993), 'Czechoslovakia: The Creation, Federalization and Dissolution of a Nation-State' in *Regional Politics and Policy*, vol. 3, no. 1, pp. 69–95.

Kirscht, John P. & Ronald C. Dillehay (1966), *Dimensions of Authoritarianism: A Review of Research and Theory*, Lexington, Ky.: University of Kentucky Press.

Kitaj, Torben (1991), *Østeuropa i kort og tal*, Copenhagen: Mellemfolkeligt Samvirke.

Knudsen, Olav Fagelund (1993), 'Utviklingen i Baltikum: Militære og politiske forhold' in *NUPI-Notat*, no. 488, February.

Kohn, Hans (1955), *Nationalism: Its Meaning and History*, Princeton, N.J.: Van Nostrand.

Kolstø, Pål and Andrei Edemsky with Natalya Kalashnikova (1993), 'The Dniester Conflict: Between Irridentism and Separatism' in *Europe–Asia Studies*, vol. 45, no. 6, pp. 973–1000.

Košuta, Milan (1993), 'Media and the War in Croatia' in *Medicine and War*, vol. 9, pp. 141–4.

Krausing, Helge (1992), 'Bessarabiens betydning for rumænsk/russiske relationer 1877–1992' in *Krigshistorisk Tidsskrift*, vol. 28, no. 2, pp. 14–21.

Križan, Mojmir (1992), 'Nationalismen in Jugoslawien: Von postkommunistischer nationaler Emanzipation zum Krieg' in *Osteuropa*, vol. 42, no. 2, pp. 121–40.

Kusin, Vladimir V. (1990), 'Czechs and Slovaks: The Road to the Current Debate' in *Report on Eastern Europe*, 5 October, pp. 4–13.

Laitin, David D. (1991), 'The National Uprisings in the Soviet Union' in *World Politics*, vol. 44, no. 1, pp. 139–77.

Lane, Jan-Erik (1990), 'The Epistemological Foundations of Public Choice Theory' in *Scandinavian Political Studies*, vol. 13, pp. 65–80.

Lauristin, Marju & Peeter Vihalemm (1991), 'Current Media Politics in Estonia' in Svennik Høyer, Bjarne Skov & Line Sandsmark (eds), *The Role of Media in a Changing Society*, Oslo: University of Oslo.

Leff, Carol Skalnik (1988), *National Conflict in Czechoslovakia: The Making and Remaking of a State, 1918–1987*, Princeton, N.J.: Princeton University Press.

Levi, Margaret & Michael Hechter (1985), 'A Rational Choice Approach to the Rise and Decline of Ethnoregional Political Parties' in Edward A. Tiryakian & Ronald Rogowski (eds), *New Nationalisms of the Developed West*, Boston: Allen & Unwin, pp. 128–46.

LeVine, Robert A. & Donald T. Campbell (1972), *Ethnocentrism: Theories of Conflict, Ethnic Attitudes, and Group Behavior*, New York: John Wiley & Sons.

Lewin, Leif (1991), *Self-Interest and Public Interest in Western Politics*, Oxford: Oxford University Press.

Lieven, Anatol (1993), *The Baltic Revolution: Estonia, Latvia, Lithuania and the Path to Independence*, New Haven: Yale University Press.

Lijphart, Arend (1971), 'Comparative Politics and the Comparative Method' in *The American Political Science Review*, vol. 65, pp. 682–93.

Mack, Raymond W. & Richard C. Snyder (1957), 'The Analysis of Social Conflict – toward an Overview and Synthesis' in *Journal of Conflict Resolution*, vol. 1, no. 2, pp. 212–48.

Malesic, Marjan (ed.) (1993), *The Role of Mass Media in the Serbian–Croatian Conflict*, Stockholm: Styrelsen för psykologiskt försvar.

Maley, William (1995), 'Does Russia Speak for Baltic Russians?' in *The World Today*, January, pp. 4–6.

Mamatey, Victor S. and Radomír Luža (ed.) (1973), *A History of the Czechoslovak Republic 1918–1948*, Princeton, N.J.: Princeton University Press.

Markotich, Stan (1993), 'Ethnic Serbs in Tudjman's Croatia' in *RFE/RL Research Report*, vol. 2, no. 38, 24 September, pp. 28–33.

Markotich, Stan (1994), 'Serbia' in *RFE/RL Research Report,* special issue on 'The Politics of Intolerance', 22 April, pp. 95–100.

Martin, Peter (1990a), 'The Hyphen Controversy' in *Report on Eastern Europe*, 20 April, pp. 14–17.

Martin, Peter (1990b), 'The New Governments' in *Report on Eastern Europe*, 27 July, pp. 9–13.

Martin, Peter (1990c), 'Relations between the Czechs and the Slovaks' in *Report on Eastern Europe*, 7 September, pp. 1–6.

Martin, Peter (1991), 'Economic Reform and Slovakia' in *Report on Eastern Europe*, 5 July, pp. 6–13.

Marx, Karl (1963 [1869]), *The 18th Brumaire of Louis Bonaparte*, New York: International Publishers.

Mastnak, Tomaz (1992), 'Yugoslavia: And Is No More' in *East European Reporter*, January/February, pp. 3–11.

Matuska, Peter (1989), 'Relations between the Czechs and the Slovaks' in *Radio Free Europe Research*, 30 March, pp. 3–8.

Mazowiecki, Tadeus (1992), *Human Rights Questions: Human Rights Situations and Reports of the Special Rapporteur and Representatives. Situation of Human Rights in the Territory of the former Yugoslavia*, report for the 47th session of the UN General Assembly on 17 November, UN document no. S/24809.

McKay, James (1982), 'An Exploratory Synthesis of Primordial and Mobilizationist Approaches to Ethnic Phenomena' in *Ethnic and Racial Studies*, vol. 5, no. 4, pp. 395–420.

Meadwell, Hudson (1989), 'Cultural and Instrumental Approaches to Ethnic Nationalism' in *Ethnic and Racial Studies*, vol. 12, no. 3, pp. 309–28.

Meissner, Boris (1990), 'Die staatliche Kontinuität und Völkerrechtliche Stellung der baltischen Staaten', in Boris Meissner (ed.), *Die baltischen Nationen: Estland, Lettland, Litauen*, Köln: Markus Verlag, pp. 192–218.

Misiunas, Romuald J. & Rein Taagepera (1983), *Baltic States: The Years of Dependence, 1940–80*, London: C. Hurst.

Moore, Patrick (1991), 'Where is Yugoslavia Headed?' in *Report on Eastern Europe*, 6 September, pp. 30–5.

Moore, Patrick (1994), 'Croatia' in *RFE/RL Research Report*, special issue on 'The Politics of Intolerance', 22 April, pp. 80–2.

Morgenthau, Hans J. (1960), *Politics among Nations: The Struggle for Power and Peace*, 3rd revised edn, New York: Alfred A. Knopf.

Motyl, Alexander J. (1990), *Sovietology, Rationality, Nationality: Coming to Grips with Nationalism in the USSR*, New York: Columbia University Press.

Musil, Jiri (1992), 'Czechoslovakia in the Middle of Transition' in *Daedalus*, vol. 121, no. 2, pp. 175–95.

Nahaylo, Bohdan (1992), 'Ukraine and Moldova: The View from Kiev' in *RFE/RL Research Report*, 1 May, pp. 39–45.

Nannestad, Peter (1992), 'Paradigm, School, or Sect? Some Reflections on the Status of Rational Choice Theory in Contemporary Scandinavian Political Science', paper prepared for presentation at the conference 'Political Science in Scandinavia – Trends and Challenges', arranged by Scandinavian Political Studies at Voksenåsen, Oslo, May 22–24, 1992.

Nativi, Andrea (1991), 'The Yugoslavian Tragedy' in *Military Technology*, no. 12, pp. 92–8.

Nedelciuc, Vasile (ed.) (1992), *The Republic of Moldova*, report drawn up by the Foreign Relations Committee of the Parliament of the Republic of Moldova, Chisinau.

Newman, Saul (1991), 'Does Modernization Breed Ethnic Political Conflict?' in *World Politics*, vol. 43, no. 3, pp. 451–78.

Nielsen, François (1985), 'Toward a Theory of Ethnic Solidarity in Modern Societies' in *American Sociological Review*, vol. 50, no. 2, pp. 133–49.

Nielsson, Gunnar P. (1985), 'States and "Nation-Groups": A Global Taxonomy' in Edward A. Tiryakian & Ronald Rogowski (eds), *New Nationalisms of the Developed West*, Boston: Allen & Unwin, pp. 27–56.

Nørgaard, Ole (ed.) (1994), *De baltiske lande efter uafhængigheden – hvorfor så forskellige?*, Århus: Politica.

Obrman, Jan (1991), 'Czechoslovakia' in *Report on Eastern Europe*, 30 August, pp. 5–8.

Obrman, Jan (1992a), 'The Czechoslovak Elections' in *RFE/RL Research Report*, 26 June, pp. 12–19.

Obrman, Jan (1992b), 'Czechoslovakia: Stage Set for Disintegration?' in *RFE/RL Research Report*, 10 July, pp. 26–31.

Odling-Smee, John (ed.) (1992), *Economic Review: Moldova*, Washington, D.C.: International Monetary Fund.

Olien, C.N., G.A. Donohue & P.J. Tichenor (1984), 'Media and Stages of Social Conflict' in *Journalism Monographs*, no. 90, pp. 1–31.

Olson, Mancur (1965), *The Logic of Collective Action*, Cambridge: Harvard University Press.

Opp, K.-D. (1984), 'Rational Choice and Sociological Man' in *Jahrbuch für Neue Politische Ökonomie*, vol. 3, pp. 1–16.

Pehe, Jiri (1989), 'The Widening Sources of Dissent in Czechoslovakia' in *Radio Free Europe Research*, 14 April, pp. 5–8.

Pehe, Jiri (1990a), 'Czechoslovakia: An Abrupt Transition' in *Report on Eastern Europe*, 5 January, pp. 11–14.

Pehe, Jiri (1990b), 'Economic and Constitutional Change' in *Report on Eastern Europe*, 13 July, pp. 10–14.

Pehe, Jiri (1990c), 'Power-Sharing Law Approved by Federal Assembly' in *Report on Eastern Europe*, 21 December, pp. 6–9.

Pehe, Jiri (1991a), 'The Instability of Transition' in *Report on Eastern Europe*, 4 January, pp. 11–16.

Pehe, Jiri (1991b), 'Bill of Fundamental Rights and Liberties Adopted' in *Report on Eastern Europe*, 25 January, pp. 1–4.

Pehe, Jiri (1991c), 'Growing Slovak Demands Seen as Threat to Federation' in *Report on Eastern Europe*, 22 March, pp.1–10.

Pehe, Jiri (1991d), 'Political Conflict in Slovakia' in *Report on Eastern Europe*, 10 May, pp. 1–6.

Pehe, Jiri (1991e), 'The Emergence of Right-Wing Extremism' in *Report on Eastern Europe*, 28 June, pp. 1–6.

Pehe, Jiri (1991f), 'Bid for Slovak Sovereignty Causes Political Upheaval' in *Report on Eastern Europe*, 11 October, pp. 11–14.

Pehe, Jiri (1992a), 'Czech–Slovak Conflict Threatens State Unity' in *RFE/RL Research Report*, 3 January, pp. 83–6.

Pehe, Jiri (1992b), 'Czechoslovakia's Political Balance Sheet, 1990 to 1992' in *RFE/RL Research Report*, 19 June, pp. 24–31.

Pehe, Jiri (1992c), 'Czechoslovakia' in *RFE/RL Research Report*, special issue on 'The Media', 2 October, pp. 34–8.

Pehe, Jiri (1992d), 'Czechs and Slovaks Define Postdivorce Relations' in *RFE/RL Research Report*, 13 November, pp. 7–11.

Pehe, Jiri (1992e), 'Czechoslovak Parliament Votes to Dissolve Federation' in *RFE/RL Research Report*, 4 December, pp. 1–5.

Pehe, Jiri (1993), 'Czechoslovakia: Toward Dissolution' in *RFE/RL Research Report*, 1 January, pp. 84–8.

Pehe, Jiri (1994), 'The Czech Republic' in *RFE/RL Research Report*, special issue on 'The Politics of Intolerance', 22 April, pp. 50–4.

Pehe, Jiri & Jan Obrman (1989), 'Whither Czechoslovakia?' in *Radio Free Europe Research*, 26 January, pp. 17–21.

Petković, Ranko (1991), 'Proposals for the Settlement of the Crisis and Regulation of Relations in the Yugoslav Community' in *Review of International Affairs*, vol. 42, 20 June, pp. 1–28.

Pettai, Vello A. (1993), 'Estonia: Old Maps and New Roads' in *Journal of Democracy*, vol. 4, no. 1, pp. 117–25.

Plamenatz, John (1976), 'Two Types of Nationalism' in Eugene Kamenka (ed.), *Nationalism: The Nature and Evolution of an Idea*, London: Edward Arnold.

Posen, Barry R. (1993), 'The Security Dilemma and Ethnic Conflict' in *Survival*, vol. 35, no. 1, pp. 27–47.

Price, Vincent (1989), 'Social Identification and Public Opinion: Effects of Communicating Group Conflict' in *Public Opinion Quarterly*, vol. 53, no. 2, pp. 197–224.

Pruitt, Dean G. & Jeffrey Z. Rubin (1986), *Social Conflict: Escalation, Stalemate and Settlement*, New York: Random House.

Radu, Michael (1992), 'Moldova: The Next Ethnic Powder Keg?' in *The World and I*, July 1992, pp. 144–9.

Ramet, Sabrina P. (1992), *Nationalism and Federalism in Yugoslavia, 1962–1991*, Indianapolis: Indiana University Press.

Raun, Toivo U. (1987), *Estonia and the Estonians*, Stanford: Hoover Institution Press.

Raun, Toivo U. (1994), 'Ethnic Relations and Conflict in the Baltic States' in W. Raymond Duncan & G. Paul Holman, Jr., *Ethnic Nationalism and Regional Conflict: The Former Soviet Union and Yugoslavia*, Boulder, Col.: Westview Press, pp. 155–82.

Reynolds, Vernon (1980), 'Sociobiology and the Idea of Primordial Discrimination' in *Ethnic and Racial Studies,* vol. 3, no. 3, pp. 301–15.

Ritzer, George (1992), *Sociological Theory*, 3rd edn, New York: McGraw-Hill.

Rogowski, Ronald (1985), 'Causes and Varieties of Nationalism: A Rationalist Account' in Edward A. Tiryakian & Ronald Rogowski (eds), *New Nationalisms of the Developed West*, Boston: Allen & Unwin, pp. 87–108.

Rose, Richard (1992), *Czechs and Slovaks Compared: A Survey of Economic and Political Behaviour*, Glasgow: Centre for the Study of Public Policy.

Rose, Richard & William Maley (1994), *Nationalities in the Baltic States: A Survey Study*, Glasgow: Centre for the Study of Public Policy.

Saar, Ellu & Mikk Titma (1992), 'Migrationsströme im sowjetisierten Baltikum und ihre Nachwirkung auf die baltischen Staaten nach Wiederherstellung der Selbständigkeit' in *Berichte des Bundesinstituts für ostwissenschaftliche und internationale Studien*, September.

Sampson, Steven (1992), '"Kiss Me I'm Serbian!": Etniske konflikter i Østeuropa' in *Politica,* vol. 24, no. 4, pp. 393–407.

Schaller, Helmut (1987), 'Sprache und Nationalkultur in Südosteuropa' in *Südosteuropa Mitteilungen*, no. 1, pp. 25–9.

Schlesinger, Phillip (1991), *Media, State and Nation: Political Violence and Collective Identities*, London: Sage Publications.

Schöpflin, George (1973), 'The Ideology of Croatian Nationalism' in *Survey: A Journal of East and West Studies*, vol. 19, no. 1, pp. 123–46.

Schroeder, Gertrude E. (1986), 'Social and Economic Aspects of the Nationality Problem' in Robert Conquest (ed.), *The Last Empire: Nationality and the Soviet Future*, Stanford: Hoover Institution Press.

Shaw, Marvin E. (1981), *Group Dynamics: The Psychology of Small Group Behavior*, 3rd edn, New York: McGraw-Hill.

Sheehy, Ann (1987), 'Cultural Concessions but no Autonomy for Gagauz' in *Radio Free Europe Research*, 12 November, pp. 1–4.

Sheehy, Ann (1993), 'The Estonian Law on Aliens' in *RFE/RL Research Report*, vol. 2, no. 38, 24 September, pp. 7–11.

Sherif, Muzafer (1966), *Group Conflict and Co-operation: Their Social Psychology*, London: Routledge & Kegan Paul.

Shils, Edward A. (1957), 'Primordial, Personal, Sacred, and Civil Ties' in *Center and Periphery: Essays in Macrosociology. Selected Papers of Edward Shils, vol. II*, Chicago: University of Chicago Press, pp. 111–26.

Singer, J. David (1981), 'Accounting for International War: The State of the Discipline' in *Journal of Peace Research*, vol. 18, no. 1, pp. 1–18.

Siupur, Elena (1993), 'Von Bessarabien zur Republik Moldau – die historischen Wurzeln eines Konflikts' in *Südosteuropa*, vol. 42, nos 3–4, pp. 153–62.

Skilling, H. Gordon (1976), *Czechoslovakia's Interrupted Revolution*, Princeton, N.J.: Princeton University Press.

Smith, Anthony D. (1986), *The Ethnic Origins of Nations*, London: Basil Blackwell.

Smith, Anthony D. (1988), 'The Myth of the "Modern Nation" and the Myths of Nations' in *Ethnic and Racial Studies*, vol. 11, no. 1, pp. 1–26.

Smith, Anthony D. (1991), *National Identity*, London: Penguin Books.

Smith, Anthony D. (1992), 'Ethnic Identity and Territorial Nationalism in Comparative Perspective' in Alexander J. Motyl (ed.), *Thinking Theoretically about Soviet Nationalities: History and Comparison in the Study of the USSR*, New York: Columbia University Press.

Socor, Vladimir (1989a), 'Soviet Moldavian Writers Publish Unauthorized Periodical in Latin Script, with Help from Latvia' in *Radio Free Europe Research*, 30 March, pp. 1–4.

Socor, Vladimir (1989b), 'Recent Mass Rallies and Demonstrations in Soviet Moldavia' in *Radio Free Europe Research*, 5 May, pp. 1–9.

Socor, Vladimir (1989c), 'People's Front Founded in the Moldavian SSR' in *Radio Free Europe Research*, 29 May, pp. 1–7.

Socor, Vladimir (1990a), 'Gagauz in Moldavia Demand Separate Republic' in *Report on the USSR*, 7 September, pp. 8–13.

Socor, Vladimir (1990b), 'Moldavia Resists Soviet Draft and Seeks Own "National" Forces' in *Report on the USSR*, 26 October, pp. 19–23.

Socor, Vladimir (1990c), 'Gorbachev and Moldavia' in *Report on the USSR*, 21 December, pp. 11–14.

Socor, Vladimir (1991a), 'Political Power Passes to Democratic Forces' in *Report on the USSR*, 4 January, pp. 24–9.

Socor, Vladimir (1991b), 'Moldavians Reject Union Treaty' in *Report on the USSR*, 11 January, pp. 12–14.

Socor, Vladimir (1991c), 'Moldavia Resists Pressure and Boycotts Union Referendum' in *Report on the USSR*, 29 March, pp. 9–14.

Socor, Vladimir (1991d), 'Moldavia Proclaims Independence, Commences Secession from USSR' in *Report on the USSR*, 18 October, pp. 19–26.

Socor, Vladimir (1992a), 'Moldavia Builds a New State' in *RFE/RL Research Report*, 3 January, pp. 42–5.

Socor, Vladimir (1992b), 'Creeping Putsch in Eastern Moldova' in *RFE/RL Research Report*, 17 January, pp. 8–13.

Socor, Vladimir (1992c), 'Why Moldova Does Not Seek Reunification with Romania' in *RFE/RL Research Report*, 31 January, pp. 27–33.

Socor, Vladimir (1992d), 'Opinion Polling in Moldova' in *RFE/RL Research Report*, 27 March, pp. 60–3.

Socor, Vladimir (1992e), 'Moldovan–Romanian Relations Are Slow to Develop' in *RFE/RL Research Report*, 26 June, pp. 38–45.

Socor, Vladimir (1992f), 'Russian Forces in Moldova' in *RFE/RL Research Report*, 28 August, pp. 38–43.

Socor, Vladimir (1992g), 'Russia's Fourteenth Army and the Insurgency in Eastern Moldova', 11 September, pp. 41–8.

Socor, Vladimir (1992h), 'Moldova' in *RFE/RL Research Report*, special issue on 'The Media', 2 October, pp. 77–81.

Socor, Vladimir (1992i), 'Moldova's New "Government of National Consensus"' in *RFE/RL Research Report*, 27 November, pp. 5–10.

Socor, Vladimir (1993), 'Moldova's "Dniester" Ulcer', in *RFE/RL Research Report*, 1 January, pp. 12–16.

Socor, Vladimir (1994a), 'Moldova' in *RFE/RL Research Report*, special issue on 'The Politics of Intolerance', 22 April, pp. 17–22.

Socor, Vladimir (1994b), 'Five Countries Look at Ethnic Problems in Southern Moldova' in *RFE/RL Research Report*, 19 August, pp. 19–23.

Socor, Vladimir (1994c), 'Gagauz Autonomy in Moldova: A Precedent for Eastern Europe?' in *RFE/RL Research Report*, 26 August, pp. 20–8.

Spinei, Victor (1986), *Moldavia in the 11th–14th Centuries*, Bucharest: Editura Academiei Republicii Socialiste Romania.

Stålvant, Carl-Einar (1993), 'The Role of the Environment in the Regionalization of the Baltic Sea Area' in Gunnar Sjöstedt, Uno Svedin & Britt H. Aniansson (eds), *International Environmental Negotiations: Process, Issues, and Contexts*, Utrikespolitiska Institutet, Report no. 1, pp. 117–42.

Steele, Jonathan (1992), 'Fear and Folly in Moscow' in *The Guardian Weekly*, 1 March.

Stein, Arthur A. (1976), 'Conflict and Cohesion: A Review of the Literature' in *Journal of Conflict Resolution*, vol. 20, no. 1, pp. 143–72.

Stepan, Alfred (1994), 'When Democracy and the Nation-State are Competing Logics: Reflections on Estonia' in *Archives Européennes de Sociologie*, vol. 35, no. 1, pp. 127–41.

Stevens, Joe B. (1993), *The Economics of Collective Choice*, Boulder, Colo.: Westview.

Stone, Deborah A. (1988), *Policy Paradox and Political Reason*, London: Harper Collins.

Stone, William F. (1993), 'Psychodynamics, Cognitive Functioning, or Group Orientation: Research and Theory in the 1980s' in William F. Stone, Gerda Lederer & Richard Christie, *The Authoritarian Personality Today*, New York: Springer-Verlag, pp. 159–81.

Sumner, William G. (1959 [1906]), *Folkways*, 2nd unaltered edn, New York: Dover Publications.

Szayna, Thomas S. & James B. Steinberg (1992), *Civil–Military Relations and National Security Thinking in Czechoslovakia*, Washington, DC: Rand Corporation.

Taagepera, Rein (1991), 'Building Democracy in Estonia' in *Political Science and Politics*, September, pp. 478–81.

Taagepera, Rein (1992), 'Ethnic Relations in Estonia, 1991' in *Journal of Baltic Studies*, vol. 23, no. 2, pp. 121–32.

Taagepera, Rein (1993), *Estonia: Return to Independence*, Oxford: Westview Press.

Tajfel, Henri (1979), 'Human Intergroup Conflict: Useful and Less Useful Forms of Analysis' in M. von Cranach, K. Foppa, W. Lepenies & D. Ploog (eds), *Human Ethology: Claims and Limits of a New Discipline*, Cambridge: Cambridge University Press, pp. 396–422.

Tajfel, Henri (1981), *Human Groups and Social Categories: Studies in Social Psychology*, Cambridge: Cambridge University Press.

Tajfel, Henri (1982), 'Social Psychology of Intergroup Relations' in *Annual Review of Psychology*, vol. 33, pp. 1–39.

Tajfel, Henri & John C. Turner (1979), 'An Integrative Theory of Intergroup Conflict' in William G. Austin & Stephen Worchel (eds), *The Social Psychology of Intergroup Relations*, Monterey, Calif.: Brooks/Cole, pp. 33–47.

Tajfel, Henri, Claude Flament, M.G. Billig & R.P. Bundy (1971), 'Social Categorization and Intergroup Behavior' in *European Journal of Social Psychology*, vol. 1, pp. 149–78.

Taylor, Charles (1992), 'The Politics of Recognition' in Amy Gutmann (ed.), *Multiculturalism and 'The Politics of Recogniton': An Essay by Charles Taylor*, Princeton, N.J.: Princeton University Press.

Thompson, Mark (1992), *A Paper House: The Ending of Yugoslavia*, London: Hutchinson Radius.

Turner, John C. (1975), 'Social Comparison and Social Identity: Some Prospects for Intergroup Behavior' in *European Journal of Social Psychology*, vol. 5, pp. 5–34.

Uibopuu, Henn-Jüri (1990), 'Estland står fast på sin selvstændighed' in *Estland – Letland – Litauen: Den syngende revolution i Baltikum*, Copenhagen: SNU, pp. 21–38.

Uibopuu, Henn-Jüri (1992), 'Dealing with the Minorities – a Baltic Perspective' in *The World Today*, June, pp. 108–12.

van den Berghe, Pierre L. (1978), 'Race and Ethnicity: A Sociobiological Perspective' in *Ethnic and Racial Studies,* vol. 1, no. 4, pp. 401–11.

Verdery, Katherine (1993), 'Nationalism and National Sentiment in Post-Socialist Romania' in *Slavic Review*, vol. 52, no. 2, pp. 179–203.

Viotti, Paul R. & Mark V. Kauppi (1987), *International Relations: Realism, Pluralism, Globalism*, New York: Macmillan.

Wallerstein, Immanuel (1961), *Africa: The Politics of Independence*, New York: Vintage Books.

Waltz, Kenneth N. (1964), 'The Stability of a Bipolar World' in *Dædalus*, vol. 93, Summer, pp. 881–909.

Waltz, Kenneth N. (1979), *Theory of International Politics*, Reading, Mass.: Addison-Wesley.

Waltz, Kenneth N. (1988), 'The Origins of War in Neorealist Theory' in Robert I. Rotberg & Theodore K. Rabb (eds), *The Origin and Prevention of Major Wars*, Cambridge: Cambridge University Press.

White, Ralph K. (1984), *Fearful Warriors: A Psychological Profile of U.S.–Soviet Relations*, New York: Free Press.

Wilder, David L. (1986), 'Social Categorization: Implications for Creation and Reduction of Intergroup Bias' in Leonard Berkowitz (ed.), *Advances in Experimental Social Psychology*, vol. 19, pp. 291–355.

Wolchik, Sharon L. (1991), *Czechoslovakia in Transition: Politics, Economics and Society*, New York: Pinter.

'Zakon o oprostu od krivičnog progona i postupka za krivična djela počinjena u oružanim sukobima i u ratu protiv Republike Hrvatske' (1992). (Law on abolition of criminal prosecution and criminal proceedings for criminal acts perpetrated in the armed conflicts and in the war against the Republic of Croatia, Zagreb).

Zubaida, Sami (1989), 'Nations: Old and New Comments on Anthony D. Smith's "The Myth of the 'Modern Nation' and the Myths of Nations"' in *Ethnic and Racial Studies*, vol. 12, no. 3, pp. 330–9.

Index